THE RELIGIOUS ISSUE
IN THE STATE SCHOOLS
OF ENGLAND AND WALES
1902-1914

A NATION'S QUEST FOR HUMAN DIGNITY

THE RELIGIOUS ISSUE
IN THE STATE SCHOOLS
OF ENGLAND & WALES

1902 - 1914

A NATION'S QUEST
FOR HUMAN DIGNITY

BY BENJAMIN SACKS

ALBUQUERQUE
THE UNIVERSITY OF NEW MEXICO PRESS

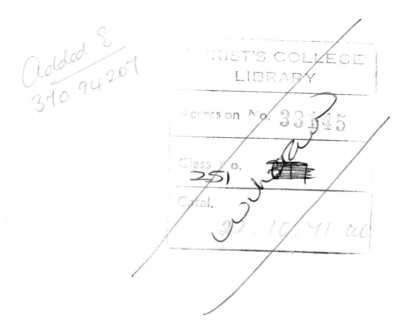

THE PUBLICATION OF THIS BOOK IS MADE POSSIBLE BY
A GRANT FROM THE FORD FOUNDATION

COMPOSED, PRINTED AND BOUND
AT THE UNIVERSITY OF NEW MEXICO PRINTING PLANT
ALBUQUERQUE, NEW MEXICO, U. S. A.

Library of Congress Catalog Card Number 61-10047

First Edition

PREFACE

Few TOPICS more steadily held national interest in Great Britain at the opening of the twentieth century than the religious issue in State schools. Should schools under the control of churches receive financial aid from public sources? Should religious instruction be included in the daily timetable of schools? Well-known men from all walks of life entered into the heated discussion—aristocrats, statesmen, members of parliament, civil servants, scholars, literary figures, journalists, educators, clergymen, industrialists, trade unionists, socialists. The immense literature on the subject bears witness to the intensity of the debate. Newspapers and periodicals carried frequent editorials and articles. The printing presses poured forth a never-ending stream of pamphlets and books. The public forum—demonstrations, parades, meetings, legislative deliberations—yielded a plethora of addresses and speeches. For the people on the British Isles the controversy provoked an emotional excitement not unlike that generated in France by the contemporaneous Dreyfus affair. The strife produced court trials, prison sentences, distraint of property, election issues, exchanges between opposing church leaders, and negotiations in political circles. The nation was in deadly earnest over the adage that he who molds the child holds the man.

There would seem to be a more encompassing value in recapturing the story than an intellectual interest in moments of the past. In France, Germany, the Low Countries, Switzerland, Canada, the United States, Australia and New Zealand (often referred to in those days as Australasia)—and wherever Western culture dug its roots—the religious issue in the schools made its appearance. The background was a reinvigorated humanism in the nineteenth century stimulating an inventory of the nature and goal of institutions. No tradition was challenged more vigorously than that of the churches as the educator of a nation's children. Nor, for that matter, has the question yet been settled with any degree of public acceptance. It still flares anew in many countries and recently, in France, Belgium, and several states in West Germany, to mention but a few, the subject has been in the public eye. It is doubtful whether an equilibrium ever will be reached, for it is a maxim that each generation must find its own answers to continuing problems. But the historian likes to think that the record and the perspective of the past can illuminate the present. So the thought is cherished that the detailed account of England's struggle might contribute to a grasp of the essentials involved.

Certainly the frequent references by English commentators to the experiences of peoples elsewhere will testify to their diligence in seeking enlightenment on their own dilemma. At the same time the varied analyses presented were not an unmixed blessing. Each circle of critics had its own interpretation of the lessons to be drawn from schemes tried abroad. Indeed, "all things to all men" would not be off the mark in appraising their conclusions. Proponents and opponents alike saw in the record of other countries supporting data for their own points of view. Actually the bewildering contradictions do not raise any issue of ignoring truth. Rather it is a matter of placing the emphasis upon those facts which best serve the dictates of a particular school of thought. The challenge for the reader is to develop his own balance sheet of what directional guides the world laboratory had to offer on the religious issue in State schools.

For Americans in particular there would seem much to be learned from the very thorough analysis given the subject by their cousins in the United Kingdom. Both countries possess the same characteristic of a heterogeneous religious incidence, comprising in significant numbers Protestants, Roman Catholics, Jews, and Agnostics. True, unlike England and Wales, the heritage in the United States has been to reserve public money for the schools administered by public authorities. Only the most nominal type of Christian overtone, and that optionally, has been allowed to permeate the school atmosphere. And, as a matter of fact, the general tendency in most of the Union has been to eschew entirely such reverent obsequies as opening the school day with a prayer, a hymn, or a passage from the Bible. But currently the cycle again is churning and once more the nation is confronted with the twin problems of State aid to parochial schools and the use of the public (common) schools to give religious instruction. The American people would do well to base their decisions on all pertinent material lest the choice or choices made be followed by unanticipated and disturbing conditions. No better opportunity is present to become acquainted with the anatomy of the question than the English story from 1902 to 1914.

Apart from the challenge of assimilating the superabundance of material, the author's task of organization was not an easy one. As familiar as the refrain is in historical circles, the sameness of much of the documentation tended to render quite indistinct significant facets of the subject. In the end I decided to pursue a chronological approach in the early chapters and a topical presentation in the later chapters. The further question arose as to how far to delve into the dynamics of political party maneuvering as compared to the arguments of the several participants in the conflict—Anglican, Nonconformist, Roman Catholic, Jew, Agnostic. The determination to develop the story with emphasis on the participants is based on the conviction that the pros and cons of the several religious adversaries offer information of an enduring nature. This is not to deny that progress is sometimes the aftermath of political calculations and it is hoped that ample consideration has been given to these. But for one who believes that the history of ideas has something to do with the evolution of a cultural pattern, a nation's thinking represents a true heritage. The study is restricted to England and Wales, for Scotland and Ireland were not parties to the controversy and domestic legislation for them required separate statutory enactments.

The conception of this study dates back to a chapter in a previous book, *J. Ramsay MacDonald in Thought and Action*, in which I presented MacDonald's approach to the everyday issues of his times. One of the topics which engrossed the attention of the Labour Party's first prime minister was the acrimonious debate over religious education in the State schools. MacDonald saw this controversy from the secularist point of view, which espoused an exclusive civic education. In the course of the preparation of that book, I was attracted to the desirability of developing the topic comprehensively. The several religious groups merited equal treatment. That each had one or more, and often shifting, points of view was well evidenced in such casual brushes as I had with the general literature on the subject. The historian's mantle of objectivity assumed special importance in this instance. No compartment of man's thinking is more tender than his religious beliefs. In the classroom this becomes obvious when the teacher turns from the discussion of politics and economics to church history. Students are prone to argue the case if the interpretation of past religious events is at variance with their beliefs. It is hoped that every side has been faithfully portrayed in the fullness of its position.

A large part of the printed material is available in the United States. Over the span of several summers I visited many depositories of knowledge. Religious newspapers and journals were located at seminaries—Union Theological and General Theological in New York, Crozer Theological in Chester, Pennsylvania, and Garratt Biblical Institute on the campus of Northwestern University. Desirable items were turned up by the well-known public libraries in New York, Boston, Chicago, Philadelphia, and Los Angeles. Private and academic collections such as those in the Athenaeum and Congregational libraries in Boston, Harvard University, Columbia University, University of Pennsylvania, and the University of Chicago yielded rich gleanings. The Library of Congress in Washington, D.C. offered from its vast holdings a number of English metropolitan dailies. The research undertaken in these extended areas was supplemented by interlibrary loans from other institutions all over the country.

The remainder of the material was gathered in England and Wales during the summer of 1957. A special debt of gratitude is owed the Ministry of Education for the opportunity to examine its files and to use the excellent pamphlet collection in its Reference Library. The British Museum and its Newspaper Library at Colindale in outer London filled many gaps in source materials. The London School of Economics and Political Science provided ready access to government publications and standard bibliographical aids. The Welsh National Library at Aberystwyth and the municipal library at Cardiff contributed valuable items for the story in the principality. Due acknowledgement is made to the officials of many religious bodies for opening their archives and sparing precious moments to arrange interviews with persons whose active years were identified with the decade before World War I. A partial list includes the central offices of the Free Church Council, the various Nonconformist sects, Unitarians, National Society, Catholic Education Council, Secular Education League, National Secular Society, Rationalist Press, and the Ethical Union affiliates. It is to be regretted that many of their archives suffered irreparable losses during the air raids of World War II.

The assistance of my own institution, the University of New Mexico, is gratefully acknowledged. From its Research Committee financial aid was obtained to carry on the project. The Library Staff was very helpful in bibliographical and reference matters. Special thanks are due Roland Dickey, director of the University Press, for his kind and patient counsel during the final revision of the manuscript. The grant from the Ford Foundation to the University of New Mexico Press toward the printing of this book is deeply appreciated. The responsibility for the study, of course, is my own.

BENJAMIN SACKS

The University of New Mexico
Albuquerque
October 1960

CONTENTS

PART I. STRUGGLES IN THE POLITICAL ARENA   1

1. *INTRODUCTION*   3
   Setting   3
   Political Corridors   10
   Balfour Bill of 1902   13

2. *PASSAGE OF THE ACT OF 1902*   16
   The Adversaries   16
   Religious Equality   30
   Prospect of Turbulence   36

3. *ACT OF 1902 IN OPERATION* (1903-1906)   42
   Passive Resistance Movement   42
   County Councils   53
   The London Scene   56

4. *THE LIBERAL GOVERNMENT'S PROPOSALS*   62
   The Several Measures   62
   The Adversaries Again   65
   Attempts at Compromise   75

PART II. TWIN VALUES OF A CHRISTIAN BASIS
         IN THE SCHOOLS   79

5. *FOSTERING CHURCH MEMBERSHIP*   81
   Anglican View   81
   Roman Catholic View   93
   Nonconformist View   94
   Secularist View   102

6. *INCULCATING MORALITY* 114
    Anglican Brief 114
    Roman Catholic Brief 121
    Nonconformist Brief 123
    Secularist Brief 127

PART III. SEARCH FOR A CONCORDAT 143

7. *UNIVERSAL FACILITIES* 145
    Anglican Proponents 145
    Anglican Critics 157
    Nonconformist Proponents 162
    Nonconformist Critics 164

8. *GENERAL RELIGIOUS INSTRUCTION* 169
    Nonconformist Proponents 169
    Anglican Proponents 172
    Anglican Critics 178
    Local Option 180

9. *THE ROMAN CATHOLIC POSITION* 183

10. *THE JEWISH POSITION* 195

11. *THE SECULARIST POSITION* 198

12. *POSTSCRIPT* 212
    Strategy of Attrition 212
    Training Colleges 215
    Act of 1944 221

13. *CONCLUSION* 224

NOTES 231

BIBLIOGRAPHY 265

INDEX 287

PART I

STRUGGLES IN THE POLITICAL ARENA

CHAPTER ONE

INTRODUCTION

THE DEVELOPMENT of armaments utilizing nuclear weapons has catapulted the importance of international relations to the fore-front in the life of the present-day generation. The frightening nature of a modern conflagration merits primary consideration of ways and means to build a peaceful world community. But this does not mean that all other issues are to be deemed pettifogging and their discussion sympto-matic of a public opinion "fiddling while Rome burns." Society must still face the challenge of meeting the everyday domestic problems. Fateful as the question of war or peace may be, only greater anarchy can follow any philosophy that the fabric of civilization in its many splendored aspects must drift along until the evil forces in world politics are halted. Man's existence on this earth may be saved but it may come to lack all of the moral, ethical, and cultural values that reflect a worth-while civilization.

SETTING

The central theme of eighteenth century Enlightenment was that the State should provide the opportunity for every individual to achieve the distinction of a dignified human being. The political program envisaged for this goal ranged from democratic government, civil liberty and social equality through freedom of press, speech, and associa-tion, and freedom of conscience to free labor, free enterprise, and free competition. The subsequent story of the struggle to commit the Western world to this noble vision of humanity includes such chapters of history as the French Revolution, the Napoleonic Empire, Revolu-tionary Europe from 1815 to 1850, and the unification of Italy and Germany under the aegis of nationalism. By the closing decades of the nineteenth century the full complement of the Rights of Man was on the march at different tempos in the various countries. Great Britain, France, and Italy were among nations in the vanguard, while Germany and Russia proceeded at a slower pace.

In the sphere of religion, the dictum of human dignity did not become stereotyped in any one rigid pattern. As progressive thought crystallized, two acceptable schemes for freedom of conscience were elaborated. Perhaps the most complete representation of this spiritual ideal was separation of Church and State, so well exemplified by the developments in America. The quest for salvation, as the first amendment to the constitution declared, must be placed on an absolutely independent basis. The role of the State was simply to see that religious bodies were not impeded in administering to the needs of worshippers. A compromise approach, adopted by many of the continental countries, was a settlement distinguishing between the religion of the majority and the several minorities. A role of primacy was accorded the faith of the greatest number of the citizenry, identified by such privileges as leading the prayers at public functions, the recognition of its commemorative occasions as national holidays, and financial assistance for buildings and salaries. However, maximum religious toleration was guaranteed minorities, emphasizing the right of public worship and no secular disabilities.

The determination of the activities necessary for the purposes of religion under either scheme provoked considerable debate. Among those under dispute none was more difficult to resolve than the custody of education. On the one hand, the school was regarded by many as a vital instrument in fostering both church membership and a moral code consistent with Christian conceptions of the afterlife. Nor would the secular and ethical training deemed so essential for the cultivation of the modern citizen be neglected. Both religious and mundane values would be given equal treatment. Certainly the tradition in the past had been to leave the education of each rising generation to the churches. On the other hand, another group of supporters of the Enlightenment questioned the supervision of education under church auspices. From the vantage point of freedom of conscience, the exposure of children of diverse faiths to a particular type of spiritual atmosphere involved religious persecution. From the vantage point of a sound civic education the stress placed upon salvation in church schools would be fatal to the prestige of the secular program. The State should administer its own school system and the churches must find their own agencies to do the work of winning youthdom to their creeds.

The steady advance of the Industrial Revolution accentuated the controversy over the respective roles of Church and State in education.

The social ills produced were of serious moment for the aims to which each was dedicated. The concentration of population in cities amid the sordid circumstances of poverty, squalor, drunkenness, and disease was not pleasant to behold. In the perspective of the churches the vulgar and base vices to which the forlorn masses were succumbing endangered the mission of salvation. Such conditions bred religious indifference and even skepticism and unless combated would produce a nation of pagans. Obviously the school could be of inestimable value to keep a child on the righteous path. In the perspective of the State the disorderly and animalistic tendencies inherent in a society living on the periphery of starvation made doubly difficult the cultivation of citizens with refined sensibilities. It was perilous to contemplate a State based upon the principle of His Majesty We the People with the dejected masses so easy a prey to demagoguery. So, if the school was needed to develop the potentialities of the individual in the new social order, it was equally vital to cope with the immediate task of inculcating elementary concepts of lawfulness and decent habits.

Great Britain, no less than other members in the family of Western civilization, was confronted with the dilemma of Church and State in the field of education.[1] The religious settlement had been along the lines of a religion of the majority. The Church of England (addressed also as the Established Church and the Anglican Church) possessed the State connection and the minorities included Nonconformists, Roman Catholics, Jews, and Agnostics. As the original locale of the Industrial Revolution, the British nation early became aware of the social problems attendant upon the birth of a proletariat. The initial leadership for popular education came from religious quarters alarmed by the spiritual apathy in the new factory towns. Two rival school systems were founded, both employing the frugal device of monitors to recruit an adequate supply of teachers at low cost. The Royal Lancastrian Association was formed in 1810 but went bankrupt in 1814 and its affairs were taken over by the British and Foreign School Society. Its leader was Joseph Lancaster, Quaker and schoolmaster, and the financial support was drawn largely from Nonconformist circles. The National Society was formed in 1811 under the active guidance of Rev. Andrew Bell, Anglican clergyman and onetime head of the Male Orphan Asylum at Madras. Its financial support came largely from Anglican circles. The major difference between the two was in their comprehension of what constituted a proper Christian basis in the schools. Where the former extolled Bible reading, the latter encouraged the study of the catechism and the Book of Common Prayer.

The formal entrance of the State into the educational picture came in 1833 when Parliament voted £20,000 for new schools, to be disbursed through the National Society and the British and Foreign School Society. Two stipulations were attached: 1) at least half the cost was to be met by contributions, and 2) preference was to be given to large towns. This grant became an annual vote of increasing proportions and in time other church educational associations, notably Roman Catholic and Wesleyan, were placed on the list of eligible participants. In 1839 a building grant of £10,000 was made to assist the above bodies in the establishment of normal colleges to train teachers and this was renewed in larger amounts as the years went on. Most significant was the decision in the 1840's to appropriate public money for maintenance purposes, parliament basing the allocation upon attendance records. The administration of the schools remained, however, in the hands of church educational associations whose personnel were drawn from clerical and lay sources alike. Intermediate responsibilities were devolved upon regional, diocesan, and urban organizations, with the bishops exercising considerable inspectorate duties. For the more detailed daily supervision of the individual school, a committee of managers was set up, composed of the local clergyman and lay members of the pertinent faith specified in the trust deed.

Educationists bent especially upon the promotion of the secular program were not prepared to let the State content itself with the role of a silent partner. In 1839 a Committee of the Privy Council on Education was created, charged with the function of disbursing directly the annual exchequer building and (later) maintenance grants and of issuing regulations related to the secular program. The curriculum was standardized and study materials independent of the Bible were introduced. The practice had been to use scriptural references as examples in teaching geography, arithmetic, writing, and reading.[2] Subsequently, based upon the recommendation of the Newcastle Commission in 1861, the State revised its school code for measuring efficient performance. Examinations came to be required for capitation grants, the so-called "payment by results." The demand was particularly pressed home that children whose faith was different from that taught in a school be excused from the religious lesson. In 1839 the church educational associations acquiesced in a statute making a conscience clause obligatory upon the trust deeds of new schools in receipt of State building grants. Finally, in 1864, its extension to all schools in receipt of exchequer maintenance grants was affirmed.

A major effort was made in 1870 to set the stage for a school system under the sole control of the State. The lever applied was the relative slowness with which the religious bodies had provided schoolplaces, thus making impossible the highly-desirable adoption of compulsory attendance. The Liberal Government under the prime ministership of William Ewart Gladstone, devout Anglican and proponent of positive religion, was won over to the importance of more accommodations. William Edward Forster, Vice-President of the Committee of Council on Education and a staunch Quaker, noted that only two-fifths (1,000,000) of the children from ages 6 to 10 and only one-third (500,000) of those ages 10 to 12 were on the school registers. True, the measure as finally passed did allow the religious bodies a five months' period of grace—until the close of 1870—to build schools in deficient districts at the expense of the State. But thereafter national grants for construction would cease, albeit annual appropriations for maintenance would continue to be dispensed. The essential victory related to districts where schoolplaces were deemed still unavailable. A local school board must be formed, of the nature of an ad hoc authority elected triennially by the ratepayers. It would be empowered to levy a rate for the erection and operation of board schools, besides having its schools eligible for exchequer maintenance grants. However, the board school was to be gratuitous only for children of necessitous families; self-supporting parents were to be charged a fee not more than ninepence weekly per child as was done in the schools of religious bodies. Thus a dual system of State schools had been brought into existence, henceforth to be composed of board and voluntary (church) schools.

If the sponsors of voluntary schools had to accept a rival system under State auspices, they insisted upon the latter possessing a Christian character. Their efforts were requited with some success. The school board was given discretionary power to include a religious lesson in the daily timetable. But differences between Anglicans and Nonconformists over the content of such instruction led to a milder prescription being adopted. Called the Cowper-Temple amendment after its author, William Francis Cowper-Temple, himself an Anglican and chairman of the National Education Union which championed the case of voluntary schools, it read "that no catechism or religious formulary which is distinctive of any particular denomination shall be taught." Furthermore, the State inspectors were not to examine the religious lesson in the board school for purposes of the exchequer maintenance grant. Some balm was derived from the concession that one or two days each year might be set aside for inspectors from religious bodies to test children of their own faiths as to the Christian quality of board school religious instruction. Less to their liking was the new type of conscience clause incorporated, applicable to all schools. It fixed the hour for the religious lesson before or after the periods devoted to the lay subjects so that the withdrawal of children to sit apart for conscience reasons would not later disturb the continuity of the school day. This could foster the idea that the religious hour was something apart from the classroom studies, to be gotten over with as early as possible or to be deferred until after the more important lay subjects were studied. But it had to be accepted to conform with the principle of religious toleration for minorities.

The Act of 1870 contributed greatly to the progress of education. The religious bodies made herculean efforts to avail themselves of the proffered building grants during the period of grace. Over the five months' respite 3,342 applications were submitted, of which the National Society accounted for 2,885, and 1,600 were allowed. Subsequently, without benefit of State assistance, the religious bodies, notably Anglican and Roman Catholic, continued to erect new schools. All told, voluntary schools increased from 8,798 in 1871 to 14,275 by 1902. Board schools too rose rapidly and reached a total of 5,878 by 1902. In terms of accommodations by 1902, the voluntary schools supplied 3,729,261 and the board schools 2,881,155 places. Many improvements were undertaken in the quality of the educational program as the result of more generous national grants and the new school board rates. The leaving age was raised to twelve years. The right of parents to free education for their children was accorded. The salary scale for teachers was driven steadily upwards. Day training (normal) colleges attached to universities were made eligible for exchequer grants. Finally, in 1899, a Board of Education was established, headed by a president, to supervise educational activities hitherto scattered among several ministerial departments.

At the same time the religious issue grew acute and the adversaries emerged more sharply in relief.[3] Nonconformists were unhappy because in many localities, notably in rural districts, only an Anglican school was available, exposing their children to an alien spiritual atmosphere. Moreover, the opportunity for a teaching career was restricted, for the voluntary school imposed a religious test upon candidates and controlled entrance to the greater number of training colleges. Agnostics, Ethicists, and Rationalists objected to any kind of Christian instruction, be it catechism, formulary, or Cowper-Templeism. Not only did it mean that children of certain minorities suffered constant embarrassment but also that the teaching profession would be a preserve for the Christian community. Anglicans and Roman Catholics were concerned for the survival of their voluntary schools, considering that Cowper-Templeism consisted of Bible reading and so gave Nonconformists their type of religious instruction in the board schools. The lack of adequate finances was the bugaboo, since only the board school could draw upon the local rate. Some relief was obtained in 1897 when parliament voted voluntary (and necessitous board) schools a special grant of 5s. per child annually. But the burden of closing the gap, even with maximum fees and liberal subscriptions, proved too much. Where in 1870 the cost per child in average attendance was £1 5s. 5d., by 1900 it stood at £2 17s. 7½d. for board and £2 6s. 4½d. for voluntary schools.[4] The Ministry of Education files contain a number of letters from Anglican bishops testifying to the budgetary difficulties of Church schools in their dioceses.[5]

Apart from expressing distress over the baneful divisions fomented among the student body by the sectarian strife, educationists interested primarily in the secular program were aroused at the continued aggressive influence exerted by the churches in the schools. The retention of the training colleges by religious bodies meant that credal would be placed ahead of civic purpose in the selection and preparation of teacher candidates. Since the greater number of these institutions were in their hands, the result would be for the staff personnel in all schools to have been impressed with the paramount importance of the spiritual side of school life. The autonomous status permitted the voluntary schools was to assure that the appointment of teachers, the choice of textbooks, and the collection of classroom wall decorations would be based upon religious predilections. What made this situation particularly reprehensible was the desperate need for an educational blueprint to strengthen the commercial position of Great Britain in world trade. The analogy could well be drawn between the British concern over the growing superiority of Germany in industry and inventiveness and today's furor in America over the impressive strides being made by Soviet Russia in the field of science. This group of educationists came to be known as secularists and took the position that the State should insist upon the supremacy of the lay subjects. Many were Christians convinced that the intransigence of the major religious bodies made a compromise between secular and spiritual aims of the school impossible and if a choice had to be made the former was the more impelling. The non-Christians—Agnostics, Ethicists, Rationalists—hostile to any kind of Christian influence in the schools, were all arrayed in the secularist camp.

POLITICAL CORRIDORS

The historical episode which provided the adversaries with an opportunity to redress the balance was the Cockerton Judgment.[6] In 1899 the London Technical Education Board challenged the right of the London School Board to organize classes in science and art at the secondary school level. T. B. Cockerton, an auditor of the Local Government Board, affirmed that this was a violation of the law that school rates could not be used above the elementary standards. The London School Board appealed the case but the courts upheld Cockerton's ruling. The complaint would appear to have been instigated by a group of Anglicans headed by Lord Hugh Cecil, youngest son of the third Marquess of Salisbury, Prime Minister of the Conservative Government.* The hope was to force an administrative reorganization which would abolish the school boards, the evil genius behind the soaring costs that were bankrupting the voluntary schools. Their idea was to show the need for a broader supervising agency if progress were to be made in secondary education so that the county council would become the local authority for elementary education as well. The advantage of the county council would be a clean slate that might enable voluntary schools to get on the rates and so avert financial catastrophe.

Educationists intent upon the advancement of the secular program were no less hopeful of the fruits which the Cockerton Judgment might yield.[7] A leader in seeking to exploit the favorable situation was Sidney Webb (Lord Passfield), student of public administration, leader of the socialist Fabian Society, and member of the London County Council. So far as his own position on the religious issue was concerned, he chose to ignore it entirely, raising his sights on the improvement of educational opportunities. He regarded the religious issue as insoluble and simply accepted the existence of the dual system. Webb deplored the lack of secondary school facilities for the masses. The endowed public schools and the sprinkling of grammar schools were available mainly for the middle and upper classes. He would designate the county council as the local authority for education and place both elementary and secondary education under its wing, thus enabling these two vital rungs in the school ladder to draw on the rates for support. Further, in return for assistance out of the rates, he proposed that voluntary schools

---

* Elie Halévy, French historian of the English scene, is in error in according the leadership to Lord Robert Cecil and, further, in listing him as the youngest son (instead of the third son) of the third Marquess of Salisbury. Halévy, *Imperialism and the Rise of Labour* (1951, 2nd rev. ed.), p. 197. For an accurate statement describing Lord Hugh Cecil as the leader of this group see Spender (1923), II, p. 61.

submit to the control of the county council with regard to the secular program. If these salutary changes were made, felt Webb, then Great Britain would be on its way to an integrated educational system offering every child a chance to develop his full faculties.

Throughout 1901 the Church of England exerted pressure upon the Conservative Government to take action. In July a joint conference of the Canterbury and York Convocations met at London to focus attention upon the "intolerable strain." A strong resolution was adopted demanding that the cost of secular instruction in all schools be borne out of public funds.[8] The Conservative Party with its tradition of supporting the Establishment was sympathetic to the Church of England. The third Marquess of Salisbury, Prime Minister, along with his three sons in the commons, James Edward Hubert Gascoyne-Cecil, Robert Cecil, and Hugh Cecil, were ardent Anglicans. Arthur James Balfour, First Lord of the Treasury and shortly (on July 12, 1902) to succeed the ailing third Marquess of Salisbury as prime minister, was born a Scotch Presbyterian and became a communicant in the Church of England at Eton. However, he held himself to be a member of both churches and was a strong advocate of the denominationalist case. Both the new President of the Board of Education, the sixth Marquess of Londonderry, and the new appointee as parliamentary secretary, Sir William Anson, distinguished scholar and Conservative M. P. for Oxford University, were members of the Church of England. Behind the scene there was Robert Morant, the new permanent secretary to the Board of Education and an active Anglican. The greater number of members in the House of Commons had an Anglican background. In the House of Lords, the Church of England hierarchy were allotted twenty-four seats and most of the peers were both Conservatives and Anglicans.

The Conservative Party was by no means exclusively Anglican in outlook. Sir Almeric Fitzroy, private secretary to three presidents of the Committee of Council on Education and clerk of the Privy Council since 1898, tells us that the discussions on education in the Salisbury Cabinet provoked heated exchanges.[9] The Radical Unionists who had left the Liberal Party in 1886 in protest against Gladstone's Home Rule Bill provided the chief opposition. Their spokesman was Joseph Chamberlain, Colonial Secretary, and at the moment occupied with the Boer War and with plans for returning Great Britain to protection via imperial preference. His religious affiliation was Unitarian and during the debate on the Forster Bill in 1870 he had been an active proponent of the secular solution. Many of his followers were Nonconformists and champions of the board schools. Chamberlain was particularly concerned lest the grant of rate aid to the voluntary schools raise the twin cries of taxation without representation and religious intoleration. In the give and take of politics, the Radical Unionists were at a disadvantage, for a second political rupture could mean an end to their public careers. Chamberlain, preferring to risk his future on what he regarded as issues of greater import, bowed to the majority of the cabinet and accepted a measure counter to lifelong convictions.[10] He was even ready to see merit in the proposed educational legislation and actually went to Birmingham, a stronghold of the secular solution, and vigorously defended the Balfour Bill:[11]

> We have a system, which is no system at all, which is a state of anarchy and confusion . . . . The authorities, which collect the taxes or the rates, are not the authorities which spend the taxes or the rates. There is no efficient control over the secular education . . . [which] in a vast number of schools [is] starved and inefficient owing to the inability of the managers . . . to provide the necessary funds. Who suffers by that? Not the managers but the children of the people. . . . All these things constitute a national weakness and a national danger in view of the competition [industrial] to which we are subjected.

While the Conservative Government was able, therefore, to muster a united front in pressing forward its scheme, an effort was made to meet the views of all plaintiffs. After all, a political party, whatever its leanings may be, must also consider the general electorate. Its hope is always to produce a compromise that will earn plaudits from all quarters and so win votes in the next election. True it was that the transfer of education from the school boards to the county councils and the grant of rate aid to voluntary schools would be great boons to the Church of England. But Balfour, who was in charge of the measure throughout the legislative stages, believed that his formula was fair to all sides. To lay the foundation for secondary education, to establish firmer State control over the secular program in all elementary schools, and to lessen the possibility of infringements upon freedom of conscience were commendable achievements. Balfour defined his position as halfway between the militant advocates of the voluntary schools and the equally militant anti-denominationalists. So far as the particular form of religious teaching was concerned, he would "see that every parent gets the kind of denominational teaching that he desires." But, more importantly, he would say

> that there are at stake issues greater than the fortune of any political party; there is at stake the education of your children for a generation,

and ... if we— ... the majority of the House of Commons—hesitate to do our duty, and to carry through this great reform, we shall receive the contempt of the parents and the children living and to be born, and that contempt we shall most justly earn.[12]

The Liberal Party constituted the refuge for those dissatisfied with the bill, notably Nonconformists. No doubt it was partly animated by the chance to attract back to its banner the Radical Unionist vote and so return to power at the next general election. But historically its tradition called for such a sympathetic position. It had championed the movement for Disestablishment. It had fought for the separation of Church and State. It had been responsible for the Education Act of 1870 inaugurating the board schools. At the moment many of its leading members bore the stamp of Nonconformity. Sir Henry Campbell-Bannerman, titular head of His Majesty's Opposition, was a Scotch Presbyterian. James Bryce, distinguished scholar and cabinet member in several previous Liberal Governments, was likewise a Scotch Presbyterian. Lloyd George, practicing Baptist, was a fiery expositor for Welsh Nonconformity. Herbert Henry Asquith, Home Secretary in the Gladstone Cabinet from 1892 to 1895, came from a Nonconformist family with traditions in Congregationalist circles. Perhaps the most active dissident in Liberal ranks to the party's attack against the measure was Richard Burdon Haldane, whose parents were Baptists and he himself a Deist. However, Haldane acknowledged frankly his isolated role as a supporter of the Balfour Bill and its meritorious aims to unify the English system of education and to raise the efficiency of voluntary schools.[13]

BALFOUR BILL OF 1902

A major overhauling of the administration of education was prescribed.[14] Henceforth the local authority for education was defined to mean the elected councils of counties (62), county boroughs (69), non-county boroughs with a population over 10,000 (139), and urban districts with a population over 20,000 (63). Where before 1902 there had been 2,214 school boards plus 736 school attendance committees (in districts with only voluntary schools) or 2,950 in all, now the number would be trimmed down to 333. The failure to make the county council everywhere the local education authority was a concession to the autonomous ambitions of urban communities. The city of London was excluded from the act, to be dealt with separately in 1903 because

of its peculiar cosmopolitan problems. For direct supervision each of
the above local authorities was to appoint an education committee, to
be filled from the elected council itself and co-opted persons in any
proportion desired. The education committee would control the disbursement of all monies, the audit of accounts, and the inspection of
the secular program in voluntary as well as council (board) schools.† It
was also to possess a veto power over the recommendation of the school
managers in the matter of teacher appointments. In the case of dismissals it was to exercise a similar veto save on grounds of religious
incompatibility. Assistant and pupil teachers could be appointed to
the staff of voluntary schools without reference to their credal convictions. In addition, the education committee was to have the right to
designate two of the six managers engaged in overseeing the affairs of
each voluntary school.

The relief of voluntary schools from their "intolerable strain" was
achieved in several ways. Naturally, the fact of prime importance was
that they would be eligible for local rate aid. As heretofore, they would
receive a national grant, although the margin was not to exceed three-
fourths of the total sum expended on education in any school district.
A modest increase in the national grant was made possible by the
appropriation of an additional £900,000 to offset the repeal of the special grant to voluntary schools (£639,270) and necessitous schools
(£219,840). The church educational associations were permitted to
retain or to share in several lucrative sources of income which the original draft bill had contemplated turning over to the local authority in
lieu of rate aid. They were to receive rent for the use of teachers' dwellings attached to voluntary schools. They were to get half of the income
secured from the school fees paid by guardians for pauper children
attending voluntary schools. They were to get half of the endowments
hitherto collected by them. The liability for ordinary wear-and-tear
maintenance was transferred to the local authority. Henceforth the
financial obligation of the church educational associations was to be
limited to the construction of new schools and structural repairs and,
initially, to reasonable improvements as requested by the local authority
prior to being made eligible for rate aid. It was on the basis of these
responsibilities that the voluntary schools became known also as "non-
provided" and the council as "provided" schools.

The preservation of the Christian basis in the elementary schools but
within the spirit of religious toleration and democratic control was

---

† If the reference to the schools of local authorities relates to experiences before 1902
the proper term is "board" and after 1902 "council."

reflected in a number of provisions. The Cowper-Temple clause featuring Bible study and to be implemented at the discretion of the local authority would remain the operating principle in council schools. The directions in the trust deed would continue to determine the nature of the religious lesson given in voluntary schools. However, its supervision devolved specifically upon the school managers by what is known as the Kenyon-Slaney amendment where hitherto the local clergyman had been deferred to as the shepherd of the flock in the voluntary school. No alteration was made in the timetable conscience clause, thus assuring pupils in all elementary schools of the right to sit apart during the religious lesson if their parents so desired. The opportunity for new voluntary school construction was liberalized to enable church educational associations to meet population trends. Henceforth a need for a voluntary school, accompanied by the names of parents representing thirty children in attendance, would receive equal consideration with a rival request for a council school. In the event of conflicting claims, the arbiter would be the Board of Education. In the new day training colleges, which local authorities were empowered to establish at the expense of the rates, the right of entry to offer prospective teachers courses in religious instruction was permissible but to be arranged for at times not interfering with the secular work.

CHAPTER TWO

PASSAGE OF THE ACT OF 1902

THE ADVERSARIES

THE EDUCATION BILL was introduced in the commons on March 24, 1902. Considering the other events of national moment that year, the sustained interest which it commanded was a testimony to its public importance. For one thing, in July the Boer War came to an end and the course of reconstruction in South Africa had to be charted. For another thing, in August the coronation of Edward VII was finally held, more than a year after Queen Victoria, his mother, had died. Yet the Education Bill was debated for fifty-nine days in the commons and nine days in the lords before receiving the royal assent on December 18, 1902. But, significantly, it was not the prospect of progress in secondary education or the improvement of the secular program in the elementary school that held the spotlight. Rather it was the religious issue that came to monopolize the bulk of attention. Anglican, Roman Catholic, Nonconformist, and secularist took over as the chief protagonists. Much as the historic parties might fret or rejoice over the political consequences of this explosive issue, those concerned with salvation as well as with education let the chips fall where they would.

Anglicans were frank in acknowledging the need for financial assistance. On the eve of drafting the measure, Archbishop Maclagan of York, in a letter to Balfour dated December 18, 1901, expressed the fear that "unless [our] schools should receive some additional support from the Government, many will succumb." How bad the financial condition of voluntary schools had become may be deduced from a memorandum prepared in February 1902 by Robert Morant.[1] The over-all findings for 1900 showed that 56% were "under water" and for the three previous years the average was 45%. In the case of the Church of England schools, apart from a momentary rebound in 1898 with the help of the special 5s. per child grant, adverse balances were recorded of £140,000 in 1897, of £50,000 in 1899, and of £105,000 in

1900. For the entire four-year-period the net adverse balance was
£280,000.

Bishop Moorhouse of Manchester attributed the deficit to rising
school expenditures geared to board school resources. For 1900 the
school board rate of £1 5s. 6d. per child could only be matched by the
voluntary schools with subscriptions of 6s. 4¾d. per child.[2] In extenua-
tion, pointed out Rev. Miller, Vicar of Tillingham, Essex, if patrons
had been unable to meet budgetary requests, it was because they were
now paying rates to finance the ambitious programs of school boards.
In this connection it might be noted that while subscriptions rose in
the aggregate from £528,483 in 1875 to £648,699 in 1901, in terms of
maintenance per child there was a decline from 8s. 2d. in 1875 to 6s. 8d.
in 1901.[3] Indeed, the School Guardian was not sure but that the plight
of voluntary schools stemmed from malice aforethought:

> The Nonconformists have endeavored so to work the School Board
> system as to supplant the Denominational School system. They have
> built schools in unnecessarily close proximity to denominational institu-
> tions [and] larger than required to entice children away and money spent
> to provide attractions we could not.[4]

The nation was reminded that Anglican patrons had dug deep into
their pockets since 1870 in response to the State plea for a network of
schools throughout England and Wales. Rev. Sidney E. Dymott,
Wavertree, Liverpool, stated that over the past thirty years the Church
of England had subscribed no less than £29,072,117 for the construction
and maintenance of their day schools and training colleges.[5] While in
1870 there were 8,281 voluntary schools educating 1,400,000 children,
as of August 31, 1901, there were 14,319 voluntary schools with
2,492,536 scholars in average attendance compared to 5,797 board
schools with 2,239,375 scholars.[6] In terms of replacement value, many
an Anglican commentator estimated that a State expenditure of
£45,000,000 would be required to build an equivalent physical plant.
This calculation was based upon the current cost of £15 per schoolplace
for the approximately three million available in voluntary schools.[7] The
School Guardian asked the nation if it were prepared to accept such a
crushing outlay in the event that these buildings were withdrawn from
education and confined to church activities.[8]

Anglicans were at pains to establish the fact that, even with the proposed rate aid, voluntary schools would have to bear financial burdens
to compensate for the time devoted to credal instruction. Subscriptions

would still be needed to purchase school sites, erect new buildings, and make structural repairs. The *School Guardian* offered an itemized account of how liberally Churchmen paid for the privilege of imparting religious instruction to children of their own faith. Not more than one of the four or five hours weekly spent in such lessons was devoted to formularies. Since the number of school hours per week was twenty-five, the proportion came to 1/25. The rent value of Church schools for secular instruction considerably exceeded 1/25 of the maintenance cost. Thus, in 1901 the figure for Church schools was £4,399,267 and 1/25 of this equaled £175,970.[9] At the modest interest rate of 3¼%, the rent value on the actual building outlay of £22,000,000 was £715,000 a year.[10] In short, subtracting £175,970 from £715,000, the remaining sum of £539,030 constituted a gift by the Church of England to the State for the latter's secular program.[11]

Anglicans were not entirely happy with the rate aid provision in the original draft, supposed to have been inserted by the Conservative Party to secure Joseph Chamberlain's support, for he feared that compulsion might bring on a recrudescence of the Church rate crusade.[12] Each community was to choose as the educational authority either the *ad hoc* school board or the county council. Since only the county council was empowered to levy the new rate aid for all schools, the *Church Times* argued that the intent to help voluntary schools could be nullified if any appreciable number of localities retained the *ad hoc* school board. True, it was commendable thinking to wish the avoidance of any apparent hostility to the more outstanding school boards. But if a community were free to make a choice, the prospect of increased rates might militate against a transfer of education to the county council. The *Western Mail* (Cardiff) was certain that in Wales, where many local authorities were dominated by Nonconformists, the bill would not be implemented. The *Pall Mall Gazette* predicted that the result would be one of uneven benefit to voluntary schools. Where a county council took over, they would flourish. Where a school board continued, they would starve. Much to the relief of Anglicans, the Conservative Government agreed to make mandatory the role of the county council as the local education authority.[13]

Many Anglicans were concerned lest the "intolerable strain" reappear through backstage machinations. The burden of structural alterations and new school construction would still be theirs. These could be very costly if hostile authorities imposed unreasonable requirements. And there was every likelihood that subscriptions would decline further as education rates rose. Accordingly, in the committee stage, supporters of voluntary schools labored to salvage revenues which the government proposed to transfer to local authorities in return for rate aid.[14] Some £50,000 annually was saved by the right to charge rent for teachers' residences attached to voluntary schools.[15] Some £75,000 annually (half of the estimated income) was retained from educational endowments previously disbursed by church associations.[16] Some £90,000 annually (half of the estimated income) was secured from the school fees paid by guardians for pauper children attending their schools.[17] In the lords, Bishop Moorhouse of Manchester pressed successfully an amendment requiring the local authority to accept the cost of ordinary wear-and-tear maintenance which he estimated as a saving of over £300,000 to the voluntary schools on the basis of almost three million schoolplaces at an average cost of repairs of 2s. 10d.[18]

Anglicans were particularly pleased with the liberal provisions for constructing new schools. Where the local authority proposed a new school, public notice was to be given and managers of an existing school or any ten ratepayers in the district could within three months after notice was given appeal to the Board of Education on the ground that it was not required or that a school by some other body was better suited to meet the needs of the district. The Board of Education was to decide with due regard for the interests of secular education, the wishes of parents, and the economy of rates.[19]

To the *Standard* the opportunity to construct new schools was vital if pace were to be kept with population movements. Hitherto the decision had been in the hands of the local authority and the law had required proof of a deficiency in schoolplaces. Few things had caused more irritation in the past than the hostile conduct of school boards who hid behind the facile plea that accommodations were already adequate to thwart new voluntary schools. Henceforth a religious need was to be a sufficient reason for authorizing a new Church school. Only the stipulation that the building funds must be raised by subscriptions was disliked by the *School Guardian*. While both voluntary and council schools would be on the rates for maintenance, the latter alone would be eligible to tap rate aid for construction purposes. The obvious danger was that the greater tempo of expansion could be in council schools.[20]

Anglicans made much of the popular control which the Balfour Bill outlined in the administration of voluntary schools in return for rate aid. An elective county council operating through a nominated education committee would have in its hands the disbursement of all monies, the audit of accounts, the inspection of the secular work, and a veto of teacher appointments on educational grounds. At the individual school level, the education committee would have the right to name two of the six managers. Even if these two non-foundation managers were in a minority their presence would guarantee full publicity for board actions.* Bishop Moorhouse of Manchester stressed that the only functions left the four foundation managers would be to nominate the teachers and to see that the religious instruction was duly given and of the character prescribed by the trust deed. As for the much maligned role of the parson, although Rev. Edward F. Taylor, diocesan school inspector for Truro, Cornwall, believed that few were guilty of interference, at any rate the so-called era of one-man domineering on the part of a vicar could no longer be charged.[21]

Some willingness was manifested to go further in popular control over voluntary schools. The leading proposal was that of Bishop Percival of Hereford, vainly introduced as an amendment in the lords. He would have had two managers named by the parish council, two by the education committee, and two by the religious association. At the same time, to protect the denominational character of a Church school, he would require that the head teacher be a member of the Church of England and that the parish clergyman have access to instruct the children under his fold. Ven. James M. Wilson, Archdeacon of Manchester and after 1905 Canon of Worcester, supported this scheme, save that he would have the parents of the school children name two managers instead of the parish council. The *Morning Post* suggested that the head teacher be appointed by the local authority subject to a veto by the foundation managers. Thus teachers would be given a sense of feeling that they were public servants while the foundation managers would be assured that the denominational basis of their school would continue. The *Pilot* would go one step further and divide authority, assigning to the non-foundation managers control over the secular work and to the foundation managers control over the religious instruction.[22] To all these proposals, however, the main body of Anglicans responded that a two-thirds majority of non-foundation managers could endanger the spiritual purpose of a Church school.[23]

Roman Catholic reaction to the Balfour Bill paralleled the Anglican point of view. The need for financial assistance was frankly acknowledged. The presence of inferior buildings, poor equipment, less qualified teachers, and overcrowded classes were not fair to children in

---

* Lord Hugh Cecil was not enthusiastic over seating public representatives on the board of managers. There was great danger of the foundation managers being cowed and subjected to bitter quarreling. In Wales, "cat and dog would be a feeble image of proceedings." He preferred that the public representatives be placed on a higher policy committee where a more independent and impartial procedure would govern. *Ministry of Education,* 1902, Bill Papers, No. 29, a memorandum attributed to Lord Hugh Cecil, 6 pp.

parochial schools. The current settlement was labeled a "gigantic system of sweating." The State should accept the principle of "an equal wage for equal work" and pay the total cost for both sets of schools. The *Tablet* described how heroic had been Roman Catholic efforts in the past to raise money for their schools:

> Little ... need to tell the ceaseless importunities of the street to street begging on Saturday nights, of the bazaars and theatricals and conjuring tricks, and the hundred other extraordinary devices by which the people were worried, or cajoled, or coaxed into giving alms to help keep afloat what with ingenious irony were described as the public elementary schools of the nation?[24]

Roman Catholics were cautious in their appraisal of the financial provisions. While the eligibility of voluntary schools to share in rate aid was welcomed, the *Catholic Times* felt that further checking was necessary to assure that "we are not overwhelmed later by a faddy authority." The fact that responsibility for structural improvements and the construction of new schools would be theirs could be a crushing obligation. Needless to say, much satisfaction was derived from the acceptance of Bishop Moorhouse's amendment making the State liable for ordinary wear-and-tear maintenance. Equal concern was evinced over the optional qualification in designating the county council as the local education authority. The *Catholic Herald* regarded its own people as very vulnerable to such a clause. Roman Catholic schools were located in large towns—Liverpool, Manchester, Leeds, Birmingham, Cardiff— where school boards were well entrenched and the communities disinclined to pay rate aid for voluntary schools. It should be made obligatory (as it came to pass) to protect parochial schools in hostile areas where rate aid was not likely to be put into practice.[25]

Roman Catholics reviewed the provision extending popular control over their schools in return for rate aid. The *Catholic Times* noted how far the measure went in endowing the education committees with authority. They possessed a veto over the appointment of teachers and could participate in the dismissal of a teacher. They had the power to choose the secular textbooks and would be master over the efficiency of all schools. Unless care were exercised, the scheme could deprive a parochial school of its character. The principal hope to check such encroachments was representation of Roman Catholic interests on the education committees. Since no opportunity existed to get a seat for a minority by the device of the cumulative vote as had obtained with the school boards, the answer was sought in a special allocation.[26] Herbert

Cardinal Vaughan, Archbishop of Westminster, wrote to Lord Edmund Talbot, Conservative M.P. and Roman Catholic,[†] for assistance, adding the argument that to give official recognition to each of the denominations whose work was bound up with education would help "weld into one the national system." Roman Catholics were, of course, gratified when the lords inserted such an amendment.[27]

Roman Catholics were divided over the appointment of non-foundation managers to their schools. On the one hand, there were some in favor of accepting even more popular control and so dissolve Nonconformist resistance to rate aid. Rev. Hugh Edmund Ford, Abbot of Downside, a settlement of Benedictine monks near Bath, contributed the leading proposal. He would allow four of the six managers to be elected by the parents of the children in actual school attendance, with the selection of the teacher to be in the hands of the two foundation managers. A variation of this scheme was put forward by John Dillon, Irish Nationalist M.P., who would assign, where only one school existed in a district, two to the education committee, two to the parents, and two to the trustees, reserving the head teachership for the religious association.[‡] On the other hand, the main stream of Roman Catholic opinion was averse to any possibility of losing the management of their schools. The *Tablet* pointed out that many parochial schools possessed a large Protestant minority. In the event of an aggressive canvass on the part of Protestants to name the two representatives of the parents and an education committee prepared to name its two representatives from the community, a parochial school could find itself with a majority of Protestant managers. Indeed, clever maneuvering could swing an election for the two parental representatives by the transfer of Protestant children from a neighboring school to the parochial school. Then there would be little security for the reality of Catholicism.[28]

Roman Catholics were at variance over what many felt was the failure of the Irish Nationalist Party to defend more energetically the Balfour Bill. They referred to the return of its members to Ireland in the fall of 1902 for consultation with local leaders on the coercive measures being applied by the Conservative Government, thereby absenting themselves during the later committee stage. The fact that

---

[†] Lord Edmund Talbot and the fifteenth Duke of Norfolk who championed the Roman Catholic cause in the House of Lords were brothers.

[‡] The *Catholic Herald* (July 25, 1902) would go along with Dillon's plan if the "two representatives of the parents" meant not just those parents who were ratepayers but all those with children in attendance. If it were only the former, it could leave the Roman Catholics in a minority position in their own schools, for as a notoriously exploited section of the population they seldom could qualify as ratepayers.

they had ignored an appeal to remain in parliament from Cardinal Vaughan created a bad impression among English Roman Catholics. The *Catholic Herald* rose to the support of the Nationalists. The first duty of Irish members was to the people of Ireland and at the moment the Balfour Ministry was pursuing a policy of repression in Ireland. It was sure, moreover, that if the Liberal Party came to power the Irish Nationalist Party would be able to wield greater influence in behalf of a just and equitable settlement for all parties. As a matter of fact, when John Redmond, chairman of the Irish Nationalist Party, returned from Ireland, he defended his party's role in forwarding the educational interests of English co-religionists. He pointed out that both on the second reading and in committee (through August) the party had voted solidly for the measure. Only when autumn came and Irish members were certain that the bill was safe had they proceeded to Ireland where their presence was urgently needed.[29]

Nonconformists reacted bitterly toward the Balfour Bill. As they envisaged educational progress, it was centered in one set of schools under popular control. Their interpretation of the Act of 1870 was that it set the sights of the nation on that goal and not on the perpetuation of the dual system. Dr. John Clifford, Baptist minister of Westbourne Park, London, and a leader in the Free Church movement, insisted that voluntary schools were intended as an adjunct to be continued so long as their sponsors made the necessary financial sacrifices. Rev. William E. Blomfield, Baptist minister and subsequently President of the Baptist College in Rawdon, Leeds, noted how in the intervening years a steady assault had been made upon the original understanding. Where in 1870 contributions were 29% and school fees were 30% of the total cost, by 1900 the former had fallen to 13% and the latter to 9%.[30] Rev. J. Monro Gibson, Presbyterian minister, St. John's Wood, London, and once moderator of the Presbyterian Church in England, commented that Anglicans had themselves to blame for the "intolerable strain." They had endeavored to exploit the final opportunity for State building grants in 1870 and so had overextended themselves financially. They should first have counted the cost of building hundreds of new schools which they could not support. Denominationalists were going beyond the bounds of propriety to have the public assume the full liability of their maintenance.[31]

Nonconformists challenged the Anglican thesis of past outlays for education at the urgent behest of the State. More often subscriptions had been wrung from reluctant local citizens by the threat of increased school rates for a board school if the Church school were forced to close its doors.* Lloyd George cited the case of a neighbor in Carnarvonshire, Lord Penryhn of Llandegai, who gave £400 a year to voluntary schools in his district whereas if he had been rated the sum would have been £2,200.† Such selfish artfulness hardly merited the description of heroic philanthropy, especially when one contemplated that inferior schooling had been the fruit of this parsimony. Dr. Macnamara, Liberal M.P., editor of the *Schoolmaster*, and active in the National Union of Teachers, contrasted the fact that in board schools 51% of the teachers were certificated while in voluntary schools its was 38%. In student ratio there was one certificated teacher for every 76 children enrolled in board schools and one for every 103 in voluntary schools.[32] Add dilapidated premises, large classes, and underpaid teachers and the so-called denominationalist largess resulted in half the nation's children being deprived of equal schooling facilities.[33]

The National Education Association, founded in 1889 to promote progressive education for all irrespective of economic status—and which became largely Nonconformist in its thinking—published a pamphlet detailing the inferior quality of education in voluntary schools.‡ The data assembled was drawn from the report of the Education Department for 1898.[34] In accuracy of knowledge and general intelligence, the maximum grant was earned by 85% of board and 62% of voluntary schools. In ability to sing by note as against ear, the maximum grant was earned by 95% of board and 84% of voluntary schools. In the first class subjects such as English, geography, history, and elementary

---

* The Anglican answer was that the public in general and Nonconformists in particular were equally guilty along with those relatively few (they hoped) of their own parishioners who indulged in such base motives. *Church Quarterly Rev.*, Oct. 1902, p. 195; *Church Times*, Aug. 15, 1902 (J. Cecil White).

† The *Journal of Education* (Sept. 1902) offered the pedagogue's awareness of this practice, submitting an incident in Sussex. The Eastbourne Voluntary Schools Buildings Committee Ltd. was formed in 1897, with capital of £10,000 (largely supplied by the ninth Duke of Devonshire) to contract, as the prospectus said, "for the building or enlarging of elementary schools in Eastbourne, so as to avoid a School Board with its heavy rates and to do this in such a way as to provide a fair interest on the capital supplied." This company had since fulfilled its promises and paid a dividend of 4% besides meeting a rent charge by the Duke of Devonshire.

‡ Wilfred J. Rowland, secretary of the National Education Association for many years, told the author in an interview that he believed the pamphlet was prepared by Anthony John Mundella, a nephew and namesake of the first president of the association, the latter also famous as a leader in the fight for compulsory education in the 1880's. Mr. Rowland stated that while the Association endeavored to be nonsectarian, its position on the religious issue had attracted greater support from Nonconformists. It is interesting to note that the National Education Association was listed under Free Church bodies, although it was described as strictly speaking not a Free Church affiliate. *Free Church Year Book*, 1902, pp. 340-41.

science, the mark "good" was given to 95% of board and 85% of voluntary schools. In the second class subjects such as domestic economy and needlework, the mark "good" was given to 96% of board and 84% of voluntary schools. In specific subjects for elder children, such as bookkeeping, shorthand, elementary agriculture, and horticulture, statistics showed children examined numbered 25% in board and 9% in voluntary schools. In cookery and laundry, taught to girls above the third standard, instruction was given to 22% in board and 6% in voluntary schools.[35]

No less false was the accompanying inference of a State indifferent to education. Rev. Gibson sketched how the State had been actually thwarted in its desire to take over full responsibility for education.* The Whitbread Bill of 1807 to establish rate-aided schools providing two years of free education for poor children was rejected because of opposition by the bishops in the lords.† It was only after the bill had been lost that the Quaker Joseph Lancaster tried to fill the gap in 1810 with the Royal Lancastrian Society. The subsequent advent of the National Society in 1811 was to forward Anglican influence among youth rather than to promote education. Even when the State had been permitted to set up schools in 1870 under public management, it was on condition that the religious associations be given first chance to supply the deficiency in accommodations. In the meantime, noted the New Liberal Review, how magnanimous had been State contributions. Between 1839 (correctly, 1833) when the first building appropriation was made and 1882 when the State closed its books on such grants, 5,676 Church of England schools had been built at a cost of £5,811,904 10s. 8d. Of this sum the State had given £1,515,385 9s. 8½d. and the Anglicans £4,296,519 no s. 11½d.[36] Again, since the 1840's public grants for the maintenance of Church of England schools (11,714) had totaled £63,700,748 9s. 9d.[37] Such expenditures hardly suggested State apathy to education.[38]

---

* The secularist Freethinker (Dec. 7, 1902) declared a plague on both houses, Anglican and Nonconformist, claiming that the true history of English education in the first half of the nineteenth century embraced the struggle of a small band of earnest educationists against the intrigues of the two great religious organizations to control the schools of the country in their own interests.

† James Allanson Picton, secularist, Independent minister, member of the London School Board (1869-78), and Liberal M.P. for Leicester (1884-94), supported this contention: "In 1807 the Archbishop of Canterbury stamped out Samuel Whitbread's scheme of national education. . . . The Bill had passed the Commons and would almost certainly have passed the Lords if the Archbishop would have allowed it." Picton, The Bible in School (1907), pp. 57, 57n. For literature on the Whitbread Bill see Barnard (1952), p. 65; Curtis (1950), pp. 208-09; Smith (1931), pp. 108-10.

Nonconformists did not ignore the Anglican threat that a withdrawal of voluntary schools would mean an enormous expenditure on the part of the State. Perhaps the most detailed analysis was submitted by Edgar T. Woodhead, an avid supporter of Disestablishment. He used the official figures for 1900-01 which set the available accommodations in voluntary schools at 3,710,998.[39] Woodhead listed two factors which would cut this number measurably. First, he referred to the case of Stockport, Cheshire, where the school board had been abolished on the ground that the 13,825 places in voluntary schools were sufficient for the size of the community. But at the commission hearing the fact was brought out that if the standard of ten square feet per scholar, as applied to board schools had governed for voluntary schools, the number would have shrunk to 8,619 places.[40] If, then, it could be assumed that the 30% shrinkage was an average occurrence and the standard was enforced in all schools, the accommodations in voluntary schools would be reduced from 3,710,998 to 2,283,000 places. Second, in the case of depopulated villages, where accommodations were now in excess of local needs, a further subtraction could be made in the original fictitious total of replacements. Obviously the figure of £45,000,000 put forward by Anglicans as the cost should be scaled down many millions and so the prospect of prohibitive cost was only a mirage.[41]

Rev. James Hirst Hollowell, Milton Congregational Church, Rochdale, active in the Free Church movement and secretary of the Northern Counties Education League,‡ answered the Anglican threat with equally formidable facts. He hammered away at the point that the original cost of voluntary schools was £25,000,000 at the most and not entirely the beneficence of denominationalists. Many thousands of pounds had been subscribed by persons of other faiths and by commercial companies, not to mention State grants. Then there were legitimate deductions that should be entered—Sunday school use of the buildings and furnishings and the money value of the forced conformity of the teachers. Even accepting the thesis of an exclusive denominationally-raised fund, the sum was small compared to the capitalized value of the £80,000,000 pledged to sectarian schools from the rates. Rev. Hollowell based this figure upon the assumption that rates would go up almost £3,000,000 annually, since the rise probably would be equivalent

---

‡ The Northern Counties Education League was organized to defend the school board system and to secure its extension throughout England and Wales. Its position was essentially that of Nonconformity, stressing popular control and no religious tests for teachers. It covered the areas of Lancashire, Yorkshire, Northumberland, Durham, Westmoreland, Cumberland, Cheshire, Derbyshire, Nottinghamshire, and Lincolnshire. For its history see Evans (1911), p. 48 ff.

to the amount of rate aid being spent on board schools.[42] Surely the
nation had no reason to fear a financial debacle if the issue were joined
with the sectarians.[43]

Nonconformists were particularly incensed over the financial concessions exacted by Anglicans at the committee stage. George White,
Baptist layman and Liberal M.P., labeled them "a distinct breach of
faith on the part of the Government and a spirit of mean huckstering
by friends of the Church which would disgrace Petticoat Lane or Seven
Dials." Nor could it be said that the revenues which they would continue to share were Anglican in origin. The Westminster Gazette recorded that the teachers' dwellings attached to voluntary schools, built
between 1843 and 1881 and numbering 3,290 units, were financed by
State building grants of £303,000.[44] Many endowments had been left
for philanthropic purposes and only later had come into the hands of
churches for administration. Dr. Clifford referred to a story told by
Rev. David Basil Martin, Congregational minister in Hereford.[45] In
the days of Charles II, Lord Scudamore left a legacy of £400 "setting
the poor people of Hereford to work." As no reasonable scheme was
devised, the money was left to accumulate until the 1850's, when it
amounted to £6,000. It was then decided to use it for a Church school.
In the matter of school fees for pauper children, Nonconformist sentiment was that rate aid should have constituted a generous compensation. As for saddling the State with the cost of wear-and-tear maintenance, Anglicans apparently intended to pay nothing for the privilege
of giving denominational instruction in 12,000 elementary schools.[46]

Nonconformists accused Anglicans of plotting to use these savings,
estimated at £500,000, as a war chest for an aggressive campaign to build
new schools. The outlined procedure patently favored the denominationalists. An education committee desiring to construct a council
school must give three months' notice and during that time if a religious
association submitted a rival plan, then the dispute must go before the
Board of Education. Since the latter was required to find its own capital
outlay, remarked the Daily News, the drain on the rates would be much
less if a church body was prepared to put up the money. So the Board
of Education, instructed to give due heed to economy, would more
often find in favor of a voluntary school. Further, the Westminster
Gazette pointed out that a zealot had only to secure the names of parents representing thirty children in attendance to establish a "religious
need" for their kind of school. The Monthly Messenger minimized
the merit of the opportunity for Nonconformists to build schools in
the single school areas where their grievances were keenest. The risk
of neighborhood retaliation if a second school were put on the rates

would deter Free Churchmen. Apart from the partisan advantage which would accrue to the Church of England, the consequences for education were lamented. The multiplication of small schools, as must follow, could be costly in maintenance and provoke a hostile reaction among the general public. It predicted that, in the end, the most ardent educator would be deterred from advocating badly needed improvements.[47]

Nonconformists were critical of the administrative provisions. Rev. W. Hume Elliot, Presbyterian minister, Ramsbottom, Manchester, defended the school board as having done much to promote an enlightened educational program. In contrast, the county council would degrade education to the level of the sewerage and drainage services.* Most serious to the *British Weekly* was the fact that the voluntary school would still be under the control of a religious body. The appointment of one-third of the managers by education committees was an empty concession since they would be outnumbered.† More likely they would have to be personally acceptable to the foundation managers and so things would go on as heretofore. The *Speaker* prophesied that the local parson would emerge as a powerful figure. Whereas previously the largest donors were usually named as foundation managers in deference to their subscriptions and had acted as a check upon a domineering clergyman, the latter could now appoint "tame managers" with the assurance that the money would be supplied by the State.[48]

The procedures related to the selection of teachers were viewed with apprehension. The education committee was to possess only a veto over the recommendation of the six managers, a role not nearly so important as that of nomination. Even less significant was the veto power in the case of dismissals, since those based on grounds of religious incompatibility were beyond the pale. It was likely that the teachers would still be recruited for voluntary schools on the basis of religious tests. In the commons, Ellis J. Griffith, Welsh Liberal M.P., referred to a statement by Lord Hugh Cecil in the *Guardian* (April 2, 1902) that "if, for instance, a teacher is not satisfying from a religious point of view, who

---

* J. Ramsay MacDonald, secularist and in 1924 Labour's first prime minister, supported the Nonconformist position in this instance. He doubted that the county council with its multifold responsibilities could actively supervise education. The danger was that a permanent official and the chairman of its nominated education committee would run the school program, with the result that pedagogical methods would be stereotyped and unresponsive to public opinion. *Labour Leader*, April 26, 1902.

† The *Journal of Education* (May, Dec. 1902) counseled Nonconformists to be more optimistic as to the value of the two non-foundation managers. Since the latter would have behind them the power of the purse, they could report any abuses of proselytism to the education committee.

cares what his teaching may nominally be." Dr. Macnamara cited a letter from a vicar in answer to an application for a headmaster's post as showing the consequences that must follow the failure to strengthen the recruitment procedure for a competent staff in the secular subjects: "Do you throw the greatest zest into your religious instruction? What experience have you had in organ playing? . . . When have you accompanied Gregorians? What Psalter was used? Have you ever accompanied a choral celebration? What voice do you sing? What are your Church views? Are you and your wife regular and devout early communicants?"[49]

Secularists joined Nonconformists in lamenting the failure of the Balfour Bill to emancipate the teaching profession in voluntary schools. The *Agnostic Journal* described how the power to dismiss on grounds of religious incompatibility would give the parson unlimited powers to stifle a teacher's initiative to express his personality and to mature intellectually:

> A joke about Joseph's coat of many colours; a candid criticism of the helpless appearance of the Dean of Canterbury at the Coronation banquet; a scoff at Archbishop Laud; a stricture on Oliver Cromwell; a word in favor of evolution, geology, or embryology; a laugh at the headgear of the parsoness; . . . a subscription to the *Agnostic Journal* fund . . . can all be treated as matters concerned with the giving of religious instruction.

Picton pleaded the wrong done every teacher by such an imposition: "Large numbers of teachers are now under an 'intolerable strain' of conscience. . . . It is a direct temptation to hypocrisy in the discharge of one of the most sacred of duties. It is not the 'Nonconformist' conscience that is most cruelly wronged by such reactionary legislation; it is rather the gifted and devoted teacher in full sympathy with the national ideal of citizenship, but unable to pronounce the shibboleth of any prevalent theology."[50]

Secularists pointed out that the prerogative of foundation managers to select the teacher must restrict the field of applicants available to voluntary schools. Lord Edward Lyulph Stanley,‡ in 1903 the fourth Baron of Alderley, commented:

> If a denomination manager is allowed to advertise, . . . coupling extraneous work with an added salary, it invites many persons of lower

---

‡ Lord Stanley himself was an Agnostic, his elder brother upon whose death he succeeded to the family title in 1903 a Mohammedan, and his younger brother a monsignor in the Roman Catholic Church and domestic chaplain to the Pope. See obituary by George Lewis Bruce in *Educational Record*, June 1925, pp. 455-61.

educational efficiency to apply with profuse expressions of eagerness to take up this work, while better teachers will reserve themselves for appointments in schools under public management where these outside duties are not suggested. A London School Board master is quite at liberty to play the organ in a church or chapel on Sunday but the body that appoints him has nothing to do with his external work.

J. Keir Hardie, founder of the socialist Independent Labour Party and Labour M.P., contrasted the measure's conception of the teacher as the vicar's assistant with the ever-widening view of State-supported activities as a civil service open to all without regard to creed:

It is absurd that the Rt. Hon. John Morley who claims to be an Agnostic[51] and spells God with a small g is eligible to become a Cabinet Minister but under this Bill would not be eligible to serve as an ex-pupil teacher in a school wholly supported by public moneys.[52]

RELIGIOUS EQUALITY

Nonconformists decried the prospect of religious equality under the Balfour Bill. Lloyd George could see no cessation of pressure upon teachers of Dissenting background to join the Church of England as a condition of promotion. They would have to remain in the classroom while headmasters expounded the sacramentarian doctrines in the catechism. They would be expected to march with the pupils to the parish church on Saints' days. No enthusiasm was manifested over Balfour's concession making it permissible for foundation managers to hire pupil or assistant teachers of other faiths.[53] Not only would it formalize the requirement that the head teacher must be of the same faith as the trust deed stipulated, declared Rev. J. Guinness Rogers, a prominent Congregational minister, but it would also be an insulting reminder that Nonconformists could not aspire to the higher posts.[54]

As for Nonconformist children, especially in those 8,000 parishes where only a voluntary school was available, their lot would continue to be deplorable.* True, parents could invoke the conscience clause, withdrawing their children from the credal lesson. But most parents feared to do this, explained Joseph Compton-Rickett, Congregational layman and Liberal M.P., lest their children be singled out as peculiar

---

* Rev. Taylor declared that only 6,108 voluntary schools were in single school districts. *The Times* (London), Sept. 19, 1902, 5f. Balfour gave the breakdown as follows: Church of England (5,600), Wesleyan (37), Roman Catholic (35), Undenominational (418), British (62), Board (1,326). *Commons*, July 30, 1902, p. 181.

and so risk an adverse psychological effect upon their school work. Furthermore, parents jeopardized their own security and faced social persecution in the village by such open hostility to the Church of England. The *British Weekly* wondered how, even if the conscience clause could be relied upon, Nonconformist children could escape the surcharged sectarian atmosphere permeating the daily school work. The head teacher was an active communicant of the Established Church. The textbooks presented the Anglican point of view on such secular subjects as history. The pictures on the walls were those identified with Anglican theology.[55]

Nor was evidence lacking that Anglicans were engaged currently in an active campaign of proselytizing. Robert Perks, Wesleyan layman and Liberal M.P., described the situation in a rural Church school in Oxfordshire, not far from his home. From one-third to one-half of the children were Nonconformists and yet on Saints' days the entire class was marched to the parish church for services. Any child who did not bow down to the altar or who did not say "Hail Mary" was caned at the school later. The *Monthly Messenger* charged that Presbyterian boys and girls were taught that "dissent" was a sin, that baptized children were regenerated, and that sacerdotalism was an instrument of divine grace. Augustine Birrell, son of a Nonconformist minister and Liberal M.P., wrote that "one has only to read what the clergy say in their own Church organs to see that they regard 'their' schools as missionary enterprises as the best means of reclaiming the masses to true views of Church authority and Sacramental grace." Perhaps the most frequently quoted evidence of the dedicated Anglican intent was a frank letter in the *Guardian* (August 4, 1897), written by Canon Pennington, for twenty years a diocesan inspector of schools in Lincolnshire. Rev. J. H. Jowett, Congregational minister in Birmingham, recalled Canon Pennington's remarks:

> Our syllabus is so arranged as to give that distinctive denominational instruction. I always saw that it was given when I was a diocesan inspector and I always asked the children, chiefly the children of Nonconformists, questions upon it. This is the case throughout Lincolnshire. Thus, in fact, we are training the children of Nonconformists to be children of the Church.[56]

Anglicans offered no apology for insisting upon adherence to the statement in the constitution of the National Society that all schools in union with it must require their masters and mistresses to be members of the Established Church. Rev. Thomas Alexander Lacey, Vicar of Maddingley, Cambridge, reminded the public that a Church school was one established for the education of children in the principles of the Church of England. Obviously the spiritual climate of a school depended upon the sincerity of the teacher who should command the confidence of the denomination and a nominal Churchman was not enough. Rev. MacColl, Canon of Ripon, let his imagination dwell upon the ordeal awaiting voluntary schools if teachers were selected without a religious test:

> Can anything be better calculated to discredit the Bible and undermine the foundation of religion altogether than to have a Roman Catholic teacher where pupils are Protestant, an Agnostic to teach Christian children? . . . The best men must be chosen, and their friendliness or hostility toward the religion which they are to teach must not count as part of their qualification. . . . And that argument must include Catholics as well. . . . We may thus have an Orange Protestant teaching Papal Infallibility and Transubstantiation in a Roman Catholic school, . . . a Unitarian teaching Trinitarian doctrine. . . . Such schools would become the breeders of religious scepticism and indifferentism.[57]

Anglicans were not prepared, however, to admit the complaints of proselytism. Insofar as the Established Church was presented in a favorable light, a Nonconformist parent naturally would object to a Church school. But if in theory the potential for proselytism was present, current experiences would indicate that the actual number of cases was small. Rev. W. Frank Curtoys, assistant diocesan inspector in Lincoln, declared that in his area of jurisdiction for 1901 only 219 out of 39,444 children made use of the conscience clause and of these 50 were Jews and 10 were Roman Catholics. Bishop Sheepshanks of Norwich reported that in his diocese only 350 out of 72,900 children were withdrawn from the religious instruction.† Bishop Davidson of Winchester, who upon the death of Dr. Temple at the close of 1902 succeeded as Archbishop of Canterbury, explained that few Nonconformist parents used the conscience clause because compared to what objections they

---

† In the commons, July 29, 1902, Henry Charles Richards, Anglican layman and Conservative M.P., asked Balfour for a count of the number of children withdrawn from religious instruction in both voluntary and board schools. Balfour answered that it was unwise to make such a canvass but so far as information was available he believed that the number was a very minor percentage of the five million children in attendance. *Commons*, July 29, 1902, pp. 16-17. Perhaps Balfour referred to a tabulated sheet submitted by the Church of England for all its schools, bishopric by bishopric. The statistics read: 1,748,772 in attendance; 5,147 (.294) wholly withdrawn; 7,596 (.434) partially withdrawn. *Ministry of Education*, 1902, Bill Papers, Appendix 6.

might have to some of the material in credal lessons they recognized the values their children were receiving in the truths of the Holy Scriptures and in the practice of a Christian life. The *Church Times* believed that Nonconformist parents appreciated the role of Church schools as a factor in the fight against the inroads of Arianism which denied Christ as a primary divinity.[58]

Actually, insisted Anglicans, the presence of voluntary schools served best the dictates of religious equality. Churchmen had never reaped the benefit of the understanding in 1870 that if the Cowper-Temple clause banned the use of formularies and catechisms, it did not bar distinctive religious instruction in the board schools. The *Pilot* quoted Rev. Robert W. Dale, the eminent Congregational divine of that time who became a secularist in the face of the unseemly Christian strife unleashed, as acknowledging that Churchmen had not opposed the Cowper-Temple clause because if "it excluded the Church catechism . . . it left the Board absolutely free to teach every one of the characteristic dogmas. . . . The formulary was forbidden but the dogma of the formulary was permitted."[59] But the passage of years had witnessed the use only of the Bible in the board school, resulting in a type of religion known as undenominationalism. This might not be the religion of the Nonconformists but it was a substitute which they could tolerate without doing violence to their consciences.‡ Rev. Dymott made much of the Nonconformist policy to transfer their schools to the local authorities as evidence of their satisfaction with board school religion, the number declining from 1,611 in 1870 to 1,510 in 1902.[60] So, if it were just for the nation to support the Nonconformist sects, it was no less just to do the same for the Church of England.[61]

Nonconformists also would leaf through the pages of history to show that the Act of 1870 had not been turned to their own advantage in board schools. The Cowper-Temple clause had not been opposed lest the cause of education be hindered. Only reluctantly did Nonconformists yield their fundamental premise that the State had no right to teach religion. Dr. Vernon Bartlet, professor of Church History at

---

‡ Frederick James Gould, secularist, active in the Ethical movement, and lecturer on moral education, supported the Anglican view: "By political accident, Nonconformist clericalism seized the Board-School system in 1870 and thrust into [them] just that Biblical method which most favors the maintenance of their forms and practices of the Christian religion. For thirty-odd years they have sat in the seat of power, assisted by the rates of Anglicans, Catholics, Jews, Unitarians, Agnostics, and Atheists. . . . The Church of England, strong as it has been socially and spiritually, has actually been browbeaten into an inferior education position. It is now protesting and demanding equality of treatment." *Literary Guide and Rationalist Rev.*, Nov. 1902.

Mansfield College, Oxford,* explained that Nonconformists had embraced Cowper-Templeism as a working compromise in order to win the assent of Anglicans to an accelerated school building program. Indeed, since then, the apparent satisfaction of the nation with scriptural teaching in board schools had influenced them to cease pressing their case for secular education in State-supported schools. So far as the charge that Cowper-Templeism approximated Nonconformity was concerned, the British Weekly pointed out that if it had any slant there was more reason to believe that Anglicanism was the chief beneficiary. A census would show that the majority of board school teachers were members of the Established Church.† Dr. John Massie, professor of theology at Mansfield College, Oxford, and active in Free Church circles, in resting the case for the neutrality of Cowper-Templeism, described how much of Nonconformity was left out:

> It does not touch the iniquity of the State patronage and control of religion, a policy which is at the root cause of Nonconformity. Neither does it touch the special differences of the Nonconformist communities. It leaves untaught the pseudo-baptism of the Congregationalist, the anti-pseudo baptism of the Baptist, the Arminianism of the Wesleyan, and the Calvinism of the Presbyterian, the sacramentarianism of the Quaker. . . . This superstructure they are content to raise by means of their organization and at their own expense.[62]

Nonconformists made an unsuccessful effort in committee to require that no student be excluded on religious grounds from training colleges aided by public funds.[63] Most of these were in the hands of religious bodies and preference was given youths of their own faiths. George Lewis Bruce, member of the London School Board for Tower Hamlets Division, discussed the inequities connected with the last examination for King's Scholarships, which entitled a recipient to three-quarters of the cost of his education for two years at any accredited institution where he could find admission. For 1901, some 10,728 candidates had presented themselves and 1,518 won first class and 4,328 second class honors.[64] For these 5,846 eligible recipients there were available 2,000 places in residential and 700 places in day training colleges; of this total, 2,300 were in the hands of the religious bodies.[65] Some 485 first class

---

* Mansfield College was founded in 1886 and supported by the Congregational churches for the study of theology and particularly for the preparation of Congregational ministers.

† Robert Blatchford, secularist and editor of the socialist Clarion, observed that Churchmen were in all cases strongly represented on school boards and often possessed a working majority. Clarion, April 11, 1902.

honors students, including many of Anglican faith, applied for the 400 places open in nonsectarian colleges (both residential and day). For the 2,300 places in the denominational colleges the selection worked out that 937 first class honors students of the required faith were admitted and the rest were drawn from second and even third class in order to recruit a religiously homogeneous student body.[66] In short, on sectarian grounds, many first and second class honors students were rejected in favor of less proficient candidates. The remaining 4,000 first and second class honors students, if they entered the teaching profession, got further training by catch-as-catch-can methods while serving an apprenticeship as student teachers. Adding insult to injury, many a Nonconformist commentator stressed the fact that the State had contributed £100,000 of the £293,000[67] needed for constructing the denominational training colleges and currently bore 94% of the annual maintenance cost.[68]

Anglicans were aware of the difficulties connected with providing accommodations in their training colleges for all who sought entrance. Suggested solutions were the establishment of hostels for students of other religions and making additional places available for day students of non-Anglican affiliations from the immediate vicinity. The *Pilot* gave support to the expansion of the nonsectarian training colleges, provided a reciprocal opportunity for denominational hostels was permitted. But so far as their own institutions were concerned, priority must go to Anglican youths. The *School Guardian* stated the case of the denominational training colleges thus:

> We built them for our own. The admission of Nonconformists into a Church College would lead to a corresponding exclusion of Church teachers and introduce friction. It would be next to impossible to maintain the religious studies in our Training Colleges if students were admitted who would claim exemption from attendance at chapel and theological lectures and from exams in religious knowledge. The students in Denominational Colleges are already exposed to great temptations to minimize the time given to their religious studies through having to compete in secular subjects of examination with students in Undenominational and Secular Colleges who can give the whole of their time to these subjects. . . . A training college is not like a college at one of the old Universities. It has more the character of a large family, and foreign elements would be destructive of its peace and unity.[69]

PROSPECT OF TURBULENCE

While the Balfour Bill was going through the legislative process, Nonconformists debated their further strategy. Basically such a Church Aid Bill could only be answered by a renewal of the fight for Disestablishment. That issue, affirmed the *Baptist Times*, had been allowed to lapse in recent years as relations between the Church of England and the Free Churches became less strained. A tolerant spirit had grown up, the former accepting the abolition of secular disabilities and the latter according a sympathetic interpretation to the role of the Established Church in preserving Great Britain as a Christian nation. But now, this spell of mutual respect was broken by Anglican use of their privileged position to get an education bill of their own making. The *Manchester Guardian* expressed well this loss of Nonconformist confidence in the ability of the Established Church to serve in the spirit of *noblesse oblige*: "To the spectator the conflict is one between the conception of clergy as public leaders in common acts of worship and as exclusive avenues of access to God."[70]

Worse yet, commented many a Nonconformist, weighing the influence of the High Church element in Anglican circles, the principles of the Protestant Reformation were in the balance. Dr. Clifford listed specifically as High Churchmen and all actively engaged in pushing the Balfour Bill, the two Cecils (Robert and Hugh), the second Viscount Halifax (President of the English Church Union, currently advocating corporate reunion of the Church of England with the Roman Catholic Church), and Athelstan Riley (a member of the Canterbury House of Laymen). The *Examiner* warned that these "most advanced and unscrupulous members" of the Establishment would not rest until they had stamped out Dissent in the villages and reduced it to impotence in the towns. Nonconformity must answer this challenge, even at the price of contention more fearsome than England had known since the days of James II.[71]

More immediately, Nonconformists debated what course to take once the Balfour Bill was placed on the statute book. Admittedly an appeal to the electorate was the ideal approach. The *Daily News* argued that the Conservative Government had been continued in office by the Khaki Election of 1900 to see the Boer War through. Nonconformists who had voted for the Conservative Party had no conception that their ballots were an endorsement of rate aid for voluntary schools. If anything, wrote Howard Evans, editor of the *Liberator* and chairman of the London Congregational Union, considering the storm of disapprobation directed at the short-lived Conservative Government's Education Bill of 1896,‡ a mandate had been given against tampering with the intent of the Act of 1870. The *Manchester Guardian* made much of the by-election trend since 1900 to attest to the unpopularity of the Conservative Government. By 1902, six by-elections had turned an aggregate Unionist majority of 8,570 into a Liberal majority of 1,912.[72] No wonder, then, that Balfour showed little disposition to risk an appeal to the nation on his school measure.[73]

Pending, however, the statutory duration of seven years to compel a general election, many Nonconformists espoused passive resistance. The dictates of conscience could best be served by a refusal to pay the school rate. If the *Baptist Times* realized that such grave conduct could only be a last resort, the occasion had arisen now as it had with John Hampden and ship money. The *Examiner* regarded the evidence as clear that the law of man which they were called upon to obey transgressed a higher law of God. To be sure, agreed Rev. Hugh Price Hughes, Methodist pulpit orator and founder of the *Methodist Times*, Free Churchmen had long paid taxes into the national exchequer, part of which had been disbursed as grants to voluntary schools. But the conscience had been spared the inner corrosion of a rate bill with a specific amount earmarked for education. Furthermore, Church of England subscriptions no longer satisfied the criterion of bearing a fair portion of the cost. Howard Evans referred to an oft-quoted speech made in June 1896 by Dr. Temple, then Bishop of London[74] (in October 1896 to become Archbishop of Canterbury) that this was the thinking in Church circles: "If our brethren in the North find the burden too heavy, I entreat them to consider whether it will not be better for the Church that they should surrender some of their schools to the School Boards than that they should put the whole body of Church schools on the slippery slope of support from the rates."[75]

Not all Free Churchmen approved of passive resistance. The *Methodist Recorder* reminded readers that it was English Nonconformity which had fought for the survival of the House of Commons against the despotic Stuarts. The *Manchester Guardian* admonished that the example of willful defiance of parliamentary government would arm every reactionary interest in the country with a weapon that could be used against progress. Walter Smith Rowntree, a relative of Joseph Rowntree, the York cocoa manufacturer, believed that the principle of representative government demanded obedience to tax measures

---

‡ Sir John Gorst's Bill was aimed to coordinate all branches of education under a single authority, to give further financial aid to voluntary and necessitous board schools, and to permit separate credal instruction in all schools where sufficient parents demanded it. The measure was withdrawn in the committee stage. Birchenough (1938), p. 167.

until they were constitutionally reversed. John Hampden's conduct would have been similar if ship money had been duly voted by parliament. John Stephenson Rowntree, grocer, onetime Lord Mayor of York, minister in the Society of Friends and brother of Joseph Rowntree, found evidence in the writings and practices of early Christians that the State must be rendered its due, notably St. Matthew who declared that government was a divine institution and taxation imposed by it should be paid by Christians. The payment of taxes was not unmoral, since the responsibility for their expenditure rested with the spender and not the taxpayer.[76]

Anglicans did not allow Nonconformist threats of passive resistance to go unchallenged. Against the argument that the Conservative Government had no mandate to enact an education bill, they submitted their views on constitutionalism. Parliament was elected not for any single purpose but to carry on the general business of the Empire. The *Standard* recalled that Gladstone's Ministry of 1869 had no special mandate to disestablish the Irish Church and to create school boards or his Ministry of 1885 to introduce an Irish Home Rule Bill. As a matter of fact, persisted *The Times*, the dictates of majority rule had been served in the case of the Balfour Bill, for Anglicans comprised more than one-half of the people of the country. The strenuousness with which Nonconformists opposed a religious census could only be explained by their fear of such a revelation. Against the plea that the payment of school rates violated the conscience, the *Church Times* reminded Nonconformists that for the past thirty years denominationalists had paid rates for the teaching of the obnoxious Cowper-Templeism in board schools.* The *Pall Mall Gazette* chided Wesleyans on the delicacy of their consciences to accept rate aid in one district for their voluntary schools and to refuse to pay rates for non-Wesleyan voluntary schools in another district. It was to be hoped that the better sense of Free Churchmen would reassert itself and thrust aside a narrowness of outlook which could end only in paralyzing the constructive will of the citizenry.[77]

Anglicans were not without their own moments of conscience strain. During the committee stage, on October 31, 1902, in an eleventh-hour move, Colonel William Kenyon-Slaney, Anglican layman and Conservative M.P., introduced an amendment to make the managers of a voluntary school responsible for the supervision of religious instruction. His announced aim was to protect Church schools from the Romaniz-

---

* Dr. Clifford answered with the statement that Anglicans had a citizen's share in the management of board schools. *Daily News*, Aug. 20, 1902.

ing tendencies of High Church clergymen.[78] Only a small section of Anglican opinion was prepared to accept the amendment. The *Church Standard*, organ of the National Protestant Church Union dedicated to defend the Protestant character of the Established Church, welcomed it as a step in the right direction. The action was inevitable against those ritualist parsons who forced their views on Mass, auricular confession, and schism upon the Church schools. The *Spectator* believed that the foundation managers, representing a generation of Church laity grounded in the true faith, offered a better guarantee that children would be protected against the encroachments of medieval theology. The possibility was discounted that clergy would be henceforth excluded, for it was hard to believe that foundation managers would not welcome the counsel of clergy worthy of the trust. More than likely, predicted the *Pall Mall Gazette* optimistically, since in most parishes the parsons were loyal to the Prayer Book, they would continue to exercise influence in the spiritual life of Church schools.[79]

The greater number of Anglican commentators, however, reacted adversely to the Kenyon-Slaney amendment.† A foreboding picture of credal instruction under the supervision of a heterogeneous body of managers was painted.‡ Athelstan Riley envisaged that the two nonfoundation managers might come from the ranks of the Dissenters, perhaps even selected with the express purpose of joining in the discussion of the religious syllabus to be used. The result could be to whittle down the parts of the catechism and Prayer Book to be studied until the teaching was identical with that in council schools. In the estimation of the *Church Times*, anarchy within Anglican ranks could follow—squires, farmers, and petty tradesmen bickering with the parson over the details of the syllabus. If both High and Low Church views happened to find supporters among the foundation managers, squabbles could be anticipated. The *Guardian* raised the question whether the

---

† The *Tablet* (Nov. 8-22, Dec. 6-13, 1902) regarded the Kenyon-Slaney amendment as a family quarrel between the Anglican clergy and their laity as to which would have the power to select the particular doctrine to be taught in the name of the Establishment. For the Roman Catholic Church there was only one catechism and the authority of the hierarchy over it was not subject to parliamentary confirmation.

‡ Balfour was nettled by the charge that the policy embodied in the Kenyon-Slaney amendment had been "sprung" upon the public. He listed three facts as sufficient to have made the nation aware of the principle involved. First, there was the resolution of the two Houses of Convocation in July 1901, agreeing to publicly-appointed managers. Second, when the clause was written up relative to the one-third non-foundation managers, the words *for every purpose* were included as to their functions. Third, during the debates, no Anglican refuted the frequent claim that the measure would mean an end to clerical tyranny. *Ministry of Education* 1902, Bill Papers, No. 331a.

concept of an episcopally-governed Church of England was not in-
fringed upon by the Kenyon-Slaney amendment. It meant that laymen
would exercise duties normally entrusted to the canonical shepherd.[80]

Anglicans joined hands to assure that the Kenyon-Slaney amendment
would not vitiate definite religious instruction. Considerable reliance
was placed upon the recognition of the diocesan bishop as a final court
of appeals in matters spiritual. The trust deed of a Church school under
the National Society contained such a provision and all voluntary
schools were urged by the Guardian to follow suit. It allowed for an
appeal to the bishop on the following points: a) the prayers to be used,
b) the religious instruction to be given, c) any regulation connected
therewith, d) any book used in school to which objection was raised
on religious grounds, e) unsound or defective teaching as a cause for
dismissal of teachers.[81] The Church Times preferred an explicit statement in the Balfour Bill itself as to the right of appeal to the bishop
and so leave no opportunity for the courts to find trust deeds open to
challenge. While an amendment was inserted in the lords,* much of its
value was regarded as lost in the ruling of Sir Robert Finlay, Attorney-General, that the right of appeal could be only on questions of
doctrine.[82] Apparently the six managers were to be supreme in de-
termining how, when, and by whom it would be given.[83]

The reaction in Anglican circles varied. Not a few voices were raised,
like that of the Church Times, in favor of leasing the buildings to the
local authority for the hours of secular education and using the rent
to hire a staff to conduct the religious instruction before or after school
hours. An occasional voice, like that of the Pilot, was even ready to
close Church schools until the vicar was restored his rightful role. However, the greater sentiment, expressed by the School Guardian, was for
the parson to remain at his post until driven from the school and for
care to be taken to secure three loyal Churchmen to serve with him as
foundation managers. Granted there might be a year or two of anxiety
but with the exercise of tact and forbearance the clergyman should
consolidate anew his position.[84]

Nonconformists followed with keen interest the Anglican family controversy over the Kenyon-Slaney amendment. At the outset, satisfaction
was expressed at this move to check ecclesiastical excesses with their

---

* Charles McArthur, Churchman and Conservative M.P., called the amendment a
repudiation of the laity's claim to a voice in the religious education of the young. They
formed part of the living Church along with the clergy. Henceforth, however, 35 ecclesiastical dignitaries (33 bishops and 2 archbishops) would control the religious instruction.
The Times, Dec. 5, 1902, 2f. For the amendment see Lords, Dec. 10, 1902, pp. 617-25
(Earl of Halsbury, Lord Chancellor).

attendant proselytism. It would be well to acquaint the public, moreover, with the lesson to be drawn from the internal quarrel. It was confirmation of the charge that Romanism was rife in the Established
Church. The *Baptist Times* affirmed that the bitter opposition of the
High Church party to the amendment smoked out its aim to capture
the children for ritualism. Subsequently, Nonconformists manifested
disappointment over the lords' amendment upholding the right of
appeal to the bishop. It would weaken the effectiveness of the Kenyon-
Slaney amendment, for past experiences had revealed how hesitant
were the bishops to halt Romanist practices. The *Liberator* was extreme
in its conclusion, observing that Church managers would hardly dare
to curb the zeal of "a red-hot Romanizer" when the chief landlord of
a parish was a man of the stamp of the second Viscount Halifax. Some
balm was derived from the ruling of the attorney-general that the jurisdiction of the bishop was restricted to questions of doctrine. At least,
the *British Weekly* reasoned, the parson could be kept out of the school
and so the danger of an ecclesiastical atmosphere proportionately
reduced.[85]

CHAPTER THREE

ACT OF 1902 IN OPERATION (1903-1906)

PASSIVE RESISTANCE MOVEMENT

In DECEMBER 1902, the National Passive Resistance League was organized under the chairmanship of Dr. Clifford. A journal was published known as the *Crusader*, for which Rev. Hollowell wrote a weekly column (as well as a song),[1] supplying readers with the latest information on the campaign.* Rev. William J. Townsend, a distinguished minister of the Methodist New Connexion, penned a series of articles on past Protestant martyrs. The *British Weekly* constituted itself a channel for passing on the tactics to be employed. The plan was to form local councils, raise a central fund to help victims, and provide legal aid. Where all schools under the local authority were council schools, no resistance would be offered to the school rate. But if there were one Anglican or Roman Catholic school in a district, then participants would be asked to deduct from their rate payments the amount estimated to go to the voluntary school. No lawbreaking would be involved, for the rate collectors could satisfy their claims by the usual method applied against tax delinquents. The constabulary should be allowed to attach personal belongings and sell them at auction for the amount deducted by the passive resister in paying his rates. The dictates of conscience would be served and, perhaps more importantly, lead to the removal of Nonconformist grievances.[2]

The active campaign got under way in May 1903, and the organizers were quite satisfied that it did focus public attention upon their trampled consciences. Great numbers of people flocked to the courts to watch the proceedings. Many of the newspapers, including *The Times*, carried accounts of the cases which went to trial. Dr. Clifford boasted that the men summoned were often pillars of society—minis-

---

* The only file of the *Crusader* located is at the British Museum Newspaper Library. The file is incomplete, beginning with issue No. 6, April 15, 1903, and would appear to have suspended publication in June 1907. It is interesting to note that it occupied the same offices used today by the *Catholic Times* at 12 Crane Court in Fleet Street.

ters, aldermen, journalists, merchants, and even magistrates. Martyrdom was achieved by those sentenced to short prison terms when their personal belongings did not bring enough to pay the school rate.† Not a few, among whom was Dr. Clifford himself, transferred their property to their wives so that it could not be attached and thereby assured for themselves a prison term. But to the *Tablet* such Nonconformist thumpings in behalf of bruised consciences was more the instinct of prudence to safeguard their property from seizure.[3] Nor did a court ruling that the education rate was part of the poor rate and failure to pay brought disfranchisement swerve passive resisters from their course. The *British Weekly* (of which Dr. W. Robertson Nicoll was editor and among those receiving a summons) declared that it need not deter from canvassing candidates and hoped that it might even spur the Liberal Party to speak out and thus garner the entire Nonconformist vote.[4]

The disposition of the 452 Wesleyan day schools was an apple of discord among Nonconformists, since it exposed the passive resistance movement to the charge of inconsistency. Rev. Hollowell argued that Nonconformists should object to pay rates for Wesleyan as well as for Anglican schools on the ground that the managers represented the Wesleyan Church and not the public. He appealed to them to transfer their schools and so strengthen the attack upon ecclesiasticism. The Scottish school system had profited in 1872 when the Free Church of Scotland and the United Presbyterian Church had joined forces to establish a national school system. Rev. Henry R. Smart, Methodist minister in Sheffield, reminded Wesleyans that by holding on to their schools they gave denominationalists a convenient argument and so exposed Nonconformist children to continued proselytism in sectarian schools. Rev. J. Scott Lidgett, a leader in Methodist circles and member of the London School Board, would go along with the transfer of Wesleyan schools provided their operation as council schools included sound unsectarian religious teaching.[5]

At Camborne, Cornwall, where the annual Wesleyan Methodist Conference was held on July 21, 1903, a compromise was suggested by Robert Perks and seconded by Dr. Lidgett. In towns where the local authority could be trusted to administer the Act of 1902 without subjection to sacerdotalism, Wesleyan schools should be transferred. Only where a Wesleyan school appeared the sole refuge from denomina-

---

† By the close of 1903 the *Annual Register* (1904, pp. 203-04), recorded 37,296 summonses, 1,504 sales under distraint, and 80 imprisonments. By the close of 1904 the *New Age* (Jan. 5, 1905) recorded 66,234 summonses, 2,274 sales under distraint, and 250 imprisonments. By April 1906 the *Liberator* (April 1906) recorded 73,816 summonses, 2,382 sales under distraint, and 280 imprisonments.

tionalism should it be retained. After a prolonged debate on the foregoing resolution which called for a national system under popular
control, Perks was defeated and a substitute resolution was adopted
"that it is the duty of managers of Wesleyan Day Schools to retain
schools . . . until such a time as the Education Act was repealed or
amended."[6]

Nonconformists did not cease to keep before the public the grounds
upon which they persevered with the passive resistance movement. The
plight of Nonconformist children in voluntary schools remained un-
alleviated. Lloyd George charged that Church schools had been em-
boldened to embark zealously upon proselytism, since they no longer
required the subscriptions of non-Anglicans. He pictured the Church
of England schools as "12,000 mission rooms" where three million
children were taught how to bow to parsons and curates. Nonconformist children heard their parents denounced as schismatics, their
Church described as heretical, and their beliefs stamped as wicked and
false. Rev. Smart claimed that Nonconformist children were being told
to receive baptism or they could not be saved and that "unless they
eat the Body and Blood of the Lord Jesus Christ in the form of bread
and wine duly consecrated, they have no life in them." Howard Evans
culled still another instance of past proselytism in a statement by Rev.
A. A. Markham, Vicar of St. Jude's, Liverpool, in the *Church Times*
(June 13, 1902), italicizing the meaningful passage:

> When I see that many of my day children are attached to Dissenters'
> Sunday-schools, I argue that it is a fortunate thing that I can teach them
> for five days out of the seven. I know, too, that the teaching will not be
> lost. *I shall find it after many days, when many of these same children
> leave their sect and seek confirmation.*[7]

Nor was there any change of heart apparent in opening up teacherships in voluntary schools. The number of Nonconformists appointed
as assistant teachers had not increased appreciably. If the Established
Church had really desired to be fair in this respect, a binding rule could
have been forced on the National Society. As it was, Rev. Robert E.
Welsh, Presbyterian minister, Brondesbury, London, understood that
the National Society had prepared a form of engagement for assistant
teachers which insisted on their teaching distinctive Church doctrine.[8]
Rev. Smart testified that in a district of his pastorate in Sheffield he
knew of neither a Methodist youth nor a maiden since 1870 who had
entered the teaching profession without being obliged as a preliminary
measure to abjure his or her faith. That it was strangling and sterilizing
Methodism went without saying. Rev. Martin recited that in Hereford

there were 17 head teacherships and of these 2 must be Roman Catholics and 15 must be Anglicans. Most brazen of all, to the *Daily News*, were advertisements in educational journals stipulating a willingness "to teach on Sunday" or "to sing in the choir" or "to play the organ." ‡ This was in express prohibition of the educational code that teachers must not be engaged for services unconnected with the school work. Obviously, the parson still ruled the roost in Church schools.[9]

The nation was asked to realize how galling it was for Nonconformists to pay directly an education rate to maintain voluntary schools. Just as the compulsory Church rate levied for the maintenance of the fabric of the parish church (Anglican) had made an earlier generation of Nonconformists resist fiercely, recalled the *Westminster Gazette*, so henceforth would the school rate be a painful reminder of religious inequality. Whether or not the cost of voluntary school buildings could be calculated to cover the expense of the credal lessons, it could hardly match the value of the sectarian incense burning the entire school day.[10]

More concretely, Rev. Elliot itemized the gleanings which the insatiable denominationalists had raked in besides rate aid:

> There are 3,000,000 places in all Voluntary Schools at, let us say, the value of £7 per place. This total of £21,000,000 at 3½% will yield an annual rent of £735,000. For day school purposes, the premises will be used an average of 36 hours per week, while for Church purposes the use is 10 hours per week. The proportion of rent for the latter would be £200,000, leaving to be paid for day school occupation some £535,000 per annum. [The Act of 1902 gave to the Churches the income from] teachers' houses (£95,000), endowments (£75,000), fees (£90,000), and wear and tear (£350,000), or all told the sum of £610,000. Since the rent in the aggregate is £535,000, it gives her a bonus of £75,000 per annum. . . .[11]

Nonconformists looked upon the unsatisfactory state of affairs in the training colleges as further justification for passive resistance. It was no consolation to Dr. Macnamara that by 1906 the number of training colleges stood at 70 or that accommodations had risen to 7,987.[12] The religious associations, mostly Anglican, still controlled the larger number of places—4,309. Stories continued to circulate of Church candidates with lower examination scores obtaining preferential treatment. Howard Evans stressed the fact that Anglican applicants could enter and did so in large numbers in training colleges operated by local author-

---

‡ The secularist *New Age* (Dec. 10, 1903) counted as many as 130 advertisements in a recent issue of the *Schoolmaster* with the forwarding address for applications that of the parish vicar. For examples see *Schoolmaster*, Nov. 28, Dec. 5, 1903.

ities and nonsectarian bodies. He cited the annual report of the British and Foreign School Society for 1903 as showing that one-third of the students in its training colleges belonged to the Established Church.[13] As for those Nonconformists who did get into Church training colleges, either as day students or lodged in an attached hostel, the *Christian World* gathered that there was no slackening in the diffusion of sacerdotalism. They remained hotbeds of ecclesiasticism in much the same temper as "Ignatius Loyola and the early Jesuits." Apart from the injustice of such mortifying exposure, the attention of the nation was called to the new figure of 95% of their income as drawn from public sources.[14] What other course was open, therefore, but passive resistance to drive home the need for transforming these closed preserves into national institutions?[15]

Nonconformists likewise kept before the public the broader issues involved in their passive resistance campaign.* The invasion of English politics by the hosts of clericalism was aimed at the destruction of the principles of the English Reformation. The intent of the High Church party which had dictated the educational settlement was to lead England back into the papal fold. Instances of the adoration of the Virgin Mary and the use of the confessional had increased to such an extent that a royal commission was now engaged in collecting evidence on the charges of ritualism.[16] Frank Smith, M.A., who described himself as a passive resister, pointed out that in recent years the Established Church had developed rapidly its priestly side and attached supreme importance to mechanical acts and a visible organization. In contrast, Nonconformity sought to remain true to the Reformation, knowing no priest but Jesus and no sacrifice but His. Salvation demanded nothing save the simple act of personal trust. Dr. Clifford called upon Dissent to regard itself as the trustee of the great evangelical traditions of the nation:

> This fight is only one struggle in a much wider contest . . . proceeding in France, . . . United States, Germany and in our Colonies, and all over the world. It is the battle with Clericalism in politics, . . . with the extreme section of the Anglican Church and its drift toward Rome. . . . For the moment clericalism wields the sceptre. The battle is set between a free Church in a Free State and a despotic Church in an enslaved State. . . .[17]

---

* Some Nonconformists clung to Disestablishment as the more permanent solution. So long as the Church of England was allowed to keep a connection with the State, it could proclaim its creed as the true religion and ordain that the educational system of the nation be molded under its leadership. *Methodist Times*, July 2, Aug. 27, 1903; *The Times*, Oct. 5, 1903, 4f (Liberation Society Circular).

As for the right to revolt, Nonconformists held it to be at the very foundation of English liberties. The *Review of Reviews*, inclined toward the Nonconformist position although secularist at heart, reached back into the pages of history. The heroic action of the barons against King John had provided the heritage of Magna Charta. The refusal of John Hampden to pay ship money had sounded the tocsin against the tyrant Charles Stuart. The fight of the Covenanters against the prelacy had given Scotland its Presbyterian settlement. The dogged acceptance by Dissenters of distraint of goods and prison sentences had won an end to Church rates (in 1868). Frank Smith averred that there was no sin in disobedience to a law where the soul in the presence of God found its conscience violated. Human progress was bound up with resistance of men against unjust laws lest they be traitors to God. Had men not been willing to go to prison, to be scourged, even to be put to death, where would liberty and religion be today? Dr. Clifford insisted that the purest patriotism sometimes required citizens to practice the "sacred duty of insurrection." The only question to be answered was "what act of the Executive Government is of such a character as to make it absolutely right and necessary?" Were not the misuse of the Khaki Election of 1900, the brazen entrenchment of the Conservative Government for the legal period of seven years in the face of national unpopularity, and the presence of a House of Lords dedicated to Church interests justifiable circumstances?[18]

Some Nonconformists continued to express disapproval of passive resistance. They repeated their anxiety over the harm anarchical conduct could do to the prestige of parliament. One F. W. H. Reed argued that John Hampden was acting in defense of the constitution against the encroachments of the Crown whereas passive resisters were defying a measure passed by their elected body. Rev. Dawson Burns, Baptist minister and secretary of the United Kingdom Alliance, a temperance society, pointed out that the Nonconformist had not refused to pay taxes for the prosecution of the unpopular Boer War and the Quaker did not allow his aversion to the military establishment to induce him not to pay taxes.† Rev. Burns turned to the words of the Apostles for guidance in proper Christian conduct. On the question of whether a Christian should pay tribute to a heathen government, foreknowing that some of the money would be used for idolatrous purposes, St. Paul gave as his judgment that "wherefore ye must needs be in subjection, not only because of the wrath but also for conscience's sake, . . . ye pay

---

† The Quakers refused to endorse passive resistance at their London meeting in 1903, advising that it was a matter for private judgment. *Friend*, May 29, 1903.

tribute also, for they are ministers of God's service, for attending con-
tinually upon this very thing." St. Peter declared that "taxes imposed
by legal authority were to be paid by Christians for the support of the
State, and they did not become responsible for their appropriation."
The saner approach was not to quarrel with the rate collector but to
appeal to ratepayers in their capacity as voters to turn out the Conservative Government.[19]

Anglicans were ever quick to defend themselves against the allega-
tion that the status of religious liberty had gone from bad to worse. John
P. Eglen, treasurer of the Birkenhead Advisory Committee of Church
schools, could not believe that there were many parsons capable of such
wickedness as Nonconformist writers depicted. The two non-foundation managers plus the Kenyon-Slaney amendment should guarantee
against the danger of proselytism. In the case of teacherships, Nonconformists had gained a valuable concession in the right to be appointed
as pupil and assistant teachers in Church schools. And they had a
valiant ally in Archbishop Davidson, who was tireless in his efforts to
have Nonconformist teachers added to Church school staffs.[20] Furthermore, Eglen reminded the nation that, even though 16,000 head teacherships in Church schools were reserved, Nonconformists did have
access to 80,000 places (especially the prize salaried posts in council
schools), including 13,000 head teacherships.‡ But, stated Rev. William Sanday, Lady Margaret Professor of Divinity and Canon of Christ
Church, Oxford, it was impossible to have non-Anglicans as head
teachers in Church schools. This was the slender thread by which foundation managers were able to preserve the religious character of their
schools.[21]

Anglicans made much of their own tempered restraint toward features
of the Act of 1902 which violated their conception of religious equality.
Athelstan Riley listed a number of provocative irritations which denominationalists faced in the future. The failure to repeal the Cowper-
Temple clause meant that hundreds of thousands of Church children
in council schools were left to the mercy of religious lessons hostile to
definitive Christianity. The introduction of a lay element in the management of Church schools could lead to the dilution of Church teaching. The appointment of pupil and assistant teachers of non-Anglican
background could corrupt the atmosphere of Church schools. The

‡ If the figures of certificated teachers (78,734) and uncertificated teachers (42,346)
are regarded as representing the number of teaching places, then the total is 121,080. If
in voluntary schools both the head teacherships (20,000) and an equal number of pupil
and assistant teachers are deducted, then 80,000 places were open to members of all faiths.
Parl. Papers, 1906, LXXXV, Cd. 3255, pp. 5-6, 28-29.

Kenyon-Slaney amendment posed a threat to the parish priest as the instructor of his flock. But Anglicans refused to think in terms of passive resistance and rather sought their relief within the letter of the law. The *School Guardian* would charge the diocesan inspector with the responsibility of assuring that religious instruction was being given in accordance with the trust deed. The *Pilot* would prod the clergy, while the situation was still viable, to undertake religious instruction themselves wherever possible. As a corollary thought, it would admonish subscribers to discriminate in making contributions. They should ascertain first if the foundation managers were according the vicar his rightful role in the spiritual life of the school.[22]

Anglicans had their complaints to register in the matter of teacher preparation. The *School Guardian* claimed that the shortage of places in training colleges affected students of all faiths.* Anglicans would like the opportunity to set up hostels in connection with the day training colleges, so that Anglican youths would want to attend knowing the opportunity existed for some spiritual devotions. The *Church Times* turned its attention to the lack of religious training for pupil teachers. Neither in the secondary schools nor in the pupil teacher centers was there any opportunity for religious instruction in the daily timetable. To establish a network of Church secondary schools was out of the question, remembering the heavy financial obligations already incurred in the elementary schools. Perhaps the answer was an arrangement in the pupil teacher centers whereby clergy could reach students before or after school hours.[23] Reference was made by Thomas Houghton, chairman of the Management Committee of Sheffield Church Schools, to a practical experiment in Sheffield where the opportunity was afforded to withdraw pupil teachers and have them taught at a local church by the clergy. Unless steps of this sort were taken, there would be a complete secularization of the teacher training programs. Would not Nonconformists be better off to join in assuring careful preparation of teachers in religious knowledge rather than to dissipate their energy in a senseless passive resistance campaign?[24]

Anglicans did not endure in silence the persistent charge that the State paid for the religious instruction given in Church schools. Patiently the financial facts in the case were repeated anew and brought

---

* Rev. J. S. Brownrigg, Canon of Bangor and secretary of the National Society, cited reports to show that Nonconformists had more than their share of places in training colleges. In 1903 there were 3,182 students in Church of England training colleges and 3,263 in nonsectarian and day training colleges. *The Times*, June 14, 1904, 7c. For his figures see *National Society, Annual Report*, 1904, pp. 13-14. The figures approximate those in *Parl. Papers*, 1903, LI, Cd. 1476, p. 83.

up to date. To begin with, the *School Guardian* recalled the past contribution of the Church of England in behalf of education. Between
1833 and 1870 the sum of £15,000,000 had been spent on construction
and maintenance. From 1870 to 1902 a further sum of £30,000,000 was
raised for the same purposes. In short, by 1902, the score stood at
£45,000,000 paid out for education.[25] Then there was the current saving
to the ratepayer in free rent use of Church school buildings. On the
basis of a capital value of £22,000,000 at the conservative interest rate
of 3¼%, the rental value came to £715,000. Since the religious lesson
took up not more than four hours weekly, the pro rata cost was not over
£175,000 annually, leaving the State the richer by £540,000. Rev.
Thomas E. Cleworth, Canon, Manchester Cathedral, reminded the
nation once again that to replace such facilities at the present cost
of £15 per place would mean a staggering bill of £45,000,000 for 3,000,-
000 places. Local authorities, already obligated for school bonds total-
ing £34,000,000 were in no position to absorb such a further outlay.[26]
Archbishop Davidson referred to the princely sums raised currently for
maintenance, noting that in 1902 the Church of England subscribed
£670,324.[27] And this did not include the cost of diocesan inspection,
support for the training colleges, necessary alterations, and the construction of new schools.[28]

Anglicans accepted the challenge to debate the broader issue of conscience involved in passive resistance. Nonconformists were not allowed
to forget that they had paid taxes, part of which since 1870 were disbursed in exchequer grants to voluntary schools. Nor were they permitted to ignore the precedent that their rates went to meet the stipends
of chaplains engaged to give denominational instruction in industrial
schools, workhouses, and asylums. Conversely, Anglicans paid taxes
and rates for a kind of religious lesson in board schools which they
abhorred. Indeed, this fact had greater significance, believing as they
did that Churchmen gave to school revenues an amount in excess of
the sum received by voluntary schools. Conscience in public matters
was a dangerous precept to follow, for opponents by conviction could
be found against an army, a navy, a land bill, in fact, against anything.
If practised by all, conscience could make defaulters of everybody.
Bishop Wordsworth of Salisbury appealed to Nonconformists as
Christians to be good citizens. He too invoked the New Testament,
reciting that Christ bade men to render unto Caesar that which was
due him, knowing fully that tribute in part went to support a false
religion, be it by the construction of a temple or a statue to honor a
pagan god.[29]

Anglicans spun their own theory of the democratic process in answering the charge that the Act of 1902 violated constitutional principles. The Khaki Election of 1900 had covered many more subjects than the Boer War. The urgency of educational reform was well known. After the abortive Gorst Bill of 1896 no one could suppose that the issue was dead. The *Morning Post* commented that to require a direct mandate on every item of business would make government impossible. A party elected to form a cabinet carried with it an approval by the people of its general position. Rev. Hammond, Vicar of St. Paul's, Beckenham, Kent, warned that this message of lawless conduct would be hailed with glee among the Irish peasantry and the natives of India. Nonconformists were "sawing off the branch on which they themselves sit." The task of the minority should be to seek redress by persuasion. It was for Nonconformists to convert the majority to their way of thinking.[30]

Roman Catholics joined Anglicans in defending the Act of 1902. The *Catholic Herald* extolled it as drawing "us out of the narrow groove in which our lot has been cast and makes our schools part of a truly national system." The *Tablet* lauded the great principle that all the nation's schools were entitled to an equal wage. Furthermore, no proselytism was practiced in a Roman Catholic school. Protestant children who attended were pointedly encouraged to avail themselves of the conscience clause. In the matter of teacherships, its editor asked Nonconformists how they could reconcile their insistence on no religious tests with their acquiescence in the Royal Declaration which forbade the sovereign to become a Roman Catholic or in the disqualification of Roman Catholics for the posts of Lord Chancellor of Great Britain and Lord Lieutenant of Ireland?[31]

The State had exacted a heavy price actually for making Roman Catholic schools eligible to rate aid. Rev. Charles Rothwell, St. John's Cathedral, Salford, Lancashire, answered the claim that the public provided most of the cost and got only one-third of the management with the assertion that the local authority had full control over the secular work through its hold on the purse strings and its right to inspect schools. And Roman Catholics raised sufficient subscriptions to meet the maxim that the protection of their children's consciences ought not to increase the financial burden of the State beyond provision made for other children. Charles Russell, a member of the Progressives in the London County Council and a solicitor in international legal disputes, would freshen the memory of the nation that the achievement of 400,000 schoolplaces at an outlay of £4,000,000 was no mean contribution to education.[32] The *Catholic Herald* contended that current financial experiences indicated a burden just as heavy as before the Act of 1902 due to stiff requirements by local authorities. In addition, the Roman Catholic role in the management of their own parochial schools was being reduced as a result of the aggressive exercise of control over the secular program on the part of education committees.[33]

Rev. W. D. Strappini, S.J., Oxford, set forth the admirable record of Roman Catholic schools, laboring as they had with limited funds. His data was collected from the Board of Education Report for 1901-02.[34] In attendance figures their schools (1,056) achieved a performance of 80.39% for 269,191 children whereas board schools (5,943) had a performance of 84.37% for 2,369,980 children. The margin of 4% was hardly significant, because board school children were better fed, housed and clothed, and more conveniently located to neutralize bad weather conditions. That Roman Catholic children came from families more poorly circumstanced could be deduced from school savings-bank accounts. Whereas 2,260 board schools had scholars wealthy enough to make deposits, only 173 parochial schools recorded deposits for their scholars. In earned government grants per pupil, board schools drew £1 1s. 7¼d. and parochial schools £1 11d. Considering that the former spent an average total of £3 5¼d. and the latter £2 3s. 5¼d. per pupil, the margin of accomplishment of 8d. more per pupil was practically negligible for the added 17s. 4d. invested by the board schools for better buildings, salaries, and teaching aids. In short, for all the greater expenditures of board schools, they could boast a mere one-thirtieth of superior secular education over parochial schools.[35]

Denominationalists drew support against the Nonconformist plea of conscience from secularist quarters.† From the vantage point of religious equality, Gould characterized the protests of Dissenters as having a false ring. Did they not accept complacently their "unsectarian" religion taught in council schools at the expense of all citizens? Did they show any solicitude for the plight of non-Christian elements like Atheists and Jews who were compelled to support Cowper-Templeism? From the vantage point of politics, Frederick Ryan, a contributor to the columns of the New Age, asked Nonconformists how they could reconcile their silence in 1899 upon the outbreak of the Boer War with their protestations of no mandate for an educational measure in 1902.

---

† The Journal of Education (July, Sept., Oct. 1903) reflected the professional educator's distress at the passive resistance movement. The important thing at the moment was to bring up the standards of voluntary schools. A state of affairs distinguished by dilapidated premises, large classes, and overworked and shamefully underpaid teachers needed immediate attention.

The Nonconformist conscience had not been outraged by the fact that the declaration of war against the Boers was not the subject of a previous election. From the vantage point of constitutionalism, Chapman Cohen, subsequently editor of the *Freethinker* and President of the National Secular Society, asked what would be the fate of education if Anglicans refused to pay rates for the teaching of unsectarianism in council schools. The proper way to prevent the unjust application of public revenue was to send men to parliament who would oppose it. As it was, by permitting themselves to be disfranchised for their refusal to pay rates, Free Churchmen were deprived of the only real means to repeal the Act of 1902.[36]

COUNTY COUNCILS

A second Nonconformist strategy was to urge county councils to enforce the conditions set forth by the Act of 1902 for rate aid eligibility. Its most extreme application took place in Wales under the fiery leadership of Lloyd George.[37] The plan was to give no money until several conditions were secured, including 1) that teachers be appointed by the local authority without any sectarian tests, 2) that teachers not be required to give instruction in any distinctively sectarian dogma, and 3) that voluntary schools be put in good condition. Meanwhile county councils would simply give voluntary schools their State grants for efficiency in accordance with reports of inspectors and have nothing to do with the appointment of their managers or teachers. The most publicized episode related to Carmarthenshire, where a public inquiry was ordered by the Board of Education. The county council had refused to pay rate aid to the 48 voluntary schools, mostly attached to the National Society.[38]

The Education (Local Authority Default) Act passed in the summer of 1904, stating that the Board of Education would pay managers of voluntary schools for any expenses properly incurred and deduct these amounts from the parliamentary grant to the county council, was denounced bitterly by Lloyd George.[39] He labeled it a Coercion Act and favored throwing upon the Board of Education the direct responsibility for all Welsh elementary schools. He would have education committees resign upon the first attempt to invoke the act. Let every Nonconformist chapel be opened for school purposes and teachers paid from contributions. The facts would indicate, however, that the Welsh threat of defiance did not materialize and the situation returned to normalcy, perhaps inspired by the hope that a Liberal Party election victory was not far off.[40]

Nonconformist commentators in England lent sympathetic support to the struggle waged by Welsh Dissent. They focussed their attention upon the phase of the revolt which contended that the Act of 1902 had stipulated that voluntary schools must be put in good shape before being given rate aid. The Welsh county councils were defended in requiring inferior Church schools to be repaired and so protect the health of children. Harsh words were directed against the Board of Education for its apparent partisanship.‡ The *Daily News* accused it of encouraging inspectors to be indulgent in pressing standards of sanitation upon Welsh voluntary schools. Often this was done even in the face of local reports as to their bad physical condition. The *Examiner* denounced the passage of the Education (Local Authority Default) Act as bound to mean educational chaos. Such coercion by the State confirmed the suspicion that its policy was essentially sectarian. Rev. Hollowell described Wales as "England's advance guard in the battle, and [we should] see that she lacks neither men nor money while she is wrestling at close quarters with our foes." The Welsh were fighting the battle of Nonconformity and subscriptions ought to be generous if the appeal came.[41]

A milder form of the Welsh strategy was tried in England, that of electing county councils pledged to enforce the Act of 1902 but not to refuse rate aid. The *Speaker* declared that there could be no objection to taking Balfour at his word and insisting upon an active voice in the management of voluntary schools. But the election results were not reassuring, reflected in the domination of the appointive education committees by large Anglican majorities. Rev. Welsh attributed Nonconformist defeats in the elections to the influence of the Church of England in local politics, the large Irish vote in towns, and the divisive effect of the varied social interests competing for votes. George White sketched the sad consequence of the Anglican triumph in the ready payment of rate aid to voluntary schools without any pressure for

‡ The *Baptist Times* (Nov. 13, 1903) charged that the Board of Education was fast becoming an Anglican outpost. Its editor termed the dismissal in 1903 of Sir George Kekewich, secretary since 1890, and Edward R. Robson, architect since 1884, to be the result of clerical objection to the efforts of these men to administer honestly the Act of 1902. While Sir Kekewich described himself as a Liberal Churchman, he identified himself completely with the Nonconformist position and spoke before the annual conference of the Free Church Council, March 1904, at Newcastle. *Free Church Year Book*, 1904, pp. 97-99. For a contrary viewpoint of the dismissal of Kekewich see Allen (1934), pp. 186-87, 189.

compliance with building standards.* Furthermore, he gathered the impression that the clergyman flaunted his authority as in pre-1902 years, refusing or neglecting as chairman to summon meetings of the board of managers and conducting correspondence without consulting other managers. Galling, too, were the accounts of how Church bodies got their new schools equipped at the cost of ratepayers and pressed forward all sorts of claims under the wear-and-tear clause to cover partitions in classrooms, asphalting playgrounds, and installing new gas fittings.[42]

Anglicans sprang to the defense of their schools. Admittedly, in Wales, some Church schools were behind in modern structures and equipment. But with the rate aid granted by the Act of 1902, money would be available to remedy these shortcomings. However, patience was not the wish of the Welsh county councils. They were out to crush voluntary schools. Rev. Berdmore Compton, Prebendary of St. Paul's Cathedral, London, labeled the exposure of children in unheated classrooms and the suspension of teachers' pay as cruel and inhuman deeds.[43]

The passage of the Education (Local Authority Default) Act was warmly supported. The *Western Mail* (Cardiff) insisted that there was no coercion in it. The local authority did not have to manage or finance voluntary schools; if it declined the government would do it instead. The threat of Lloyd George to throw the council schools into the hands of the Board of Education brought the answer that his policy of "no-education" would fail just as had that of "no-rate." If chapels were used, there would be no exchequer grants and probably no payment of rates. The *Daily Telegraph* observed that candidates who sought election to county councils bound themselves to accept the obligations of the office. The Welsh, like the English, enjoyed free institutions and their redress was through the election of a majority pledged to amend the act.[44]

Anglicans sought to ensure that in England the Nonconformists did not work the Act of 1902 against them. The most vigorous instrument in this fight was the Church Schools' Emergency League, founded locally on November 16, 1903, as the Manchester Church Day Schools' Emergency League and extended to the entire country in July 1904

---

* The *Daily News* (July 31, 1903) noted that one of the few exceptions was the Cambridgeshire County Council which voted 18 to 9 to refuse rate aid until satisfaction was given on the questions of popular control and no religious tests for teachers. The *Review of Reviews* (Aug. 1903) added the vignette that "it was in the Eastern Counties where Cromwell raised his Ironsides and the memory of the seventeenth century still lingers in the neighborhood of the fens."

when its more permanent title was adopted. The militant Rev. Cleworth became its fighting secretary. Its sponsors were unhappy with what they felt was a failure of the National Society to supply more energetic leadership against the conduct of hostile administrative bodies. Members of education committees, managers of Church schools, and others were invited to join in the preservation of voluntary schools and their religious purposes. Its regularly published leaflets contained the manifold activities engaged in to resist encroachments upon Church schools.[45] It provided publicity and counsel when violations in the spirit of the Act of 1902 occurred and the list was endless—paring down the time for religious instruction, refusing to provide furniture for new schools, docking teachers' salaries for time spent in denominational instruction, requiring expensive repairs, evading responsibilities under the wear-and-tear maintenance clause. It sought out members of parliament and arranged for deputations to government officials to register complaints. It participated actively in county council elections, seeking the views of candidates as to fair treatment for Church schools.[46]

Roman Catholics were no whit behind Anglicans in preparing to contest deviations from the Act of 1902. Rev. Hugh Edmund Ford favored a working agreement between Roman Catholics and the Church Schools' Emergency League. But the Catholic School Committee preferred to leave the defense to its regular agencies. Furthermore, in 1905, the Catholic School Committee was replaced by the Catholic Education Council, a body established to integrate primary, secondary, and college functions for the better implementation of the Act of 1902.[47]

THE LONDON SCENE

Particularly bitter was the strife between Nonconformists and Anglicans in London. The first round took place in connection with the passage of the London Education Act of 1903. The metropolitan area had been excluded from the Act of 1902 in order to give special consideration to its administrative problems. Actually the final form of the bill was not too different from the parent measure. The original draft had contemplated designating as the responsible educational authorities the twenty-nine metropolitan borough councils which functioned somewhat autonomously in certain matters not delegated to the central London County Council. But eventually the latter was named as the responsible body† and was empowered to appoint, for continuous supervision, one comprehensive education committee, partly drawn from the ranks of its own London County Council and partly co-opted from the citizenry. The role reserved for the borough councils was two-fold: first, to name two-thirds of the managers of each council school (the other one-third to be named by the education committee) and second, to consult as to the site of any new schools within their districts. Otherwise the education committee of the London County Council was to be in direct administrative contact with council schools. In the case of voluntary schools, the education committee would exercise supervision over their secular work and name one-third of the managers (one each by the borough council and the London education committee). For the rest, the financial and religious provisions of the Act of 1902 were extended to London.[48]

Nonconformists castigated the measure as possessing all the objectionable features of the Act of 1902. It was a clerical bill putting the voluntary schools on the rates without either adequate public control or any guarantee of no religious tests for teachers. It would increase the power of the clergy and stifle the expansion of new council schools. The *Presbyterian* believed that the two non-foundation managers, one from the greater and one from the lesser local authority, would oppose each other often enough to permit the foundation managers in voluntary schools to have their own way. In the commons, Francis A. Channing, Liberal M.P., son of an eminent American Unitarian divine and later first Baron Channing of Wellingborough, warned that the endowment of Church schools in London was far more serious than elsewhere, for in the metropolis they were particularly under the pressure of "Romanish" clergymen.[49]

Nor was the proposed liquidation of the London School Board any more palatable. Its exemplary service and educational leadership had been outstanding. The *Speaker* harbored the suspicion that Anglicans wanted its demise because it would have insisted upon an efficient performance in return for rate aid. Perhaps the only source of comfort to Nonconformists was the defeat of the original proposal to decentralize management among the borough councils. That could have made easier Anglican influence, for the well-organized diocesan associations would swamp the many education committees with nominees more concerned

---

† The literature on the London Act of 1903 suggests that Sidney Webb (Lord Passfield) was also influential in the behind-the-scene activities to replace the London School Board by the London County Council. Allen (1934), pp. 206-07; Beatrice Webb (1948), p. 252 ff; Sidney Webb, *London Education* (1904), pp. 209-12.

over the welfare of Church schools than the extension of secular knowledge.[50]

Anglican literature is meager on the London Education Act of 1903, considering that 438 voluntary schools were placed on the local rates. The explanation of the *Guardian* was that there seemed no reason to debate issues which for good or evil had already been settled in 1902. The scattered comments suggest the same range of friendly and unfriendly views as over the parent measure. The *Standard* regarded rate aid for non-provided schools as an act of equality inasmuch as all schools offered special religious instruction. The *School Guardian* was not alarmed over the appointment of two non-foundation managers by the education committee, confident that they would be drawn from the faith which the school represented. In contrast, the *Church Times* was critical of the extension of the Kenyon-Slaney amendment to Church schools in London where children needed especially strong spiritual guidance to combat the mundane values of a commercial center. The *Pilot* expressed itself as unhappy over the failure to obtain the right of entry into council schools for credal lessons. A great number of Anglican children would thus be left uninstructed in the faith. Bishop Percival of Hereford was worried by the deepening Nonconformist hostility at what the latter termed a new violation of conscience. The Established Church courted increased danger that the "slippery slope" of rate aid would end in public control of voluntary schools.[51]

Roman Catholic comment was directed toward the proposal in the original draft for representation on the education committees in the metropolitan boroughs. Whereas previously the cumulative vote had always assured them of seats on the London School Board, henceforth it would have to be by the vicarious method of co-optation. When the measure was amended to establish a central education committee, the Catholic School Committee passed a resolution asking for not less than 3 of the proposed 25 co-opted members.[52]

A second round in the metropolitan rivalry occurred during the election, in March 1904, of the London County Council. In January of that year Bishop Lang of Stepney (who became Archbishop of York in 1909) had called upon Churchmen to take an active part in the campaign. If he confessed to a dislike for ecclesiastical embroilment in politics, the blame must rest with Nonconformists who were asking candidates if they would insist upon a special inspection of all voluntary school buildings before granting rate aid. What else, then, could the Church of England do but ascertain that candidates pledged to carry out the act were returned if voluntary schools were to get fair play?[53] In particular, suspicion was pointed at the Progressives as representing the disciples of predatory radicalism. While the results of the election found the Progressives retaining a majority over the Moderates, Churchmen did not feel that their efforts had been in vain.[54] Apart from the fact that the Progressives' majority had been cut from 53 to 49 (which should have a sobering effect upon these extremists), some 97 of the 118 elected members were regarded as having answered satisfactorily the questions propounded by Churchmen.[55] The duty now was to maintain vigilance to see that the pledges were carried out.[56]

Nonconformists blamed the Established Church for injecting sectarianism into the London County Council election.‡ Apparently such Churchmen as Bishop Lang of Stepney and Bishop Talbot of Rochester were prepared to intervene even in civic life in order to advance ecclesiasticism. The *Speaker* noted that their approved candidates were the Moderates whose views on social reform were reactionary. Vital legislation on sanitation, hygiene, and housing all were to be sacrificed upon the fetish of orthodoxy. As Nonconformist commentators analyzed the cause of good education, it rested with the election of the Progressives. The *Examiner* commended their past record and was astounded that their good work could be endangered "because they refuse to bow the knee to the ecclesiastical Baal." The *Daily Chronicle* liked their forthright stand that every school should be treated with the yardstick of educational efficiency. The Progressives would not permit church associations to escape the responsibility of putting their schools in proper repair in return for rate aid. Great was the elation of Nonconformists at the retention by the Progressives of a working majority. Upon the occasion of its congratulatory message, the *Daily News* reminded the Progressives that they were pledged to administer the London Act of 1903 impartially.[57]

The *Catholic Herald* warned Roman Catholics against identifying themselves exclusively with any political party. They should make it their business to secure friends in both camps. The fact that some Roman Catholics chose to connect themselves with the Moderates impelled the editor to welcome the presence of other co-religionists on the Progressives' ticket as a counterbalance. Furthermore, it proved that in the field of social politics communicants were under no compulsion from the hierarchy. The Roman Catholic as a citizen could decide for himself on such municipal schemes as tramways and housing.[58]

---

‡ Once again secularists pronounced a plague on both sides for introducing the religious issue into politics. Anglicans and Nonconformists alike were guilty of displaying indifference to the problems of municipal life and of making children the shuttlecock of feuding sectaries. *Justice*, Feb. 6, 1904; *Labour Leader*, Dec. 26, 1903, Mar. 5, 1904.

A third round transpired in connection with the inspection report of school buildings ordered by the newly-elected London County Council. The publication of the survey was made in April 1905 and to the Nonconformists it was a devastating disclosure.[59] Only 64 of the 438 voluntary schools were noted as in a suitable condition, while 92 (25%) were so bad as to warrant being closed at once or as soon as alternate accommodations could be found.* No restraint was shown in flaying Church authorities for this sorry state of affairs. The facts were obvious to the naked eye—ill-lighted and ill-ventilated classrooms, defective drains, and inadequate playground space. The presence of only one narrow staircase exposed children to great hazards in the event of fire. Where now were the boasts of denominationalists that they had saved the ratepayers large sums of money? The *Daily News* regarded the report as an object lesson on a large scale of the meaning and cost of clericalism in education. Much of the blame rested with the Board of Education which had steadfastly winked at the low standards of Church schools. George Lewis Bruce expressed doubt that Churchmen could raise the money for the staggering job of renovation ahead. If the London County Council was called upon to assist, then it should demand popular control. At any rate, it was to be hoped that from these findings would come a buildings program of significance to the health and educational progress of hundreds of thousands of children.[60]

Anglicans were not to be shamed into any contrite spirit by the buildings survey. The report was surfeited with malice. The intent was not only to damage the reputation of the voluntary schools but also to "squeeze them" out of existence. The yardstick for building standards applied by surveyors was preposterous, greatly in excess of what had been the minimum. Indeed, few buildings anywhere of any kind could meet such standards. If, observed the *Guardian*, drains did not stand the water or smoke test, "the same would be true of most Park-lane houses if subjected to the finicking and unnecessarily rigorous tests . . . used

---

* The *School Government Chronicle* (April 22, 1905) regarded the findings as a vindication of Circular 321 issued by Arthur H.D. Acland, vice-president of the Committee of Council on Education, in January 1893, to inspectors to ascertain the physical condition of all grant aid schools in England and Wales: "But Circular 321 was a failure. Reactionary agitation was stimulated into tenfold activity; intrigue was set on foot in all directions; and by a thousand channels such pressure was brought to bear upon Mr. Acland. . . . The 'schools warned' lists, after assuming quite appreciable proportions, soon began to dwindle. Smaller by degrees and beautifully less they grew; until their disappearance became a hardly perceptible incident of the first days of the Board of Education. Meanwhile, the state school buildings have been growing worse. . . . [It is to be hoped] arrears will now be caught up." Acland's circular may be found in *Parl. Papers*, 1893, XXVI, Cd. 7089, pp. 482-83.

by the County Council inspectors." The *Standard* wondered how many of the children's parents inhabited dwellings in which a zealous inspector would not find fault with the drainage. It was not denied that improvements and alterations were in order. No sensible person would defend the use of unsanitary premises. But repairs could proceed in an orderly fashion and not be discouraged by sweeping condemnation. Each school should be reviewed on its merit, the extreme cases of defectiveness tackled first.† *The Times* warned the community of the problem ahead to find 26,940 places lost by rigidly enforcing the ten-square-feet per child rule and 41,884 places lost by the proposed closing of 92 schools at once.[61] The financial outlay would be heavy.[62]

Roman Catholic comments varied. The *Catholic Herald* was prepared to accept the report in good faith and to make the necessary repairs. The *Catholic Times* qualified its position to the extent that the demands should be opposed when not referring to sanitation but merely to up-to-date alterations. The *Tablet* expressed gallantly the Roman Catholic determination to raise the necessary money for repairs "even if it means foregoing the adornment and elaboration of our churches—painted glass, peals of bells, ornamental towers."[63]

A postscript may be added that in 1914 the situation had not changed very materially. A London County Council Report showed that 124 condemned voluntary schools accommodating 54,545 children were still unimproved. They lacked adequate provision for playground space, rest room facilities, lighting, and ventilation.[64]

---

† Henry W. Burrows, consulting architect for the National Society, declared that many of the schools condemned completely were reparable, citing as one instance St. Anne's Limehouse School. *Guardian*, April 26, 1905; *The Times*, April 25, 1905, 10 e-f. For data on St. Anne's see *London County Council Report*, 1905, p. 125.

CHAPTER FOUR

THE LIBERAL GOVERNMENT'S PROPOSALS

THE SEVERAL MEASURES

THE SWEEPING TRIUMPH of the Liberal Party in the General Election of January 1906, brought renewed hope to Nonconformists. Undoubtedly, its victory was partly owing to the return of many Radical Unionists to its ranks as a result of the Education Act of 1902. Its program of social reform to improve the condition of the masses included the field of education, especially to redress the existing imbalance in favor of the Anglicans. As a result of pledges by Liberal leaders during the election campaign, the Free Church Council took an active part and raised money to defray the expenses of many Liberal Party candidates. This body was organized in 1896 to embrace all evangelical denominations in order to carry the Gospel more effectively to people in the urban areas.[1] Rev. Thomas T. Law, secretary of the Free Church Council, estimated that some 200 Free Churchmen * were returned to the new House of Commons as contrasted with 120 in 1900.[2] The selection of Augustine Birrell, an avowed champion of the Nonconformist cause, as President of the Board of Education in the Liberal Government was hailed with joy. Nor were the succeeding education ministers, Reginald McKenna in January 1907, and Walter Runciman in April 1908, less active in seeking the amelioration of Nonconformist grievances. And, to cap the climax, Herbert Asquith, who replaced the ailing Campbell-Bannerman in April 1908 as prime minister, was a Nonconformist and sympathetic to their plight.

Three major attempts were made by the Liberal Government between 1906 and 1908 to fulfill their promise to Nonconformists. Indeed, Lord Fitzroy gathered from a conversation with Lord Crewe on March

---

* Halévy gives the figure as 180 Dissenters (*Free Church Year Book*, 1906, p. 306). In addition he lists 13 Scotch Presbyterians, 16 Jews, 80 Irish Catholics, 10 English Catholics, and 300 Church of England members. Further, he comments that with a loss of only 40 more seats the Church of England would not have possessed a majority in the commons. Halévy, *The Rule of Democracy, 1905-1914* (1952, 2nd rev. ed.), Book I, pp. 64-65.

23, 1906 "that in return for their contribution to the ministerial majority, they [Nonconformists] seemed determined to exact their pound of flesh and make the Bill as crude a triumph for ultra-Nonconformity as the complaint is that the last Act was for the Anglican Episcopate." The Birrell Bill of 1906 passed the commons but was so drastically amended in the lords as to influence Campbell-Bannerman to drop it. The McKenna Bill did not get beyond the second reading stage in May 1908. The Runciman Bill was withdrawn in December 1908, while still in the committee stage. What happened was that Anglicans and Roman Catholics, hostile to the Liberal proposals as unfair to the interests of positive religion, found formidable champions in the political arena. The preponderance of the membership in the lords was identified with the Conservative Party and defended the Act of 1902. The Irish Nationalist Party, some eighty strong in the commons and whose support the Liberal Government was anxious to retain, lent a restraining hand. In the end the Liberal Government took refuge in negotiations with the various religious groups in the hope that a *modus vivendi* might be worked out.[3]

The Birrell Bill of 1906 sought the solution of Nonconformist grievances by restricting exchequer and rate aid to council schools.[4] It was envisaged that the loss of State money must ultimately put voluntary schools out of business. Where it was desirable the local authority could negotiate the transfer of a voluntary school. If agreement failed as to the compensatory amount, then recourse was to be had to an appointive commission whose decision would not be subject to review. A grant of £1,000,000 was requested to cover the initial anticipated cost. At the same time the Liberal Government was prepared to meet the needs of the various Christian faiths for religious instruction. While the Cowper-Temple clause would be the operating principle in both council and transferred schools, in the latter ordinary facilities (twice weekly) for credal lessons were to be optional. Also, in urban areas, defined as a minimum of 5,000 population, the local authority was to have discretionary power to set up extended facilities (daily) for credal lessons provided the petitioning parents represented four-fifths of the children registered. For the parent opposed to any or all types of religious instruction a new conscience clause was to prevail, embodying Anson's model by-law which permitted children to remain at home during the religious hour.† To assure that the appointment of teachers would be based pri-

---

† Anson, hoping to mitigate the Nonconformist complaint of proselytism, had issued in July 1903, a model by-law, optional for local authorities, to this effect. *Commons*, July 9, 1903, pp. 244-45; *Ministry of Education*, 1913-14 (Box 104), I (J).

marily upon their qualifications for the lay subjects, no teacher was to be required to subscribe to any creed or to give credal lessons in a transferred school. However, a teacher could volunteer where extended facilities were authorized. The right of teachers to impart Cowper-Temple lessons was not prohibited.

The McKenna Bill of 1908 sought the solution of Nonconformist grievances by a proposal more lenient to Anglicans and Roman Catholics.[5] Only in single school areas would exchequer and rate aid be restricted to council schools although no mention was made of compensation in the event of a compulsory transfer of any voluntary school. From these places, in which the Church of England had a monopoly of education, had come the greatest number of Nonconformist complaints of proselytism. But in multiple school districts, voluntary schools could contract out with the loss of rate aid, to be offset by increased exchequer grants. However, the latter was not to exceed 47s. per child (hitherto 41s.) and not more than 75% of the total cost. In addition, the Board of Education must be satisfied 1) that the number of children was not less than thirty in attendance and 2) that all conditions of efficiency with regard to staff, premises, and curriculum were met. A Christian basis in council and transferred schools would be maintained through the operating principle of the Cowper-Temple clause, with the opportunity in transferred schools for credal lessons before or after school hours. In the contracting-out school, the credal instruction specified in the trust deed would govern. As in the Birrell Bill, the dictates of religious toleration would be served by permitting those parents who desired to keep their children at home until the religious hour was over. While religious tests were banned in the engagement of teachers, the regular staff was forbidden only to give the credal lessons in transferred schools. No such prohibition was imposed upon teachers in contracting-out schools with regard to credal lessons or upon teachers with regard to Cowper-Temple instruction wherever given.

The Runciman Bill of 1908 sought the solution of Nonconformist grievances by a proposal even more lenient to Anglicans and Roman Catholics.[6] Like its immediate predecessor, it called for the restriction of exchequer and rate aid in single school areas to council schools. It contained a schedule of rent payments for the lease of voluntary schools with an alternative of outright purchase. Similarly, in multiple school districts, voluntary schools could contract out with the loss of rate aid (but with increased exchequer grants) and subject to satisfying the Board of Education as to need and efficiency. Where the two measures differed was in the willingness of the Runciman Bill to meet the desire of Anglicans for a more positive Christian tone in all schools. The Cowper-Temple clause was made mandatory in council schools from 9 to 9:45 A.M. and a religious instruction committee was authorized to draft a syllabus in each school district. Ordinary facilities (twice weekly) for credal lessons were to be permitted not only in the transferred but also in the council schools, the cost to be borne by the denominations. In the contracting-out school, the credal instruction specified in the trust deed would govern. While the ban on religious tests in the appointment of teachers was reaffirmed, greater latitude was allowed the teaching staff to participate in the credal lessons. Eligibility to volunteer was given incumbent head teachers in transferred schools and assistant teachers on a permanent basis in both transferred and council schools. In the contracting-out schools, the entire staff could be used for the daily credal lesson specified in the trust deed. No prohibition was imposed upon teachers with regard to Cowper-Temple instruction. As in the two previous measures, the conscience clause permitted a child to stay at home until the religious hour was over.

THE ADVERSARIES AGAIN

Anglicans labeled the financial provision in all instances as confiscatory in nature. The proposed appropriation of £1,000,000 in the Birrell Bill was not a large sum and if the State took any appreciable number of voluntary schools the compensation would be small. Dean Ridgeway of Carlisle, later to be Bishop of Chichester, saw a modern Star Chamber in the appointive commission of three endowed with the final word in the event of a dispute. The absence of any schedule of payments in the McKenna Bill drew from Bishop Knox of Coventry, who replaced Dr. Moorhouse in Manchester in 1903, the strong words that "as a specimen of class legislation, of unscrupulous rapacity, and of religious intolerance in the twentieth century, the Bill will no doubt deserve a place in historical archives by the side of racks, thumbscrews, boots, and other engines of torture." The contemplated range of £3 to £4 10s. on an absolute transfer in the Runciman Bill was compared by the National Society with an actual cost of £8 per place on a calculation of ten square feet. What breaches of faith these proposals were from a State which had encouraged religious associations to promote education! New facets of past financial sacrifices were unfolded. Rev. Cleworth observed that by 1870 the churches had built 6,382 schools at a cost of £6,200,000 and only £1,766,000 of that amount was contributed by the State.[7] More recently, between 1902 and 1905, he estimated that the Church of England had spent £3,000,000 on repairs to satisfy county councils.[8] *Blackwood's Magazine* stressed that since 1870, when the State had discontinued building grants, the Church of England had raised £20,000,000 for new schools.‡ Churchmen would not have spent all this money unless there had been a distinct understanding that their efforts would be recognized.[9]

Anglicans took a dim view of the ordinary facilities twice weekly. Both Birrell and McKenna Bills limited it to the transferred schools, to be given by outside teachers and at the cost of the denomination. In the case of the McKenna Bill, it had to be done before or after school hours. Children would not find the catechism alluring at times ordinarily given to play and tea. *Blackwood's Magazine* felt that it was asking too much for untrained clergymen and laymen (assuming sufficient numbers could be gotten) to possess the same authority over the children as the regular teachers. Nor did ordinary facilities in council schools in school hours plus the right of assistant teachers in all schools to volunteer represent a fairer compromise under the Runciman Bill. The well-known opposition of regular staffs in council schools to the right of entry (or to any kind of religious lesson) would neutralize its effectiveness. Mrs. Watkin Williams, wife of the Vicar of Monkton, Thanet, Kent, conjured up the horrifying apparition of a clergyman presenting a lesson on the Incarnation to the tune of "a sneering smile from a certificated Unitarian teacher sitting at a desk apparently occupied with school registers." Samuel Butcher, classical scholar and Unionist M.P. for Cambridge University, argued that children would be apt to look upon the denominational instruction as an "extra," considering that the entire teaching corps would give Cowper-Temple lessons. The total effect would be to discredit such lessons in the eyes of the public, local authorities, and teachers generally.[10]

Anglicans were no more enamored of the greater concessions for credal instruction in urban centers. They doubted whether under the Birrell Bill extended facilities would benefit the Church of England since these were restricted to urban areas with more than 5,000 population. George Wyndham, Conservative M.P. and staunch Anglican layman, referred to a specially-prepared government table showing that only 25.6% of Church schools would qualify whereas 100% of the Jew-

---

‡ The annual report of the National Society (1903, p. 16) lists £8,495,751 as the amount spent on construction since 1870. However, statements in Anglican literature would suggest that many building expenditures were often not included in the official accounts, chiefly local outlays before and after the actual contracted sum had been recorded. It was these which brought the sum to £20,000,000. As an example see the notes of Rev. A. Goodall in the *Wakefield Diocesan Gazette*, reprinted in *Church Schools' Emergency League Leaflet*, XXXIII, Dec. 1905.

ish, 77.1% of the Roman Catholic, and 52% of the Wesleyan schools were located in the affected urban areas.[11] The *Western Mail* (Cardiff) predicted that in Wales it would be confined to Roman Catholic schools, because in most Church schools the number of Nonconformist children was usually more than one-fifth. Disapproval of the contracting-out provisions under the McKenna and Runciman Bills likewise was registered. The proposal of the government to increase the national grant from 41s. to 47s. per child would still leave a considerable margin to raise by subscription. With the average cost of education 63s. per child at the moment, a sum of 16s. per child would have to be found in the future, an utter impossibility.* The *Commonwealth* lamented that if it were adopted, once more foundation managers, dreading increased expenditures, would be forced into the detestable position of obstructors to educational progress.[12]

Whether or not Anglicans felt by 1908 that they had already sufficiently expressed themselves on the subject of giving statutory effect to Anson's model by-law, the collected literature is confined to the Birrell Bill of 1906. Their conclusion was that to permit children to remain at home during the religious lesson would invite secularism by the back door. Indifferent parents would keep their children home to do housework, hawk in the streets, or indulge in playground games. Probably many of these children came from the homes of the poor and stood most in need of spiritual sustenance. Certainly the optional nature of the religious lesson would not enhance its dignity for those who participated. Children would take the hint that it was an extra, not important enough to be made an integral part of the daily timetable. It could be anticipated too that the withdrawn children would come to school in a straggling trickle, perhaps seeking some shelter out of the cold and so disturb the solemnity of the religious period. Or perhaps, if it was a pleasant day, those children engaged inside at the devout services would be distracted and unhappy at the hilarious shouting of schoolmates enjoying an early recess. As they saw it, the result would lead to the corrosion of the Christian tone of a school. The traditional conscience clause requiring children to remain at school during the religious hour should be restored.[13]

Anglicans were greatly concerned over the prohibition of religious tests for teachers. Archbishop Davidson challenged the theory that the

---

* The official compilation placed the average cost for the entire country at 64s. 10d. per child. Broken down, it was 57s. 4d. in counties, 60s. in boroughs, 64s. 7d. in county boroughs, 64s. 9d. in urban districts, and 94s. 3d. in London. *Parl. Papers*, 1908, LXXXII, Cd. 4406, 8 pp.

teacher was a civil servant and hence must be free from tests. The principal object in civil service was administrative efficiency and the individual as a distinctive personality was subordinated. But in the educational profession a chief purpose was to kindle the vision of divinity and for this the personality of the teacher was paramount. To put it bluntly, tests were necessary and teaching was not a career for anyone who did not accept the responsibility of promoting the nation's Christian aims. Lord Robert Cecil argued that all other public servants whose duties involved a religious function were tested as to their qualifications. The State did not appoint chaplains in the navy, army, or prisons without first asking about their professional affiliations. What the repeal of the Test Act had meant, contended the *Church Times*, was that public service ought not to be reserved exclusively for adherents of a particular denomination. So, if in a Church school a teacher was required by the trust deed to be a member of the Church of England, the comparable interpretation for a council school teacher held true that he should be Christian in outlook. As a matter of fact, Anglicans were skeptical that no religious tests could be enforced, for managers could ill afford to exempt teachers from giving religious instruction. Much was made of the admission (in committee) by Thomas Lough, new parliamentary secretary to the Board of Education, that if a teacher would not give the Cowper-Temple lessons he would be dismissed.[14] The Liberal Government should think out the inconsistencies of its position.[15]

Roman Catholics were caustic in their appraisal of the several measures.† Rev. Peter Gallwey, S.J., London, termed the compensatory features for taking over voluntary schools "as a wholesale spoliation which will stand in our history side by side with Henry VIII's violent seizure of the monasteries." And as transferred schools their atmosphere would be difficult to retain. At best, remembering that Cowper-Templeism would be given thrice weekly, Protestantism would gain a favored position. At worst, remembering that no religious test would be required of the teacher, the tone could well become secularist. Rev. Sydney F. Smith, editor of *Month*, saw no value in facilities twice weekly; it was pedagogically an impossible task to teach the doctrines

---

† The Irish Nationalist Party in the commons and Roman Catholic peers in the lords were the recipients of many grateful acknowledgments for their role in defending English Catholic schools during these hectic years from 1906 to 1908. Perhaps the only dissident note related to the first Marquess of Ripon, a Roman Catholic convert from Anglicanism, who supported his Liberal Party's Birrell Bill as a reasonable compromise and for which he suffered much painful obloquy at the hands of his co-religionists. Wolf (1921), II, pp. 280-84.

of the Roman Catholic Church at one sitting to a collection of children ranging from five to fourteen.[16]

The plight of Roman Catholic teachers in transferred schools evoked sympathy. They would be restricted from giving the credal lessons which many treasured as a precious trust confided by God and conceived of as in the nature of an apostolic office. They would find their innermost convictions strained on the three days Cowper-Templeism was given. Indeed, Rev. Smith wondered if many teachers of Roman Catholic faith would be hired any more, steeped as local authorities were in the Protestant tradition. So long as any kind of religious teaching was permissible, local authorities would take every means to ascertain the beliefs of candidates. It was to be doubted if the provision of no religious tests would do any more than help Nonconformists break down an Anglican monopoly.[17]

Scarcely attractive were the alternatives offered to salvage the identity of Roman Catholic schools in urban centers. Under the Birrell Bill, the negative propensities of the four-fifths majority seemed too many. Rev. Smith pointed out that the poll must represent an absolute four-fifths of all the children actually in attendance and there would always be some parents unable to vote for health or other reasons. Particularly vulnerable would be those parochial schools not running at capacity and which might be compelled to fill up with Protestant children in lieu of a new council school. There was the further discomforting fact that the migratory habits of the Irish could dissipate quickly a four-fifths majority.[18]

The attractiveness of contracting-out under the McKenna and Runciman Bills rested in the financial terms. The *Tablet* deemed the margin between the national grant of 47s. and the current average cost of 64s. 10d. too great to overcome by subscriptions and the maximum school fee of 9d. weekly.‡ The result would be a return to the old days of raffles, jumble-sales, bazaars, and concerts. The English nation should remember that most Roman Catholic parents were poor and

---

‡ The secularist Lord Stanley of Alderley dealt roughly with the Roman Catholic protest that the proposed national grant of 47s. per child was not enough. That was far more than they got in France, Italy, Switzerland, Germany, the United States, and the British colonies where no recognition of private schools as such was given in the form of national grants. As for their argument that conscience forbade any use of the council school, the answer was that they accommodated themselves to circumstances. In the United States there were two million Roman Catholic pupils of whom one million went to the common schools. In short, Roman Catholics naturally tried for all they could get. *Nineteenth Century and After*, April 1908, pp. 544-47. For his estimate of American school attendance see an article written by Rev. Morgan M. Sheedy, an American Roman Catholic priest, in *Annual Report, Commissioner of Education* (U. S.), 1903, I, p. 1089.

already overburdened to pay rates for council schools. Msgr. William
F. Brown, Rector of St. Anne's Vauxhall, London, and a member of
the old London School Board, lamented that once again the Roman
Catholic Church would be left with inferior school buildings, larger
classes, and uncertificated teachers. It was a cruel form of reparation
that made the lot of slum and alley children more degrading and harder
to bear by unequal schooling opportunities.[19]

Nonconformist reaction to the various bills, designed as they were to
meet their grievances, varied from clause to clause. The proposed rental
payment for transferred schools was defended against the Anglican re-
proach of base ingratitude for past sacrifices. Rev. Hollowell repeated
anew the facts pertaining to the construction of Church schools. A fair
proportion of subscriptions had come from individuals and corporations
who sought to avoid the heavy rates imposed by a school board. Moreover, if one granted that spiritual zeal alone had raised the entire sum,
Anglicans should reckon in the balance sheet the use of these buildings
for night meetings and Sunday schools and the time devoted to credal
lessons by State-paid teachers. And the grant of rate aid in 1902 was
the finishing touch to any illusion of a labor of virtue. George Lewis
Bruce believed that the State would be better off if it refused to rent
the antiquated voluntary school buildings and erected new council
schools. Calculating the rental cost of transferred schools at the budgeted £1,000,000 under the Birrell Bill, the State could borrow £30,-
000,000 at 3¼% interest and provide the nation with a brand new
physical plant. The *Methodist Times* felt that such a move might draw
a more heartfelt public interest in the schools. Where the transferred
school must bring with it the sectarian habit, a new council school
would be part of a fresher community life.[20]

Whether the provision for twice weekly facilities would serve the
criterion of religious equality was another question. As confined to
transferred schools under the Birrell Bill and utilizing outside teachers
at the cost of the denomination, Nonconformists were amenable to it.
The *Daily News* understood that very few Church schools devoted
more than that amount of time now to catechetical instruction. As
proposed under the McKenna Bill with similar conditions plus exclusion in school hours, Nonconformists offered even less objection. The
Daily Chronicle expressed doubt that Anglicans would avail themselves
of such limited facilities and it seemed foolish to let the idea of entry
be a stumbling block to a settlement. But the concessions under the
Runciman Bill aroused great opposition. Rev. Hollowell protested the
right of the incumbent head teacher to give credal lessons in transferred schools. That meant a continued sectarian atmosphere for some

time to come in several thousand schools. Most disturbing was the
right of entry in the council school and the use of the assistant teacher.
Alfred Hutton, Liberal M.P., anticipated frequent visits from the diocesan inspector to see that the credal lessons were given properly. Under
such circumstances peace would dwell no longer in the council school
and the *esprit de corps* which had come to distinguish its life would be
first demoralized and then destroyed.[21]

Nonconformists were quite wrought up over the offer of extended
facilities. As contemplated under the Birrell Bill via a petition representing four-fifths of the school children, the *Methodist Times* declared that such a school would imply the presence of a minority breath-
ing in the sectarian incense. While it was true that a council school must
be available on demand, Rev. Hollowell wondered if the distance to
travel might not always compel some Nonconformist parents to send
their children to a school where credal lessons were the order of the
day. As contemplated under the McKenna and Runciman Bills, the
contracting-out school would reflect the essence of extended facilities.
Rev. C. Silvester Horne, Congregational minister and Liberal M.P.,
was ready to recognize the necessity of compromise. It was to be granted
that Roman Catholics and Jews should not be compelled to put up
with Protestant teaching. But the crux of the problem centered in the
financial terms. It was surely not asking too much of those who wanted
their own doctrines taught to find some of the money themselves. Furthermore, a sizeable margin of subscriptions was highly desirable lest
too many schools come under the contracting-out provision and so perpetuate the dual system. As it was, the Anglican demand for almost
complete State support along with the right to build new contracting-
out schools drew from Dr. Clifford the charge that the Church of England aimed to make contracting-out the rule rather than the exception.
Sectarianism would achieve an impregnable position in towns and
many Nonconformist children by virtue of convenient proximity might
have to go to them and thus be exposed to proselytism.[22]

Nonconformists were divided in their interpretation of the new conscience clause. On the one hand, some feared that children would stay
at home during the religious period and so weaken the Christian basis
of council schools. Between the parent who would use the opportunity to put his child out to work early in the morning and the parent
who would yield to the desire of his child to sleep longer, withdrawal
might become the normal practice. It was especially objectionable to
have the inference prevail that religious instruction was an extra and
optional subject.[23] On the other hand, some felt that it offered a more
effective means of combating proselytism. It was contrary to human

nature to expect a child to separate himself and sit apart as was currently the law. The mere threat of a Nonconformist minority to keep children at home until the lay subjects were taken up could serve as a lever to secure a more reasonable religious syllabus. Anglicans might profit by a like threat in the council schools if the quality of Bible teaching was strained too thin. As for the danger of children being exploited, proper child labor legislation would prevent that. The *British Weekly*, however, did not think that the proposed new conscience clause went far enough to protect against proselytism. A better scheme was that employed in the Irish National schools where it was assumed that the children of minorities must not be present in the same room at the time of the religious instruction.[24] Only if a parent of a minority faith signed a certificate in a special book could his child be taught in the tenets of another denomination. The Liberal Government's proposal was faulty in that the initiative was put on the parent to get the exemption. The result would be that the timid parent who dreaded the irascibility of a local squire would continue to suffer in silence.[25]

Nonconformists were only partially satisfied as to the effectiveness of the prohibition of religious tests in the appointment of teachers. The statement in both the Birrell and McKenna Bills specifically forbidding the regular teacher to give the ordinary facilities in transferred schools was deemed an adequate protection. The *Examiner* hoped that it would end the "manufacture of hypocrites" and enable the schools to get more than second and third rate teachers who "swallow the prescribed shibboleths." Less favorably received under the Birrell Bill was the provision that in extended facilities schools the regular staff might volunteer to give it. Bruce pointed out that such schools as qualified under the four-fifths formula would necessarily demand teachers of their own faith who were prepared to give the credal lessons and so religious tests would be unavoidable. Most harshly judged was the right of the assistant teacher in both transferred and council schools to volunteer for facilities instruction under the Runciman Bill. Dr. Clifford regarded religious tests as inevitable under that contingency.[26]

Secularists could see only the word ecclesiasticism writ large over the horizon of the several bills. These bills were but attempts to adjust rival Christian influences in the elementary schools. Nonconformist gleanings were dwelt upon at length. Their favorite Cowper-Temple lessons were to be extended to transferred schools. Indeed, under the Runciman Bill, Cowper-Temple lessons were to be made compulsory in both transferred and council schools with the regular staff to impart it at the expense of the State. The *Ethical World* reminded the nation that the school board syllabuses in vogue with their selected passages from the Old and New Testaments reflected particularly the Protestant views of Nonconformity. The dividends accruing to Anglicans were reckoned as bound up with the facilities and contracting-out provisions. If they were modest under the Birrell and McKenna Bills, Joseph McCabe, onetime Franciscan monk and rector of St. Bernardine's College, Buckingham, who left the fold in 1896 to become a vigorous advocate of secularism, emphasized their greater significance under the Runciman Bill. Not only was the right of entry extended to council schools but assistant teachers could volunteer for it. The choice to contract out meant the practical preservation of voluntary schools in urban centers. Whether the bargain would be acceptable to the two parties and so produce a state of equilibrium was to be doubted. As Theodore Rothstein, a Russian emigrant and active in the Social Democratic Federation,* saw it, the wheels of fortune, pointing to the Nonconformists in 1870 and to the Anglicans in 1902 and now apparently to the Nonconformists again, would continue to spin around in this unseemly game which Christian bodies were playing.[27]

Secularists were skeptical of the merits of the new conscience clause to provide an escape valve for children caught in the middle of this sectarian quarrel. Gould felt that it would still place a strain upon the parent who wanted his youngster to avoid ostracism. A child who came to school after the religious hour was just as much singled out as one who sat apart from fellow students while the religious lesson went on. MacDonald recounted his own reflections as a father weighing the cruel alternative to keep his child away until the lay subjects were taken up: "He had a child at a council school and he objected to Cowper-Temple-ism because it did not satisfy his ideas of what religious education should be; but was he going to withdraw his child . . . and expose him to be the butt of his fellows in the school?"[28]

On the brighter side, McCabe pointed out that the statutory Anson model by-law might serve as an opening wedge for secularization. He would make thoroughly known the optional character of the religious lesson to every parent and perhaps invite a wholesale use of the opportunity to keep children at home and to a forced elimination of the devotional period. George W. Foote, founder of the *Freethinker* in 1881 and President of the National Secular Society from 1890 to 1915, spoke in the same vein, arguing that the effect was to make religious instruc-

---

* Rothstein returned to Russia in 1920 and rose to prominence in Soviet ranks, holding such positions as Chairman of the Universities Reform Commission, Minister to Persia, and membership in the Collegium of the People's Commissariat for Foreign Affairs.

tion permissive instead of obligatory and so set in motion a lever that could wreck the use of the schools by the sectarians.[29]

Secularists aimed severe strictures at the well-intentioned efforts to eliminate religious tests for teachers. So long as religious instruction remained in the schools, it was impossible to appoint teachers for secular competency alone. MacDonald asserted that logic would make it impossible to abandon tests. Schools with only one teacher could not indulge him in conscientious objections and the percentage of teachers in schools with a larger staff who would be spared must be very small. Secularists no less than Nonconformists were concerned over the right of assistant teachers in both transferred and council schools to volunteer for ordinary facilities instruction under the Runciman Bill. That would increase the pressure for religious tests as managers maneuvered to match teachers with demands for specific types of credal lessons. Philip Snowden, secularist and Labour M.P. and later Chancellor of the Exchequer in the first Labour Government (1924), was a witness to the episode in the commons when Thomas Lough was asked what would happen to a teacher who refused to give the Cowper-Temple lessons. As Snowden recalled Lough's answer, it was the impulsive remark, "sack him." Foote referred to the case of Gould and the consequence of his petition to be relieved from giving the Cowper-Temple lessons in the London board school where he taught. While Gould was granted his request,[30] he received no promotion and eventually left the teaching profession (in the 1880's). Foote added that the sectarians had already won the real battle, since the denominational training colleges handled the larger number of students and operated as sieves, eliminating "unbelievers" and inculcating a Christian outlook among their student teachers.[31]

Secularists placed their own solution before the commons. In the committee stage MacDonald submitted an instruction "that education given in school hours and by civil servants must be in secular subjects." Because of a higher ranking in the order paper, however, a somewhat similar amendment by Frederick Maddison, also a Labour M.P., was considered to the effect "that no religious teaching should be permitted during school hours." When the commons divided on the Maddison motion, the secular solution was badly beaten by a vote of 477 to 63. Philip Whitwell Wilson, Liberal M.P. and an earnest Congregationalist, described the sixty-three negative voters "as mostly Nonconformists and rationalists." Wilson gave as his reason for being one of the sixty-three the fact that apparently Churchmen would have none of Cowper-Templeism and so an end to all religious teaching seemed the only possible solution.[32]

ATTEMPTS AT COMPROMISE

On the occasions of both Birrell and Runciman Bills, strenuous efforts were made to compose the differences between Anglicans and Nonconformists. In the instance of the Birrell Bill, King Edward VII, according to his biographer Sir Sidney Lee, was instrumental in persuading the Liberal Government and the House of Lords to meet in conference. The amendments introduced by the latter were proclaimed as ensuring religious equality and a positive Christian tone in education.[33] Religious instruction was made compulsory in all schools. Local authorities must take over voluntary schools when the latter were willing to negotiate. Provision of ordinary facilities was made meaningful by allowing them to be given daily in transferred schools upon petition of twenty children and assistant teachers could volunteer. Extended facilities were to be made mandatory upon local authorities at the request of only a two-thirds majority and the restriction to urban areas with more than 5,000 population eliminated. Two discussions took place on December 18, 1906, the first at the home of Lord Crewe, Lord President of the Council, in Curzon Street, and the second later in the evening in Balfour's room at the House of Commons. Among those present were Balfour, Lord Lansdowne (formerly Foreign Secretary), Dr. Davidson, Lord Crewe, Asquith, and Birrell. The critical items in the negotiations related to the opportunity for extended facilities in rural areas and the liberty of teachers to give ordinary facilities. Birrell's attitude was that to concede these points would leave many transferred schools as much sectarian agencies as they were now. Hence his decision to accept the defeat of his bill.[34]

In the instance of the Runciman Bill, a settlement failed by the narrowest of margins. Typical of the spirit of compromise between Anglicans and Nonconformists was the unanimous resolution carried at the Wesleyan Methodist Conference meeting presided over by Rev. Lidgett. In return for popular control, no religious tests for teachers, and compulsory simple Bible instruction, the special session was willing to go along with contracting-out and the right of entry. But the gravamen of the negotiations found the Liberal Government and the Archbishop of Canterbury at odds over the financial provisions for contracting-out. Dr. Davidson asked for a grant of 57s. per child. Runciman countered with an offer of 50s. based on his own estimated average cost of 60s., leaving as he felt only a small margin to be raised through subscriptions and school fees. The proposition was placed before the Representative Church Council on December 3, 1908, a body formed in

1903 to recommend legislation to the Church of England. Dr. Davidson spoke to the delegates of the three houses—bishops, priests, laity—urging a settlement. But the sentiment of the gathering was against accepting Runciman's offer. Since the lords would follow the views of the Anglicans, Runciman felt that it was useless to persevere with his bill and withdrew it in the committee stage.[35]

Subsequently the Liberal Government made no further major effort to meet the needs of Nonconformists. While the corridor talk was always thick with plans to bring in a bill at the "next session," nothing was done. Nor were the several private member bills offered between 1909 and 1912 acceptable to Asquith. Part of the explanation rested with the pressure put upon Asquith to proceed with other parts of the Liberal program. A good deal of the time of parliament between 1906 and 1908 had been devoted to the religious issue in the schools. Especially imperative was the obligation to deal with the working conditions of the proletariat. Such matters as old age pensions, sickness and unemployment insurance, minimum wages, and housing had been also in the forefront of their campaign pledges. Again, part of the explanation rested with the necessity of first dealing with the veto power of the lords, brought to a head by the latter's rejection of the Budget Bill in 1909. This occupied the Liberal Party until 1911 when it was successful in reducing the lords' power to a suspensory veto for two years. Afterwards the Irish Home Rule Bill and the Disestablishment of the Church of England in Wales absorbed the attention of the nation.

Nonconformist literature during 1913 and 1914 suggests a growing sentiment for a concentrated attack upon their worst grievance, namely, the single school area. Indeed, the question was raised whether the entire problem would not have to be solved in a series of stages. The Free Church Council spearheaded the campaign and a draft bill was formulated as a basis for negotiations. Schools in districts where only one was available were to be placed under council school conditions. The State should make the necessary grants to meet the rent and capital charges that might be involved. No teacher should be required to give religious instruction and the church association whose building it was previously would be permitted to take its children to another place during the religious hour if the parents so desired. But Nonconformist opinion was adamant against any further concessions such as contracting-out or the right of entry into council schools.[36]

The responses of Joseph Albert Pease, who replaced Runciman as President of the Board of Education in 1911, indicated frankly his fear of another humiliation for the Liberal Government. There was not enough time left in the life of the current parliament, whose five years would be up in 1915, to override the probable veto of the lords. Pease preferred to join the issue at the next general election and, if victorious, then to bring in a bold measure. Interestingly enough, in the Ministry of Education file boxes for 1914 there are to be found several draft bills which apparently circulated among responsible officials, all along lines favorable to the Nonconformists. The outbreak of World War I in August 1914 put an end to any further developments, social reform being shelved for the time being.[37]

PART II

TWIN VALUES
OF A CHRISTIAN BASIS
IN THE SCHOOLS

CHAPTER FIVE

FOSTERING CHURCH MEMBERSHIP

ANGLICAN VIEW

THE PRECIOUS INHERITANCE at stake was kept before the public throughout the years from 1902 to 1914. Anglicans proclaimed the mainspring of their fight to be that of fostering church membership. The *Saturday Review* was convinced that unless a child were attached in youth to some denomination he was likely to emerge from adolescence unattached to Christianity itself. Such an individual might eventually become a nominal member but never a worthy communicant and, indeed, might become a soul lost for salvation. During the debate on the Balfour Bill of 1902, in a speech thereafter quoted frequently, Lord Hugh Cecil declared that the merit of a voluntary school was its "two doors":

> It has been said, allegorically, that a board school is a school with only one door; the child goes in, learns a great deal that is valuable, and goes out again into the street. A Church school, a Wesleyan school, or a Roman Catholic school are schools with two doors, and the other door leads on into the Church or Chapel, and brings the child into contact with and under the influence of this or that denomination.[1]

The Church school was pictured as oriented to connect a child with the visible body representing divinity on this earth.[2] The atmosphere imparted to the classroom was that of a heavenly-given Home. A child learned about an active Church with symbolic sacraments. The central place was accorded the catechism, the appointed manual of Church training which set forth that all life was gathered within the Church. Archbishop Davidson commended the catechism which explained the Apostles' Creed, the Ten Commandments, and the Lord's Prayer as "one of the best handbooks in the world for a teacher who wishes to bring practically and methodically to a child's mind the lessons of the Bible." The *Commonwealth* stressed that Jesus was portrayed as coming down from Heaven to illuminate what the Father was like and to

bring the human race back into the light of the Home. The child was told that Christ is God and that He took man's nature upon Him and suffered and died for mankind. The words of Christ upon baptism, the Eucharist, and the ministry were read to the pupils. Instruction was given in the Holy Trinity, Incarnation, and the Divinity of Christ. In short, the fundamental Christianity of a Church school followed the redemption of humanity through the Cross and Passion of the Incarnate Son of God.[3]

The merits of Bible lessons as part of the daily religious instruction were acknowledged. The Bible was described as possessing for Churchmen the supernatural meaning of the history of a gradual self-manifestation on the part of God.* Rev. J. Llewelyn Davies, Vicar of Kirby, Lonsdale, Westmoreland, affirmed that a good acquaintance with the New Testament enhanced for youth the significance of Church services and hymns. But the value of the Bible rested with its interpretation by the churches. The child should have some explanation to see how the biblical stories conveyed a revelation of God's existence. Lord Robert Cecil insisted that to help a child capture its tidings the teacher should state what was meant by the Kingdom of Heaven and emphasize that Christ intended His ministry to endure after Him. Bible lessons by a trained Church teacher and suffused with the doctrinal convictions of the catechism touched off the element of divinity in the sacred books.[4]

Anglicans reviewed the experiences of the board school with the Bible under the Cowper-Temple clause. Given a teacher with a zealous belief in the efficacy of his own faith and he would present his slant upon the Bible, the legal exclusion of catechisms and formularies to the contrary. Sincere religious education was impossible without being given some form. What response, declared Rev. MacColl, could a pious teacher give but his own conviction if a child asked, "Was Jesus, who preached the sermon on the mount, God?" To equivocate must demoralize the affinity between master and pupil. A devoted Roman Catholic would find the dogmas of papal infallibility and transubstantiation inscribed in the Bible. Trinitarians and Unitarians would find their contradictory beliefs on the divine personality laid down in the Bible. Rev. Hugh Price Hughes and Dr. Clifford, conscientious practitioners that they might be, would find baptism sanctioned or con-

---

* The Guardian (Nov. 11, 1903) cautioned against cramming the minds of children with merely a store of facts about biblical history. It referred to an article written by Rev. Charles Marson, Curate of Hambridge, Somerset, entitled "Huppim and Muppim," from two minor Benjamite personages in Genesis, as a fit criticism of the dullness with which the Bible was all too often taught. See Commonwealth, July 1901, pp. 201-04. It was reprinted in 1903 as a pamphlet.

demned in the Bible. Where, therefore, a teacher was ready to interpose comments in reading the Bible to his class, there would be many "to box the compass of sectarianism from Agnosticism to Ultramontanism, from Esoteric Buddhism to Papal Infallibility."[5]

However, the brand of sectarianism most often disseminated in board schools was that of Dissent. Rev. Clement F. Rogers, St. Botolph without Aldersgate, London, and an active social worker, made much of the acceptance of the Bible as the basis for Christian fellowship by the sects cooperating in the Free Church Council. Apparently Nonconforming bodies had relaxed their insistence on such tenets as predestination, baptism, and conversion. Dean Thomas Bank Strong, Christ Church, Oxford, gathered the impression that the contents of their distinct theologies had become subordinate to a body of central truth. So their potion of Fundamental Christianity was now satisfied with the primary facts of the Old and New Testaments. But to an Anglican a historical study which simply told of the existence of God, the life of Jesus of Nazareth, and the hope of immortality did not bring into the life of man the love of God, the sacrifice of Christ, and His risen life.† No wonder, commented Rev. Hugh Legge, Head of the House of Laymen, Trinity College, Oxford, that undenominationalism as the offspring of Cowper-Templeism was so dear to Dissenters. The definite doctrines of the Established Church had no place in it and children, taught such lessons, if they clung to Christianity at all when they grew up would gravitate to the Free Churches.[6]

Still another brand of Cowper-Templeism frequently to be encountered was described as unsectarianism. It was born of the desire to avoid any appearance of being partial to Nonconformity and consisted of the residuum of the creed when every controversial subject had been withdrawn. Many school boards admonished their teachers to follow the dictum that, while preserving the element of divinity, any tincture of sectarianism should be eschewed. In this respect Archbishop Davidson singled out Dr. Clifford's prescription that the religious instruction must consist of carefully-selected portions of the Bible which were non-credal and non-theological. That could mean nothing was to be said about the Bible as containing a revelation from God or about Christ

---

† The Church Times (March 9, 1906) turned to India as an example of the futility of the external study of Christianity. For years missionaries gave Hindu boys careful instruction in the Holy Scriptures. While many Indians became familiar with Christian history, they had not the least intention to be converted. They had learned as Hindus things which should be taught to communicants as members of a Christian body. See Strachey (1911), pp. 342-43.

coming to this world as the Saviour.‡ Rev. Morley Stevenson, principal of Warrington Training College, interpreted such restrictions to require that the teacher should be on guard constantly to avoid awkward subjects—confirmation, the ministry, the Christian Year. Ven. Charles C. Mackarness, Archdeacon of East Riding, Yorkshire, labeled this so-called unsectarianism as sectarianism of the narrowest form, fixing upon it an oft-repeated phrase of Gladstone,* "a moral monster borne of the State's supposition that it possessed a charter from heaven to authorize a new religion."[7]

Where the teacher sought to avoid bruising the sensibilities of any students, Cowper-Templeism shaded off into a sort of theism. To be sure, observed Daniel C. Lathbury whose journalistic career included the editorship of the *Guardian* and the *Pilot*, such Bible lessons taught something about Jesus Christ, explaining that to the orthodox He is God, that to the Arian He is the first of created beings, and that to the Unitarian He is the most perfect exemplar of manhood. But the result was a mere recitation of scriptural passages, just as one would teach English history or excerpts from Shakespeare. Bible teaching drifted into the narration of ancient tales like Aesop's Fables or even as only Hebraic history on a level with that of Greece and Rome. Rev. Cleworth recounted the story told him by a friend who went into a council school and listened to the religious lesson. The subject was the execution of Jesus and it might very well have been the description of a State execution taking place in England at the present time. As such Cowper-Templeism was a body without a soul, a crude bibliolatry, and could only end in the dissemination of sterile facts common to all forms of belief. Rev. John Wakeford, Vicar of St. Margaret's, Anfield,

---

‡ The *Guardian* (July 16, 1902) quoted from Bryce's book on America a definition of unsectarianism which reflected the vague state of Christian thinking in a nation whose education also lacked the denominational tone. The definition was taken from the foundation deed of Leland Stanford Junior University in California which described its spiritual basis in the words, "the immortality of the soul, the existence of an all-wise and benevolent Creator, and that obedience to His Laws is the highest duty of man." See Bryce (1895, 3rd ed.), II, p. 688n2.

* An instance occurs in a reply of Gladstone to a political supporter who placed before him his difficulty in voting at the coming London School Board election in 1894, fought on the issue of the religious instruction to be given: "In my opinion . . . an undenominational system of religion, framed by or under the authority of the State is a moral monster. The State has no charter from Heaven such as may belong to Church or to the individual conscience. It would, as I think, be better for the State to limit itself to giving secular instruction—which of course is no complete education—than rashly to adventure upon such a system." *The Times*, Nov. 9, 1894, 7e. See Lathbury (1910), II, pp. 126-30.

Liverpool, warned that it could actually be harmful, hardening the soul through a familiarization with words apart from the spirit of Christ. Simple Bible reading "is the betraying of our Lord with a kiss."[8]

Lord Hugh Cecil was convinced that if this theistic trend triumphed it must be fatal to Christianity:

> I believe that we are in the presence of a religious movement not unreasonably comparable to the Protestant movement of the sixteenth century or the Puritan movement of the seventeenth century, save that it is much less beneficent than the first and much more pernicious than the second. This movement is characteristically undenominational, just as Roman Catholicism is Papal or Independency is Congregational. It rejects successively belief in hell, sin, grace, the ministry of grace, and with the ministry of grace all the ecclesiastical organizations and their rites which are concerned with it, . . . and finally belief in redemption and Incarnation. This movement widely and deeply prevailing is, rather than Nonconformity, the antagonist of the Church. No Churchmen that I have ever met fear that fifty years hence Methodism or Congregationalism or Anabaptism will be the dominant religion of English people, but Churchmen are keenly afraid of some sort of general decay in religious belief.[9]

Finally, to run the gamut of recorded experiences under Cowper-Templeism, there was the case of the indifferent and even the anti-Christian teacher. Since formal religious tests were not applied in the appointment of board school teachers, they might belong to no religion at all.† Rev. Edward B. Ottley, Vicar, St. Marylebone, London, declared that he knew of one teacher who was a secretary of an Atheist Society in London. Rev. Henry Charles Beeching, professor of Pastoral Theology, King's College, London, wrote of a conversation he had with a board school master:

> I should be very sorry if the clergy were to defend the School Board teaching of the Bible. I will tell you of two incidents that came within my knowledge in my own school. I asked a master if he was willing to teach the Bible in his class and his reply was 'Teach the Bible? Of course, or anything else. I would teach Buddhism if I was paid for it!" On another occasion, I heard a master say to his form, "Well, that is what the Bible says; you can believe it if you like, I don't!"

---

† Picton as a secularist agreed with Anglicans on this point: "Those who talk so glibly of unsectarian Bible teaching ignore the fact that whatever part of the Bible is taught the teacher must regard it as either true or false. There is nothing yet in our Education Laws to impose a test upon teachers in the board schools. A Rationalist is quite entitled to be a Board School master." *Westminster Gazette*, April 12, 1902.

Imagine the toll upon the Christianity of children to be taught the story of Crucifixion by an unbeliever who made innuendoes after the manner of Gibbon in his *Decline and Fall*. Athelstan Riley averred that "had I as a parent the hard choice between Board School Undenominationalism and a Wesleyan school, I would prefer the latter as a guarantee of my child being taught by Christian teachers."[10]

Surely a range of irresponsible heterodoxies parading under the nomenclature of Cowper-Templeism would be a negative force in attaching a child to a church body. The spiritual confusion of a child would mount as he went from one standard to another, receiving in each a different, often a contradictory, and possibly even a skeptical interpretation of the Bible. Such training was more likely to foster an air of amicable contempt which induced a child at the age of discretion to throw overboard instruction based on bewildering inconsistencies. Frederick Platt-Higgins, Conservative M.P., quoted Dr. Robert W. Dale of Birmingham, Congregationalist (and secularist), to the effect that undogmatic instruction ended in detaching children from all denominations.[11] By whatever name Cowper-Templeism went—unsectarianism, undenominationalism, fundamental Christianity—it was an imposture. Rev. MacColl poured scorn upon Cowper-Templeism as an avenue to religiosity: "There is no halting place between Denominationalism and Secularism pure and simple and I should prefer the latter as infinitely less damaging to Christianity and religion in general than a system which, while professing to teach religion, in reality plants the seeds of dissolution at its roots."[12]

Anglicans submitted evidence to support their view that thirty years of board school religious teaching had not fostered church membership. It was very noticeable how children fell away from religious observances after leaving the board school. The Lord's Day was but slightly revered. Public worship was neglected. Millions of working folk never went to a place of worship. Apparently the religion they learned under Cowper-Templeism had not been penetrating. Lord Robert Cecil blamed the disheartening disclosures in the study of Charles Booth, wealthy shipowner and philanthropist, of religious torpor in London as due to the vogue of undenominationalism in its board schools.[13] He discussed at length the findings of Booth's trained investigators. They had encountered some religion in the wealthy and upper middle classes and even in the lower middle strata. But when they came to the working class, save for Roman Catholics, most remained outside the religious bodies, and these were the people who had been largely educated in board schools.[14]

Charles F. G. Masterman, writer and Churchman (who in 1907 joined the Secular Education League because of the seemingly intransigent position of both sides) probed further the failure of Cowper-Templeism in board schools. He granted that the teachers were energetic and devoted to their profession. He paid tribute to the palatial buildings generously supported by ratepayers. He acknowledged that board school religious teaching was excellent. The child could repeat by heart the fifty-third chapter of Isaiah and the fourteenth chapter of St. John and knew the history of the people of Israel and the chief events of the Gospel story. Yet there was the damning fact of a population practically heathen in South and East London. The explanation reposed in the fact that the board schools were unrelated to the life of the community in which they were planted. They were centers of an alien civilization and exercised only a transitory influence on the strange life surrounding them. A wave of population entered at nine in the morning and vanished at four-thirty in the afternoon. The teachers arrived by train or bicycle for work and disappeared immediately after their classes ended. When the children attained the age of fourteen, the vast majority were lost in the shuffle of a teeming population and unconcerned with a religious life. The children had learned their knowledge as a thing apart, with no relation to the real world of their daily existence. Something infinitely more intimate and consistent, woven into the very fabric of life, was required to cope with the disintegrating forces of the modern city. Christianity supplied that society and the child ought to be helped by his school to find a Home. That was the secret of the superiority of voluntary schools, forlorn as their buildings were and deplorable as was the pay of their teachers.[15]

Nor was there any prospect that future teachers, devout as many were, would be adequately prepared to get what possible good there was in Cowper-Templeism. If the substance of board school teaching had given a reasonably sound Christian foundation (although not so positive a church membership as the catechism), wrote Rev. MacColl, it was because the majority of the teachers had been trained in denominational colleges. Both Archbishops of Canterbury for the period commended the latter's role in behalf of the board schools. Dr. Temple believed that in the past their saving quality had prevented undenominationalism from leading to a complete spiritual collapse. Dr. Davidson cited figures for the London board schools that out of 1,468 teachers, 860 had gone to Church of England, 73 to Wesleyan, and 10 to Roman Catholic training colleges. Only 88 had come from the day training colleges operated by local authorities and the remaining 134 had a pupil training background.[16] But henceforth the proportion would change, for the day training colleges were being expanded and they provided no religious instruction. This was particularly crucial in the face of the rising tide of biblical criticism, especially of Old Testament history.[17] Unless some acquaintance were given teachers in the interpretation of recent archaeological findings in the Holy Land, the Bible and with it Christianity might well come into ridicule.[18]

Equally ominous were the attacks being made upon the existence of voluntary schools. They had operated as a stimulus for more effective Bible teaching in board schools. T. Martin Tilby, secretary of the Church Committee (formed in 1896 to defend voluntary schools), believed that only their competition had compelled many school boards to retain even a modicum of Christian teaching. Voluntary schools had served as a stabilizing factor to prevent Cowper-Templeism from running completely amuck. So long as they were present to keep the public conscious of the vital importance of religious education, council schools would be forced to do something in that respect. Sacrifice the voluntary school, admonished Ven. Wilson, and England would then have taken the fatal step of severing its spiritual destiny. The Church of England was fighting the battle, not merely of teaching the catechism to its own children, but of religious teaching itself.[19]

Even at that, Anglicans acknowledged that the benign influence of their training colleges and voluntary schools was not sufficient to overcome entirely the indifference and the hostility of many school boards. Reference was made to the returns of a questionnaire sent out by the Committee of Council on Education in 1888 at the request of the lords.[20] The purpose was to ascertain the degree to which the Cowper-Temple clause had been implemented. Rev. Beeching noted how 494 (out of 1,941) school boards in England expressed themselves as having no syllabus of religious instruction at all. Furthermore, such resolutions as they had called for reading the Bible without note or comment, "an ordinance worthy of Laputa." Nor did the syllabuses adopted by the rest of the school boards make pleasant reading for those who still thought of England as a Christian country. Most of them omitted any express recognition of the fundamental articles of the Christian faith. Very few school boards made provision for inspection of the religious instruction. None would appear to have entered into arrangements for adequately preparing their pupil teachers in biblical knowledge. Worst of all, commented George Frederick Chambers, barrister and member of the Canterbury House of Laymen, was the record in Wales where out of 295 school board districts the Bible was not taught in 116 and only a few brief portions were allowed in another 102. Thus, in two-thirds of the Welsh school board districts, the Bible was practically excluded.[21]

More frequent were comments on the failure of an investigation in 1894 to show any material improvement in the implementation of the Cowper-Temple clause. This second inquiry was again initiated by the lords and the same questions were used.[22] The National Society computed the answers contained in the voluminous report published by the lords in 1895 and distributed its analysis in printed form for public examination.[23] Perhaps the most authoritative observations to refresh the nation's memory were by the two successive Archbishops of Canterbury. Dr. Temple generalized on the essential returns (from 2,079 English and 313 Welsh school boards) to the effect that many schools excluded the Bible altogether while others permitted only the reading of the Bible without note or comment and often but for ten minutes (and that included prayers and hymns). Dr. Davidson employed concrete figures, noting that as many as 316 school boards followed this routine prescription of Bible reading without comment or note. No attempt was made by 700 boards to have the religious teaching inspected. In 57 school board districts (48 in Wales, 9 in England) the Bible, opening prayers, and hymns were all banned. These facts did not suggest that faith could be placed in Cowper-Templeism to keep kindled the Christian spark among the nation's children.[24]

Bishop Percival of Hereford came to the defense of Huddersfield which was singled out by many Anglican commentators as a "Godless" school district. This town had set an example in regard to infant mortality, reducing it by one-half compared to the over-all English statistics of 120 to 200 of every 1,000 children dying within the first twelve months of life. There must be some local reasons why religion in its schools was restricted to a brief rendition of hymns, prayers, and reading a passage from the Bible. For that matter, these observances hardly merited the picture of Huddersfield children being brought up in a pagan atmosphere. It might be added, to fill the gaps in Bishop Percival's account, that Huddersfield had reduced its mortality figures by requiring information of the birth of a child within 36 hours in order that a female health visitor or other competent woman could tender personal advice to the mother on nurturing her child. As a matter of fact, in 1907, the Liberal Government passed a private member bill (sponsored by Lord Robert Cecil) entitled the Notification of Births Act and modeled on the Huddersfield experiment. During the debate on this measure Arthur Sherwell, Liberal M.P. for Huddersfield, informed the commons that in the first nine months of its experiment

(1906-07), his constituency had cut the mortality rate to 85 per 1,000 as against an average of 118 per 1,000 for the previous ten years.[25]

Arthur H. D. Acland likewise took issue with his fellow Anglicans. He found that of the 57 school boards which made no provision for religious instruction, 51 with an average attendance of 8,264 scholars were in Wales and Monmouthshire and 6 with an average of 842 were in England. In contrast, the remaining 2,335 school boards with an average attendance of 1,885,837 all provided religious instruction. Disagreement on the religious issue was sharp between Charles T. D. Acland and his elder brother Arthur H. D. Acland. The former was a strong Churchman, served for many years on the Ecclesiastical Commission, and was a member of the Canterbury House of Laymen. The latter was ordained a clergyman in 1872 but resigned his orders in 1879. He was concerned only with progress in the secular program and was critical of the denominationalist position.[26]

Even less comfort was drawn from an investigation undertaken in 1906 as to the degree of enthusiasm for religious instruction to be expected from county councils and their education committees. In that year, for a third time, the lords requested an inquiry into the extent of Cowper-Templeism in council schools. The announced purpose was to find out the reaction of the new administrative bodies set up by the Act of 1902 and so to bring more information to bear upon the Birrell Bill, then under debate. The questions were worded differently but the main points covered were likewise about the issuance of regulations or syllabuses, the extent of inspection, and the presence or absence of religious instruction.[27] The results were printed in a voluminous paper in July 1906.[28] The National Society tabulated the results, singling out as significant that 68 out of the 333 education committees had not issued any schemes of religious instruction and that of the 225 which had done so, 125 provided no inspection. Archbishop Davidson expressed himself as no happier at these findings. The salient impression he derived was that in two-thirds of the educational areas either no arrangements at all were made for religion or if given the value was weakened by the lack of official inspection. The record in Wales continued to be particularly bad: 60 out of 75 schools in Cardiganshire and 69 out of 104 in Carmarthenshire gave no religious instruction.‡ Were not these

---

‡ The *School Guardian* (Sept. 23, 1911) called attention to the report in 1911 of the Director of Education for Cardiganshire on the status of religious education. The figures showed little improvement in the implementation of Cowper-Templeism over those of 1906. Out of 83 council schools, 56 had no religious instruction of any kind, 14 had only hymns and prayers, and but 13 had provision for religious instruction in their timetables. *Cardiganshire Education Committee*, Proceedings, Sept. 7, 1911, p. 449.

statistics proof "of the foolhardiness of leaving a question of such magnitude to the popularly-elected councils."?[29]

If Anglicans discounted the ability of Cowper-Templeism to build a Christian foundation, they were no more impressed with the Nonconformist thesis that home and Sunday school were the places to impart further instruction in doctrinal beliefs to children. In most working class homes, even if parents were themselves well instructed, they had neither time nor energy for systematic religious training of their children. The eighth Viscount Midleton, once President of the National Protestant Church Union, believed that it was asking too much of the tired artisan or the overworked mother to spend evenings at the hard task of teaching. In many more homes, unpleasant as it was to admit, rich as well as poor parents were lax or indifferent to religion. Thomas C. Horsfall, writer on education, civic leader in Manchester, and Anglican, observed that the statistics of church attendance did not speak well for the zeal of parents, especially in the working class districts of East and South London. It might be interpolated that Richard Mudie-Smith, a member of the *Daily News* staff who undertook a religious census for his newspaper,[30] estimates the average church attendance in East London at between 15 and 28 per cent.[31]

While the instructional staff of the Sunday schools comprised well-intentioned amateurs, they were no match for the trained teachers in the elementary schools. Rev. W. Hartley Carnegie, Rector of Cathedral Church, Birmingham, was skeptical that much could be achieved within the limits of one or two hours before or after services one day a week. Since participation was voluntary, discipline was apt to be lacking. Sunday school attendance figures were hardly encouraging. Canon Henson of Westminster and later Bishop of Hereford and then of Durham, reckoned that in London at least 250,000 children of school age did not belong to Sunday schools.* There was no other educational agent but the day school. The fast tempo of town life, the advent of compulsory education, and the rise of the idea that the child belonged to the nation had replaced the parent by the teacher as the dominant influence in religious education.[32]

Anglicans turned to America as an example of a nation whose people learned too late that an undenominational system akin to that of council schools spelled secularism. In the beginning, recalled Butcher, schools in the United States offered Bible reading without comment, the Lord's Prayer, and hymns. Then the question was raised whether

---

* Average school attendance in London for 1902 was: voluntary, 175,426; board, 462,000. This meant that two-fifths did not attend Sunday schools. *Parl. Papers,* 1903, LI, Cd. 1476, pp. 12-13.

this was not sectarian teaching. The High Court of Wisconsin ruled that it was, and therefore could not be paid for out of public money under the state constitution. That judgment would seem to have affected other states and the reading of the Bible was dropped or contracted to the narrowest limits.[33] Horsfall referred to an official American report that by 1904 the Bible was banished from all schools in four states and not used in many schools where states permitted it.† He gathered too from his reading that many thoughtful Americans such as the well-known Congregational pastor, Rev. Josiah Strong,[34] were concerned over what they regarded as a decline in religious fervor and were setting up an agitation to obtain admission for the reading of extracts from the Bible. Rev. Arthur Jephson, Vicar of St. John's Walworth and a member of the old London School Board, reporting on his visit to America in the fall of 1903 as a member of the Mosely Commission,‡ declared that Roman Catholic and Lutheran schools were springing up everywhere to protest the vogue of secularism in the common schools.* America was growing aware of the danger which secular schools posed to the Christian foundation of the country.[35]

The experiences of two Anglo-Saxon peoples were drawn upon to show that reliance upon Sunday schools was a risky gamble in winning young people for the churches. Rev. Thomas L. Papillon, Vicar of Writtle, Essex, and onetime fellow and tutor of New College, Oxford, described Sunday schools in America as he observed them on his visit in 1903, also as a member of the Mosely Commission. He saw enough to satisfy him that they did not make up for the lack of religious instruction in the schools. Americans were aware of this situation, notably Dr. Nicholas Murray Butler, President of Columbia University and a progressive educational leader, who confessed in a speech that "one of the most pathetic sights in America is the ordinary Sunday

---

† The reference is to information collected by the United States Education Office in February 1904 from inquiries sent out to communities with a population over 1,000. Some 1,098 cities replied: 830 cities conducted religious exercises, comprising Bible reading, prayers, hymns, sacred songs; 530 out of 818 had Bible reading but forbade comment. The banished list came to include Wisconsin, Montana, Wyoming, Idaho, Washington, and Oregon. *Annual Report of the Commissioner of Education* (U.S.), 1903, II, pp. 2444-48.

‡ This was a private project undertaken by a wealthy business man, Alfred Mosely, to investigate the conditions of education in the United States. Mosely was convinced that education was responsible for America's material prosperity. *Mosely Education Commission to the United States of America* (1904).

* The Annual Report of the American Commissioner of Education (1903, II, pp. 2304-06) showed 4,235 parishes with Roman Catholic schools and 1,031,378 children in attendance and 5,522 Lutheran schools with 247,871 children in attendance.

school, taught by untrained persons, not properly coordinated, with textbooks of the poorest and ideals the most vague."[36] Rev. Beeching made much of the decline in Sunday school attendance in the Australian state of Victoria where, since 1872, a secular school system had been in operation, modified only by a meaningless right of entry after school hours by outside teachers.[37] Whereas in 1883 some 71½% of the children of school age attended Sunday school, in 1890 it had gone down to 39%.[38] The verdict was that without religious teaching in the State schools, the Sunday schools did not prosper.[39]

ROMAN CATHOLIC VIEW

Roman Catholics recognized no compromise in the purpose of their schools to train children as practicing communicants. The *Dublin Review* declared that if a boy's religion was to influence him, then it must be definite even if it approached bigotry. Religious flabbiness bred the pretentious spirit of latitudinarianism. Rev. Joseph Keating, S.J., asserted that an occasional hour snatched from the secular routine was not enough and gave undue prominence to the other subjects. God had first claim on the youthful soul and it was His right that His revelation should be put in the forefront. Rev. Smith stated frankly that a Roman Catholic school was intended to nurse faith, sown divinely in the first instance, to full growth in its youthful charges:

> We want children to know that Christ is God, . . . that Christ is sacramentally present in the Holy Eucharist, that they may learn to converse with Him as their priest—in Holy Communion and in their daily visits; we want them to know what Catholic duties are such as hearing mass. . . . We want them to know what sin is that they may learn to avoid it, . . . we want them to know of the Sacrament of Penance and to make regular and devout use of it; to know about the blessed Virgin and the saints, . . . to know what authority belongs to the Pope and Bishops . . . and what power has been confided by our Lord to the priests. . . .[40]

Roman Catholics were no less adamant on the importance of the interpretation given biblical material in the classroom. Where Protestants believed in the Bible as the sole source of dogmatic belief, Catholics refused to accept the Bible alone as the sanction for faith or as a matter of private judgment. To accept Cowper-Templeism was to admit the right of the individual in the extraction of creeds from the Scriptures. This issue had been the very cry which had produced the schism in the Church of Rome. Certainly, in England, emphasized Rev. M. F. Glancey whose career included service as rector at Solihull, Warwickshire, and as principal at St. Charles, Begbroke, near Birmingham, the Bible read in the council school was the Protestant Bible. Add the process of rationalistic criticism in fashion among Protestants and the end could well be to undermine the foundations of positive Christianity. At any rate, Roman Catholics could find no spiritual sustenance in simple Bible reading without note or comment. There was no heavenly light in the hazy afterglow of unctuous affirmations.[41]

Roman Catholics regarded actual experiences with Cowper-Templeism in much the same way as Anglicans, running the gamut from sectarianism to theism and even to deism. At its best, the product was a brand of Protestantism. "Is not," John Dillon asked rhetorically, "the teaching of the divinity of our Lord . . . one of the greatest dogmas? . . . Why do they speak of Bible teaching? . . . Is it not a dogma to say that the Bible is a sacred book?" William Samuel Lilly, writer, barrister, and secretary to the Catholic Union of Great Britain (a lay body watching over Roman Catholic interests), wrote that "the existence of God, or the authority, in however attenuated a form, of the Bible, is as much a dogma as Transubstantiation or Justification by Faith." To be sure, the minds of children were instilled with a sense of Divine Providence and a familiarization with the sacred scenes and pregnant precepts of evangelical history. But the State had no right to impose this upon children whose parents preferred more definite teaching. Archibishop Vaughan commented that simple Bible teaching which avoided any sectarianism made of religion a shallow thing, presenting to the young no visible living institution to claim their obedience and affection. Its content often was something which made of the Bible a mere story of ethical conduct, not much different from the material taught by Confucius and Seneca. Dillon was convinced that the full cycle of Cowper-Templeism must bring a sad finale: "If you are logical, the moment you break with the principle of sectarian teaching, you must banish the Bible, or else you must bring the Bible in as it was brought in in the days of the French Revolution, as a beautiful poem to be placed beside the poems of Shakespeare and the Dialogues of Plato."[42]

NONCONFORMIST VIEW

Nonconformists challenged the denominationalist thesis that church membership was best fostered by definite religious instruction in the schools. Bryce asserted that Lord Hugh Cecil attributed to children a far greater power of grasping abstract propositions than experience had proved to be the case. A child could not possibly understand the parts of the catechism relating to the sacraments of baptism and the Lord's Supper. Children were only repelled by metaphysical formularies and lost the faculty of reverence. Children were better served if they were not bogged down in the quagmire of highly theological disquisitions. Doctrinal instruction was the business of clergy to be inculcated carefully as the communicant matured. The *South Wales Daily News* insisted that the catechism was beyond a child's comprehension. When he recited from the creed that "He descended into Hell," surely he could not attach to it the idea of Gehenna. What was needed was "milk for babes and strong meat for men." [43]

Bryce referred to developments elsewhere as bearing upon this abuse of pedagogical wisdom in the sphere of religious instruction. In Scotland, the Act of 1872 set up school boards and gave them discretion as to the religious material to be taught. With few exceptions the Presbyterian majorities included the Shorter Catechism of the Presbyterian Church of Scotland along with the Bible. [44] Yet, Bryce came away with the impression that Scottish youth showed surprising independence in developing its own spirtual opinions. In Protestant Germany, where the schools were largely denominational, churchgoers were only a small fraction of the number in America where many states did have religious instruction of an unsectarian type, albeit in an abbreviated form. [†] The conclusion was that credal lessons had nothing to do with disposing young people to attend church as adults later on. [45]

To fill gaps in Bryce's account of Germany, the facts in the case are worth stating. While the administration of education in Germany was in the hands of the state governments, the religious settlement in schools was fairly uniform and best illustrated by Prussia. All forms of religion were endowed. Where children of one faith were present in sufficient numbers, a school with teachers of that faith was supplied. Where there were not enough children to form a separate school, then a mixed school was set up and children received religious instruction

---

[†] No statistical comparison of actual communicants for Germany is offered in the various almanacs and yearbooks, but for America the 1890 figures indicate a total of 20,612,806 communicants out of a population of 62,622,250. However, William Harbutt Dawson, a writer on contemporary German history, regarded church-going as very poor in Germany. J. Ellis Barker, also a student of German history, estimated 800,000 scholars attending Sunday schools which he deemed a low figure compared with England's. Barker (1915, 5th and enl. ed.), pp. 462-63; *Contemporary Rev.*, Oct. 1906, p. 522 (Barker); Dawson, *Germany and the Germans* (1894), I, pp. 316-21.

from teachers of their own faiths appointed in proportion to the incidence of religious distribution. In 1896 there were 24,487 Protestant,
10,725 Roman Catholic, 246 Jewish, and 680 mixed schools.[46]

At the same time Nonconformists were no whit behind Anglicans in
their desire to have schools participate in fostering church membership.‡
But the content material should aim simply to build a foundation of
Christian outlook as a preparation for concurrent church indoctrina-
tion. What a child needed, wrote Dr. Robert F. Horton, a leader in
both Congregational and Free Church circles, was for his soul to be
awakened and a personal response secured from him to the Christian
verities. At a tender age, when the child might be left a prey to dark
thoughts and terrible fear, perhaps even to lapse into baser realms of
instinct, the aid of the school should be enlisted to impart knowledge
of the personality of God. Rev. John Brown Paton, principal of the
Congregational Institute, Nottingham, contended that a child early
manifested its spiritual nature. A child's imagination soared at once
beyond the present and into the unseen. It was of infinite importance
that the child should know of God who blessed the good and denounced
the evil. Bryce identified this approach as the Christianity of the first
three centuries, an epoch free from the attachment of any formularies
or catechisms. True, controversies were not wanting in the primitive
Church but no creed was officially imposed by Church authority until
at the Council of Nicaea in A.D. 325. Only after that date did Christians begin to separate themselves into sects. Nevertheless, there still
were many Christian truths which could properly be taught to children
of all faiths.[47]

How, then, could the further instruction necessary to assure church
membership be obtained? Home, chapel, and Sunday school were light-
houses to help a youth find his spiritual haven. The opportunities were
endless. The example of a devout father could strengthen the religious
element in his child. Confirmation classes and study guilds were available. Bible classes in the evening frequently were offered. The *South
Wales Daily News* stressed the Sunday school for dogmatic instruction
—that was the Welsh method of diffusing religious strength. Dr. Clifford supplied a statistical picture of Nonconformist exertions in the
promotion of Sunday schools. They had 3,275,257 scholars and 383,778

---

‡ The *British Weekly* (March 17, 1904, Sept. 28, 1905) played its part in the school
controversy, but frequently lamented Nonconformist perseverance with religious instruction in schools. The State, it announced, could only be a temporary makeshift in religious
training and the variety of creeds simply could not be harmonized. It was a great calamity
for Nonconformists to abandon the principle of separation of Church and State in favor
of what was called undenominational teaching.

teachers as against 2,841,862 scholars and 203,902 teachers for the Established Church.[48] Neither conscience clause nor the limitations of the Cowper-Temple clause need be wrestled with in the House of God. Distinctive tenets could be taught there to the heart's content without touching the sensibilities of children of other faiths. Anglicans would be much better advised if they spent their money to improve their Sunday schools.[49]

The Bible was extolled as the best instrument through which to warm the divine impulse in a child. Rev. J. Guinness Rogers described it "as containing the message that God was in Christ reconciling the world to Himself." Bryce dwelt upon the opportunity afforded through the Old Testament to develop the greatness of the Creator and the duty to love Him and to keep His Commandments. In the New Testament, he liked the sacred precepts, especially those delivered by Christ Himself and expressed in language so beautiful that the fancy of a child was touched and his heart opened to a spiritual awakening. Dr. Richard Glover, a Baptist minister in Bristol, lauded the passages which familiarized the child with the great Personality and moved him to love God's goodness, to see His help, and to follow His lead. The Bible taken as a whole and studied in the most natural way was endowed "with the singular power of leading souls, even very young souls, to conversion." Rev. Paton applauded the way in which the Bible appealed to the imagination and emotions of a child: "What can transcend the conceptions which it unfolds of God as our Holy Fatherhood, of the brotherhood of man . . . and of the love of God, revealed in Christ, as a love full of tender sympathy, of inflexible righteousness, and of the passion of redemptive purpose."[50]

A glowing picture was painted of how well the Bible was taught under the principle of Cowper-Templeism. What could be more reverent, asked Dr. Macnamara, than the religious hour in the council school? Every morning school was opened with the gathering of all pupils for prayer and singing of hymns. Then each class went to its own room where for a period from thirty to forty-five minutes a Bible lesson was given. It was based upon a carefully-prepared syllabus which prescribed not only readings in the historical parts of selected portions but also the committal to memory of some of the Psalms, the Book of Proverbs, and Christ's teachings.[51] Nothing could exceed the solemnity of these services in the elements common to all Christians. It should be an advantage for the child to arrive at Sunday school well versed in the Bible story and the language of prophets and apostles. Birrell would go further and say that council school religion contained four dogmas common to all orthodox Christian churches: 1) the existence of God, 2) the authority of the Scriptures, 3) the life hereafter, 4) the judgment to come.[52]

Dr. Clifford differed with his Free Church brethren as to what Bible teaching should consist of under Cowper-Templeism. The Bible itself was certainly the citizen's best book. The facts of the Gospel were "Christian," supplying the "history of the Founder of Christianity and speaking for Him better than any and all creeds." But the portions should be selected prudently, suited to the capacity of children, and least likely to provoke controversy. As he interpreted these injunctions, the use of the Bible must be "literary, historical, ethical, devotional but never theological or ecclesiastical."* Where better could a child nurture his spiritual happiness than in the Parable of the Good Samaritan? What greater inspiration was there than in the twenty-third Psalm, the Ten Commandments, the Lord's Prayer, and the Beatitudes? Dr. Clifford would have the Bible take its place in universal literature along with the histories of the devout Queens par excellence—Elizabeth and Victoria, with Milton's spiritual poems—L'Allegro and Il Penseroso, with religious novels—J. H. Shorthouse's John Inglesant and Charles Kingsley's Two Years Ago. The Bible belonged to humanity and it was no more Protestant than the saintly literature which it had inspired.[53]

Nonconformists took issue with Anglicans and Roman Catholics as to the lessons to be deduced from American experiences. To begin with, it was not true to say that the common schools in America were secular. As they interpreted the findings of the inquiry instituted in 1904 by the Education Commissioner, it showed that in most schools the Bible was read and prayers were conducted at the opening of each day.[54] Out of 1,098 city superintendents reporting on the presence of religious exercises in the daily schedule, 818 had Bible reading, 827 a morning prayer by the teacher, and 915 hymns or sacred songs. This cross-section survey meant that the American common schools approximated English council schools in their religious lessons.† For instruction in dogmas America

---

* Some Nonconformists were highly critical of Dr. Clifford's views on Bible lessons. Rev. J. Edward Roberts, Union Chapel, Manchester, declared that if the Scriptures were to be taught it must be as the inspired revelation of God in Jesus Christ. Baptist Times, Feb. 23, 1906. Rev. J. Guinness Rogers asserted that if the Bible were to be read simply as a great work of literature, he would rather it be excluded altogether. Nineteenth Century and After, Aug. 1906, pp. 341-42.

† After 1910 a steady increase occurred in the number of states requiring Bible reading in the public schools. Since World War I, the entire subject of separation of Church and State has been reopened and today American society is confronted anew with the issue in the public school system. See A. W. Johnson (1934), 332 pp.; Butts (1950), 230 pp.; Thayer (1951), 257 pp.

had gone to a highly expanded Sunday school program,‡ the derogatory remarks of denominationalists to the contrary. Edgar T. Woodhead quoted Sir Joshua Fitch, for many years inspector of training colleges, "that in America the separation of the secular from religious education [that is, credal lessons] has quickened the zeal of the Churches to their own responsibility in furthering Sunday schools."[55] In terms of attendance, Bryce regarded the figures (a total of 20,612,806 communicants out of a population of 62,622,250 in 1890) as speaking for the excellence of an unsectarian instruction which had laid such a good foundation for membership in the churches later. America was an example of a nation which had reaped well spiritually as the result of its tone of Christian reverence in the common schools.[56]

Nonconformists had their own interpretation of the answers to some of the questionnaires initiated by the lords on the implementation of Cowper-Templeism in board schools. The facts for the Return of 1895 were not quite so bad as Anglicans made them out to be. The replies of most school boards did indicate that the day was opened with hymns and prayers and that the Bible was read. Howard Evans pointed out, as had A. H. D. Acland, that the list of school boards which provided no religious instruction represented only a fraction of the total school children in attendance. In England the 9 delinquent school boards had less than 1,000 scholars and in Wales the 48 delinquent school boards had an average attendance of 7,200 scholars. Furthermore, the erring English school boards were in rural districts where ample religious instruction was given in the home and the Welsh school boards were in areas well covered with Sunday schools.[57]

Dr. Macnamara set forth a serious weakness in accepting the Return of 1906 at face value. Many of the negative answers to the question "Has the authority put forth any regulations or syllabus for religious instruction for the use of its council schools?" simply meant that the education committees were content to continue the regulations of the school boards whose work they took over under the Act of 1902. He knew personally several of the counties credited with negative responses where religious instruction continued to flourish—Northampton, Peterborough, Chester, Batley, Devon, Isle of Ely. Again, he had made a point of personally visiting "Godless Huddersfield," recipient of Anglican criticism for having no regulations on religious instruction. He, like Bishop Percival of Hereford, found its schools comfortable and up-to-date and concerned for the physical health of their children. Further-

---

‡ The Annual Report of the American Education Commissioner (1905, I, pp. 198, 409) carries statistics for 1904, showing 140,519 Sunday schools with a total enrollment of 13,209,114 out of an estimated population of 17,815,300 for the ages from 5 to 18.

more, the school day was opened with hymn singing, the master read
the Parable of the Sower, and the children recited the Lord's Prayer.
Philip Whitwell Wilson undertook to answer those who continued to
fix upon Wales, especially the counties of Cardigan and Carmarthen, a
bad reputation for irreligiosity.[58] It should be well known how vigorous
Nonconformity was there and how extensive was its Sunday school
system.[59]

Exasperation was manifested at the Anglican charge that if Cowper-
Templeism were any brand of Protestantism it was Nonconformity. Dr.
Clifford was voluble in protesting that the Free Churches gained noth-
ing by simple Bible teaching any more than they did from the use of
Milton or Shakespeare. Justification by faith, the central feature of
Dissent, was nowhere to be found taught in council schools. The Pres-
byterians had their printed creeds and catechisms. Methodists had their
theological standards in the four volumes of Wesley's sermons. The
Congregationalists and Baptists were more opulent in positive beliefs
than the Established Church. Not one portion of the entire range of
Nonconformist doctrines was taught in council schools—the ministry,
sin, "conversion" as the basis of church fellowship, the eternal life.*
What the Cowper-Temple clause represented, affirmed Mundella, was
a practical application of the principle that the duty of parliament was
to hold a balance between the various sects and to secure that the
schools were not used in the interests of a particular sect.[60]

There were many facts to belie the Anglican contention that Nonconformity ruled the roost in council schools. The pages of history
would describe the Cowper-Temple clause as a pure Anglican product
and say that the Free Churches had yielded to it reluctantly. The
Examiner insisted that Cowper-Templeism "was invented by members
of the Church of England and pushed by them against the opposition
of many Nonconformist leaders." It was to be regretted now and apparently it would have been better in 1870 to have insisted that the State
confine itself to secular education and leave religion to the churches.
The Christian World argued that the Cowper-Temple clause was the
work of a very good Churchman, William Francis Cowper-Temple,
and that it was approved by a House of Commons with a Church of
England majority. Also, directly through the elective process of naming
the school board (and now the county council) Anglican parents had

---

* Rev. Walter Wynn, Baptist clergyman, Colne, Lancashire, spoke at further length
for his Church alone: "Where in any Board school . . . is baptism of adults by immer-
sion [taught] . . . which we believe to be the only true form of Apostolic baptism, . . .
[and that] is only a fragment of the New Testament beliefs held by Baptists, which are not
taught in Board schools. . . ." The Times, Jan. 6, 1904, 8d-e.

expressed themselves on the nature of the syllabuses. The *Monthly Messenger* observed that between the Church of England monopoly of training colleges and its social predominance, the greater majority of teachers appointed in board schools were members of the Established Church. So, for thirty years, Anglicans had been influencing Cowper-Templeism in board schools and the presumption could be made against its flavor being Nonconformist.[61]

Anglicans were called to task for their disparagement of Cowper-Templeism. If it left out the creeds and the polity of denominations, the omission was respectful and not an act of antagonism.† Nothing was said to lend any impression that it was wrong to join a church. The *Westminster Gazette* did not believe that Cowper-Templeism had weaned Anglican children away from the family faith. The true parental demand should be that neither ecclesiastic nor politician stand between the child and the light of the Great Book. The proposition that the Bible was the Book of the Church as distinct from the people was an intellectual theorem against which the Reformation was an emphatic and final protest. The Bible belonged to all churches. Dr. Clifford charged that a change had come over the Church of England since 1870. The Established Church was fast being saturated with Roman ideas and an insidious growth of sacerdotalism was overtaking it. Sad and heavy were the words of Robert Masters Theobald, a student of the Shakespeare-Bacon riddle who described himself as a political Dissenter: "It is melancholy to think that most of the bishops and their High Church followers do not believe in the Bible at all, that it is not a divine book carrying a divine message, and that only the consecrated presence of a clergyman could keep the devil from the schools."[62]

Anglicans were reminded that their own leaders had spoken in praise of Cowper-Templeism. Reference was had to speeches by two Archbishops of Canterbury. The immediate background for both statements was the controversy in 1894 over the desired inclusion of the Doctrine of Trinity in the syllabus of the London School Board.[63] In the lords, during the debate on the Balfour Bill in 1902, the fifth Earl Spencer, first Lord of the Admiralty in previous Liberal cabinets, recalled the comment of Archbishop Benson in defense of Cowper-Templeism against the attacks of more extreme Anglicans:[64]

---

† Rev. Hollowell stated the case for the philosophy underlying Cowper-Templeism: "A nation may wish its children taught to revere God . . . without desiring them to be taught sacramentarianism and ecclesiastical refinements. The House of Commons may wish to open its proceedings with prayer, without having a lecture on transubstantiation from its esteemed chaplain." *Daily Chronicle*, April 28, 1902; *The Times*, April 28, 1902 9f.

I am persuaded that in a very great number of board schools there is a very good religious teaching indeed. Those terrors of a polymorphous religion, in which a child is being taught in one standard by a Baptist, and in the next by a Congregationalist, and in the next by a Roman Catholic, and in the next by an agnostic do not exist . . . I do say that in the Board School teaching in London, we have a very great amount . . . of that which is practically and really the teaching of the Church. . . .

Again, during the debate on the Birrell Bill in 1906, Bryce recalled the comment of Archbishop Davidson,‡ then Bishop of Rochester, on the satisfactory nature of Cowper-Templeism in the metropolis: "It is almost inconceivable that any Christian who knows the facts can speak of the Christian teaching given in the London school board as worthless because it is undenominational. Such instruction lays the foundation on which the ampler teaching of the Christian faith can be securely built."[65]

SECULARIST VIEW

Secularists constituted a fourth party actively engaged in the controversy over the role of the school in fostering church membership. Christian and non-Christian, cleric and layman, worker and lord, as the preceding pages should disclose, were to be encountered in their ranks. For many of them, if the issue rested on the grounds of reason alone, the weight of logic was against the State undertaking a religious function in education. MacDonald submitted the principle of no taxation at the expense of conscience, since citizens would have to pay for the propagation of beliefs which they did not share. Again, MacDonald confronted Protestants with the argument that parents who professed a rationalist outlook merited the right to have their children educated in the doctrines of the positivist Auguste Comte or the freethinker Charles Bradlaugh. Harry Quelch, editor of the socialist *Justice*, pictured the bedlam that must follow if all churches demanded an altar in

---

‡ For Dr. Davidson's speech see *Guardian*, Oct. 31, 1894. In the lords, he took exception to Bryce's use of his statement and replied that it related only to London and certain other places but not to the entire country. *Lords*, Aug. 2, 1906, pp. 1234-35. Apparently Dr. Davidson was bedeviled even by his own hierarchy for his commendation of Cowper-Temple teaching so that he felt it necessary to defend himself before the Upper House of the Canterbury Convocation on May 3, 1906. The full context of his speech would show that his remark had as its background an emphatic introductory reservation "that the Cowper-Temple teaching left much to be desired and was inadequate compared to Church school teaching." *The Chronicle of Convocation*, May 1-4, 1906, pp. 198-99.

the schools—Mohammedanism, Shakerism, Christian Science, the Peculiar People, and even Voodooism. Religion in the schools could not be reconciled with the doctrine of separation of Church and State, a central principle of contemporary Western civilization. In short, the obvious conclusion to be drawn was that the schools should be confined to secular subjects and avoid the inconsistencies that would follow indulgence in obsolete traditions.[66]

How, then, did they answer those who predicted, as MacDonald understood their thinking, "that the secular solution would leave tens of thousands of children to grow up without the knowledge of anything higher than the gutter" and "that the teeming millions of the towns and cities would pass their lives in darkness." The firm reply was that the responsibility rested with family, church, and Sunday school. Rev. Stewart D. Headlam, Anglican clergyman, Christian socialist, and member of the old London School Board, argued that church membership was best done at Sunday catechizing and least of all, by memorizing facts about Huppim and Muppim and Ard. Both Charles T. Gorham, a joint editor of *Ethical World* after 1916 when it became known as *Humanist*, and Harry Snell, active in the Ethical movement and after World War I a Labour M.P. until 1931 when he was raised to the peerage, asserted that the sectarians had wealth, numbers, organization, and an inherited prestige. The country was covered with a network of religious establishments. Every parish had its beneficed clergyman and a commodious building at his disposal. There were many Dissenting chapels and a host of lay preachers and Sunday school readers. It was for those who really lived their religion to impart to children adequate training in what they held to be precious. The State as a secular body should say to all churches that they alone could teach religion so that it stirred a child's heart to a spiritual awakening.[67]

Many secularists held that the idea of "conversion" involved an even more complete neutrality on the part of the parent. Ernest E. Hunter, active in the socialist Independent Labour Party, described the duty of the State to train the mind and to develop the intellect so that when the child reached the age of discretion he could either accept as truths or reject as fallacies the tenets of the various sects. If MacDonald admitted that the time was yet remote, he treasured the hope that the parent would eventually accept this higher sense of duty. It seemed to him that a really conscientious parent, while arousing within his child a sense of the divine, would abstain from proselytizing for his own sect. Rather, that parent would be anxious "to protect the mind of his child against sectionalism and historic error in religion, and prepare him for the supreme moment when he becomes conscious that the finite has a relation to the infinite." When that day came, the child, now a man and free from the prejudices and conclusions of his parents, would possess a mind clear to choose fearlessly and intelligently how his religious nature should express itself.[68]

John Dillon, the ardent Irish Nationalist, construed MacDonald's remark as a plea for reviving Spartan practices: "When the honourable member for Leicester gives expression to such principles as these, he is tilting against a very ancient principle of humanity which is too strong for him. It is nearly 2,500 years since the philosopher Plato laid down the principle in his *Republic* that every child within a few weeks of birth should be taken from the father and mother. More than 2,000 years have elapsed since then and even with that great authority [in its favor] that doctrine has not made much progress."[69]

The secular solution had functioned well in English-speaking countries. In the United States, to be sure, agreed Picton, the practice of hymn singing, formal prayers, and the reading of a verse from the Bible without note or comment was observed in a majority of the schools. But there was nothing like the English attempt "to reduce to a theological jelly the common beliefs of Evangelical sects." At any rate, the apparent flourishing of churches would not suggest that America had lost its spiritual vigor. Rev. W. E. Coller, Congregational minister and Manchester agent of the Liberation Society, referred, like Bryce, to figures that nearly one-third of the American nation (20,612,806 out of 62,622,250) held membership in religious bodies.[70]

In those Australasian states with a secular school system, Picton declared that letters from friends living there gave him the impression that piety had lost nothing by the exclusion of religious instruction from the curriculum.* Puritan devoutness and Sunday-go-to-meeting habits survived with great freshness and simplicity. Their Sunday schools and missions were no less prosperous than those of the mother country. What had happened abroad was not a decay in Bible veneration but a spiritual resurgence due to the free play of common sense in a new environment. Harrold Johnson, secretary of the Moral Education League (formed in 1897 to promote systematic non-theological moral instruction in the schools) countered the Rev. Beeching's statistics on Sunday school attendance in the secular state of Victoria with a set of his own. Whereas the figure in 1891 was 149,812, it rose to 163,796 in 1896 and 168,230 in 1901, a remarkable achievement in a period when

---

* The secular states in Australasia were Victoria, Queensland, South Australia, and New Zealand, in all of which only the right of entry outside school hours by outside teachers was permitted. See Browne (1927), pp. 84, 245; *Parl. Papers*, 1900, XXII, Part I, Cd. 417, pp. 308-09, 419-20, 470, 635-36; Paton, *Colonial Handbooks* (1914), Nos. 3, 4, 5, 8.

population growth was very slow (from approximately 1,140,000 in 1891 to 1,200,000 in 1901).[71] So, however much Rev. Beeching might show a decline in Sunday school attendance from 1883 to 1890, the more recent years had witnessed an upswing.[72]

Secularists saw nothing in the record of church statistics at home to suggest that religious instruction in the schools stimulated membership in a church body. Every sect was deploring a diminished attendance. Rev. Coller cited Liverpool and London, where church records estimated attendance at one-fifth of the population, a poor comparison with the American proportion of one-third. Over-all, in England and Wales, the population numbered 32,526,075, with communicants of Christian sects approximately 5,200,000. The *Truth* believed that a study of how many children from Church schools became in later years regular worshipers and attended church services on Sunday would show that denominational teaching was a sham and a delusion. Dogmas learned mechanically faded away or remained barren formulas. Indeed, fostering among clergy of the lulling notion that a child taught the catechism was a proselyte for life had resulted in the assumption that no further effort was needed to win his adherence. The *Truth* would exclude only the Roman Catholics from its statement that catechisms and formularies left no telling impression toward a spiritual life with a church body. This was because of the influence of the priest who, by consent of the people, was supreme, not merely in the school but also in the home and had, therefore, no difficulty in keeping each member of his flock under control from youthdom up.[73]

So far as the plea of Nonconformists for religious equality was concerned, secularists could distinguish little between the sectarianism of Dissenters and Churchmen.† Frederic Harrison, president of the English Positivist Committee, charged that Nonconformists had been as bigoted to maintain the ascendancy of the Scriptures as Churchmen had been to further their own catechism. Cowper-Templeism favored the general trend of religious thought among the Free Churches. For the State to select the Bible and teach it at public expense was just as much a violation of the principle of neutrality as it was to select the Thirty-nine Articles and teach them. What moral force, inquired the *Social Democrat*, could they possess in their cry against "Rome on the rates," considering how much undenominationalism approximated

---

† Cohen traced the extent to which Freethinkers found themselves in a position of religious inequality: "All Churches and Chapels are free from taxation which clearly equals a grant of money from the State . . . whereas a purely secular hall pays rates. No liberty of bequest exists for us as for the Churches. . . . The Sunday laws stereotype the religious frame of mind. . . ." *Freethinker*, April 27, 1902.

their religious views and was supported by rates? How could Nonconformists expect their children to command sympathy for their plight
in Church schools when they heeded not the cries of Atheists and
Agnostics against their children having to attend Bible lessons in council schools or being subjected to the insults of fellow students if the
conscience clause were requested? What sincerity, asked *Justice*, could
be accorded their protest against religious tests for teachers, considering
that they expected teachers in council schools to give Cowper-Temple
teaching? Nonconformists must be as understanding of other points
of view as they expected others to be of theirs.[74]

Secularists regarded Nonconformists as mainly responsible for the
perpetuation of the dual system. The National Secular Society at its
annual conference in London, May 18, 1902, passed a resolution that
"the present difficulty has been chiefly caused by the recreancy of Nonconformists to their professional principle of the complete separation
of the State from religion." Cohen reproached Free Churchmen on
their professed belief in the severance of all bonds between Church and
State. If they had united back in 1870 to banish religious instruction
from board schools and had taken their stand logically for secular education pure and simple, a more formidable opposition might have been
arrayed and all the points contended for won long ago. As it was,
scolded John Mackinnon Robertson, Liberal M.P. after 1906 (and for
many years identified with the freethinker Charles Bradlaugh's journal,
National Reformer), Nonconformists had paid the penalty for devia-
tion from the principle of separation of Church and State in the
unhappy form of the Act of 1902. They had themselves to thank for
the Church of England having succeeded in getting its dogmas taught
in so many schools at public cost. Rev. John Page Hopps, Unitarian
minister, London, pronounced the current dilemma of Nonconformists exposing their children to proselytism to be of their own making:‡

> The Nonconformists surrendered the fort when they succumbed to
> the temptation to include what they called "religious instruction" in
> the list of subjects to be taught in Board schools. From that moment
> their overthrow was only a question of time; for, if it is right to teach a
> religion of compromise watered by timidity, it is right to teach a religion
> of thoroughness fortified by zeal.[75]

---

‡ The *New Age* (Nov. 5, 1903) recalled Gladstone's comment to John Bright in 1874
as to the uncertainty within Nonconformist ranks: "The fact is that Nonconformists have
not yet as a body made up their minds whether they want unsectarian religion . . . or
simple secular teaching, so far as the application of the rate is concerned. . . . The former
is in my opinion glaringly partial and I shall never be a party to it." See Morley (1903),
II, p. 311.

From 1906 on, when the proposals of the Liberal Government brought the religious issue to a climax, secularists were more than ever convinced that Nonconformists were responsible for the presence of the religious lesson in schools. The place of honor in all the successive measures was reserved for Cowper-Templeism. Simple Bible teaching was the concrete expression of the Nonconformist adherence to the open Bible with the right of private judgment.* Picton recalled his own youthful days as a Congregationalist. The teacher related nearly all the doctrines that Picton heard from his parents at home—the fall of man, the calling of the chosen people, the sacrificial types of Christ, Incarnation, Crucifixion, and Resurrection. The omission of forms of church government and the sacraments signified little for the Nonconformists attached small importance to them. Charles Callaway, who described himself as a former Nonconformist and now a Freethinker and by profession engaged as a geologist, declared that if the chapels in Wales were closed tomorrow the children would continue to be nourished in orthodox Dissenting dogma at the expense of the State. What made this state of affairs in council schools alarming was the implication of a new Establishment to replace the Church of England. Foote warned that this posed a fresh danger to separation of Church and State, for whereas the Church of England was an old and enfeebled enemy, the Free Churches were young and vigorous.[76]

Secularists saw nothing ahead but trouble in the determination of Christians to use the schools for fostering church membership. Each sect had its own ideas on how that should be achieved and none was powerful enough to force an answer. Each sect had its own Bible and none would agree on the parts to be used. George W. E. Russell, one-time Liberal M.P. and described as a High Churchman, referred to Gladstone's comment on the reading of the third chapter of St. John by a schoolmaster who explained the passage on baptism in the sense of the Prayer Book and the Articles. Gladstone replied that "the Dissenters would say that this is instruction in the doctrine of the Church of England." † And, opined Russell, the Dissenters would say the truth.

---

* Foote seriously questioned if Dr. Clifford himself wanted the Bible taught as a purely ethical, literary, and historical document. His advocacy of the London County Council syllabus must mean a book of religion, for it contained nothing which was related to "civic" or any other uses of this world. Once get the children to read the Bible as the fountain of "faith and morals" and they were made raw material Christians. *Freethinker,* Aug. 23, Nov. 15, 1908.

† Gladstone said this in justifying the need for the National Society to put in a conscience clause and so reconcile the integrity of religious instruction with the sensibilities of children of other faiths. Gladstone continued: "Now it is utterly impossible for you to tell the Church schoolmaster or the clergyman that he must not in the school

There was no dogma held by any body of Christians which could not be presented as biblical. One "M," writing in the *Labour Leader*, declared that it would surpass the wit of man to devise a system of Christian instruction which would satisfy Roman Catholic,‡ High Churchman, and Nonconformist, even leaving out the views of non-Christians. Granville George Greenwood, Liberal M.P., barrister, and Rationalist, who frequently used the pseudonym of "George Forester," was particularly wroth at the failure of the nation to be conscious that the teaching of the Christian faith in any form was repugnant to non-Christians. Yet in all discussions the latter were treated as infidels, formulas always being sought to reconcile only the entreaties of Anglicans, Roman Catholics, and Nonconformists for religious equality.[77]

In reality, Christianity itself was the loser, for the circumstances surrounding the religious instruction defeated the goal of vibrant church membership.

First, the Bible was forced into the pedagogical framework of the school, ordinarily given during the first period of the day and followed by the lay subjects. The child was invited to apply the common denominator of mundane values to both. Edmond Holmes, inspector of schools for the Board of Education, regarded the idea as ridiculous that when the hands of the clock pointed to a quarter to ten the religious education of a child was over and his secular work began. The essence of religion was an emotional experience and to give it a timetable appointment was to dull that conception.[78]

Equally bad was the requirement in most council schools that the Bible must be read without note or comment. That was scarcely respectful of the sacred text and turned the lesson into a ritual exercising little effect on a child's imagination. MacDonald believed that the result was to reduce the Bible to a textbook like a Royal reader or a Todhunter's algebra book. It was a real secularization of religion to proceed on the same plane as though the multiplication table was being committed to memory. He called upon his own Scottish school memories to illustrate the routine nature of the religious lesson:

---

explain any passage of Scripture in a sense to which any of the parents of the children, or at least any sect objects; for then you would in principle entirely alter the character of the religious teaching for the rest of the scholars, and in fact upset the whole system." Morley (1903), II, p. 300, citing Gladstone's Letter to Lord Granville, dated 1865.

‡ "M" was sympathetic of the Roman Catholic position to seek protection against the onslaughts of Nonconformist and Anglican: "Let any fair-minded person turn for a moment to where school histories record the religious conflicts in the time of Mary and her designation as 'bloody.' There, in every adjective, every phrase, every conclusion, Protestantism was taught as it was in an Orange manifesto or in Foxe's Book of Martyrs." *Labour Leader*, Dec. 5, 1903.

What happens in schools where the Bible is used? At nine o'clock the school assembles, the teacher opens a book which happens to be the Bible. He reads in a great many cases verses out of it. He then asks his pupils to sing a hymn. The book is then closed. He opens a geography or history book and the lessons go on in the ordinary way. . . .

The English schools, so far as I can gather, are pretty much in the same position. The Bible is used as a textbook for the purpose of telling some story or other to the children in precisely the same way that the geography or arithmetic lesson is used. . . .[79]

Second, the content material of the Bible covered in the religious lesson was scarcely conducive to imbue a child with veneration. Mc-Cabe recounted how infants were drilled in the stories of Creation, the Fall, and the Flood. Older children were forced to memorize the plagues of Egypt and the very Oriental ways of Solomon, Jezebel, and Elisha. MacDonald insisted that to teach the outside facts of Bible history was not to teach religion. Christianity was a thing of the heart and not of the head. Unless Church and Chapel faced honestly the psychological effect of Bible teaching in the schools, the apocalyptic quality of religion as implied by the term "conversion" would remain an elusive hope. In contrast, he related the story of the Welsh districts of Cardigan and Carmarthen where, out of 179 schools, 129 (corrected tabulation) had a timetable purely secular and yet these areas were reputed to be the center of emphasis upon "conversion" as the catalyst to win the soul.[80] So far from condemning the spiritual indifference of the principality, these facts ought to be put in the forefront of the reasons Christianity was such an invigorating movement in Wales. Holmes described a visit to a Church school where children were being crammed with metaphysical phraseology:

All boys over Standard III were grouped for a religious lesson and the assistant teacher who was giving it delighted in long words which he rolled out in ore rotundo and then chalked up on the blackboard. It was obvious that he was making no impression whatever on his audience. The boys, one and all, reminded him [Holmes] of the "white-headed boy" in Dickens' village school [The Old Curiosity Shop], who displayed "in the expression of his face a remarkable capacity of totally abstracting his mind from the spelling on which his eyes were fixed."[81]

MacDonald penned a dispirited passage in 1909 after it had become apparent that the crusade for secular schools had failed:

To impart "religious instruction" by State machinery is to offer religion without its spirit, to give the husk without the kernel, the chaff without the wheat. And who can measure the deadening influence upon a nation's spiritual life of generation after generation being subjected to a drill in the mere knowledge of facts which are supposed to be the special carriers of religious convictions, but which are imparted without that transforming enthusiasm, without that alchemic quality which is religion itself. That is really to deprive a nation of the chance it has of being quickened into a religious life. The spiritual delusion and darkness in which the people live who set value upon what is called "religious instruction" in our State schools can only appal one with the conclusiveness of its evidence how little we have yet gone on the way of spiritual life.[82]

Third, the attitude of many teachers worked against touching off any regenerative sparks in the child. MacDonald offered his analysis of the difficulty. Whatever the obsession gripping the teacher, an impelling devotion to the secular program or a credal belief at variance with the denominationalism to be expounded upon, he would appear to have regarded the religious lesson as a chore, to be gotten over with as rapidly as possible, as something exempt from the obligations of wholeheartedness. No doubt the religious test to which many had to subscribe, formally or informally, to get an appointment fanned the smoldering embers of resentment. Submitting with mental reservations, just as others had done when the Thirty-nine Articles had to be signed for admission to the historic universities, teachers probably felt no compunction in sloughing off the work of the religious period. In resting his case upon this score, MacDonald commented grimly:

> If teachers are to give Scriptural lessons, they ought to believe what they are teaching. A Unitarian, equally with a Positivist or an Agnostic, cannot teach the London Education Committee syllabus properly, whilst the influence of a teacher who believes indifferently will be more deadly than that of one who does not believe at all. We are to have sincerity and keenness in the teaching of every subject on the timetable, except that which demands the greatest degree of enthusiasm.[83]

Picton explained similarly the quandary of the teacher. Nonconformists took too much for granted to think that the Bible could be thrust into the hands of any instructor without asking him what were his opinions. Most teachers adopted an attitude of conventional acquiescence which guarded their mental comfort but which emptied their scriptural presentation of all conviction. They told the story of the Old Testament without any pretense of discriminating reality from fiction, even in their own minds. It was both vain and wicked to ignore the fact that whenever the Bible was treated with candor and honesty, questions arose upon which one could never be sure of the teacher's convictions. If he should think the lessons false but be anxious to keep his position, the result must be hypocrisy, an approach hardly calculated to foster respect for the Bible. In closing his brief upon this vitiating ingredient, Picton recalled a distressing letter from a board school teacher:[84]

> One does lose a certain amount of self-respect in standing before a class and teaching for truth what one believes to be false. But . . . I ask myself: "Why be honest? Why trouble at all about the matter? The Scripture lessons occupy little time after all, and the harm done cannot amount to much. . . . But one must get a living somehow; so I personally comply with the terms of my agreement with my employers, and let conscience go hang."[85]

Secularists predicted that the "New Theology" would increase the confusion of the teacher. Many scholars in biblical history now regarded the greater portion of the Old Testament and not a little of the New Testament as a collection of myths. No less a personage than Rev. R. J. Campbell, successor to Dr. Joseph Parker at City Temple (Congregational), London, wrote Picton, described the first book of the Bible with its stories of the Deluge and the adventures of Abraham, Isaac, and Jacob as simply of Babylonian origin.[86] The new writings in biblical history questioned the dates and the authority of the Old Testament books. They were at variance on the Messianic prophecies, the Atonement, the extent of the inspiration of St. Paul, and the historical value of Gospels like that of St. John. George Greenwood quoted Dr. Cheyne, professor of the interpretation of Holy Scripture at Oxford and one of the editors of the new Encyclopaedia Biblica, as saying that such stories as the moon and sun standing still at the command of Joshua and the walls of Jericho falling down at the sound of Joshua's trumpets were "purely legendary."[87] As Snell appraised the simple Bible lessons anchored to a storehouse of learning whose foundation was being badly shaken, it meant trying days ahead to recount the usual stories of Creation, the Flood, Noah and the Ark, the Virgin Birth, Resurrection and Ascension, and the miracles.[88]

For many a teacher, commented Picton, this new learning obviously posed an additional challenge. Hitherto, the vexatious problem had been that his religious beliefs were at variance with the syllabus he taught. Henceforth his intellectual integrity was at stake. The wide circulation of newspapers and journals had laid bare before the nation the new findings. It would be little credit if the teacher did not seek light from all available sources of scholarship. What thoughts and emotions, then, must pass through his mind when such a syllabus as that of the London County Council was put into his hands. It directed him to give young children "simple stories from the Book of Genesis," lessons from the "life of Moses," and lessons from the "Book of Joshua." Suppose he had come to the conclusion, as many had and more would, that these simple stories were pure fable and that no single event in the life of Moses, for example, could be pronounced to be definitely historical. But the teacher must satisfy an education committee whose orthodox views made it cling to the Bible as infallible and divine inspiration. Picton cited a series of articles by Henry W. Nevinson, journalist, describing his visits to elementary schools during the hour for religious instruction. Nevinson noted as painful to behold the evident anxiousness of the council school teacher to avoid any suspicion of eccentricity.[89] Surely, the cynicism born of narrating discredited material must only add to the hypocrisy nourished by serving as a false preacher.[90]

Secularist that he was in the school controversy, MacDonald insisted repeatedly that his protestations were inspired by a desire to arouse greater religious fervor. Indeed, he was prepared to say "that unless there was a better spiritual life among the people, they could educate them as much as they liked, but the country was not thus going to remain great and maintain its leading position in the world." A significant evidence of MacDonald's deep concern for a strong religiosity among the nation is to be found in his touching biography of his wife, Margaret Ethel:

> She was in the Ladies' Gallery of the House of Commons one day when I was trying to express that view [that the religious lesson had brought Christian life to a low state] and when I had finished she came down and beamed on me: "They cannot get over that argument of yours," she said. "We of the secular solution value the Bible; I don't think the others do in quite the same way."[91]

Picton, denying that he was either an Atheist or an Agnostic in the literal sense, declared "that I am more certain about the being of God than I am of my own personality. I can no more conceive of humanity without a religion than I can conceive it without a sense of the relations of part and whole." The Bible was an age-long vision of truth disentangling itself from error, of right slowly conquering wrong. One need not be a fanatical "individualist" to hold that some inner sources of character and will were of priceless worth to the community and should be held sacred in every man. Among these could surely be counted the feeling of solitary accountability to the Eternal Power and for the refurbishment of these transfigurative moments the Bible was an inspiration. But the inheritance of this noble treasure was the trust of the family and the church and not the school.[92]

Admittedly, however, the prospect that those primarily responsible would pass on their religious beliefs to children was not promising. MacDonald listed the many obstacles which stood in the way of even that modest objective. For the most part, parents preferred to delude themselves that by the payment of rates and taxes they were guaranteeing the performance of the religious lesson by the school. The nation as a whole appeared willing "to live in a fool's paradise," accepting Cowper-Templeism and credal lessons as adequate religious training. The State persisted in believing that bills could be drafted to propitiate faiths absolutely opposed to each other. The deplorable result of such temporizing would be a lack of pressure to force the responsible agencies to acknowledge their trust. The prospect was a sad one:

> Religious instruction in the schools . . . marks—and the feverish demand for its continuation even at the expense of political and educational unsettlement— . . . the decadence of both Church and home, and admits their failure to perform their most precious functions in society. . . .
>
> One must contemplate . . . with uneasiness and disquietude . . . that the school should be regarded as the only barrier against "a generation that knows not God." The more one clings to the school as the sole or essential custodian of religion, the deeper one sinks into the mire; the longer we postpone the day of honest confession that the Church and family are being malformed by modern conditions of life and of equally honest confession that school religion is of little value at best, the more do we allow both Church and family to degenerate into something meaner and more unworthy than they now are. By their present opposition to the secular solution, Church and Chapel alike are confessing that they care more for religious appearances than realities and that they fear to face the essential problem: "What is there in modern society weakening the moral and spiritual functions?"[93]

CHAPTER SIX

INCULCATING MORALITY

ANGLICAN BRIEF

IF ANGLICANS claimed for definite religious instruction the merit of fostering church membership, they were equally positive of its efficacy in enhancing the moral tone of society. Modern civilization was the product of a Christianity founded on the doctrine of the Incarnation. Christian manhood had been the basis for the world's noblest examples of patriotism. Civic helpfulness was part of the vocation of every Christian man and woman. Canon Henson praised the New Testament as a summary of the ethical code prevalent in the Western world. He listed the indebtedness as including a strong sense of personal rights, a widely diffused spirit of humanity, an exalted standard of female chastity, and a respect for the innocence of children. Rev. Dymott quoted Sir James Stephen, noted English jurist, to the effect that "the criminal law may be described with truth as an expansion of the second table of the Ten Commandments." * Especially salutary, in the estimation of Rev. MacColl, had been the influence of Christianity in behalf of the masses in past centuries. In the days of the Roman Empire, when slaves constituted a large segment of the population and were treated harshly, "Christianity without making war on slavery directly, planted in the heart of humanity principles which have been fatal to slavery wherever they have had fair play."[1]

The moral influence which the Established Church had exercised on the English scene had been particularly gratifying. Rev. Dymott believed "that the sense of duty so characteristic of Englishmen and which had found expression in Nelson's famous signal at Trafalgar is largely the result of the impress that three hundred years teaching of the Church Catechism has left." Rev. MacColl was convinced that the

---

* The first table, consisting of the first five commandments, is grouped as the precepts of piety and the second table, consisting of the last five commandments, is grouped as the laws of probity. For Stephen's statement see A History of the Criminal Law of England (London: 1883), III, p. 366.

reason the working class had not used its overwhelming political power to dispossess other classes was due to the Church's inspiration. But dissipate that enriching spiritual atmosphere and they would cease to think of a hereafter where wrongs were redressed and virtue was rewarded. Irresistible might be the temptation of the toilers to make their heaven on earth with as little delay as possible and with scant respect for the rights of others. In view of the basic self-interest of society to guard against revolution, Rev. MacColl asked if it were wise to substitute for the creed of Christendom "that vague and unpalpable religious abstraction called undenominationalism which is all very good in fair weather but which will at the critical moment sink beneath its advocates like the whale on which Sinbad and his companions had cast anchor in mistake for an island." National well-being depended upon national character which ultimately must depend upon religion to determine whether mankind looked upon the world as an instrument for pleasure or a stage for an immortal destiny.[2]

The school was hailed as the touchstone in awakening a nation's righteous instincts, developing character as well as the dissemination of information. Rev. Carnegie asserted that intellectual sharpness without a corresponding moral impulse reduced the social usefulness of a human being. The training of the mind alone tended inevitably to make men worse because it was a device and not a beneficent power. An improved intellect served merely to guide the passion to its coveted object, be it good or bad. Rev. Cleworth argued that the result of an exclusive secular education was that children grew up to be clever worldlings, slaves of the universe and not its conquerors. If education meant anything at all, it was to foster man's ethical nature, otherwise the materialism and egotism of mankind would destroy the very foundations of civilization.[3]

However, for the school best to shape personal conduct, definite religious instruction should be the prescribed approach. A vague, formless creed was not likely to inspire fervent loyalty to itself; the belief should be syncretic if it were to be effective.† Imagine a morality built up by the Bible used without note or comment. Unless the teacher dealt with biblical material as possessing the inspiration of the Holy Writ, the child could derive no ethical stirring. Rev. Dymott turned again to Sir

---

† Rev. Isaac Gregory Smith, Great Sheffield Rectory, Lambourne, and Canon of Worcester, turned to the pages of history as witness to the intimate affinity of religion with conduct: "One of the greatest thinkers that ever lived [St. Augustine], eye witness himself of the crash of the Roman Empire, has portrayed in colors indelible the hideous results of the pagan mythology of Helos." I. G. Smith (1903), p. 8. See Aurelius Augustinus, *The City of God*, I, Book 2, trans. by Rev. Marcus Dods (1870).

James Stephen, quoting him to the effect that "the statement in the Catechism of the positive duties of man to man corresponds step by step with the prohibitions of a criminal code."[4] Dogmatic religion cultivated restraint and cleansed what was evil in a child's nature and strengthened what was good. Boys and girls should be brought up to believe in something concrete and so acquire firm roots for social ethics or else they were apt as they grew older to drift into a blunted sense of right which whispered that morality was either useless or futile.[5]

Alfred Lyttelton, Conservative M.P. and Chancellor of the Diocese of Rochester and an older brother of Rev. Edward Lyttelton (Headmaster of Eton College), was convinced that the future of the rising generation depended upon denominationalism supplying the ethical guidance:

> Let anybody who knows London ask the great workers in the East End —men like Mr. Booth, Canon Barnett [President of Toynbee Hall, Whitechapel, a university settlement], or the heads of the Oxford and Cambridge Houses—what is likely to be the effect . . . upon a child 13 or 14 years of age who leaves the board school without association to attach himself to or to guide him in the difficult three or four years which he has to spend before he gets settled in life. . . . Many will tell you that the great hope for the derelict poor of London is that some denominational body should get hold of these children. . . . A boy looks to these bodies for approbation if he does well; and he fears their disapprobation if he does ill. . . . This system interests a body comparatively small in the welfare of the pupils. . . .[6]

The English record on morality had been good in the second half of the nineteenth century. Ven. Wilson referred to the number of indictable offenses which the Department of Justice regarded as "the best general criterion of the amount of crime."[7] There had been a steady decline in the number of criminals per 100,000 of the population for the nine five-year periods beginning with 1859-63 and ending with 1899-1903. The readings in round numbers for persons tried annually at the Assize and Quarter Sessions for indictable offenses over these quinquenniums were 91, 90, 72, 63, 57, 49, 41, 37, 33.[8] Rev. William G. Edwards Rees, Vicar of Pendleton, Manchester, offered an equally favorable picture of English statistics of crime. For his comparison he took the two periods of 1857-60 and 1900-04. The number of persons per 100,000 annually tried for graver offenses fell from 90.39 to 34.17.[9] The number of persons per 100,000 annually tried for less grave offenses in courts of summary jurisdiction fell from 172.30 to 128.30.[10] Only the number of persons charged with non-indictable offenses showed some increase, due apparently to the multiplication of offenses by new legislation.[11] Ven. Wilson attributed the heartening record to the fact that until the last thirty-five years England had retained the connection of centuries between education and the religious bodies. Credal lessons had exuded therapeutic sustenance.[12]

Rev. David Jones, Vicar of Penmaenmawr and Prebendary of Llanfair, Bangor Cathedral, contrasted the superior record of England to that of Wales where the school boards were so delinquent in the implementation of Cowper-Templeism. His statistics included Monmouthshire, traditionally identified with Welsh history.[13] In serious crime, in 1873 England averaged 1 in every 541 people and Wales 1 in every 633 people while in 1903 it was 1 in 375 and 1 in 428 respectively, admittedly in favor of Wales. In lighter offenses, in 1873 England averaged 1 in every 38 and Wales 1 in every 43 while in 1903 it was 1 in every 44 and 1 in every 35 respectively, a decidedly worse performance for Wales. But it was in arrests for drunkenness that Wales came off most unsatisfactory. The figures showed that in 1873 England averaged 1 in every 124 and Wales 1 in every 138 while in 1903 it was 1 in every 131 and 1 in every 97 respectively.[14]

Still, if the condition in regard to crime had been healthy in England, signs of trouble ahead were not wanting. The School Guardian saw in the recent outbreaks of hooliganism the suggestion that a moral failure was taking place. At night, in the streets, there was an increase in ill-behavior. Rude and insulting conduct was visited upon passers-by, especially women, practical evidence of the absence of respect and self-control. The number of offenders against minor laws was on the increase, perhaps suggesting a strategy of conscious transgression with the least risk of punishment. To interpolate, the cases of summary jurisdiction from 1881-85 averaged 675,025 a year, whereas in 1896-1900 they rose to 758,969 annually.[15] And the worst could be yet to come in the following decades when there would be fewer youths in close contact with religion as council schools arrogated more and more the educational function. The effect was cumulative and would not reach its crescendo, unless halted, until another generation by which time the influence of definite religious instruction would have exhausted itself.[16]

Anglicans found in the experiences abroad ready evidence of the sequence between secularism and moral deterioration. In the United States, where Horsfall described the religious instruction at best as no more than that in English council schools, many facts offered pertinent testimony. The American boy, bright as he was, developed into a youth, sensual but not spiritual, sharp but not scrupulous, politic but not truthful. Again, he called attention to the public utterances of several distinguished university presidents—Eliot of Harvard, Hall of Clark, Harper of Chicago—attributing the low standards of personal conduct to the absence of religious training.[17] Finally, he quoted the American journal, McClure's Magazine, to the effect that there were four and one-half times as many murders and homicides in 1900 for each million of people in the United States as there had been in 1881.[18] Ven. Wilson unfolded a similar melancholy story of criminal statistics. Whereas in 1850 there were 292 offenders in prison per million, the most recent figure (1894) showed 1,320 offenders in prison per million.[19] Rev. Rees was not optimistic that the record would improve in the future, noting first the statement of Rev. William Douglas Morrison, Rector of St. Marylebone and a chaplain in His Majesty's Prison Service, that there had been an increase in American juvenile delinquency and second the statement of President Hall of Clark University that the average age of first commitments grew steadily younger.‡ Such was the dismal story of America where definite religious instruction was banned from the common schools.[20]

Nor did the criminal record of the Australian state of Victoria make pleasant reading. Secular education had been introduced in Victoria in 1872 and statistics for the years from 1880 to 1890 should reflect the life of the first generation of graduates under that system. Rev. Beeching relied again upon the figures cited by Bishop Moorhouse of Manchester at the Church Congress at Folkestone, Kent, in 1892. In 1880 male criminals summarily convicted or held to bail amounted to 12,469 and in 1890 the number was 20,189. In 1880 persons arrested for robbery with violence was 245 and in 1890 the number was 465. In 1880 persons arrested for the serious crimes of murder and manslaughter came to 36 and in 1890 the number was 56.[21] Considering that the male population in Victoria had increased by less than a third over the decade (from 452,083 in 1881 to 599,172 in 1892), the Church Quarterly Review regarded this two-fold bulge in crime as startling in its lesson of the fruits of secularism.[22]

In the case of New Zealand, Wilfred Seymour de Winton, a director of Lloyd's Bank and a member of the Canterbury House of Laymen,

---

‡ Rev. Morrison stated that in 1890 the inmates in juvenile reformatories was 15,000, an increase of nearly 30% in ten years. But it should be noted that he does not take into consideration the increase in population. In 1880 there were 11,468 inmates and a population of 50,155,783 and in 1890 it was 14,846 and a population of 62,622,250. Thus the ratios were 229 and 237 per million in 1880 and 1890 respectively, still an increase but not 30%. Morrison (1900), p. 277. Dr. Hall's specific statement was 14.23 as the average age of juvenile inmates in reformatories in 1890. Hall (1904), I, p. 327. For the official figures see U.S. Census, 11th, 1890, III, Part II, pp. 518, 574.

found the criminal record of graduates of secular schools since their inception in 1877 bad.[23] The number of persons arrested or summoned in 1890 was 18,247, rising to 22,674 in 1899 and 28,076 in 1902.[24] Considering that the rise in population for the period had been 28% (from 625,508 in 1890 to 832,505 in 1903), the criminal increase of 53% did not speak well for the moral influence of the New Zealand secular school system.[25]

Rev. Rees presented the better record of New South Wales where since 1880 general religious instruction was given daily in school hours and supplementary facilities were allowed for denominational religious instruction.[26] True, in terms of absolute figures, the advantage would appear to have rested with Victoria.[27] In 1902, persons charged for all offenses in New South Wales numbered 60,373 or a ratio of 42 per 1,000 with convictions at 50,776, while in Victoria it was 45,198 or a ratio of 37 per 1,000 with convictions at 33,461. In the higher courts, convictions averaged .55 per 1,000 in New South Wales and .32 per 1,000 in Victoria. But in terms of relative figures, New South Wales made the better showing. Thus, in 1902, New South Wales had 60,373 persons charged with offenses and in 1905 it had 61,062, an increase of less than 1% as against an increase of 2.04% in population (correctly, a fraction of 1%), while in Victoria with a population almost stationary charges rose from 45,198 to 48,345 or crime had outstripped the increase of population by nearly 6%. The estimated population figures in official sources are as follows: New South Wales 1,400,000 (1902) and 1,430,-000 (1905); Victoria 1,205,000 (1902) and 1,210,000 (1905). What made all these statistics the more significant were the adverse conditions under which New South Wales labored. Rev. Rees summed up a statement of E. T. Drake, Victorian Government statist, on this point:[28]

> The population of Victoria was never a convict stock like that of New South Wales which has had in recent years to combat the hereditary criminal tendencies of a section of its population. . . . Also New South Wales has a greater floating and foreign population . . . which tends to augment crime. Also Victorian justice is more lenient whereas in New South Wales the magistrates *must always convict* a person found guilty and the conviction *must always be recorded.*[29]

As a matter of fact, continued Rev. Rees, the aggregate figures of crime in New South Wales as well as in Victoria compared ill with those of the mother country. The number of persons in 1904 charged with indictable and criminally non-indictable offenses totaled 149,214 in England and Wales[30] and 13,919 in Victoria.[31] In proportion to population the ratio was 1 for Britain to every 3 for Victoria. In

New South Wales there was the damaging occurrence, for example, of growth in youthful first offender cases, rising from 62 in 1896 to 371 in 1905, albeit the population was almost stationary.[32] Illegitimacy had increased conspicuously in relation to the general birthrate. Where the former had risen 30% between 1885 and 1905, the latter had only gone up 10%.* To Rev. Rees the existence of voluntary schools in Britain was the difference in putting across effectively denominational instruction compared to credal lessons under the right of entry as given generously in New South Wales and niggardly in Victoria.[33]

Nor was there anything in the record of France to commend the secular system, even buttressed as it was by purposeful instruction in social ethics. Its foundation was laid in 1882 by the Ferry Act which provided that national grants would be restricted to State schools and in these only lay teachers would be appointed.[34] Then, in 1886, systematic moral instruction of a non-theological content was introduced in place of credal lessons. So sufficient time had elapsed to permit some comparisons in matters of turpitude. Rev. Rees noted that the number of criminal cases of graver character increased from 514,761 per annum in the quinquennium 1896-1900 to 543,636 in 1904.[35] In short, while the population had increased 1.5% (from 38,517,000 in 1896 to 38,-961,000 in 1901), crime had gone up 6%. He regarded as symptomatic of the lack of moral fiber among the French their record in suicides and divorces. Suicide figures showed an upswing: 1,739 (1826), 8,541 (1888), 8,885 (1903). The number of divorces mounted from 4,123 in 1885 to 10,186 in 1903.[36] The only possible conclusion was that in France a better antiseptic was needed than a secular school system dispensing jejune and insipid moral lessons.[37]

Anglicans were at odds over whether Germany provided an example of a good moral record based upon denominational instruction in schools. Dr. Arthur Shadwell, physician and a student of industrial development, was lavish in his praise of the rewards which that system had yielded in Prussia. To it he would trace the sense of duty and responsibility, the respect for law, and the self-restraint of the German citizen. He believed that it had contributed to material prosperity through ensuring the loyal cooperation of the worker. Bishop Wilkinson for Europe (North and Central) expressed similar approval of the dividends which had accrued to the German nation in the form of order, discipline, obedience, and honor. On the other hand, Rev. Rees (and Canon Wilson) did not feel that the actual data of crime justified commenda-

---

* The statistics of birth rates and illegitimacy are: 1885, births—35,043, illegitimate births—1,612; 1905, births—39,501, illegitimate births—2,912. *Statesman's Year-Book*, 1890, p. 227; 1907, p. 327.

tory generalizations. Thus, from 1882 to 1896, Dr. Edgar Loening, German statistician, found that the rates of increase for juvenile and adult crime were 22.7% and 16% respectively.[38] As Rev. Rees interpreted the apparent paradox, the answer was that the denominational instruction was too much under the control of the State. The result was a lesson overly routinized and constricted, lacking in spontaneity. In England the advantage of retaining an autonomous status enabled the voluntary school to offer a stimulating adventure in religious education.[39]

ROMAN CATHOLIC BRIEF

Roman Catholics affirmed that in their schools religious and moral training were indistinguishable. The strengthening of the mind and the will must be identified with right action. Mental culture made only "clever devils." Lilly observed that "man is not merely an intellectual but a moral being . . . and [the] former is a means to the latter." But the State, which had intervened to require education, "must obtain the aid of religion as an instrument of ethical culture."† Roman Catholic teaching brought forth in all their shining moral armor the Lord, Jesus Christ, Mary, Joseph, and the saints to win the heart of the child. In a parochial school, wrote Rev. Michael Maher, professor of Mental Science, Stonyhurst College, Lancashire, the actual emulation of the Christian life fulfilled its mission. Moral reflections abounded in the teaching and example of Christ and His saints, in the frequent preparation for the sacraments, and in the periodic examination of the conscience. The more intimately religious motives were associated with a child's conduct, the more completely the impulse of doing good would animate his whole life. The answer to temptation should be that the omnipresent all-seeing God had forbidden such acts because they were in conflict with His all-holy and that He would punish those who were disobedient by banishing them from His sight.[40]

Roman Catholics advanced evidence both at home and abroad that anything less than denominationalism, be it unsectarianism or secularism, yielded evil products. In the populous centers children leaving council schools at the end of each day exhibited abominable manners

---

† Dillon reminded the nation that "when it was a question of reforming waifs and strays the common sense of the country, instead of trusting to Cowper-Templeism, handed them over as far as possible to the denominations to which they belonged, thus recognizing that denominational instruction was the most likely to reform and prepare them to take a better part in the life of the nation." Presumably the reference is to Roman Catholic industrial schools maintained by the State. *Commons*, July 8, 1902, p. 1111.

and their language was quite often shocking. The recent outbursts of hooliganism were testimony to the irreverence wrought by Cowper-Templeism. Bishop Burton of Clifton regarded the American schools with their spasmodic and indifferent simple Bible teaching as breeding a generation with no ethical standards. It was a matter for anxiety to read Dr. Arthur Shadwell's statement that responsible Americans were now disposed to trace "the corruption in public life, the growth of lawlessness, violence, and juvenile crime, the increasing prevalence of divorce, and taste for foolish, false, and degrading literature and for immoral and unwholesome amusements to the want of reverence and the failure of the Churches."[41] Rev. Edward Myers, professor of Dogmatic Theology and Patrology, St. Edmund's College, Ware, and later Archbishop of Berea in the Near East, noted that the first generation of French children educated in *la morale laique* and now grown men and women in their thirties manifested personal decorum hardly calculated to recommend it.[42] Timothy M. Healy, Nationalist M.P. for Louth North, Ireland, was himself convinced "that the whole reason for these anarchist movements which disturbed Europe and which have led to the assassinations of the presidents of the United States and the French Republic have been due to the expulsion of God from the schools."‡ To weaken religion was to relax the bonds which knit a civilized people together and to unleash the wildest forces of human passion.[43]

Rev. Smith was perturbed by the efforts to make systematic non-theological moral instruction a part of the school curriculum in England. Such a course had been included as a secular subject in the Code of 1906 by the Board of Education.[44] This meant that it could earn grants as well as be outside the operation of the conscience clause. Admittedly there was some value in it for children in large cities where poverty bid fair to crush all sense of social obligations. But behind the Moral Instruction League was the Ethical movement which disavowed God as the fountainhead for supreme authority.* Its civic morality was based on the premise of independence of the Supreme Being. It aimed to form a type of character for which the will and commands of God counted for nothing. Its syllabus, for example, taught truth by dressing

---

‡ The assassinations were those of Abraham Lincoln (1865), James Garfield (1881), Marie F. Sadi-Carnot (1894), William McKinley (1901).

* The *Catholic Herald* (April, 1906, April 29, 1913) warned Roman Catholics away from the Moral Instruction League. It was anti-Christian in its whole conception of morals and its opinions of life were such as any pagan might hold. Its purposes contained no ultimate ideals of a constant nature, especially none suggesting the promised punishment by a divine authority for offenses against eternal truth. It might be noted that the Moral Instruction League and the London West End Ethical Society share today the same offices at 13 Prince of Wales Terrace.

up the so-called celebrated conscience cases of Copernicus and Galileo. The notion was fostered that "priests" and the "Church" were the opponents of truth-searching. The popular subjects of the moment—the ill-considered theory of socialism and the inhuman practice of vivisection—were treated on the same plane as external principles of justice. Earthly men and women were adequate models for right conduct. Socrates exemplified noble courage. Pericles represented the quintessence of magnanimity. George Washington personified single-heartedness. Florence Nightingale was the epitome of stalwart impassionateness. Children were to be made moral by grand talk.[45]

Rev. Smith lamented the failure of the Roman Catholic Church to take a more active part in the inquiry initiated by Michael E. Sadler, professor of history and education, Owens College, Manchester, into the state of moral education in the schools of the world. Representatives holding all points of view were invited and it behooved advocates of the role which religion should play in the concepts of morality to muster their full strength. Otherwise the field of ethics would be abdicated to non-Christian bodies. As it was, only three Roman Catholics were on the program of the First International Moral Education League held in September 1908, at London. Rev. Smith listed them:[46] 1) Msgr. W. F. Brown whose topic was Roman Catholic moral training in Sunday schools, 2) Rev. Michael Maher who contributed two papers on the methods of moral training in Roman Catholic voluntary schools, 3) Rev. Edward Myers who discussed moral instruction in French schools.[47]

NONCONFORMIST BRIEF

Nonconformists were no less ready to avow the role of the school in strengthening the moral fiber of the nation. Education was not merely the training of the intellect and the cramming of the brain with knowledge. It was also the mission of education to discipline the conscience. While there might be other social sanctions for morality, none were substitutes for religion. As Christians, Free Churchmen were in accord with the belief that to place the mind of the young under the great realities of the historic faith was a purifying pilgrimage. But, insisted the Daily News, "it can best be done apart from rigid dogmatic statements which [children] can not possibly understand and which serve to block the stream of renovating thought instead of creating a channel for its flow." Imagine the effect upon the average rough and unemotionally healthy lad in a town alley or a country village to listen to talk about rinsing mouths and the importance of the Blessed Sacrament. The *Manchester Guardian* admonished that it was even dangerous to attach completely moral truths to specific sets of supernatural doctrines, considering the scientific inroads being made upon them in the modern world. Surely, without violating the sanctuary of private worship, the sacred name of God could be uttered to cultivate a detestation of vice, a love for veracity, civility without flattery, and a peaceable demeanor.[48]

The Holy Scripture was stoutly defended as the best moral restorative. Was it not better to hold the point of view of one great religious community inclusive of a hundred different churches and seek spiritual sustenance for the righteous growth of man in the venerable "Rock of the Ages"? For centuries the Bible had been providing the inspiration for exalted public life and gracious social usages. Indeed, the ethical content of the Bible formed the basis of Western civilization, emancipating society from the pagan world of old. Rev. Joseph Agar Beet, professor of Systematic Theology, Wesleyan College, Richmond, pleaded the case for the Bible in the phraseology that it evoked a consciousness of sin and sinfulness. The Bible enlisted the heart and the will on the side of goodness, holding up to view the beauty and strength of the single soul in whom dwelt righteousness—the Christ. To drink at the fountain of the sacred books and to learn what God required the soul to be was the indispensable gateway to master rightly the elements of earthly lore. Banish the Bible and one of the few refining influences in life would be gone.[49]

Nonconformists discoursed at length how the Bible nourished good conduct. Both Old and New Testaments were replete with stories of enlightenment on truth, purity, temperance, and courteous manners. The history of Israel reflected the development of the human race and its rise and fall furnished excellent lessons. The stories of the patriarchs —Isaac, Jacob, Joseph—set a fine pattern of justice for the home. The Book of Proverbs with its condemnation of slander and Ecclesiastes with its critical views on shame and pride offered conceptions of dignity in ordinary social intercourse.The denunciation of stealing in the Ten Commandments suggested to the citizen that there was a God above to whom one was answerable. Then there were the opportunities for the biographical approach to depict lives of constructive deeds—Abraham, Moses, Samuel, David, Solomon, John the Baptist, Peter, Paul. The great historic facts of Christ's life and death and the image of a righteous and merciful God redeeming man from evil supplied an enhancing answer to what was right and wrong. This wealth of material was ample testimony of the ability of the Bible to crystallize morality into forms easily understood.[50]

Dr. Clifford was in the forefront of those extolling the use of the Bible to prepare children in the duties of citizenship. The Scriptures offered the child access to the best source for ethics through its sublime poetry, inspiring history, and ennobling literature. As he would familiarize children with the stories of good and bad kings—Alfred, John, Charles I, Cromwell—so he would place in their possession analogous accounts from the Bible. For awakening the humanitarian impulse, along with the message from Shakespeare's *Merchant of Venice* beginning with "the quality of mercy is not strained," he would choose the story of the Good Samaritan. The dignity of natural wonders suggested in the line from Milton's *Paradise Lost*, "Hail, Holy Light, offspring of heaven first born," could be matched with the transcending address to the Creator and Sustainer of the Universe in Psalm 104. The representation of the ideal wife in the Miltonic picture of Adam and Eve in *Paradise Lost* could be set down for elder children side by side with the words of wisdom in the Book of Proverbs. However, Clifford made clear that theological material should be eschewed, mentioning Shakespeare's references to Atonement *(Measure for Measure)* and Milton's allusions to Predestination *(The Christian Doctrine)*.[51]

The charge that Cowper-Templeism was responsible for the lowered morality of the masses was challenged. Bryce urged the home secretary to include in the tables of criminal statistics information as to the type of elementary school attended and so provide a more scientific method for judging the relative performance of graduates from provided and non-provided schools. Howard Evans cited statistics on the experience of Manchester with its youth. In 1895 a return was obtained by the school board as to the number of children committed to industrial schools because of unmanageableness, truancy, or circumstanced with ne'er-do-well parents.† It was found that 387 Protestant and 897 Roman Catholic children attended. Considering the fact that board schools had 77,905 children and parochial 11,275,[52] the conclusion could be drawn that the latter were the perpetrators of the hooliganism so recently bewailed by Roman Catholics.[53]

On the broader canvas of England and Wales, Lewis Williams, chairman of the Cardiff School Board, quoted the observations of Lord Avebury (Sir John Lubbock), eminent archaeologist and ethnologist. Since the inception of the board school system in 1870 and allowing

---

† The industrial school lodged children up to fourteen years of age whose surroundings and conduct threatened a career of delinquency unless taken under closer State custody. An alternative type of industrial day school was permitted school boards which would allow a youth's rehabilitation without leaving home. See Balfour (1903), pp. 53-62; Barnett (1913), p. 20 ff.

for the one-third increase of population by 1899, the criminal class in the jails had gone down from 20,080 to 13,000, a reduction of 66%. Again, where the average number of persons sentenced on indictment to penal servitude in 1869 was 1,978 out of a population of 21,681,000, in 1899 it was down to 770 out of a population of 31,061,000, a reduction of almost 80%.[54] The *Baptist Times* regarded as a high compliment the words of Whitelaw Reid, American ambassador to Great Britain, delivered at a New York State Teachers' Association convention, in December 1907,[55] that English schools did turn out "well-behaved, orderly boys and girls."[56]

The Welsh record was singled out for special examination. The *South Wales Daily News* challenged the soundness of Rev. David Jones' interpretation of the superior performance of England compared to Wales in criminal statistics. In the case of offenses, the answer lay in the large proportion of foreigners in Welsh mines, men either from England or the Continent. In the case of drunkenness, the answer rested in the large influx of holiday-makers from the midland counties and Lancashire who abused the hospitality of Wales. By way of more positive proof in behalf of Wales, Philip Whitwell Wilson observed that "Cardigan's crime record per 100,000 is lower than in any other county of England and Wales . . . and Carmarthen comes as high as twelfth in the list with only 115 crimes per 100,000." An inquiry to the Home Office produced a partially different set of figures for crime during 1905 per 100,000: Cardigan (88) and Carmarthen (292). However, Carmarthen was twelfth on the list as Wilson stated, although Cardigan was second to Cornwall whose rate was 87. The principality of Wales, with its preponderance of council schools, did not come off badly as an exemplar of morality.[57]

Nonconformists gathered their tidbits of evidence from experiences across the English Channel. Rev. Hollowell saw in the events on the Continent damaging marks against the influence of a sectarian school system. He mentioned the rise of socialism in Germany and the numerous political murders in Russia, countries fully committed to credal instruction. As for "Godless France" and its criminal record, if the Anglican indictment were true, then what a tremendous failure this was for the Roman Catholic Church which had dominated the French schools until recently. Philip Whitwell Wilson waxed sardonic over the way in which the Roman Catholic Church had employed its theological primacy, seeking to transform the educational system into an unscrupulous engine for the destruction of the Third French Republic. It had helped produce the potential dictator, Boulanger, and had promoted the anti-Semitic Dreyfus episode to a high pitch. The French nation had been well advised to rescue their schools from the grip of Ultra-montanism and to assert the supremacy of the State in its proper sphere.[58]

Nonconformists were divided on how apt was the citation of Anglo-Saxon peoples overseas as illustrations in behalf of the moral benefits deriving from the religious settlement in their schools. Dr. Clifford came forward for the affirmative and discussed the situation in New Zealand and the United States, so-called secular countries but both of which he regarded as offering in various voluntary ways the essence of his ideas on the ethical application of the Bible. He recounted his trip to New Zealand in 1897 and his visits to schools where only the right of entry outside school hours was permitted. He had been impressed with the Christian quality of teaching there and its fitness for making good and useful citizens. He quoted for his American information Dr. Joseph Henry Crooker,[59] Unitarian clergyman and active in American educa-tion: "American teachers . . . are the most thoughtful, earnest, hard-working, painstaking and self-sacrificing class in the State. . . . There is not a priesthood in the world that outranks them. . . . Is it not a frightful slander to call our public schools irreligious when, in fact, they are taught by as noble and saintly a band of workers as ever consecrated themselves to the service of humanity?"[60]

Dr. Horton came forward for the negative, describing America and Australasia as a warning of the consequences of what he believed were their secular school systems. Their populations seemed to him on a lower plane than nations which had grown up in the happy posses-sion of great truths concerning God, man, and the universe. A like judgment was rendered by the *British Congregationalist* which claimed that "America is finding that the secular character of her day-school system is producing ill results in national character."[61]

SECULARIST BRIEF

While secularists challenged the ability of any kind of Christian in-struction to develop the moral sense, some were not without an appre-ciation of the qualities which the Bible itself possessed as one source among many. Harrold Johnson acknowledged that if the Bible were employed as Dr. Clifford wished, it could well be studied along with other elevating literature. Many were the beautiful thoughts contained therein. William Thomas Stead, apostle of pacifism and editor of the *Review of Reviews*, granted that, even if the Bible were to be excluded from the curriculum, it had by no means been cast out of the school.

The Christian graces were the basis for the secular handbook of ethics. The Ten Commandments permeated the ordinary lessons devoted to character, conduct, and citizenship. The sublime precepts of Jesus of Nazareth had passed so thoroughly into the texture of the thought of mankind that it was no longer necessary to recall the biblical pronouncements on forgiveness for injury and compassion for the suffering. In ceasing to be merely Christian and becoming human, wrote George E. O'Dell, assistant to Dr. Stanton Coit in the work of the English Ethical movement and later field secretary of the American Ethical Union, the biblical injunctions against theft and in praise of the golden rule attained to a greater worth and dignity.[62]

But, many secularists insisted firmly, the reading of the Bible under current usage vitiated any potential moral effectiveness. In such an avowedly Christian country as Britain, the Bible could not be contained within the realm of literature. Hardly a passage, observed Picton, could be perused without the question arising of its truth. Was it possible for teacher and pupil to avoid linking the Bible with divine sanctions? It was highly problematical that many clergy would accept any treatment of the personality of Christ save as predicated on the acknowledgment of His life and mission. Such humanitarian stirrings as were to be derived from religious instruction, MacDonald averred, would be only incidental to the confession of faith. Regrettable as the fact must be, therefore, a large number of secularists were not prepared to support the use of the Bible in the schoolroom. The chances were too great that teacher and children would be engulfed in disquisitions on dogma and theocracy.[63]

Certainly the portions of the Bible used did little to commend it for moral purposes. How could David be said to be a man after God's own heart when it was his habit in war to slay or torture the people he conquered. His relations with Achish, son of the King of Gath, could only be described as replete with treachery and duplicity. What was the moral to be drawn from the story of Joseph and his devotion to the interests of the Egyptian dynasty rather than to the welfare of its subjects? By the royal monopoly Joseph gathered in all the money and the cattle of the people. Then Joseph forced these men, women, and children to sell themselves into serfdom to escape starvation. How damaging, commented Herbert M. Thompson, M.A., Llandaff, Cardiff, must it be to a child's sensitivity to read the account of Elisha and the children of Bethel: "And he went up from thence unto Bethel; and as he was going up by the way, there came forth little children out of the city, and mocked him, and said unto him, Go up, thou bald head. . . . And he turned back, and looked on them, and cursed them in the name of the Lord. And there came forth two she-bears out of the wood, and tore forty and two children of them." [64]

Again, the attendant pedagogical methods defeated any possible benefits. A trying ordeal awaited those who taught a syllabus based upon "Bible reading without note or comment." Gould described the process of teaching under these restrictions as a dull undertaking. One need not be astonished if it habituated young minds to accept unproven marvels for history and so weakened their capacity in the sphere of ethics. Picton insisted that the final enforcement of the moral principle demanded before all things "truth in the inward parts" and that could not be achieved by accepting "as actual historic fact Jewish folklore about the creation of the world, the deluge of Noah, the talking of the serpent and of Balaam's ass." MacDonald placed the blame "not upon the Bible but because it has been dragged in by the scruff of the neck to make timetables look moral and quieten the hesitating minds of people who pay homage to the letter because that excuses them from taking the trouble to understand the spirit." More, the allocation of a separate period for the religious lesson tended to convey to the teacher, as well as to the child, the false idea that the sacred and the secular belonged to two different realms of thought. As a result the teacher was even discouraged from exploiting the potentialities of the lay subjects for moral purposes. [65]

Particularly bad were the pedagogical methods employed in voluntary schools. There was no chance to stir the conscience of a child by forcing a rigid set of theological beliefs upon him, none of which he could grasp. A. W. Merriman, who described himself as having taught in Church schools, recalled how details rather than principles were wanted. The catechism, the Prayer Book, selected portions of the Bible were "crammed up" for weeks before the examination in factual religious history. Children wrote out from memory long passages of the Scriptures with capital letter and punctuation mark correct. One Miss A. S. Furnell told that in many schools children were expected to master the names of the Kings of Israel and Judah, to list Jacob's sons, and to know the towns visited by St. Paul on his journeys. It would mean a loss of marks in an examination to plague Egypt with locusts before she suffered from the frogs. Picton recounted a visit he made to a voluntary school. Questions were asked as to the reasons for Jacob's partiality to Joseph, the significance of Joseph's dreams, and the unreasonableness of brethren and father in objecting to his conjurations. Explanations were given on the inferiority of Herod's claim to be King of the Jews as compared with that of Jesus. To look for moral results from such material was "to expect grapes from thorns and figs from thistles." [66]

Granting, however, that the religious lesson could be organized to exploit the moral potential of the Bible, secularists did not believe that it answered the problems besetting a child. Genesis with its epynomic patriarchal history and saturated with ideas of polygamy was hardly sound material. The Ten Commandments might have been very well adapted for a pastoral tribe living in a state of semi-savagery but was quite unsuited for the twentieth century. What had children from five to twelve years of age to do with the admonition not to make unto themselves graven images? It was ludicrous to teach a child that he must not covet his neighbor's wife, or his oxen, or his ass. Children did not comprehend fully what was meant by murder and adultery. Indeed, the Ten Commandments told a child not to do a number of things which he never dreamed of doing but which he saw others doing every day without the least apparent discomfort to conscience. The net result could be for a child to grow up in an ethical vacuum, perhaps cynical of social propriety and indifferent to elementary moral conduct.[67]

Especially obsolete was the traditional view of the close connection between religion and civic virtue. Gustav Spiller, Ethical lecturer and after 1904 secretary of the International Union of Ethical Societies, noted that in the past the State had demanded of all its citizens belief in the Church of England. From the humblest servant to the highest minister, all in the employment of the State had to prove doctrinal soundness.‡ But today the State had discarded orthodox theology as essential to its well-being. A good character was still the recognized commendation for public service but its source of strength transcended the confines of sectarianism.[68]

MacDonald submitted a discerning analysis of this old thesis that the mutual interests of Church and State required the Established Church to cast its benign influence over the schools of the nation:

> So long as it was maintained that the sacrament, taken according to the Church of England was a test of civic rectitude, it could properly be imposed upon servants of the State, and the right of parents belonging to the Church of England to have their children educated in the creed was consequently valid. The secular belief then was "No Church, no State." But all that has gone. No religious tests are now applied to can-

---

‡ References are to the Corporation Act of 1661 and the Test Act of 1673. The former laid down that all officers of municipal corporations must be comunicants according to the rites of the Established Church. The latter required that all persons holding public office should receive the sacrament according to the Established Church, take the oath of supremacy, and subscribe to a declaration against transubstantiation. Both were repealed in 1828.

didates for public office, and when the State ceased to be denominational the claim of every parent that his right to teach his children his
private religious beliefs (provided they were those of the Established
Church, for the argument from this point of view was never sound
further than that) should become a responsibility of the State, became
invalid. This claim urged against the State by parents is therefore nothing
but the final remnant of those preposterous pretensions of the Established Church, that outside her pale was the Land of Moab and beyond
her sacraments the Abodes of Sin. . . . The contention that religious
dogma is necessary to the existence of the State, happily, . . . has been
settled. The State has become a secular organization after a long conflict
during which every consideration involved in this claim has been fought
over and settled adversely to those now making the claim. The State
takes no cognizance of creed, except ceremonially, and no cognizance of
rival ethical sanctions.[69]

Secularists spelled out the moral issues confronting modern day society in terms of the various age groups. A child's need was correction in
little failings—personal uncleanliness, petty pilfering, cruelty to dumb
animals, unkindness to playmates. The adolescent should have brought
home to him the importance of thrift, courtesy, and intellectual honesty. For the adult the moral complement included a wide range of responsibilities. The State should encourage its citizens to possess a
social conscience and the civic enthusiasm to eradicate poverty and to
promote healthy recreation. These vital reforms in human engineering
were detailed as better housing, improved working conditions, and
assistance to the aged. The ethical philosophy of today should hold
that nations fell and rose of their own doing and not by the vicarious
fiat of a divinity revealed through the Bible. Spiller complained that
even when religion sought to provide answers for contemporary problems its instinct was to stress passive duties—humility, meekness, obedience, resignation. Granville George Greenwood proposed an oath mir-
roring a righteous frame of mind:

> To do to all men as I would they should do unto me: To hurt nobody
> by word or deed: To be true and just in all my dealings: To bear no
> malice and hatred in my heart: To keep my hands from picking and
> stealing, and my tongue from evil speaking, lying, and slandering.[70]

The surface facts of human behavior bespoke the barren results of
religious instruction. The adults of today, wrote MacDonald, whose
schooling had included the Bible or the catechism could not boast that
theirs was an incorruptible society. The practice was all too common to

swear and to use obscene expressions. The English language showed no signs of being less profane and coarse. Picton referred to an editorial in the *Westminster Gazette* (Sept. 6, 1901):

> We would gladly see the resolution passed by the East Ham Council to stop offensive language on tram-cars adopted by other local authorities. The use of language of this sort is disagreeable enough to many, wherever heard; it is particularly so on public conveyances where other passengers are compelled to listen to it.

Was it not a scandal that elementary schools should have been powerless to mold the speech of children who had attended them for six or more years? Dr. Washington Sullivan, active in the London Ethical movement, criticized the prevalent indulgence in horse betting, which often drifted into vice and deceit. On the public streets, vulgar exhibitions of horse-play and jostling were growing more frequent, often bordering on the indecent side. Then there were the outbreaks of rudeness and the disregard for the rights of others which made Bank Holidays so odious. Snell directed his censure toward the twin evils of drinking and infidelity which had become crying national shames.[71]

The surface facts of law and order likewise denied the claim that the religious lesson had yielded optimum returns in rectitude. Picton noted that wilful damage to public parks and private property was on the increase. Acts of desecration at picturesque places were nullifying the efforts to preserve historic spots. The statistics of juvenile delinquency, declared MacDonald, lent no comfort that divine intercession would vanquish lawlessness.† The increase in the number of policemen (from 39,749 in 1896 to 46,027 in 1906) was alarming.[72] Whether these figures were cause for concern would seem to depend on the ratio of population and the number of new laws requiring police supervision. Snowden was especially critical of the sectarian school and its so-called moral influence. He referred to a return given the commons as to the religious faith of all prisoners according to a census taken in 1906. It showed that out of 21,000 prisoners 16,000 had associated themselves with the Church of England and 4,000 with the Roman Catholic

---

† The official figures per 100,000 population (*Parl. Papers*, 1907, XCVIII, Cd. 3314, p. 57) for indictable offenses were not good, although in ratio terms they showed signs of improvement:

	1893	1905	1893	1905
12 years to 16	6,595	6,042	261	218
16 years to 21	9,298	9,443	321	275

Church.‡ Surely, if religious teaching had an effect upon character, it would manifest itself in the conduct of the adult generation. Whatever it was in the religious lesson, its compartmentalized approach, its unsound pedagogical methods, or its blood-curdling content, it stood self-condemned.[73]

McCabe presented the case of America in a favorable light. The criminal statistics cited by denominationalists required careful analysis. There were not only the colored inhabitants to equate but also the constant immigration of illiterates from Europe. Thus, taking the Census Report for 1890, prison statistics indicated 57,310 whites and 25,019 negroes in jail. The whites of native parentage amounted to 6 out of every 10,000 in jail. In contrast, for the white natives of foreign parentage and for foreign born immigrants the ratios were 13 and 17 out of every 10,000 respectively.* It was the European countries with full religious teaching which swelled America's criminal record. McCabe found positive testimony in favor of the American character in observations made by Dr. Frank Herbert Hayward, whose career included service as an organizing teacher for Mid-Devon, principal of Torquay Pupil Teacher Center, and inspector of schools for the London County Council from 1905 to 1933. Dr. Hayward referred to the remark of a Bristol philanthropist well acquainted with America that "he heard more foul words in the street in one day in Bristol than he heard in three months in America."[74] As McCabe followed American developments, the only serious opponent to the modified secular system was the Roman Catholic Church. And the best answer here was contained in a work by an American Methodist clergyman, Rev. Richard Harcourt, who held a pastorate in San Francisco. Rev. Harcourt charged that the Irish (taught in parochial schools) comprised an abnormal percentage of the criminal class. He noted that in Philadelphia, in 1890, of 8,034 persons engaged in the saloon business (of whom 6,418 had fallen foul of the law) 3,041 were Irish and only 205 were native Americans.[75] McCabe commented that these facts should place the American record in its proper perspective.[76]

---

‡ Actually, the return of March 28, 1906 cited by Snowden simply indicated the religious creed of prisoners and no question was asked about what school was attended and so it could be questioned if the voluntary school should bear the entire blame. The breakdown is as follows: Church of England 16,089, Roman Catholic 4,395, Jews 257, Wesleyans 352. Parl. Papers, 1906, XCIX, No. 138, 4 pp.

* The figures work out close to McCabe's ratios. In 1890 the native born population was 53,372,073 and the foreign born population was 9,249,547. In 1890 the approximate number of prisoners of white native born was 23,000, of white foreign parentage 14,000, and of white foreign born 16,000. U.S. Census, 11th, 1890, I, Part I, LXXIX, III, Part I, p 149.

Secularists refused to accept the sectarian presentation of criminal statistics for Australasia, stressing the greater significance of relative to absolute figures. Their outpourings constitute a veritable fairyland of interpretive excursions. To begin with, the challenge was accepted to examine the record of Victoria, the most secular state of all. Cohen made use of the compilations of Thomas A. Coghlan, Australian statist and Agent-General for New South Wales in London.[77] The beneficent result of the accumulative effect of secular education in Victoria was evidenced by the steady drop in the number of arrests per 10,000 population over the last thirty years from 1875 to 1904: 380 (1875), 382 (1880), 347 (1890), 254 (1900), 242 (1904). Particularly pertinent were the number of arrests of males under thirty years of age for 1881 and 1891 compared to those over thirty.† Not only was it much less but it decreased in 1891 as compared with 1881 whereas the opposite was true for those over thirty years of age. The point was that those males below thirty were brought up under a system of secular education (since 1872) while those over thirty had been favored with religious instruction.[78]

In a letter to *The Times*, Coghlan declared that he had compiled these statistics at the request of the Agents-General for the several Australian states. He explained that he did not wish to intrude any opinion upon the Birrell Bill currently under debate. Indeed, he preferred to draw from the combined statistics for New South Wales and Victoria the broader conclusion that the development of Australian industrial and social conditions tended on the whole to the betterment of the community and the reduction of crime. Thus the over-all number of persons apprehended per 10,000 declined from 380 in 1875 to 242 in 1904 and the number of persons committed for trial by jury declined from 16 in 1875 to 8 in 1904. In conclusion Coghlan observed that "the Australian has become resolutely well-behaved, his face is set steadily against drunkenness and its concomitant evils, and statesmen of all shades of opinion are united on this common ground that the surest defense the country possesses against crime is the education of its people."[79]

Even better for the case of secular education in Australasia, in the

---

† The breakdown is as follows for arrests per 10,000 at each age period for males:

Age Period	1881	1891	Age Period	1881	1891
10—15	111	96	30—40	865	869
15—20	335	305	40—50	721	1,053
20—25	720	688	50—60	623	760
25—30	823	777	60 & over	661	586

thinking of McCabe, was a comparison between the various states.[80] For every 1,000 of the population the convicted persons in New South Wales (the religious state *par excellence*) stood at 9.68, but it was 2.27 in South Australia, 3.60 in New Zealand, 4.33 in Victoria, and 6.73 in Queensland (all secular colonies). Again, over the years from 1890 to 1903, although Victoria's population increased from 1,000,000 (correctly, 1,140,000) to 1,250,000 (1,208,000), that most secular state had dropped in summary convictions from 24,494 to 15,741 and in number of prisoners from 1,862 to 978. In contrast, in New South Wales, where the population was (1,132,000) in 1890 and (1,415,000) in 1903, summary convictions rose from 48,102 to 51,379 while the number of prisoners in 1903 was 1,882 or twice that of Victoria (and populations were practically identical). In Western Australia where, like New South Wales, daily general religious instruction plus supplementary facilities were in force, there were 12,758 summary convictions in 1903 for a population of 185,000 (220,000) compared to Victoria's 15,741 for a population of 1,208,000. In South Australia, there were 5,102 summary convictions in 1903 (for a population of 365,000), an equally creditable performance for the secular school side. Summing up the facts, McCabe proclaimed that the ratio of crime mounted almost in direct proportion to the degree of religious instruction given.[81]

Australasian crime statistics by 1908 were regarded as further proof that the moral accomplishments of a secular education system was no transitory feat.[82] The Secular Education League (founded in 1907 to work for the exclusion of religious teaching from the State-supported schools),[83] described the progress made in Victoria. For offenses against the person, where the number had been 4,091 in 1890, it was 1,932 in 1905, and 1,793 in 1908. For offenses against property, where the number had been 5,036 in 1890, it was 4,032 in 1905, and 3,894 in 1908. For the incidence of drunkenness, where the number had been 18,501 in 1890, it was 14,458 in 1905, and 13,102 in 1908. Their significance was even more remarkable, considering that its population had increased from 1,140,405 in 1890 to 1,258,140 in 1908. Again, comparing Victoria and New South Wales in 1908 for offenses against person, property, and drunkenness per 10,000 population, it was 141; 308; 1,036 respectively for Victoria against 229; 427; 1,766 respectively for New South Wales, another feather in the cap of Victoria.[84]

Secularists had their own set of statistics to counter the denominationalist indictment of the French crime record. It was only in 1886, pointed out a study of the Secular Education League, that religious instruction ceased in the newly-established State schools. Furthermore, the change to a completely national system was gradual and many private schools continued in existence.‡ But even at that some facts did place secularism in a favorable light, considering that the population of France was 38,517,975 in 1896 and 39,252,245 in 1906. The Secular Education League regarded prison records as a more serious barometer of morality than criminal records (which the sectarians used) because increased police activity and new laws made difficult a common denominator in criminal records over the years. In terms of the number of persons received in prison establishments, the annual average for 1897-1901 was 406,000 whereas for 1902-06 it had gone down to 368,000. In terms of the aggregate number of days of confinement, the annual average for 1897-1901 was 11,775,000 whereas for 1902-06 it had gone down to 9,106,000.[85] McCabe referred to the figures of Alfred Jules Fouillée, French sociologist, that between 1826 and 1880 the criminality of boys had quadrupled and that of girls had tripled. But from 1896 to 1901, McCabe found that the number of boys in reformatories had lowered from 5,023 to 3,528 and the number of girls from 1,095 to 690.[86] How, then, could it be maintained that secular education in France had led to an increase in crime? Rather, the "Godless" Third French Republic had taken over a heritage of delinquency, especially in juvenile ranks, and had done its job well.[87]

Secularist literature was prolific on the content of non-theological material to develop sounder moral values. One category of outpouring related to an outlined course of study as it would proceed from standard to standard according to the capacity of children.[88] A favored schematic approach was to develop such admirable traits as kindliness, truth, and restraint—from personal virtues into civic attributes. Another way to phrase the charted course was from self-mastery for the individual to a like achievement for a nation. In the early standards, precepts and exhortation were best, drawing the examples from nature, history, and the social environment. Herbert M. Thompson liked the moral tales to be found in Charlotte Yonge's Book of Golden Deeds of All Times and All Lands (1866), typifying true ideals of bravery, manliness, and fortitude. Both biblical and secular stories are included, for example, David and the Cup of Water, Leonidas and the Pass of Thermopylae, and The Last Fight in the Colisseum. In the middle standards, when explanations were possible, the broader issues attached to concepts of brotherhood, justice, and respect could be discussed.* In the later standards,

---

‡ In 1911 there were 4,592,634 in public primary schools and 1,062,160 in private primary schools. Hayes (1930), p. 37.

* Arnold Smith, M.A., and assistant lecturer in English Language and Literature at the University College of South Wales and Monmouthshire, Cardiff, recounted as an instance of promoting respect the story of an old man who substituted for the regular

when children had matured and were ready to examine topics like patriotism and the power of self-knowledge in terms of comparative advantage and disadvantage and of relative right and wrong, the multiple implications could be more fully explored.[89]

A second category of material related to the exploitation of the secular subjects for moral ends. Lady Agnes Grove, active in the suffragist and anti-vivisectionist movements, would invest geography with a living interest by the introduction of the ethical element. The earth's inhabitants and the impact of different habits and customs could be translated into a session on human understanding. The contributions of the different countries toward the daily needs of life could be a constant reminder of the unity of the world and the shortsightedness of international jealousies. Citizenship could be made a dramatic and exciting odyssey. The idea of freedom could call up the glories of Thermopylae and Marathon, the resistance of the Dutch Republic, and the heroics of the American Independence War. All embraced the record of man's march from slavery and serfdom to emancipation. Gould saw in the biographies of national heroes the opportunity for setting noble patterns. Alfred, Wyclif, Elizabeth, Cromwell, Cook, and Gladstone were idealized by the schoolboy.† Literature could murmur the message of the beauty and revelation of the world through the voices of Chaucer, Shakespeare,‡ Milton, Wordsworth, Byron, Burns, Tennyson, and Scott. The arts could nourish the youthful soul by the vision of the domes and towers of Wren, the grace of Flaxman's marble, and the rich hues of a Gainsborough, a Reynolds, or a Turner canvas.[90]

---

porter one morning to take the names of absentees. A few boys smiled and one laughed at the obvious nervousness of the old man in appearing in the classroom. The teacher waited quietly until he had left and then told without comment the story of the Spartan envoys who, in the crowded theater at Athens, rose from their seats of honor to make room for an old man who was seeking a place. Thereupon the Athenians all stood up and applauded the action. It was an appeal to the imagination and showed how an ethical influence could be exerted by drawing upon the pages of history. *Westminster Rev.*, Aug. 1906, pp. 148-49.

† Conversely, John S. Mackenzie, professor of Logic and Philosophy, University College of South Wales and Monmouthshire, Cardiff, and active in the Ethical movement, believed human weaknesses could occasionally be an asset to the teacher of morals. The ill-temper of Milton, the arrogance of Johnson, and the waywardness of Ruskin could serve to enhance their beneficent influence by acknowledging their imperfections and so reduce suspicion of more to conceal. *International Journal of Ethics*, July 1909, p. 407.

‡ Picton was especially enamored of the many gems of moral truth in Shakespeare. He cited such sayings as "the quality of mercy" (*Merchant of Venice*), "truth hath a quiet breast" (*King Richard the Second*), "love's best habit is a soothing tongue" (*The Passionate Pilgrim*), and "never anything can be amiss when simpleness and duty tender it" (*A Midsummer-Night's Dream*). *The Bible in School* (1907), p. 49.

A third category of material related to the importance of finding a rational basis of sanction for personal conduct. Agnostics and Freethinkers in a joint declaration resolved that the case for virtue was in the altruistic motive of human compassion, together with the egoistic motives of self-respect, the approbation of fellow-citizens, and the happiness of a well-ordered life. Charles Watts, for many years secretary of the National Secular Society, set forth several examples. The case for honesty rested in the fact that stealing was an infringement upon the rights of others. The case for honor due parents was not because children might live long under their doting care but for the reason that children were indebted to their parents for life and training. Drunkenness should be condemned because it brought ill-health to the drunkard, misery to his family, and disaster to the nation and posterity. The emphasis upon the penal consequences of crime should have no place in moral education and the law should only be explained as a regrettable necessity which more abiding restraint might tend to remove. MacDonald liked the suggestion of one of His Majesty's Inspectors for the western division of Scotland to combat crime. A direct and concise treatment of moral problems should be essayed by the headmaster. After they left school, many pupils came into collision with the law through sheer ignorance of the pitfalls that beset their path. A frank discussion of the actual temptations confronting the pupil when he was sent forth to fend for himself would, therefore, answer the purpose better.[91]

Secularists engaged in a lively debate whether non-theological moral instruction should be given as formal lessons at set hours. Sir William J. Collins, Liberal M.P., argued that unless made definite and systematic it would be nobody's duty. To make moral instruction incidental and dependent upon the teacher being alert to exploit casual occasions would put an end to it. Direct and separate lessons enabled the teacher out of the fullness of his ethical sense to communicate appropriate notions and sentiments. George P. Gooch, Liberal M.P. and historian, wanted it to be set for the first hour of the day as was the case with the religious lesson. Perhaps the most doctrinaire on the subject was Dr. Stanton Coit, leader of the West London Ethical Society, who insisted that instruction in righteousness must bear the stamp of formal religious lessons. Unless declared a supremely sacred study, it would fail to impart the inwardness which was the essence of true character. Furthermore, there was the grave danger of exposing ethical literature to become the mere teaching of outward rules of conduct, to be enforced by so-called shifting social sanctions. Dr. Coit would begin the daily lesson with some great "Words of Life" which committed the spirit to the higher sphere and prepared the soul to meet its destiny with valor. Then, he would use as an equivalent to a hymn either the Marseillaise tone of "England arise! The long, long night is over,"[92] by Edward Carpenter, writer and socialist, or that wonderful message of hope "Each eve earth falleth down the dark, . . . Behind tomorrow's door,"[93] by William Morris, poet, artist, and socialist. Finally, the content proper of the moral lesson would be given.* Only a religion could replace a religion and that of a secularist must be Moral Idealism.[94]

Some secularists were afraid that a formal methodology would produce moral lessons as dry a mental pabulum for youth as a catechism or collects. Rev. E. G. Maxted, Vicar of Tilty, Essex, writing in *Justice*, felt that moral training should be given as the chance arose throughout the day and so assimilate itself into the atmosphere of the school. He objected especially to any substitution of a non-theological moral lesson as inviting an outcry for equal facilities from religious bodies. The *Ethical World* advised against investing moral instruction as a premier subject with a spiritual basis and so bringing it into rivalry with the orthodoxies. Furthermore, teachers were not qualified in the mass to handle it with such skill or conviction as would justify its classification as "religious" in the highest sense of the term. James Oliphant, M.A., examiner for the University of London, warned that the lesson would be task work and wind up as something to be forced upon pupils. The sympathies of children were better enlisted when they were taken unawares. In a region of perception where it was of great moment that everything should be spontaneous, a formal presentation would breed distrust and introduce a note of constraint.[95]

Secularists pressed actively the use of their scheme in schools. The Moral Instruction League had been formed in 1897 to promote the idea of systematic non-theological moral lessons.[96] Gould, whose career became identified with this body as a lecturer and demonstrator after his severance with the London school board system, participated in drawing up a comprehensive syllabus. One of the earliest adoptions took place in Leicester, largely the result of the presence there of Gould who had taken service with the National Secular Society, succeeding McCabe in 1899 and staying until 1908. Gould had won a seat on the Leicester School Board, polling second place among the fifteen members returned, by making moral instruction his chief plank. Subse-

---

* Gould felt that textbooks should be used only by the teacher in the preparation of the lessons and not by the children. The ethical instruction should proceed through the living and impromptu voice and not degenerate into a reading exercise, and any examination on it was to be regarded as educational folly and an outrage. *Literary Guide and Rationalist Rev.*, Aug. 1, 1906.

quently, in 1906, the movement received a stimulus when the Board of Education was persuaded in its code to approve moral instruction as part of the curriculum, either incidentally or formally. However, it might be noted that the exultation was short-lived for many secularists when the London County Council ruled out systematic moral instruction altogether and decreed that only incidental moral teaching would be allowed.[97]

Harrold Johnson, the secretary of the Moral Instruction League, recorded, nevertheless, encouraging results by 1908, noting that 100 of the 133 local authorities had returned positive replies to his inquiry as to what definite action had been taken to provide such instruction. He counted 40 local authorities who had set time apart and 50 who had a syllabus connected with it. In particular, there was the welcome fact that 20 local authorities, including Bucks, Cheshire, Devonshire, Surrey, and West Riding, had accepted the official syllabus.† A similar campaign was waged to have training colleges incorporate systematic non-theological moral instruction in their curriculum. Gooch made this provision part of his motion in the commons on March 16, 1909, when he was seeking its authorization in the elementary schools.[98]

Secularists were enthusiastic over the progress being made in moral instruction elsewhere in the world. In America, the Ethical Culture schools were pioneers. In Australasia, many states provided for set lessons. In Canada, the province of Nova Scotia and the Northwest Territory had entered the field. In Japan, ethical lessons had been adopted after the political upheaval of 1868. In France, if Johnson thought that the results had not been too auspicious, the answer rested partly in undue emphasis on moral education instead of moral training and partly in the adverse external influences of a licentious press and an increasing alcoholism (which the French Government did its best to encourage). But over-all the outlook was bright for the ultimate ascendancy of non-theological moral instruction wherever a progressive civilization prevailed.[99]

Some would still find a place for the Bible in moral instruction. The *Ethical World* declared that there was no need to allow any appearance of boycotting it. The Bible could be employed alongside other great humanistic literature but, as Dr. Clifford would say, "exclusively of an

---

† The Moral Instruction League suffered serious setbacks before long. The first was the changing of its title in 1909 to Moral Education League, which many of its members disliked as implying a more confining task and therefore they left the movement. The second was the resignation in 1913 of Harrold Johnson as secretary and his resumption of his earlier career as a Unitarian minister. He became pastor at Evesham, Worcestershire. Spiller, *The Ethical Movement in Great Britain* (1934), pp. 153-55.

ethical, historical, and literary character." It ought not to be difficult to make moral training in its illustrations so scriptural as to satisfy the wishes of parents desiring their children to be acquainted with the Bible. Mrs. Hypatia Bradlaugh Bonner, writer and lecturer on ethical subjects and daughter of the freethinker Charles Bradlaugh, pointed out its value for folklore study. Through the Bible children could learn much of the primitive thought the world over and the essential brotherhood of the human race. Excellent examples of its hortatory value were the stories of Jonah and the whale, the widow who succored Elijah with a handful of meal and a little oil, and Samson with his strength in his locks. The parable of the Good Samaritan was an admirable model for conveying the story of "who is my neighbor." Gould was firmly convinced that given time and purposefulness the extreme narrowness of the Protestant interpretation would gradually be relaxed and the Bible would find its natural place in the moral instruction of the schools.[100]

But many secularists remained adamant against any use of the Bible for moral instruction for the simple reason that they did not believe it could be taught in a totally mundane sense. Gilbert K. Chesterton, well-known journalist and author, argued that to the orthodox man, for example, Isaiah meant first and foremost the prophecy of a world-shattering event. Spiller felt that any lesson including the Bible would take in too much scope—belief in a deity, a heaven, a hell, the fall of man, and miracles. By the time the classroom discussion had run its course the original quest for moral lessons would have been forgotten. Ethical issues of necessity would tend to become incidental or to be shunted to the side, otherwise the Bible was being worshipped without being proclaimed. To Walter J. Baylis, M.A., who described his career as being identified with schoolboys, the psychology of youth would make shambles of any moral lesson which allied itself with the saintly figures enshrined in the Bible. As a rule a schoolmaster who wished to reprove a boy for misconduct did so by pointing out that it was beneath the standard of conduct expected from a young gentleman. He would not dream of saying how different would have been the behavior of Jesus, for to do so would create an opposite effect. To tell boys that they should follow Jesus as a model was like telling them during a painting lesson that they should try to paint like Michelangelo. It was better to set them an easier model in ethics, perhaps the Satires of Horace, no less than in painting. The youth of England were really more akin to the hardy Romans for whom Horace wrote than like the ascetic Christian saints.[101]

PART III

SEARCH FOR A CONCORDAT

CHAPTER SEVEN

UNIVERSAL FACILITIES

ANGLICAN PROPONENTS

F ROM 1902 UNTIL 1906, as the battle raged over the Act of 1902, many Anglicans were troubled that the net result might be the triumph of secularism. The *Saturday Review* feared that a sickened public might decide to exclude religious instruction entirely from the schools. Then, indeed, the future of England as a Christian nation would be in jeopardy. For the spiritual well-being of the people a concordat was imperative. A favorite thought was to accept a national school system, with facilities for denominational instruction in all schools. The dual system had been maintained at the cost of a mischievous awakening of religious bitterness. Here was a chance to foster a better spirit between Nonconformist and Anglican. Peace and goodwill among Christians were assuredly treasured prizes. The *Pilot* declared it was for Churchmen to make up their minds what was the most that could be expected from a country where nearly half the active religious life was alienated from the Established Church and in which all the religious bodies together formed but a diminishing minority of the population. Out of a population of 32,526,075, religious membership for England and Wales in 1901 included: Church of England, 2,004,493; Dissenting bodies, 1,946,951; Roman Catholic, 1,500,000.[1]

Self-interest also dictated this solution. Each year an increasingly larger number of Anglican children attended board schools. The *Pilot* recited that for 1902 in average school attendance there were 2,327,946 pupils (correctly, 2,545,437) in voluntary and 2,796,000 (2,369,980) in board schools.[2] In London, for the year ending March 25, 1903, accommodations were available for 572,649 children in board and 217,088 in voluntary schools.[3] The ability to build new voluntary schools and to keep existing ones in repair would not be easy, since subscriptions would go down as school rates went up. Was it not a matter of paramount concern, asked the *Saturday Review*, to contemplate hundreds of thousands of Church children left wholly to the mercy of Cowper-

Templeism, a teaching hostile to positive Christianity? It was for the Church of England to follow its children into the council schools and instruct them in Anglican tenets.[4]

There was the question of whether the importance of religious atmosphere was not unduly exaggerated. Was it likely that the denominational spirit could survive in the voluntary school now that two non-foundation managers would be present at board meetings? The *Pilot* believed that foundation managers would instinctively seek to mollify the local authority representatives by watering down the catechetical element in the credal lesson. Churchmen were often to be encountered defending themselves against accusations of proselytizing with the response that there was nothing in the religious lesson to which Nonconformists could object.* More than this, the desire to assure Anglican children an equal opportunity to win scholarships would invite the temptation to take for granted the spiritual fervor of a teaching applicant in the search for a competent instructor in the secular subjects. Was it worthwhile to keep schools of which it could be said that the teachers did not any more possess an ardent zeal to impart the true faith?[5]

A special plea was made to the Anglican clergy to heed the gravity of the situation. The Kenyon-Slaney amendment would work henceforth against their role in Church schools. They should be aware that the alteration of a few words in the management clause could turn the one-third public representatives into a majority. Were they prepared to risk the formal enthronement of Cowper-Templeism in voluntary schools with no guarantee anywhere thereafter of denominational instruction? If the clergy would but agree to the transfer of Church schools, the precious freedom to give definite religious instruction in every school in the kingdom might be obtained. The *Saturday Review* asked "how can bishops and clergy be satisfied to have vast numbers of Church children in schools where no religious teaching is given in the principles of the Church of England? [Are] they not as important as to retain the small remnant left to Church control?" True, agreed the *Pilot*, it would require time on the part of the clergy to follow their

---

* That this practice was not rare might be guessed from a speech by Helena Powell, principal of the Cambridge Training College, before a gathering of Diocesan Church School managers and teachers of the Cambridge district. Miss Powell warned against those who, in their desire to be fair to children of Dissenters, forgot their duty to Church children and mutilated the catechism by cutting it short at the end of the "desire" and left off the sacramental portion. To teach the duty without showing the means of grace was to lay a yoke upon their necks. It deprived Church children of that which they had a right to expect. Better it would be to excuse Nonconformist children from the Prayer Book lessons. Powell (1905), pp. 6-7.

children into council schools. But that would be a much worthier occupation than attendance at cricket clubs or bazaars. Anglican clergy should take to heart the words of the great nineteenth century Congregational minister (and secularist), Dr. Robert Dale: [6]

> When a great moral duty incumbent on all men was recognized by the Church she had no choice but to discharge it by herself. . . . Thus the Church had created hospitals and had taught Europe to care for the sick, but when the lesson was learnt the Church had ceased to maintain hospitals of her own and had left their support and management to society at large. The Church had established schools for secular as well as for religious instruction but when the nation had learnt to care for education, secular teaching might be left to the care of the nation and the Church would then be free to deal with the religious instruction of the people. [7]

After 1906 the presence of a Liberal Government pledged to remove Nonconformist grievances spurred on to greater efforts Anglican advocates of universal facilities. On the occasion of the Birrell Bill, they lent support to Chamberlain's amendment to substitute the right of entry for the Cowper-Temple clause as the operating principle for religious instruction in all schools. [8] In 1908, when the McKenna and Runciman Bills were being debated, they urged that the proposal for facilities in transferred schools be broadened to apply to all schools. Subsequently, the fact that Church schools continued to lose ground provided the impetus for agitation. Between 1902 and 1911, noted J. H. Seaborne, who described himself as a Church school teacher, the loss was about 400 Church schools (correctly, from 11,711 in 1902 to 10,952 in 1911). [9] Lathbury renewed the appeal to the clergy to support universal facilities as the only real form of neutrality to carry out effectively the twin principles of parental right and religious equality:

> The clergy will never brace themselves to play their proper part in the teaching of religion, . . . will never develop the immense mass of voluntary agents who are only asking to be made useful, will never divert the funds that have hitherto gone to the support of Church schools to the payment of religious teachers where volunteers are not to be had until they are forced to do these things by the impossibility of employing secular teachers. . . . [10]

Anglican literature was prolific on details of a satisfactory scheme of universal facilities. [11] A composite picture of the highlights should serve the purpose. The transfer of voluntary schools must be at a fair rent.

The Cowper-Temple clause should be repealed in council schools, with right of entry to prevail in all schools, the cost to be borne by the denominations. Stress was placed upon facilities being given in the schoolrooms during the regular hours as established by the marking of the attendance book. A creed register was favored to determine the wishes of parents, perhaps indicated by a written note handed the teacher on the opening day. Only a few, like Rev. MacColl, were prepared to think in terms of an exclusively outside staff paid from the rent income of Church school buildings. The advantage would be sincere teachers, trained specifically for the responsibility. The greater number, however, demanded that the regular teaching staff should be eligible to volunteer. Canon Henson pointed out the disparity between the available 15,000 clergymen and the schools' teaching staff of 153,492.[12] At any rate, the number of amateurs ought to be kept at a minimum, lacking as they did both the pedagogical and the disciplinary ability of the professional instructor.[13]

Reference was made to practical instances at home with schemes of universal facilities. The *National Review* called attention to the fact that the State applied the principle in the case of the army, navy, poor law schools, and prisons, clergymen being assigned to administer to members of their own faith. It was just as right for a child to be given definite religious instruction if his father were living as for a child sent to a poor law school upon the death of his father to be taught the parental faith at the expense of the State. Surely the contingency should not be that a parent must die or a child commit a crime to obtain this inalienable right. The industrial day school was singled out as pertinent to a scheme of universal facilities. The principle of the right of entry was applied in connection with the religious instruction, clergymen coming in to attend to the needs of children of their own faith. The *Saturday Review* dwelt at length upon the Drury-lane Day Industrial School, set up in 1895 by the London School Board, as a working model.[14] Some 120 boys and girls attended, the religious incidence being 80 Anglicans, 30 Roman Catholics, a few Wesleyans, and one Jewish child. Here, then, was a creed register in operation and a recognition of the right of parents.[15]

Abroad, the essence of universal facilities was found to exist in many places.† In Germany, the mixed school (*simultanschule*) of Prussia served as a prototype.[16] True, granted the *Saturday Review*, it did represent an extreme form with the State holding initiative and responsibility

---

† Currently, in America, the practice in many schools to give religious instruction in the form of dismissed and released time approximates the idea of facilities. Johnson and Yost (1948), pp. 74-90.

for the religious instruction. But a Board of Education Report attested to its practicality, commenting on one district "that under one roof and in the same block, with separate teachers and textbooks, were two complete and independent schools, one a seven-class Protestant and the other a fourteen-class Catholic school, living in peace and concord with one another."[17] Rev. Cleworth praised especially the requirement that teachers must be appointed with religious affiliations in the same proportion as the faiths of the children in the school.[18]

Two Australian states were identified as successful examples in the use of facilities.[19] Cyril Jackson, chairman of the London County Council Education Committee and once head of the Education Department of Western Australia, described the plan in vogue there. The religious instruction was given during school for three half-hours a week. When children were enrolled, the parents were invited to declare their denomination and classes were arranged on the basis of this creed register. If the lay or clerical instructor recruited was inexperienced, the State school teacher stayed in the classroom to keep order. W. A. J. Wells, Dawlish, Devonshire, referred to New South Wales where the schools were open to clergy of all denominations twice a week in the ordinary school hours. Even in the secular states of Queensland and Victoria at least the husk of the scheme was present in the right of entry once a week after school hours by clergy or their representatives.[20]

If a choice were possible, many Anglicans preferred the implementation of universal facilities through the dual system. There was no reason to go out of the way to lose the rich spiritual values of the voluntary school because minorities might chance to attend them. In parliament, the most ardent exponent was Lord Hugh Cecil, even to the extent of offering the scheme as an amendment to the Balfour Bill.[21] The basic premise was the right of parents to have their children taught their beliefs. The Cowper-Temple clause should be repealed and the right of entry allowed in council schools. Conversely, the voluntary schools would offer facilities to Nonconformists for the religious instruction of their children.‡ From the vantage point of proselytism, wrote the *Church Quarterly Review*, Nonconformist parents should prefer this settlement to reliance upon a conscience clause, a sort of negative justice implying "that we do not mind if our children are brought up without knowledge of religion provided that they do not learn what we

---

‡ References were made frequently to the scheme which figured in Clause 27 of the ill-fated Gorst Bill of 1896, proposing that every school should be open on reasonable demand to external teachers of every denomination for credal lessons different from those regularly featured in a particular school. See *Commons*, May 5, 1902, p. 748 (A. Lyttelton). For the provisions of the Gorst Bill see *Parl. Papers*, 1896, I, Bill 172, p. 14.

think wrong." In all schools the religious instruction would be in school hours and the regular staff would be allowed to volunteer. Archbishop Davidson favored appointing Nonconformists as assistant teachers in Church schools and hoped in turn that council schools would let their staffs express preferences as to which type of religious lesson they wanted to give.[22]

The years between 1906 and 1908 offered unparalleled opportunities to lay the foundations for the right of entry under a dual system. Both the Birrell Bill with its extended facilities in Clause 4 schools and the McKenna and Runciman Bills with their contracting-out provisions required only further elaboration to fit into a dual system plan. In the urban centers, observed Rev. Clement F. Rogers, there could be separate schools for Anglicans, Roman Catholics, Free Churchmen, and Jews as well as council schools. In single school areas, where usually only two religions needed to be considered, the school could provide instruction for each. The head teacher would be of the faith of the majority and the assistant teacher of the minority. Rev. W. H. Hornby Steer, Lambeth, St. Philip's, pointed out that such an arrangement was already legally possible in voluntary schools by the Act of 1902. Let every teacher say in which type of school he would like to serve and then assign him accordingly. This would get rid of the difficulty of religious tests. Each set of schools could correct any theological overdoses or dilutions and the result would be better religious teaching all around.[23]

As a means of bringing their scheme before the public more forcibly, a Parents' League was founded in December 1907, approved by the National Society but distinct from it in the hope of attracting Nonconformists as well as Anglicans. The nation must be made aware of the parental right to have a child educated in his faith. Lord James Edward Hubert Gascoyne-Cecil, eldest son of the third Marquess of Salisbury, who succeeded to the title in 1903 as the fourth Marquess, was named president. Both archbishops and many bishops signified their support of the campaign. An organized effort was made to establish chapters in parishes throughout the land. By June 1909, the National Society reported that branches were functioning in 2,200 parishes with 150,000 members, of whom 7,500 were Nonconformists. Demonstrations were held, the first in London being recorded on July 13, 1908, at which the Marquess of Salisbury presided and Arthur Balfour spoke.[24]

A series of leaflets was issued, stating the case for parental rights as a feasible scheme. It was argued that in most villages not more than two kinds of religious teaching would be needed—church and chapel—and most of the schools contained two classrooms and two teachers. Several

Church schools were cited as already providing both facilities and an assistant teacher of Nonconformist faith: Oakham Church School, Rutland; Orsett Church School, Essex; Martock and Bower Hinton Church Schools, Somerset; St. Nicholas Girls School, Lincoln. Indeed, often as not, the minority were apt to be all Wesleyan or all Congregational, so they could even have their own credal lessons in place of undenominationalism. Where classrooms were lacking or the desire was to exploit the convenient presence of a church, opportunity for withdrawal should be possible just as was the case for swimming, cookery, and laundry. In towns there could be a choice of schools and facilities would not be necessary, for each school would boast a student body homogeneous in its faith.[25]

Rev. John H. Thorpe, Vicar of St. George's, Stockport, Cheshire, answered those who objected to parental rights on the twin grounds of its unmanageableness and the danger of religious tests being riveted upon the teachers. As he examined the first objection, the supposed multiplicity of sects producing pandemonium, the theory outran the reality of things. Most of these fringe creeds, Moravians, Mormons, Moslems, Irvingites, Plymouth Brethren, Quakers, and the like, could claim comparatively few adherents and in many districts none at all and should be ignored. These sects would have to console themselves with Birrell's comment that minorities must suffer and should seek to avoid it by uniting.* Many of the respectably-attended creeds did not differ about doctrinal beliefs and could be treated as one, like the Methodist bodies. As he examined the second objection, his answer was that schools existed for the education of children and not to provide persons with teaching situations. While he would not defend the ancient imposition of religious tests to qualify for a purely secular occupation, the analogy was not the same for teachers in elementary schools. They were not civil servants of the Imperial Government but employees of local authorities. Even if they could be designated as civil servants, it was part of a universal procedure to make inquiries as to fitness to fulfill all the duties of a position. Not to do so was to abdicate control of religious teaching to the staff and the result would be to place religion in a position of contempt and expose children to a bewildering assortment of interpretations as they passed from standard to standard. Religious instruction to be effective should be constant and continuous and in

---

* Reference is made to Birrell's introductory speech in connection with his Education Bill in 1906. In discussing the inability of the conscience clause to meet every case, Birrell stated that "all minorities must suffer. It is the badge of their tribe." At the same time Birrell hastened to add that he hoped the enlightened policy of the Liberal Party would avoid unnecessary hardships. *Commons,* April 9, 1906, p. 1033.

harmony with that which a child received in the home. Absence of religious tests, he declared, was a cry for secularism in disguise and a denial of parents' rights.[26]

From 1909 on, Anglican literature suggested a determination to fight for facilities only within the framework of a dual system. The concordat must be a reciprocal grant of the right of entry, embracing the repeal of the Cowper-Temple clause, a creed register in all schools, and the appointment of teachers in proportion to the children's faiths. G. Lawder-Eaton, successor to Rev. Cleworth after the latter's death in April 1909 as secretary of the Church Schools' Emergency League, stated that if Nonconformists could complain of 5,704 Church schools in single school areas, Anglicans could do likewise in the case of 1,996 council schools.[27] More than this, it was reiterated that the dual system constituted a guarantee of religious instruction in all schools. Samuel J. G. Hoare, Conservative M.P., member of the London County Council, and Anglican layman, pounded away at the theme that if Church schools were abandoned, then the religious instruction in the State schools would be at the mercy of a future secularist or anti-Christian government as France had found out to her disillusionment.[28]

The thought was frequently voiced that the Church of England should make the first gesture toward entry all around. Even as the Balfour Bill of 1902 was going through the legislative mill, Bishop Ingram of London urged that facilities in Church schools be offered Nonconformist parents. Attention was called repeatedly to the resolution passed at the Convocation in 1901 to that effect.[29] Many an editorial and pastoral sermon discussed the desirability of Church schools opening up assistant teacherships to Nonconformist candidates and establishing a concurrent class in Cowper-Templeism. In single school areas particularly, the foundation managers ought to ask every parent his creed to facilitate the scriptural alternative to the catechism. It would have the merit of eliminating the supreme grievance of proselytism complained of by Nonconformists in rural areas and show that Anglicans intended to be fair.† Rev. Joseph Nunn, Upton House, Ardwick and a past chairman of the Manchester School Board, discerned a cor-

---

† Rev. Arthur C. Headlam, principal, King's College, London, pointed out the fallacy in the reasoning of some that facilities were not really needed since most Church schools gave Bible instruction four days a week and devoted only one day to the catechism and the Prayer Book and a withdrawal on the fifth day should dissolve the Nonconformist grievance. The Bible teaching for four days was not the undenominationalism of the council school and a Nonconformist parent could protest quite rightfully the number of places where distinctive religious teaching entered into the Bible lessons in a Church school. A. C. Headlam (1903), p. 26.

ollary advantage for Anglicans in that credal lessons could be taught more freely and fully when Nonconformist children were not present. Welcome, then, were the resolutions of the National Society in 1912 urging foundation managers to offer minorities their kinds of religious teaching and of the Canterbury House of Laymen in 1913 reaffirming the right of entry as a just policy.[30] Whether or not these generous terms would invite reciprocal concessions in council schools should not be calculated. The course advocated was honest and it was not for the Established Church to wait until others were ready to follow the Golden Rule.[31]

The suggestion was weighed that the Nonconformist conscience might be squared with the dual system if the individual ratepayer were allowed to determine what school should receive his rate. Bishop Ridgeway of Chichester saw special merit in it for the single school area. Parents earmarking their rates would have the right to a teacher on the staff qualified to give instruction in their faith or, failing that, to nominate a suitable person and have the cost borne by their payments. One J. S. Redmayne favored the broader form in which it was applied in parts of Canada toward the support of specific schools.[32] In Quebec, Roman Catholics and Protestants had separate schools and the Department of Public Instruction was assisted by two committees: a Roman Catholic committee including archbishops, bishops, and laymen; and a Protestant committee of laymen. At the school level, committees of similar denominational nature supervised the schools. These committees participated in decisions on organization, textbooks, teacher appointments, and inspection. In Ontario, a public school system prevailed featuring Bible lessons from which Roman Catholic children were exempt. Where Roman Catholic numbers warranted it, they were allowed separate schools. Both in Quebec and Ontario, the parents earmarked their rates, making up any deficit by personal assessments.[33]

On the other hand, some questioned whether earmarking would be practical and, even if it were, whether the sums would be sufficient to meet the wishes of all parents for definite religious instruction. As Sir Theodore C. Hope, Indian civil servant and member of both the Canterbury House of Laymen and the Representative Church Council, studied the proposition, the task would be formidable in the categories of compound tenants, "inclusive" tenants, and lodgers. To serve declaration blanks on these occupiers and fix even approximate rates in each case would be difficult, for rents varied from week to week and tenants came and went. It was problematical if the blanks would ever reach the addresses and if they did whether many would be filled out and returned. Furthermore, annual allocations could not be made up to the minute and from a triennial or quinquennial entry system no reliable poll of parental desires was likely to be obtained. Again, as in London, some 44% of rateable properties were in the value of £20 and under with the rates paid on them only 10% of the whole tax roll. Hence, in school rate allocation, their weight would be low compared to that of the owners of commercial properties, even though their claim numerically might be heavier. In addition, the wealthier classes paying higher rates for their more resplendent residences would wield great influence, even though they made little use of the nation's elementary schools. Earmarking could be no standard at all in relation to parental rights.‡ There were many consciences which would not be on the rate rolls.[34]

Advocates of facilities under a dual system, no less than those under a national system, claimed as successful experiments the several instances to be encountered at home. Rev. William Gascoyne-Cecil, second son of the late third Marquess of Salisbury and Rector of Bishops, Hatfield, Hertfordshire where the Salisbury estate was located, averred that no one would dream of compelling men in the armed forces "to attend a State-created device." The military took care to assign chaplains for the various faiths. Rev. Philip Vernon Smith, Chancellor of the Diocese of Manchester and Durham and a writer on church law, pointed out that criminals and paupers received their own religious rites in prisons and workhouses. A Parents' League leaflet, printed in 1909, noted public acknowledgment of parental rights in reformatories and industrial residential and day schools, with the single exception of decent parents of well-mannered children whose natural desire for denominational instruction was ignored. Athelstan Riley discussed the Drury-lane Day Industrial School, established in 1894 by the London School Board when he was chairman.[35] Since the school was under the Industrial Schools Act of 1876, no Cowper-Temple clause was required and so credal lessons could be given. He was high in his praise of the results, listing four participants—Anglican, Roman Catholic, Free Churchman, Jew. The children were divided into their "religious persuasions" and received instruction from teachers appointed as being properly qualified in the opinion of the local ministers of religion. How-

---

‡ In 1902, on the eve of the Balfour Bill and at the insistence of Joseph Chamberlain who wondered if an allocation scheme might not avoid the pitfall of passive resistance if voluntary schools were put on the rates, Morant requested the Local Taxation Commission for an opinion on earmarking. The reply was submitted by T. Llewelyn Davies, assistant secretary, dated February 11, 1902. Davies was pessimistic of its feasibleness and believed that the difficulties were underestimated. In general, his objections paralleled those of Sir Theodore Hope. *Ministry of Education*, 1902, Bill Papers, No. 174.

ever, Riley added, in most voluntary schools the right of entry would be needed for only one minority.[36]

In Scotland and Ireland, the essential feature of the dual system stressing the denominational basis of schools could also be recorded. Talbot Baines, successor to Rev. J. S. Brownrigg as secretary of the National Society, commended the application of parental rights in Scotland through the complete freedom given the elected school board to determine the religious instruction.[37] If almost all board schools taught the Shorter Catechism and radiated a Presbyterian atmosphere, remarked Sir Charles Elliott, member of the London County Council Education Committee and Anglican layman, no one seemed to be outraged by that fact. Further, where there was a majority of Episcopalians or Roman Catholics, the school board would have their special doctrines taught at public expense. In Ireland, denominational schools in the nature of the religious instruction taught plus teachers of the requisite faith preponderated and every penny was paid out of taxes.* Butcher listed 6,671 out of the 8,500 Irish national schools as autonomous in their religious instruction. In the remaining 1,829 mixed schools a right of entry was provided.[38] It was not a matter of bargaining; the religious instruction desired by parents was accorded. The teachers could give it or some one, cleric or layman, could be brought in from the outside. But the facilities were regarded as a second best expedient, useful as a supplementary arrangement to meet unusual difficulties or to satisfy theoretical grievances. The national school with an autonomous religious status was the more highly esteemed as security for a sound Christian foundation.[39]

Even more applicable to the essence of a dual system was the scheme in Prussia. There the State endowed all forms of religion. Where children of any one faith were present in sufficient numbers, a school was provided including teachers of that faith. The religious character of a school was normally determined by the profession of the majority of the local population as established by the census. In the event, explained the *School Guardian*, that for five successive years two-thirds of the children in a school should be adherents of a different creed, then the teacher must be changed to meet the new religious incidence of the

---

* The Irish school system was planned in the 1830's to be strictly unsectarian. But as it evolved, the clergyman of the parish became the manager of the local school and appointed a teacher of his own faith and in time the schools assumed a rigidly denominational character. Eventually the State acceded to the demand for schools bearing the religious background of its pupils. See Graham Balfour (1903), pp. 109-10; Gwynn (1904), pp. 85-88; *Parl. Papers*, 1897, XXV, Cd. 8447, pp. 222-33.

school. As for children of other faiths who might be admitted to such a "confessional" school, the *Church Quarterly Review* understood that they were not allowed to attend the catechetical lesson. If the minority numbered at least twelve pupils, the State had to supply them with their own religious instruction at public expense. Where there were not enough children to form separate schools, then a mixed school was set up and the children received religious instruction from staff teachers of their own faith. In mixed schools, commented Horsfall, the head-master was chosen from among the members of the church to which the majority of parents belonged and the second teacher represented the religion of the minority.[40] When, however, in mixed schools there were more than sixty children of either faith, the parents could apply to the education authority for a denominational school.† Besides, Prussia recognized the need for careful religious preparation of teachers by fully supporting denominational training colleges.[41]

Elsewhere on the Continent the story was an eventual triumph for a system enthroning the denominationalist ideal. In Switzerland, a referendum in 1882 threw out an attempt to introduce a syllabus of undenominationalism and each canton made its own adjustments.[42] But, remarked Rev. Clement F. Rogers, the Swiss constitution did state in Article 17 that every canton was bound to provide children of any denomination with a teaching not prejudicial to their beliefs and by Article 49 parents had the right to decide in what religion their children should be indoctrinated. Except for Geneva, all cantons had provided definite religious instruction, either facilities or autonomous denominational schools. In Holland, for many years after 1806, wrote the *Pall Mall Gazette*, public support had been confined to schools which were either neutral or undenominational, with clergy (under the Act of 1857) allowed to enter out of school hours.[43] However, the Roman Catholic Church had fought this exclusion and in 1888 the Dutch Government agreed to State aid for all schools. Since then education had prospered and denominational schools had become very popular. In Belgium, reported the *Church Times*, after a period of conflict (over the Act of 1878 which established a secular system with right of entry before or after school hours), an accord was finally arrived at in 1884.[44]

---

† The discussion in this paragraph on Prussia includes the changes made by the Prussian Act of 1906 which strengthened the denominational basis of schools by requiring teacher vacancies to be filled by candidates of the same faith and by making it easier for children to be withdrawn from mixed schools and to have organized for them separate denominational schools. See *Annual Report of the Commissioner of Education* (U.S.), 1906, I, pp. 35-68; Dawson, *The German Empire* (1919), II, pp. 326-27; Fife (1918), pp. 355-56; Helmreich (1959), pp. 62-63.

There were to be two types of schools, one under the local authority with parental choice of religious instruction and the other of denominational character, the costs of both met by the State. In the former, the religious instruction was that of the denomination to which the majority of the pupils belonged. But any minority over twenty in schools with two or more masters could have their spiritual needs met in the school. If the number fell below twenty, then the religious instruction must be held at a place determined by the local minister.[45]

ANGLICAN CRITICS

Opponents of the idea of facilities under either a national or a dual system were many in Anglican ranks. The foremost objection was the problem of assembling a competent staff. In view of the intransigent attitude of Nonconformists and teachers' unions to anything possibly involving religious tests, the use of the regular staff was to be discounted.‡ That meant reliance on outside volunteers and the skill and disciplinary ability of such amateurs was to be doubted. A lesson given to a disorderly class was always repulsive to a well-disposed child. In such hands the outcome could be to associate credal lessons with disagreeable memories in the minds of children. The task of recruiting a staff would be difficult. Where were the thousands of voluntary workers to be found who would be available during school hours? The *Spectator* declared that it would be a heavy chore to maintain a full complement of teachers over a long span of time. It was quite likely that after a couple of years of wearied effort volunteers would tend to shirk their responsibility. Obviously their personal careers would take precedence over any obligation to appear in the schools. This would be especially true of local clergymen who, with their manifold engagements, could hardly be depended upon to discharge the pedagogical function with either punctuality or regularity. Under these contingencies the right of entry would not fulfill the religious aims of the nation's schools.[46]

Still other factors militated against the success of facilities. The apathy or hostility of many parents would nullify the usefulness of a creed register. Many children would get no religious instruction at all because of parents who needed them at home to work. One S. M. B., writing in the *Pilot*, questioned if a half hour of denominational instruc-

---

‡ The most comprehensive professional organization was the National Union of Teachers with a membership of 45,000 in 1902 and 88,000 in 1914. It regarded as the only satisfactory solution a national system based upon popular control and free from all tests but those of character and capacity. See Tropp (1957), p. 106 ff.

tion in a council school would possess any real value, dividing as it must the life of a child into compartments, with most of the time reserved for the lay subjects to the exclusion of the spiritual stream. Furthermore, the division between the spiritual and the secular subjects would be even more sharply drawn if only volunteer teachers could be used. The regular teachers would be discouraged from bringing in the religious element to play upon the moral potential of the secular lessons. Actually the religious beliefs or unbeliefs of the regular teacher must still be reckoned with in the study of history and literature. Lawder-Eaton observed that Anglican, Roman Catholic, and Nonconformist had different viewpoints on the Tudor, Commonwealth, and Stuart periods. The right of entry could not build up a protective shield about the spiritual life of a child buffeted by the random contradictions and the insinuations expressed during the secular work.[47]

The right of entry into voluntary schools was particularly disliked. Rev. Douglas Macleane, Codford, St. Peter Rectory, Wiltshire, declared that to open the doors of the voluntary school to every variety of teacher would encourage instead of check indifferentism. Clergymen were not prepared to "stomach" the specter of Baptists, Ranters, and other schismatics having free entry into their schools. Rev. Curtoys raised the haunting thought that the unity and atmosphere of Church schools would be undermined. He conjured up an unhappy prospect in some rural areas where Nonconformist children might constitute a majority in a Church school. The Nonconformist minister would do his teaching in the main room and Anglican children would have to be shunted to some out-of-the-way place in the school building. The central fact was not so much the dogmatic teaching given two or three times a week as the reverent overtone of the school itself. And in the end, the reciprocal right of entry in council schools could prompt the query of why continue the unnecessary expense of the dual system. It was sounder policy to keep the distinctively Church schools for the two million children of the Anglican faith who sought in them the glorification of God.[48]

Anglican critics had their quiver of practical examples where the right of entry had failed. At home the foremost episode was the substitution in Birmingham (1873-79) of a scheme of facilities for simple Bible lessons.[49] Bishop Knox of Manchester reviewed his experiences as a member of the Birmingham School Board. The use of voluntary teachers in the day schools twice a week could not be depended upon for regular religious instruction. Classes were disrupted and it required all the tact and discretion of head teachers to keep the peace in the face of the rivalry which developed between sects to win children over to their views. J. Allen Bell, formerly chairman of the School Management Committee of the Birmingham School Board, described the chore of full coverage of all children. At best, 22,700 out of 60,000 children received religious lessons and inadequate at that for the ratio of teacher to pupils eventually rose to 1 to 220 for Church children and 1 to 280 for Nonconformist children. Bell too called in as a witness Dr. Robert Dale, referring to his admission that sufficient volunteers could not be recruited.* So the Birmingham School Board was compelled to return to Cowper-Templeism, while a legacy of sectarian animosity among the citizenry of Birmingham plagued the subsequent history of the community.[50]

Anglicans found in the Australian state of Victoria the classic fiasco with facilities.† One F. J. Chandler quoted Bishop Moorhouse of Manchester as recalling that children refused to get up earlier or to stay a half hour later or to give up their playtime.[51] Ministers were irregular in their attendance and the whole system broke down. Most reprehensible to the *Pall Mall Gazette* were the secularizing tendencies which the right of entry outside school hours had promoted during the study of the lay subjects. The Victorian Government had come to read the word "secular" to mean "non-religious" in an extreme sense. An expurgation of the textbooks was undertaken, thereby spinning a tale of literary barbarism without modern parallel. The name of Christ was forbidden in the classroom. Robert Burns' *The Cotter's Saturday Night* was eviscerated to omit such verses as told "how guiltless blood for guilty man was shed." Longfellow's ballad, *The Wreck of the Hesperus*, was attacked because of the verse which told how the maiden "thought of Christ Who Stilled the Waves on the Sea of Galilee." This was secularism gone wild. In the face of public indignation the Victorian Government had later passed a resolution directing that the deleted passages

---

* Dr. Dale, eminent Congregational minister, was a member of the Birmingham School Board from 1870 to 1880. Although an advocate of a secular school system, he went along with the use of the Bible as a great English classic rather than as a supernatural revelation or a divine rule of life. When the School Board accepted the right of entry for denominational instruction in 1873, Dr. Dale joined the Birmingham Religious Education Society to provide for the needs of Nonconformist children. But he found that the clergy remained aloof and that the difficulty of recruiting volunteer teachers mounted as more classes were organized. Alfred W. W. Dale (his son) (1899), pp. 477-82.

† If Lathbury, a proponent of facilities, would agree with critics as to its failure in Australasia, the reasons were the vastness of the area to be covered and the frequent absence of the minister from the school locality as he made the itinerary of his pastorate. Therefore, volunteers could not easily be persuaded to go into the classroom. But in England, a thickly-populated country, the minister was readily at hand. *The Times*, Feb. 13, 1907, 18a-c.

should be restored‡ Canon Henson stamped the entire affair as a dem-
onstration of what grotesque insults to Christian sentiment the notion
of a "neutral state" could invoke under the right of entry.[52]

A similar sad experience with facilities was registered in New Zealand.
Rev. T. Flavell, Plymouth, who had seen service in the province of
Nelson, described the Act of 1877 as permitting ministers to come into
the schools before or after school hours. He recollected how for many
years he stood alone in Christchurch in meeting his youthful charges.
The Nonconformist ministers—Wesleyan, Congregational, Presbyterian—utilized the privilege for a month and then withdrew, never to try
again. Bishop Neligan of Auckland, visiting in England in 1908, estimated that about one-third of the children of school age (50,000 out
of 160,000) received no religious instruction.[53] Unless such a lesson was
a normal part of the school day, "it produces in a child's mind the conviction that God is an extra and not so important as the table of weights
and measures."[54]

For the story in the South African colony of the Transvaal, the
Guardian opened its columns to communications from Rev. J. O. Nash,
an Anglican clergyman in Johannesburg. In 1903 the right of entry was
tried for the first time there. But its shortcomings quickly became evident. Religious friction was engendered among the children. The regular teachers disliked the intrusion of amateurs and the injury to school
discipline. The task of teaching children of all ages together for two
half-hours was hopeless. Ultimately the facilities were replaced in 1907
by regular undenominational lessons for all children.[55] Rev. Nash regarded it as incredible that for a worthless right of entry the Church of
England should dream of surrendering 11,000 schools which educated
half the nation's children.[56]

Disagreement was voiced for the analogy drawn between a dual system integrated with a facilities scheme and the settlement in Prussia.
While it was true that every child received the religious instruction his
parents desired in a Prussian school, Sir John Kennaway, a member of
the Royal Commission on Ecclesiastical Discipline in 1904 and Conservative M.P., argued that the circumstances were different from those
in England. In Prussia the nation was roughly divided into Roman
Catholics and Lutherans, and most districts were one or the other and

---

‡ The *Pall Mall Gazette* obtained its information from a series of articles contributed
to the *London Tribune* by W. H. Fitchett, editor of a popular Australian journal, *Life*.
The several examples cited are to be found in the issue of Feb. 24, 1906. The second
article (Feb. 28, 1906) includes more illustrations of how far the Victorian Minister of
Education went in removing the Christian nexus from the schools.

not scrambled as in England. Rev. Lacey challenged the effectiveness of the religious teaching in either the separate or the mixed schools, controlled as both were "under the heels" of the Minister of Education. This kind of denominationalism supervised by public authorities, even to the extent of actively participating in drawing up the content of the religious lessons, was to be looked on with suspicion. He understood that the result was for Christian doctrine to be taught in the same manner as Greek mythology.[57] The credal lessons were dispensed too much in the nature of task work and lacked spontaneity.* Religion never thrived when it had been made a matter of State patronage.[58]

As Anglican critics of facilities analyzed the future, the battle of the Established Church was yet to be fought against the forces of indifference, vice, and infidelity. The stake was the very existence of revealed religion in the British Isles. The *Western Mail* (Cardiff) believed that the cause of Christianity was especially imperiled in Wales, where only the Church schools were "pledged to keep burning the lamp of religious knowledge." The nation should be made to realize the superior merits of the unshackled voluntary school in the epic crusade ahead. Ven. Robert C. Fletcher, Archdeacon of Blackburn, boasted that the Church schools imparted credal lessons in their most sanctifying fullness. The sincerity and competence of Church teachers was ensured through their selection by foundation managers. Nor ought the country be allowed to forget the millions of pounds poured into education, stipulating only the right to instruct children in the duties of life as defined by the formularies of the Church. It would be a betrayal of faith to surrender their school buildings and to violate their trust deeds. The *Pilot* was berated for advocating the transfer of voluntary schools in return for universal facilities.† Better it would be, Rev. Lacey fumed, for the Church of England to accept frankly the position of a minority group like the Roman Catholics and demand special treatment. At least some of the Church schools might be preserved to keep Christianity alive in England.[59]

---

* Ernst C. Helmreich, American historian, although favorable to religious education in his study, mentions the excessive memorization work and the importance of the school grade in the subject as often linking it with unpleasantness in the minds of students. Helmreich (1959), p. 89 ff.

† The *Pilot* (Aug. 23, 1902) defended itself, declaring that it would not close a single Church school so long as it was able to maintain itself by voluntary subscriptions and the parliamentary grant. Even if it were possible to save the best Church schools, the fact remained that the relinquishment of the weaker voluntary schools was worth the gain of making denominational teaching available in all schools.

NONCONFORMIST PROPONENTS

Some Free Churchmen were not averse to a national school system with universal facilities. But their conception of what its details should be differed considerably from that of its Anglican sponsors. Dr. Clifford acknowledged the reasonableness of paying a fair rent for the use of Church schools in school hours. The repeal of the Cowper-Temple clause in council schools was more than compensated for in the extension of popular control to and deletion of religious tests by voluntary schools. However, the facilities ought to be outside school hours and the attendance register should be marked at ten in the morning when the secular instruction began. The *Examiner* was hopeful that a definition of school hours could be phrased which would enable satisfactory attendance for the religious lesson under facilities. Nor did it think that the Birmingham failure in the 1870's was an argument against it any more. The fact should be remembered that since then the Free Church Council had arisen and Nonconformists were better organized to provide religious instruction for their children. Nonconformists could set up a teaching staff to travel in circuits just as was done currently with itinerant teachers of music and cookery. If the *British Weekly* admitted facilities would be expensive, that appeared the only way out of the religious controversy, for Anglicans apparently would not accept Cowper-Temple teaching. And it did bring Nonconformity back to the logic of its principle of separation of Church and State.[60]

Nonconformists were adamant against the recruitment of the regular teachers even on a voluntary basis. To permit this, insisted Dr. Clifford, would mean religious tests. It passed the wit of man to devise any scheme under which a teacher could be allowed to give credal lessons without his religious affiliation being probed at the time of his appointment. The *Examiner* believed that removal of religious tests would actually enhance the spiritual life of the nation. The distressing thing had been that the aim was not merely to possess a statement of a man's opinions for the time being but as a guarantee that he would continue to hold them. Such an oath in perpetuity fettered a man's freedom of thought and became a barrier against progress if he were conscientious. The alternative was to promote hypocrisy and it was a cruel system that subjected young people on the threshold of maturity to self-deception. As the *Examiner* saw it, the whole system of religious tests implied a low and mechanical notion of spiritual things:

If it is more important *how* a man believes than *what* he believes, then tests can be of little use, for the *how* of the matter they do not touch. The more earnestly a man's beliefs are, the less able will he be to pour them into any rigid mold that others may have made. Of all a man's mental and spiritual furniture, his religious ideas are least capable of remaining in fixed and stereotyped forms. . . . The fundamental ideas of Christianity remain the same but that does not mean they can always be expressed in the same way. Men grow more and more deeply into them as their experience matures. It has always been the glory of the Free Churches that they have stood resolutely against the imposition of religious tests and articles of belief. It is not because they have any love for a vague latitudinarianism but their faith in liberty of conscience stands high. They do not claim yet to have attained the whole truth and they would leave their minds room to grow.[61]

Only a very few would express themselves as sympathetic to facilities within a dual system, albeit popular control might be strengthened. Those who did were prompted largely by the realistic thinking that for the time being it was better than nothing. However, the *Methodist Times* qualified its support with insistence that in single school areas a council school should prevail, with some provision for denominational teaching according to the trust deed of the transferred school. In urban districts, where a choice was possible, the voluntary school would not be an extreme irritant. John Alfred Spender, editor of the *Westminster Gazette*, took a more elevating point of view that even a minimum compromise was best for Protestantism in the face of the threat from ritualist quarters. He saw nothing objectionable in "denominational teaching in regulated hours" and he would be willing to concede it in both types of schools as an alternative to universal undenominational teaching. The important thing was that the Church of England abstain from pressing forward its atmosphere theory, otherwise Nonconformists would find the value of facilities weakened by the steady incense of ecclesiastical surroundings.[62]

More persons were prepared to accept the dual system if it were applied in the form of contracting-out. The *Baptist Times* felt it was better frankly to recognize that schools insisting upon denominational instruction should stand outside the regular State system. The *Methodist Times* was careful to emphasize that children in such schools ought not to suffer educationally. They should have secured for them medical inspection and eligibility in scholarship schemes. But the teachers should be protected from falling back under "one man" management. Further, contracting-out was acceptable only where sufficient council school accommodations existed. So far as the size of the parliamentary grant was concerned, there ought to be a margin of financial responsibility for those who would demand contracting-out. If Dr. Clifford regretted this type of a concordat, he would insist that the parliamentary grant be given only for the child who passed the examination in the secular subjects. Further, contracting-out should be rigidly governed by a strict ballot of parents and so kept to the smallest limits, or it would thwart a national system of education.[63]

NONCONFORMIST CRITICS

Nonconformist criticis of facilities under any system were biting in their denunciations. Philip Whitwell Wilson objected to a child starting his school life with a denominational label affixed to it. There was no more baleful anti-civic influence than a formally-fostered sectarian animosity. It was tragic to divide children on dogmatic differences and to have them regard each other with distrust, as if they did not hold either a common Christianity or a common citizenship. In colorful phraseology, many depicted the havoc that would descend upon the classroom when the hour for facilities struck. Two of the observations should reflect their general tenor. The first is that of Asquith, repeated frequently thereafter:

> The children are all sorted out into separate theological flocks, and each flock is herded off into a little ecclesiastical pen of its own, there to be grounded and confirmed at the cost of the State in the doctrines, or it may be in the negations, which are dear to its parents.

The second‡ is that of Lloyd George who conjured up a military forage:

> Hundreds of little theological Fashodas all over the country, . . . one sect fighting another. They would have at one time a child belonging to one sect and in another week or a fortnight there would be a successful Jameson Raid, or there would be some local Major Marchand who would have the child taken away.[64]

---

‡ The *Journal of Education* (March 1906) offered the pedagogue's version of this theme that pan-denominationalism meant pandemonium: "Fifty little Church of Englanders taught by the Anglican arithmetic master, a score of little Primitive Methodists taught by the Methodist music master, a Quaker pupil-teacher and two Quaker infants taught by the Friend sewing mistress, and a job lot of no particular persuasion handed over to the agnostic drill sergeant." For a satirical dramatization of a morning session with facilities, see *Journal of Education*, Feb. 1909, pp. 106-07.

The *Liberator* examined the historical basis behind the Anglican cry of parental rights upon which was predicated the advocacy of facilities. The Established Church had not always spoken thus. Back in 1807 when the Whitbread Bill was under debate to provide two years of free education for poor children, the Church hierarchy in the lords threw out the bill because it did not give sufficient power to the clergy over the schoolmaster. When the National Society was formed in 1811 the Church of England required that all children in its schools must be taught the catechism and attend Church services every Sunday. Only the fear of loss of government grants in 1864 impelled the National Society to admit children under a conscience clause. In single school areas where a Church school held forth, Nonconformist parents had never been granted facilities for their children. The right of a parent to have his children educated in his own religion at the cost of the State had never been the guiding principle in Church educational policy. This new cry (and its instrument of propagation, the Parents' League) was mainly for political exigency. Under its guise the hope was to perpetuate the power of priests. A parent had a right to teach his children what religious belief he liked but he had no right to call upon the secular State to do it for him.[65]

Nonconformist critics went over old ground in arguing against the educational consequences of allowing the regular staff to volunteer as most Anglican schemes for the right of entry demanded. Obviously the elimination of religious tests would be impossible.* It would not be difficult for an ecclesiastic at the time of appointment to find out the willingness of a teacher to give denominational instruction. A teacher who refused to "volunteer" would have no chance of winning a post. The *Westminster Gazette* lamented the fact that the teacher would continue to be the symbol of the sectarian quarrel and his capture would be the hallmark of victory. Afterwards the tempting bait of promotion could be brought into play. The ample funds flowing to the Church of England from the lease of their voluntary schools would be an added allurement to teachers desirous of extra earnings. The *Christian World* affixed a postscript to the dilemma in store for local authorities in the event that a teacher who had been giving the Baptist lessons left a school. Would another Baptist be hired and what steps would be taken to find out?[66]

---

* While the *Presbyterian* (March 30, 1904) was no admirer of facilities, it was quite perturbed by the insistence of Nonconformists upon the abolition of every kind of religious test for teachers. To think in terms of appointing even an avowed Freethinker to a post in an elementary school to meet the analogy of the civil service would encompass the complete secularization of the schools.

Nor would facilities do the greatest good for the greatest number. Children from the poorest and most morally-necessitous families would get no religious education because their parents were attached to no denomination. The *Liberator* warned that all the forces of clerical bribery and church prestige would be brought to bear upon the meek to list their children as Church sheep. There was the fact that while Nonconformity comprised more than half the actual worshipping population, when it came to creed registers nearly all inmates of prisons and workhouses without a religious affiliation were set down as Church people. Nonconformity would be particularly at a disadvantage in caring for the religious instruction of its children. It was debatable whether the Free Churches could muster an outside staff of teachers (even if this less objectionable type of facilities were adopted). Compton-Rickett did not think financial resources were available to recruit a large body of religious teachers. In contrast, the Anglican Church would start with the great assets of its comprehensive parish system and numerous clergy. Rev. Hollowell was sure that only the sectarians would use the right of entry. Free Churchmen would suffer for their high sense of honor against using State property for denominational purposes. So the end would be the entrenchment of the priest in the school.[67]

The idea of facilities integrated with the dual system was especially objectionable.† The *Westminster Gazette* pointed out that this meant the atmosphere theory rather than the regulated theory would prevail. The orthodoxy and the zeal of the head teacher would guarantee a sectarian incense burning all day long in the school. Rev. Welsh observed that history books could be selected which stigmatized the Reformation and Cromwell and glorified "the martyr Laud" and Charles Stuart. Obviously, the facilities granted Nonconformist children could not overcome the effects of a surcharged sacramentarianism. In the small village school, where only one teacher was possible, Nonconformists would have a hard time to obtain even an outside volunteer. An overworked minister whose flock was scattered in several villages or a willing artisan with no teaching experience were slender reeds upon which to rely. In the meantime, the head teacher, a paid servant

---

† Critics were not enthusiastic toward the use of either contracting-out or earmarking of rates to reduce the objection of passive resisters to the dual system. In the former case, the danger would be to deprive children of good educational opportunities, since with the disappearance of rate aid the "intolerable strain" would reappear. In the latter case, the objection was that the Church of England schools with centuries of ecclesiastical and social tradition behind them would reap the windfall of unallocated rates. *Contemporary Rev.*, Feb. 1908, p. 144 (George White); *Daily News*, Oct. 14, 1907; *Methodist Times*, March 19, 1908; *Nation*, Jan. 2, 1909 (Massie).

of the State but named by the foundation managers on the basis of a searching religious test, would give the distinctive credal lessons without expense to the Church of England.[68]

Only a few of the examples at home and abroad cited by proponents in behalf of facilities were accepted as relevant and in these the results had been disappointing. The Birmingham experiment had proved the difficulty of securing a sufficient and continuous supply of voluntary teachers. Bryce gained the impression from his reading that the ministers of religion had not been good for discipline and had disturbed the daily program. The total score had been that of unleashing the forces of bigotry among the population of Birmingham. In the case of the industrial school, whatever might be the degree of success with the right of entry, Birrell did not think that the analogy was the same. In such institutions children were taken away from the custody of parents and the State had to accept a sectarian obligation. If the State sought the redemption of the child criminal partly through the reform potential of clergymen, then it had to give consideration to the religious preference of the parents. Parents of law-abiding children, on the other hand, had many more choices for their religious training—the home, the church, and, most ideally, the option offered by Cowper-Templeism. Dr. Clifford made much of the findings in the Transvaal where a commission had been appointed to inquire into the use of facilities in the State schools.[69] Among the complaints brought to light were the irregularity of the clergy in attendance, failure to inform school authorities beforehand of their absence, and disregard of the time limit allotted them in school.[70]

The fewness of religious groupings was regarded as voiding the significance of several examples cited by proponents as fulfilling the conditions of a dual system. In Ireland, where 75% of the population were registered as Roman Catholics, schools with an autonomous religious character were possible. For the record, the census of 1901 showed 3,308,661 Roman Catholics out of a population of 4,458,775 or 74.2%. The main minorities comprised two, Episcopalians (581,000), and Presbyterians (453,173), and arrangements for them were feasible. For that matter, Philip Whitwell Wilson wondered if the acute religious difficulty in Ireland between Protestants and Roman Catholics could not be partly traced to denominationalism in the classroom. Children were insulated in their own school systems and refused to listen to "the other side" when they grew up.[71]

In Scotland the population was practically unanimous in its theological beliefs and the board schools could take a Presbyterian slant. For the record, the census of 1901 showed 3,985,200 Presbyterians out of a population of 4,472,000. Roman Catholics and Episcopalians in Scotland numbered 365,000 and 121,800 respectively. At the same time, Rev. Hollowell believed that the Shorter Catechism was but an exposition of scriptural theology and contained neither ecclesiastical nor sacramental teaching.[72]

In Prussia the population was distributed generally between two established churches, Lutheran and Roman Catholic, with a concentration of Jews in a few towns. For the record, the census of 1900 showed 21,817,577 Protestants, 12,113,670 Roman Catholics, and 392,322 Jews. Separate schools for denominations did not impair education while the few mixed schools had to provide facilities for no more than two religious bodies. Furthermore, observed William Harbutt Dawson, these established religions were controlled by the State to a larger degree than in England and so could be conditioned toward a sound educational program.[73] In contrast, the varieties of Protestantism in England and Wales were so numerous and the distinctions so sharp as to make the prospect of administering definite religious instruction in whatsoever form devised a veritable nightmare.[74]

CHAPTER EIGHT

GENERAL RELIGIOUS INSTRUCTION

NONCONFORMIST PROPONENTS

THE FAVORED SCHEME of Nonconformists was a national system featuring general religious instruction plus supplementary facilities.* Its chief recommendation was the guarantee of Christian teaching in all schools. Denominationalists ought to welcome the opportunity to rectify their complaint that a large number of council schools had little religious instruction. Moreover, by their own admission, Anglicans were aware that in many Church schools the religious instruction had been modified to fit the tender susceptibilities of mixed faiths. Why not, then, accept frankly a settlement which included a catechetical lesson once or twice a week as was now most often the case. More importantly, all devout Christians should be concerned for the children of the poor who, if they were not taught the Scriptures in the day schools, would be entirely ignorant of them. The prize at hand, wrote the Rev. John H. Shakespeare, editor of the *Baptist Times,* was the mass of children in the slum quarters of the great cities who might grow up as "white heathens." † Were they, he asked, to be reared in a darkness like that of pagandom, never hearing the name of Jesus except in blasphemy? At the annual conference in 1904, at Newcastle-on-Tyne, the Free Church Council voted overwhelmingly in favor of a

---

* A number of specific schemes along these lines are to be encountered, notably, Bishop Edwards of St. Asaph's Bills of 1904 and 1908 and the Durham, Hibbert, and Manchester proposals in Northern England between 1903 and 1908. The most elaborate effort was that of the Educational Settlement Committee, formulated over the years from December 1908 to June 1910, culminating in a printed plan entitled, *Towards Educational Peace: A Plan of Resettlement in English Elementary Education.*

† The professional educational periodicals, notably *Schoolmaster, Journal of Education,* and *School Government Chronicle,* felt the same way and were favorably inclined toward general religious instruction. In the words of *Schoolmaster* (March 24, 1906), if religion were excluded from the schoolroom, it meant that tens of thousands of poorer children in the towns would be shut off from "the sweetening and beautifying influence of the elemental truths of Christianity as revealed in the Bible."

national system under complete public control with no religious tests for teachers and providing simple Bible lessons subject to a conscience clause.[1]

The plan called for the State to pay a fair rent upon the transfer of a voluntary school to the local authority. The negotiation for a transfer was to be optional with the church educational association but where no agreement could be reached and the circumstances warranted it a new council school would be built. The lease was to be for the school hours and the entire complement of six managers was to be appointed by the education committee. The teaching staff would have status as civil servants and be given the right to claim exemption from participating in the general religious instruction.[‡] A representative Christian body should be designated to draw up a syllabus and attendance of children subject to a conscience clause. Supplementary facilities could be given once or twice a week, the teachers to be recruited from the outside, and the cost borne by the denomination.[2]

The supplementary facilities constituted the most controversial feature of the plan, the vital question being whether these should be permitted in school hours. Dr. Macnamara and others could see a reason for doing so in transferred schools since the tradition of definite religious instruction was deeply rooted and a period of transition might be desirable. Many Free Churchmen were quite willing to let the incumbent head teacher volunteer his services, but the right of entry into council schools in school hours was another matter. The *Methodist Recorder* pointed out that a compulsory right of entry would be an infringement upon the freedom of the education committee to make plans for religious instruction in its own schools. The idea of facilities in any form in the cherished council schools of the nation was unpopular to men like Rev. Hollowell. Even under the precautionary conditions of being placed outside school hours, at the expense of the denominations, and with volunteer teachers, the nonsectarian roots of the council school might be weakened. The vital danger was that the supplementary facilities might so overlay a national system with denominationalism as to destroy the civic character of the schools.[3]

As to the content of the general religious instruction, Dr. Horton suggested that the syllabus embrace the great truths of the Christian revelation and the great principles of Christian ethics. English children should be taught "to speak the tongue which Shakespeare spoke," and

‡ In the fall of 1903, Archbishop Davidson and Dr. Horton exchanged letters on the merits of the scheme featuring general religious instruction, concluding that the stumbling block was how, without religious tests, to assure the competency of the teacher to give it. *Liberal Magazine*, Dec. 1903, pp. 707-09.

"to hold the faith and morals which Milton held." In every school there should be the sense of God, the habit of prayer, and the reading of the Book "which is at once the supreme religious treasure of the world and the greatest masterpiece of English literature." Dr. Clifford liked the Lord's Prayer, the twenty-third Psalm, the leading facts in the life of Jesus, and the bearing of the laws of Moses on the "poor," the "stranger," the "fatherless," and the "widow." Thomas Hodgkin, Quaker and author of a classic treatise on the barbarian invasion of Italy, regarded as a sound Christian foundation simple lessons from lives of biblical figures—Joseph, Moses, Samuel, Elijah, Daniel, the Parables and Miracles of Christ, the story of His Death and Resurrection, and the Acts of the Apostles.[4]

Assuredly, all sects could get together and draft a syllabus which would have nothing offensive in it to members of the Christian churches of the country. George White mentioned the Adult School Movement in which hardheaded working men of all denominations met every Sunday morning for Bible study, including Anglicans and Roman Catholics.* Elizabeth Boyd Bayly, a writer of popular stories who identified her background as Nonconformist although her youthful upbringing was Anglican, pointed out that the churches cooperated in such worthy causes as the Y. M. C. A., Y. W. C. A., Dr. Barnardo's Homes for Orphans, Bible and Trust Societies, the Ragged School Union, and the Railway Mission. Rev. Lidgett, who became editor of the *Methodist Times* in 1907, affirmed that the religious teaching under Cowper-Templeism neither promoted nor injured the interests of any denomination. Rather it served the destiny of a common Christian civilization.[5]

Nonconformist proponents listed examples to show how widely their scheme was applied. The Scottish use of the Bible and the Shorter Catechism was described by Dr. Macnamara as a prototype of general religious instruction. The plan in vogue in Ontario was interpreted by Lloyd George as one in which the teachers gave the general religious instruction (Protestantism) and Catholic parents were encouraged to bring in the priest at a specially-appointed hour.[6] The custom in the United States of giving Bible reading without note or comment conformed to the essence of the proposed concordat. Rev. Hollowell quoted that in 1896, out of 946 reports received from school superintendents in 14 states, 454 superintendents indicated that the Bible was

---

* Wm. C. Braithwaite, President of the National Council of Adult Schools Association estimated that there were 60,000 members and 700 schools. The movement was fostered by the Society of Friends for the purpose of developing the Christian spirit through the study of the Bible. Mudie-Smith (1903), p. 331.

read in all their schools. Only 197 superintendents stated that no religious instruction at all was given.[7] This sample poll sponsored by the Chicago Woman's Educational Union is not to be mistaken with that previously mentioned as initiated in 1904 by the American Commissioner of Education and which yielded about the same findings.[8]

Particularly apropos were the facts for Australia. Thomas Edmund Harvey, Liberal M.P. and a Quaker, referred to Western Australia where denominational teaching supplemented the Bible lessons. In Queensland a popular referendum in 1910 had endorsed general religious instruction plus the right of entry at the option of the local authority.[9] The settlement in New South Wales resembled closely the scheme favored by Nonconformists, the demand for facilities to supplement the general religious instruction being met by having ministers come in at a scheduled time of the day.[10]

Rev. William T. Whitley, Baptist minister, Preston, Lancashire, and later a historian of the Baptist movement, believed that the trend in the secular state of Victoria was to restore the Bible. In 1900 a Royal Commission had reported unanimously in its favor and, if adopted along with the current right of entry allowed out of school hours, would represent a satisfactory concordat.[11] Rev. Whitley's observation was made before the unfavorable results of the Referendum of 1904 had come to pass. As reported by W. H. Fitchett, an Australian journalist and editor, in a letter to the London *Tribune* (March 5, 1906), three questions were submitted to the voters: 1) Are you in favor of the Education Acts remaining secular as at present? Yes, 89,229; No, 62,980. 2) Are you in favor of the Scripture lessons recommended by the Royal Commission being taught in school hours to children whose parents desire it (subject to a conscience clause exempting teachers who object)? Yes, 70,094; No, 70,119. 3) Are you in favor of the prayers and hymns selected by the Royal Commission being used? Yes, 79,289; No, 69, 839. Whether or not it was the confusion of interpreting the several overlapping and seemingly contradictory questions, the Victorian Government voted against scriptural lessons. It should be added that Victoria has continued to be a secular state.

ANGLICAN PROPONENTS

Support for a scheme of general religious instruction plus supplementary facilities was not lacking among Anglicans. Self-interest dictated the thinking of those who favored this plan no less than it did those who espoused universal facilities as the ultimate concordat. Rev.

Henry Russell Wakefield, Rector of St. Mary's, London, reasoned that since voluntary schools were now financed almost completely by the State they were unlikely to be a permanent feature of the educational system. The payment of rates entitled the local authority to exercise full public control. Rev. Screeton, St. Thomas's Vicarage, Hyde, near Sheffield, stressed that subscriptions were falling off in proportion to total expenditures and were bound to decline further as donors struggled under the strain of rising school rates. The result would be increasing difficulty in repairing old schools and constructing new ones. Statistics about schools and their accommodations were not comforting. The *Guardian* counted close upon 1,000 voluntary schools shutting their doors between 1902 and 1906 (from 14,268 down to 13,487).[12] For Church schools alone, the score was 11,711 in 1902 with accommodations for 2,813,978 and 11,377 in 1906 with accommodations for 2,743,876.[13]

An even worthier treasure for this band of Anglicans was that general religious instruction would help retain the Christian roots of the nation. It would bring justice to Nonconformists in rural areas where the Anglican clergy had done well in behalf of their own flock but not for those of the Dissenters. Canon Henson pointed out that the morally-destitute children of the slums gained nothing from the fact that select groups of the better-to-do children were taught their denominational doctrines in appointed classrooms. Impoverished parents were either indifferent or ill-equipped to give religious instruction at home. Nor could children of such families be coerced into attending Sunday schools. If Cowper-Templeism were made compulsory, it would provide a barrier against the secularization of the schools. Bishop Diggle of Carlisle asked where the outside teachers could be recruited from if religious lessons in the school were left to amateur efforts. The churches had no adequate machinery to keep up with the increase in population. Bishop Ridgeway of Chichester went to the core of the entire problem: "Who will care for children whose parents do not label themselves as members of any denomination or where denominations are too weak or poor in localities to provide religious teaching for their children?"[14]

The years 1906 to 1908 witnessed urgent appeals to the Church of England to throw itself behind this type of concordat. The evident intention of the Liberal Government to legislate along the lines of general religious instruction plus supplementary facilities was to be found in the proposed clauses to continue Cowper-Templeism (and even to make it compulsory under the Runciman Bill) and to allow facilities twice weekly for credal lessons. Canon Henson pleaded with Church prelates to join in the crusade to give children the priceless benefits of a

Christian education. Half the professed Christians of the country were Nonconformists and harmony could be achieved only on a Protestant basis. Unless Christianity were capable of being taught apart from the dividing dogmata of the denominations, it could not be taught at all with State sanction and by State teachers.[15]

The Established Church of a Protestant nation lay under a special obligation to come forward as the champion and exponent of fundamental Christianity common to all Protestants.† Canon Henson reminded his brethren that hitherto it had been the Anglican boast of constituting the most tolerant and comprehensive of all denominations. The National Church ought not decline into a sect. Rev. Rosslyn Bruce, Rector of Clifton, Nottingham, pleaded: "It must not be said that the limbs of that Holy Body (Church of Christ) are so torn asunder that the mouth is unable to deliver the message of its Divine Founder in such a way that the little lambs of the flock can receive it, unadulterated with our unhappy divisions."[16]

The tendency of many clergy to belittle use of the Bible in council schools was distressing. Such disparagement was not likely to incline local education committees toward general religious instruction. Bishop Diggle of Carlisle reminded the clergy that the nation had as much right as churches to teach the Bible. States, no less than churches, were divinely ordained with corresponding responsibilities imposed on them. A major key to the Reformation was the translation of the Bible into the language of the people and its unfettered circulation among them. John Wyclif had trumpeted that the sacred books should be read by every husbandman at his plough and by every weaver at his loom. The very heart of the Reformation was that the Old and New Testaments constituted a free library. The Church of England should support the effort to anchor the national school system to the impregnable rock of the Holy Scripture. No other than John Milton, recalled the *Spectator*, enshrined the books of the Bible in words of hallowed reverence:[17]

> In them is plainest taught, and easiest learnt,
> What makes a Nation happy, and keeps it so,
> What ruins Kingdoms and lays cities flat;[18]

---

† Rev. H. Gresford Jones, the Vicarage, Bradford, Yorkshire, recalled that in 1828, in the face of Lord Eldon and a host of Churchmen who cried "We are betrayed," the Archbishops of Canterbury and York and all the bishops except two led the lords in the repeal of the Test and Corporation Acts and so placed the administration of public affairs on a basis of religious equality. *The Times*, Nov. 14, 1908, 10e-f. The Archbishop of York spoke in the lords, announcing his intention to vote for its repeal and also that the Archbishop of Canterbury, at the moment indisposed, would do likewise. *Lords*, April 17, 1828, pp. 1482-83.

A lively discussion took place in these Anglican circles as to the content of general religious instruction. If the lessons followed the syllabuses now in print, there was nothing with which to cavil. They contained the Decalogue, the Lord's Prayer, the Sermon on the Mount, and the parables and miracles of the New Testament. Particularly, the Apostles' Creed should be included as the surest foundation upon which to build the further dogmas of all creeds. Bishop Edwards of St. Asaph eulogized it as a general statement of Christian faith just as the Ten Commandments were a creed of conduct. A precedent for its use was at hand in the six areas listed in the Lords Return of 1906 as including the Apostles' Creed—Oxford, Somerset, Sussex West, and Worcester County Councils and Bath and Birkenhead County Boroughs.[19] He recalled the views of Gladstone in 1870 when the Cowper-Temple clause was under debate "that it [the Apostles' Creed] appears to me not to be a distinctive formulary in the sense of the Act. . . . It sets forth in the simplest shape a series of the leading facts on which Christianity, the least abstract of all religions, is based."[20] Canon Henson contended that the Church catechism, apart from a sacramental prelude and epilogue, both easily separated from the rest of the document, was non-denominational. But he was not averse to children having an option between that of the Church of England and the Free Church catechism.[21] Both affirmed the Fatherhood of God, the Redemption in Christ, and the helping power of the spirit of God. The final word might be yielded to Archbishop Davidson, who would remind all that an acceptable syllabus must mean "the idea of Revelation, of Jesus Christ dying for us on the Cross and rising again, . . . of the Incarnation and the Atonement."[22]

Anglicans hoped Nonconformists would join in a course of action. Bishop Carpenter of Ripon favored a request to the Board of Education to call an advisory committee composed of representatives of the various denominations and have them draw up a religious syllabus. Canon Henson preferred an ad hoc elected committee in every locality to decide on a common Christianity. He drew an appreciative picture of the extent to which Christian churches were already in close connection. In many parishes Nonconformists used the local Church facilities for baptism, confirmation, marriage, and burial rites. The congregations of chapels often came to the parish church on the occasions of Harvest Festival, Christmas, and Good Friday. Many Nonconformist chapels were leased on trust deeds which expressed doctrine in the language of the Thirty-nine Articles. In charitable enterprises, both at home and abroad, Nonconformist and Anglican clasped hands. All congregations had the same favorite hymns. Cardinal Newman's "Lead, Kindly Light" and Faber's "Hark, hark, my soul" could be heard in any Christian church. The most widely circulated weekly religious newspaper was the *Christian World Pulpit* (which contained sermons from clergymen of all faiths), read by Anglicans and Nonconformists alike. Many were the holy men associated with the history of a particular faith who were respected by all Christians—John Bunyan (Baptist), Thomas à Kempis (Catholic), Jeremy Taylor (Anglican), Richard Baxter (Puritan). Was it unreasonable, asked Canon Henson, to believe that a basis for an educational concordat could be found?[23]

Confidence was expressed in the sincerity and competence of the council school teacher to give the general religious instruction. Canon Henson placed considerable stock in the belief that the general law of adequate qualifications which governed in other fields of employment would apply to teachers. The profession should attract devout men and women by virtue of the obvious fact that the school system was intended to be Christian. Bishop Carpenter of Ripon was confident that teachers were devout in the main and that their consciences would lead them to diffuse the Christian spirit. Tests did nothing to protect against exceptional misconduct and did much to render the religious teaching nominal and lifeless. Conversely, religious lessons would educate teachers and so gradually imbue them with the spirit of reverence. The *Spectator* felt that the majority of teachers in council schools valued the Bible lessons very highly in helping them to stir the better side of their students' natures. At the same time, assuming religious tests would be abandoned in appointment, teachers should be qualified to give general religious instruction. Why not, after engagement, have a committee of good citizens—a "Board of Triers," to use the Cromwellian phrase—ascertain the interest and preparation of a teacher to conduct the religious lesson? Rev. F. Daustini Cremer, Eccles Vicarage, close by Manchester, recommended the Oxford, Cambridge, and Manchester University local examinations‡ as free from any sectarian stamp. A corollary benefit might be that pupil teacher centers and day training colleges would be prompted to include religious instruction in their curriculum.[24]

It was urged that the supplementary facilities be made meaningful. Rev. J. Frome Wilkinson, Barley Rector, Herts, supposed that the Cowper-Temple clause in council schools would be repealed and the right of entry made statutory and scheduled in school hours, with the regular staff allowed to volunteer. The cost would be borne by the

---

‡ Scriptural knowledge was in the list of subjects in which students from 16 to 18 were examined to measure achievement in the secondary schools and to provide a means for the award of scholarships and prizes.

denomination from funds made available by the lease of voluntary schools on a fair rental basis. As a possible compromise, bowing to the obstinate attitude of many Nonconformists in the matter of the regular teachers giving credal lessons, some Anglicans thought the chances were better for the whole scheme if the right to volunteer were restricted to the assistant teacher in council schools but permitting the head teacher to give it in the transferred school. Bishop Edwards of St. Asaph hoped that a derivative value of an effective system of supplementary facilities would be to set a standard of excellence for the general religious instruction and so act as a further security against secularism.[25]

The British Empire offered proof that Christians of all sects could work together. Canon Henson discussed at length the Jamaica Catechism drawn up by the ministers of the various denominations present in the West Indies.[26] It contained seventeen questions and answers on "God and Man," for the most part in the familiar language of the Scriptures and Protestant formularies. This was followed with eighteen questions and answers on "Man's Duty," of which the text was the Decalogue, with every article separately explained. Next came a summary of the Ten Commandments in the words of Christ with sections on the Beatitudes and Prayer. The Lord's Prayer was elucidated in nine questions and answers, followed by a concluding section on "Resurrection, Judgment, and the Life to come." Bishop Carpenter of Ripon regarded as a somewhat analogous example the experiences of Bishop Smyth of Lebombo, in Africa,[27] who described mission work in an area where natives had been converted previously by another sect. The challenge was to give the native continued spiritual guidance and yet avoid possible confusion in his mind about Christianity and the answer was found in the open Bible, psalms, and hymns.[28]

Rev. William Emery, Archdeacon of Ely, called attention to a pamphlet written by Rev. Christopher, recounting the story of an experiment in Martiniere near Calcutta.[29] Rev. Christopher had served as headmaster of a school there from 1845 to 1848. Religious instruction for the school was predicated on the principles held in common by the Christian faiths represented by the student body—Anglican, Roman Catholic, Presbyterian. It included the Being of God, the Bible as a revelation, the mystery of the adorable Trinity, salvation through grace by meritorious sacrifice and redemption of Christ, the indispensable obligation of repentance toward God, and sustained prayer for the grace of the Holy Spirit. For further instruction in their own faiths, the students attended church services on Sundays.[30]

New South Wales was hailed by Bishop Frodsham, back from a tour of duty in North Queensland (1902 to 1913), to take up his new post as Canon Residentiary of Gloucester, as an example of the comprehensive scheme. In 1881, it had adopted the Irish Textbook, consisting of selected passages of the Old and New Testaments. The government required this to be taught to all children in the state schools by state teachers and to be examined annually by inspectors as in other subjects. There was ample provision for supplementary facilities in school hours by outside teachers. When a child was first entered in the school register the religion of the parent was posted and at the hour when the teacher of that religion appeared the scholar was sent to him. The churches raised their own funds to employ volunteers and by allowing the hour to be set up flexibly a teacher could cover many schools. Bishop Frodsham quoted Senior Inspector Lobban[31] (a Presbyterian) on its success:

> I know nothing that has done more to remove sectarian bitterness and religious misunderstandings between members of the various Churches than the possession of this inestimable privilege [parents' rights] in the public schools of this State. The teachers are selected without reference to their religious denomination and hence members work together on the same staff and learn to respect each other as friends and co-workers and never interfere with each other's religious beliefs. Children of various denominations are ranged side by side in the classes and read the Scripture lessons together; but no reference to churches is allowed—the child's religion is held sacred. When they separate to go for special religious instruction to their pastors, no more notice is taken of the fact by the pupils than if the classes had been broken into sections for special instruction in secular work.[32]

ANGLICAN CRITICS

The thesis of a common Christian foundation was disputed by Anglican critics. Nonconformist literature repudiated any use of the idea of Revelation or of Jesus Christ dying for mankind on the Cross and rising again. As Dr. Clifford demanded it, Bible teaching would be exclusively ethical, literary, and historical. Bishop Knox of Manchester wrote of the experience of the Birmingham School Board when that body decided in 1879 to end its trial with facilities and to return to Bible lessons. Besides Bishop Knox, the school board included a Wesleyan, a Congregationalist, and a Unitarian. To satisfy the Unitarian it was found necessary to omit from the hymn "Hark the Herald Angels Sing" the verse which began "veiled in flesh the Godhead see." Lathbury referred to the London School Board episode of 1894 when Athelstan Riley sought to have included in the syllabus the Doctrine of Trinity.[33] The desire was to ensure that a definite Christian interpretation of the

Bible would be placed before the children.* Nonconformists had raised the cry of "no dogma" and prevailed upon the London School Board to turn down the request. Athelstan Riley added his own postscript, recalling that not only did the London School Board deny his motion but it refused also to inquire into the fitness of the teachers to give the Cowper-Temple lessons.[34] Rev. Taylor was certain that the outcome of any compromise would be nothing more than the Gladstonian "moral monster," a State-defined religious teaching and "a twentieth century Act of Uniformity."[35]

This proposition of a fundamental Christianity showed a complete ignorance of the niche which the catechism occupied in the voluntary school. The *School Guardian* asserted that the catechism was not something over and above the Bible. It was the Bible reduced to order and clothed in the authoritative language of the Established Church. The public impression that Church schools watered down their religious instruction was not true. What existed was a diversity of credal lessons ranging from a minimum of dogma to an excess of theology. Any concessions which could be made by some voluntary schools would not necessarily be possible in others without sacrificing their distinct personality. The inference attached that anything other than general religious instruction was superstructure not only erred, commented Rev. W. Trevor Nicholson, the Vicarage, Egham, Surrey, but it was also to be doubted that in practice the teaching of the Scriptures could remain the so-called fundamental Christianity. The simplest moral passage could be connected with dogma if the teacher willed it. Bishop Gore of Birmingham affirmed that the Bible could not be taught without assuming definite religious truths. Every book of the New Testament was written for those who had already received and accepted the primary teaching of the Established Church. The catechism taught young people the truth of their own spiritual origin as children of God by regeneration.[36]

Especially reprehensible was the lack of dignity present in the role assigned to denominational instruction. Facilities would stand forth shabbily in contrast to the exalted position accorded general religious instruction by its being given daily in school hours by the regular teacher at public expense. Labeled as supplementary, restricted to twice

---

* The London School Board controversy stemmed apparently from an incident in class when children were marked correct in an examination upon supplying the name of Joseph as the answer to the question, What is the Name of the Father of Jesus? Riley protested the answer as reflecting Unitarianism and asked that teachers be allowed to give the Doctrine of Trinity. See *Examiner*, Dec. 24, 1903 (Hugh B. Philpott); Philpott (1904), pp. 105-09.

or even once weekly, and taught by amateurs at the expense of the denominations, credal lessons would be regarded as sectarian idiosyncrasies foreign to the Christian faith of children. Bishop Knox of Manchester portrayed the denominations in the role of intruders, branded with the stigma of seeking purely ecclesiastical interests. The ordinary application of the plan was not pleasant to contemplate. Church teaching would refer the child back to its baptism as the foundation of its spiritual and moral life. Cowper-Templeism would instruct the child that baptism had nothing at all to do with these saintly qualities. The Church would train the child in the catechism as the key to the true knowledge of the Scriptures. Cowper-Templeism would assure the child that no interpreter was needed. The Church would urge the child to prepare for the solemn rite of confirmation as its highest aspiration. Cowper-Templeism would throw out hints that confirmation was an unhappy survival of medieval superstition. In the end, between contradictions on alternate days and the mingling of children of all and no faiths, Blackwood's Magazine predicted that the general downward tendencies of the atmosphere of such a school would vitiate the value of supplementary facilities.[37]

LOCAL OPTION

Nonconformists discussed frequently an alternative approach to general religious instruction known as "local option." David Brynmor Jones, Liberal M.P. for Swansea, focussed attention upon it in 1902 when he introduced an amendment to this effect. The proposal would give each district the power to meet the wishes of its ratepayers, sanctioning whatever syllabus the majority desired. The Cowper-Temple clause would be repealed and national legislation would be confined to the establishment of full public control over all schools. In the case of the voluntary schools, the process would be completed by purchase or lease. A wide range of views circulated, however, as to the choices of religious instruction which should be open to the local authority. At one extreme, Dr. Clifford insisted that only those passages should be used as were not the battleground of the churches and in a sense exclusively ethical, historical, and literary. At the other extreme, the Christian World imposed no restrictions at all upon the local authority, leaving it free to follow public wishes. Rev. Hollowell took a middle-of-the-road view that the popular vote simply include a statement whether or not to have Bible reading without oral exposition. He believed that the Bible was capable of exerting its own charm. So far as justice for minorities was concerned, the British Weekly felt confident that their rights would be respected, since each side would triumph and lose equally in elections and so be anxious not to expose its own children to proselytism elsewhere.[38]

The Scottish system was cited as a successful prototype of local option. Rev. Elliot claimed that since 1872 Scotland had had a universal system of school boards, popularly elected by the ratepayers who controlled the religious instruction through their representatives. The lessons were in the main scriptural, the Shorter Catechism including the Ten Commandments and the Lord's Prayer. The Baptist Times opened its columns to James Wishart, a Scotsman from Kirkcaldy, near Edinburgh, to explain in detail to Nonconformists its operation. The school board had the headmasters meet and draw up a syllabus. It was given the first thing in the morning, although the roll was not called until the time to take up the lay subjects so that a child whose parents so desired for conscience reasons could stay home until then. In addition, the school board arranged for any thirty children, at the request of their parents, to have a different kind of religious instruction in a separate classroom but at their own cost. Perhaps, suggested Wishart, the special instruction could be made obligatory in England and meet the needs of minorities. What more could be wanted, asked Dr. Horton, than the Scottish plan which left each local authority at liberty to teach any religion it pleased in its schools, embracing even universal endowment through facilities.[39]

Not all Nonconformists were prepared to endorse local option. The Examiner disapproved of it, contending that this formula of the will of the majority gave away the whole case against an Established Church as a violation of the principle of separation of Church and State. Religious equality would be transgressed no matter whether Nonconformists or Anglicans won the victory or whether the vote approximated a near unanimity. James Henry Yoxall, Liberal M.P. and like Dr. Macnamara a leader in the National Union of Teachers and an editor of Schoolmaster, questioned the adaptability of the Scottish plan to England. In Scotland most scholars, teachers, and managers were of the same faith and agreement on dogma was fairly general. But in England, the fact should be apparent to all that religious differences were too pronounced. The Westminster Gazette commented that most every school contained children of different creeds and under local option both the syllabus and teacher appointments would become footballs.[40]

Sentiment was present in Anglican quarters for the idea of local option. Charles T. D. Acland would accept a concordat calling for the repeal of the Cowper-Temple clause and leaving each community free to handle any religious difficulty that might occur. Rev. Henry Scott Holland, Canon of St. Paul's and editor of the *Commonwealth*, favored having the local authority form a committe out of the representatives of the religious bodies to make arrangements for religious instruction in the schools. If they agreed on general biblical teaching for all children, then well and good. At least it would not be an abortive fabrication of civic authorities who had no right or qualification for defining the fundamentals of the Christian faith. Frederick E. Smith, Unionist M.P., felt that local option had special merit for assuring religious instruction. Where the local authority was favorable to religious education, that sympathy could be made the fullest use of by parents. Where the local authority was hostile or indifferent, the pressure of the parents could be enlisted in aid of religious teaching. The net result would be for the predominant religious views to prevail in each district and Lord Hugh Cecil was sure that in England the Established Church would not fare badly. Since the majority of the nation were Anglicans, its tenets would be taught in most districts and at public cost.[41]

Anglican sympathizers agreed that the Scottish plan was an appropriate illustration of local option in successful operation. Dr. Davidson was receptive because it actually provided denominational schools and appointed teachers on a credal basis, be they Presbyterian, Anglican, or Roman Catholic. If it were a matter of choice, the *Pilot* would select the Scottish approach rather than general religious instruction, for the former at least allowed a definite religion to be taught instead of a State-manufactured amalgam. Indeed, it was prepared to contemplate with equanimity the likely advent in Wales of a variety of Calvinistic creeds in all schools under local option in preference to a mere spectral syllabus of so-called biblical instruction.[42]

Anglican critics of local option centered their objections on the dangers for denominational instruction. Rev. Cleworth asserted that a parental vote in school management was the worst way to parents' rights. Few would take the trouble to vote and fanatics could take over control. R. W. Burnie, perhaps a barrister of the Middle Temple, counseled that local option would develop into a kind of Kenyon-Slaneyism, with a lay committee wielding control over Church teachers and the syllabus. Lathbury presented the vulnerable point against the appropriateness of the Scottish plan to England. He declared that the majority of the Scottish people were of one religion, the members of which were not divided among themselves on vital doctrinal matters. In England, the incidence of religion was diverse and theological views hopelessly entangled.[43]

CHAPTER NINE

THE ROMAN CATHOLIC POSITION

THE POSITION of Roman Catholics was one of implacable hostility to all concordats. The idea of a national system with universal facilities had no attraction. In its best form, during school hours but using volunteers, Rev. Smith believed it was impossible to give denominational instruction to children of all ages at the same time. An amiable homily or a pious talk was one thing, a catechetical instruction was another thing. In its worst form, outside school hours and still using volunteers, Archbishop Bourne characterized the right of entry as "a miserable triviality." After school hours the children were least amenable to religious instruction, exhausted by the day's school work and intent upon play. In the meanwhile, during the week, children would be receiving anti-Catholic doses from the Protestant teachers of the school. What defense was there, asked Bishop Hedley of Newport, if the teacher chose to promote the historical lies of the Gunpowder Plot, the Titus Oates slander, and the Reformation as a product of Papal corruption? What defense was there against the atmosphere of negation produced in simple ethical references, in comments on life and manners, and in contacts with children of the more socially-accepted faiths? Rev. Rickaby, S.J., London, declared that it would be unendurable to see Catholic children driven into schools where everything "valued was ignored, tacitly set aside, and even exposed to mockery and formal repudiation."[1]

Roman Catholic resistance to the idea of a scheme of general religious instruction was no less vehement.* Archbishop Bourne affirmed that in England the Bible instruction would be the endowment of Protestantism. The very appointment of teachers in council schools without

---

* Rev. Hugh Edmund Ford was the only Catholic writer to favor negotiations with Anglicans and Nonconformists on the basis of the common elements of Christianity and so ensure that religion would be a part of the school and that the nation would remain Christian. Tablet, May 24, Aug. 6, 1904, Feb. 17, 1906 (Ford).

religious tests implied an abiding trust that their outlook would be that of the Reformation. There was acute danger of Catholic children growing up to be Protestants, because of the great receptiveness of children to environment. Father Bernard Vaughan, S.J., worker among the poor in the East End, branded Bible instruction as "boneless, fibreless, structureless, colorless, tasteless religion, absolutely wanting in every constituent needed to build up the Christian character." A child formed under undenominationalism, taking a few isolated truths out of context, would come to look with contempt upon all the various churches as absurd receptacles of differences which had nothing in them but conceit and intolerance. Adding to the prospect of secularism was the fact that religious tests would not be required of teachers of general religious instruction. Thus the Bible lessons could fall into the hands of Agnostics and Atheists.[2]

Nor would any scheme of general religious instruction be more palatable by the addition of supplementary facilities. Archbishop Vaughan was dubious that denominational instruction twice weekly would counteract the Reformation outlook in the proposed national system. If universal facilities could not erase the Protestant tone of a school built up during the other hours, the more restricted supplementary facilities could not do any better against daily lessons in the Protestant Bible. The three undenominational lessons even in transferred schools would very soon exhaust the vigor of those elements which had made it Roman Catholic. Rev. Glancey was sure that the hierarchy would not make use of such futile facilities. They had not done so in New South Wales where in 1899 priests paid only 392 visits to the schools as against 13,315 visits by Anglican clergy.[3] The predominant Protestant background among staff and student body there had been too uninviting to sustain catechetical instruction. Archbishop Bourne could anticipate one possible exception where the merit of facilities might be acknowledged, that of a few Catholic children completely isolated from the main centers of their religious life. Here the obvious solution was entry by the priest.[4]

Catholics termed local option equally dangerous to the future of their faith in England.† To be sure, observed Rev. Smith, it would meet the wishes of every sect where it could command a majority to institute denominational lessons. But for the Catholic Education Council the

---

† John Dillon was vividly conscious of English Catholics' hostility to any form of local option. He recalled how roundly he had been denounced by English Catholics for his amendment on July 30, 1902, to allocate two managers to the parents of the children attending the local voluntary schools, thus jeopardizing control by the hierarchy. *Daily News*, Dec. 6, 1906.

consequence would be the loss of many of their schools. In a number of them the majority of the children were non-Catholic because they had to open their doors to all children in the district. As for the frequent references to such a plan operating successfully in Scotland, Msgr. Brown answered that the reason was in the uniform nature of its Protestantism. The Presbyterian preponderance on Scottish school boards made denominational instruction possible. Furthermore, the fact ought not to be overlooked that there was an opportunity for separate schools with a State grant but no local rates and since the Scottish Education Act of 1872 Roman Catholic schools had increased (from 22 in 1872 to 201 in 1905).[5] In England, however, Protestantism was too disunited to adapt itself to a State system of denominational instruction. While local option might mean capture of the lion's share of council schools by the Church of England, it would be no guarantee of tranquillity. At any rate, for Roman Catholics, if the Scottish plan were emulated, it needed amendment to provide them with separate schools.[6]

Rev. Glancey made much of the educational unrest in British possessions where the practice had been to rely on facilities solely or combined with general religious instruction. He reviewed the history of "cleaning the slate" in Australia. In Victoria, the Act of 1872 withdrew aid from all schools not vested in the Minister of Education. In Queensland, aid to private schools ceased on December 31, 1880. In New South Wales, by the Act of 1880, all aid to denominational schools was cut off. But the result was not peace. In Victoria, for instance, within ten years an agitation compelled the appointment of a royal commission. Its report was presented in 1884 and the commissioners were divided evenly on the question of certifying denominational schools as entitled to aid from the State. In 1900 another commission drew up a course of religious instruction and recommended that the question be submitted to a direct vote of the people.[7] A bill with this object in view was rejected by a narrow majority in the Victorian legislature.[8]

In Canada, Rev. Glancey contrasted the calm that followed in the wake of the denominational system with the turbulence generated in areas trying the secular plan. He praised the concordat in Ontario where the Protestants outnumbered Catholics five to one and in Quebec where the latter outnumbered the former seven to one. In both provinces denominational instruction was featured, the rights of minorities being preserved by separate schools eligible to tax support.[9] But in Manitoba secularist aggression in 1890 had overturned the system of denominational schools set up by the Act of 1870 and the strife had been bitter.[10] It was the work of doctrinaire politicans who had the mistaken idea that separate schools prevented a "homogeneous Canada."

The aftermath brought Manitoba to the verge of revolution and left a deep feeling of discontent and irritation. To fill the gaps in the abbreviated account of Rev. Glancey it should be noted that the system established by the legislature of Manitoba in 1890 called for State schools which all taxpayers had to support. While private schools could exist, subsidies from the State were not granted. After a prolonged fight which included an appeal to the Privy Council in England and an embroilment in national Canadian politics, a compromise of a sort was worked out in 1897. The State schools would be opened to priests for religious instruction in the afternoon from 3:30 to 4 o'clock when the average attendance of Catholic children was ten in the rural and twenty-five in the urban school. In addition, on petition of parents, the trustees were to employ one qualified Catholic teacher if the numbers justified it.[11]

Archbishop Vaughan recounted his favorable impressions of a visit to Prussia.[12] Every religious body—Catholic, Protestant, Jewish—had its own schools fully paid for by the State which prescribed that from four to five hours every week should be devoted to religious instruction. In Catholic schools, for example, the catechism was taught and explained two hours every week, generally by the priest, plus two to three hours weekly devoted to the history of the Church, the meaning of the Liturgy, and acquaintance with devotions and hymns. The children and their teachers attended Mass together on weekdays and the teachers were well qualified to give religious instruction, having been trained in denominational colleges supported by the State.[13]

Rev. Alban Goodier, S.J., emphasized the amendments in 1906 to Prussian education laws, placing on a more legal footing what was already a workable plan. For adjustment to shifts in population, it was provided that in five-year periods if a district changed its denominational character to the extent of a two-thirds majority, then a new teacher must be appointed of the same faith as the new majority. For adjustment to increases in population, a minimum of sixty children was deemed sufficient for a religious faith to petition for a school of its own. When the minority was at least twelve, it was recommended that a teacher of that faith be included if possible on the staff or, failing that, obtain a local pastor for the religious instruction. The Prussian State, he said, acted with wisdom in supplying religious instruction in accordance with parental wishes.[14]

Catholics were sharp in their criticism of those Anglicans willing to negotiate on the basis of facilities or general religious instruction and thus surrender the conception of Christianity as an influence permeating the entire school program. Apparently a large proportion of Anglicans had no strong convictions on the subject of religious instruction. And the difference between the Anglican and the municipal alloy was only one of degree. It indicated that the support of some Anglicans for separate schools was a local idiosyncracy which had no root in any fundamental principle. In Canada, Australia, and the United States there were no State-supported Anglican schools; a common school system prevailed, based upon undenominationalism and lumping together all the Protestant sects. In England, the decline in the number of Church schools testified to the agreeableness of Anglicans to send their children to council schools and to have them corralled with children of Dissenting faiths under the Cowper-Temple clause. The *Tablet* referred to the calculations of Pease, President of the Board of Education, that from 1902 to 1911 some 759 Church schools had been transferred or closed and the average attendance figures in Church schools had declined from 1,927,633 to 1,750,094.[15] Still, the *Catholic Times* regretted any prospect of the triumph of Cowper-Templeism as presaging a blow to Christian forces in the British Isles.[16]

Catholics struggled everywhere to maintain their parochial schools. Rev. Glancey offered several instances where they refused "to bend the knee to the Secularist or Undenominationalist Baal." In France, when religious instruction had been banished from the State schools, Catholic schools had sprung up from private funds.‡ In Belgium, Catholics had met secularist encroachment by organizing separate schools. Within eighteen months after the erasure of the denominational character of the Belgian communal schools (1879), the Church had established nearly 2,000 schools and in the following two years this number had increased to 4,000. The result was to force new legislation in 1884 authorizing a dual system of schools. In Australasia, Catholics had not fallen in line with the State system and had kept up their own schools.* In Ireland, the attempt to set up a national system of undenominational schools had failed ignominiously and the Irish National Schools had

---

‡ Robert E. Hughes, English writer on education, gives the enrollment in French public primary schools in 1897 as 4,189,506, a decrease of 5½% over 1887, whereas the private primary schools, chiefly Catholic, enrolled 1,341,098 in 1897, a gain of 23% over 1889. In terms of finances, Hughes notes that French Catholics raised annually over £2,500,000 for the maintenance of their own schools. R. E. Hughes (1902), pp. 106-07. See also Bracq (1910), pp. 214-51; Farrington (1906), p. 82; Hayes (1930), pp. 35-36.

* In Victoria for 1898 there were 221 Catholic schools compared to 111 in 1876. In New South Wales 75 Catholic schools in 1882 were attended by 16,595 pupils and in 1904 some 355 were attended by 41,112 pupils. New Zealand had 133 Catholic schools in 1899. *Victorian Year-Book*, 1895-98, pp. 1076, 1093; *New Zealand Official Year Book*, 1901, pp. 170, 180-81; *Official Year Book of New South Wales*, 1904-05, pp. 556-57.

taken a denominational character.† In America, Catholics were building their own schools in the face of the growing secularism of the State system. Rev. Vincent McNabb, O.P., estimated that Catholics in the United States were educating more than 1,000,000 of their own children in parochial schools.[17] So too would be the end in England of any attempt to force Roman Catholics into a rigid pattern.[18]

Rev. Alban Goodier confined his detailed account of the struggle to the Continent. In Switzerland, liberty in religious education was adopted as a principle in 1865 and, then, in 1874 neutrality was imposed on all cantons. The result was that Catholics got training in their own doctrines in school hours by teachers of their own faith, inspected by the hierarchy. In Holland, the State took over education in 1806 and the religious teaching was Calvinistic. In 1857 a new law banished all positive religion from the State schools. Catholics persisted with their poverty-stricken schools against the competition of the well-kept State schools. But in 1889 voluntary schools were formally accepted and subsidized by the State. In Belgium, the Church battled to retain its rights. In 1879 the forces of anticlericalism and freemasonry came into power and a new law confiscated Catholic schools and made them State schools. Heroically, Catholics founded an entire new school system, totalling within twelve months 2,064 schools, built by contributions, attended by 63% of the Belgian children, and taught by 8,713 teachers most of whom had relinquished more lucrative State posts. Finally, in 1884, came retribution, a new party alignment bringing about fairer treatment. The State adopted a more equitable position, subsidizing both the public and the "free" Catholic schools. In France, the impression was that if the Catholic Church had been beaten, at the moment, it would not be for long. Despite the series of hostile acts restricting State grants to the secular schools, their private schools still persevered, 15,000 against 60,000 State schools and in terms of children nearly one-half of them.[19] Catholics would await further restitution in France. In Italy, the law of 1877 had suppressed religious teaching in the schools but in 1895 there had been a partial restoration if parents signified a desire for their children to be given it.[20] Everywhere in Europe, con-

---

† The *Catholic Herald* (Dec. 14, 1907, Jan. 18, 1913) did not regard the *de facto* advantage of Catholics in Ireland as entirely satisfactory. Its impression was that the Irish National Schools were far less Roman Catholic than those in England. Even if the "undenominational" settlement existed only in theory, the State would not appear to have abdicated its authority entirely. The fact that sacred emblems were put out of sight on the day when the inspector visited a school was quite suggestive. Separate management provided the best guarantee of a Roman Catholic school.

cluded Rev. Goodier, the acceptance of positive religion in the schools was in the ascendancy.[21]

The Roman Catholic position was firm and precise.‡ Religion must be in the forefront of education, to be taught every day by precept and example if the precious spiritual atmosphere were to be fostered. The *Catholic Times* stated flatly: "We would rather have our children know about Jesus and the lessons He taught for time and eternity than know about the use of globes." Bishop Burton of Clifton averred that the State had no inherent right to educate the children of a nation. Even less had the State the right to adopt secularism, exposing a people to its twin companion, atheism. This was to go back to "Lycurgus and Hobbes and Rousseau, and the cycle of paganism and revolution." All alike should have schools properly built and fully equipped at public cost to which they could send their children without injury being done their souls. If it were said, commented Hilaire Belloc, well-known writer and Liberal M.P. for South Salford, that Roman Catholics go to universities, the answer was that advanced disciplines fell upon a mature mind whereas the early grades took place in the formative years and molded minds yet plastic. Perhaps Protestantism could be gotten without special training in childhood in England where the entire environment was the Reformation. But that fact of alien surroundings made vital sowing securely the seeds of Catholicism. In a Lenten pastoral letter in 1906, Archbishop Bourne pontificated that a Roman Catholic education implied three things, "Catholic schools, Catholic teachers, effective Catholic oversight of all that pertains to religious teaching and influence."[22]

The *Catholic Herald* differed as to how its religious compatriots should face up to the realities of the English scene. Wherever Roman Catholics were a minority, the whole question was one of expediency and of making the best settlement possible. A multitude of ways had been found to secure the interests of their children. In the United States, except for promoting parochial schools wherever possible, they went along with the secular system as an alternative which required no sacrifice of principle. In Scotland, they managed their own schools with partial State aid. In Germany, they accepted State control in return for schools with a denominational character. In England, even if there was always room for improvement, it must be admitted that Catholic schools had not fared too badly. They had been sacramental in the

---

‡ The *Tablet* (Dec. 23, 1911) referred proudly to the figures published by Pease which showed that Roman Catholic schools had increased from 1,054 in 1902 with an average attendance of 269,191 to 1,074 in 1911 with an average attendance of 295,802. See *Parl. Papers*, 1911, LIX, Cd. 6002, 3 pp.

fullest sense and in respect of finances they were better off than those of kinsfolk in many other Protestant countries.

Whether Catholics would fare as well in the future, continued the *Catholic Herald*, depended upon their position in the current controversy between Anglicans and Nonconformists. It was obvious that the Liberal Government was pledged to redress Nonconformist grievances. Catholics could make a grave blunder by allying with Anglicans and remaining blind to the plight of Free Churchmen. Apart from questioning any cooperation with a Tory Party committed to an anti-Irish policy, the counsel should be to play a part in promoting a just and permanent concordat subject, of course, to separate treatment for Catholics. The penalty for a false step would be heavy. If Nonconformists won, they might in a spirit of vengefulness make short shrift of parochial schools. Or if the two branches of Protestantism decided to seek a *rapprochement*, leaving parochial schools alone to face the Board of Education and probably without the protection of the Irish Nationalist Party (assuming Home Rule had been won), the result could be likewise fatal to their schools. Needed in this hour of trial were diplomacy and tact to get the most for Roman Catholic children.[23]

Catholics were not keen on the idea of contracting-out as a means of preserving the character of their schools. It would revive the intolerable strain if applied as proposed in connection with the bills introduced by the Liberal Government in 1908. Voluntary schools were to be cut off from rate aid and required to make up the margin by subscriptions. Nor would the proffered increase in national grants ease the situation. James A. Doughan, diocesan representative for Shrewsbury on the Catholic Education Council, declared that, while expenditures must be budgeted on the actual upkeep of the full accommodations, the national grant would be based on average attendance, thus reducing the real value of the per capita grant. Rev. George Richardson, St. Augustine's, Manchester, and diocesan inspector of schools in Salford, was against accepting any differential for performing the same work, offering the analogy of the Cunard Company which built "Atlantic greyhounds" with public assistance. Nothing was said as to the manning of the vessels except that efficiency must be observed. The *Tablet* was bellicose, referring to the Act of 1902 as the charter of emancipation. Contracting-out would end not only in starvation and bondage but also in exposing the nation to secularism. In France the same malicious tactics had prepared the way for anticlericalism. It was first phrases, then regulations, and finally confiscation. Who could fail to see the same genesis of events casting their shadow over England under the euphemism of "contracting-out."[24]

A spirited debate was carried on in Catholic circles as to earmarking rates in order to retain the dual system. Its proponents turned to Canada for a favorable report on its operation.[25] Rev. Smith described the workable system in Ontario where the common schools served the Protestant majority of the population and the atmosphere was essentially that of the Reformation. In a Roman Catholic community, a separate school was permitted embracing trustees, teachers, and formularies of that faith. These latter schools received public assistance, albeit they were subject to complete popular control for the secular work and subscriptions were required for construction and maintenance. At present there were about 500 Catholic schools in Ontario and these were on the increase.[26] John Redmond supplied information on how rates were earmarked in Quebec as well as in Ontario.* The ratepayer filed a statement as to which denomination he desired his money to go. If it were found at the end of the year that a particular denomination had not sufficient funds for its schools, then the deficit had to be supplied from private pockets. In England, the rates paid by Catholics should be enough to provide for the wants of every parochial school.[27]

The technical problem of assuring that Catholic schools got their fair share of the rates was not regarded as formidable. W. D. Gainsford, Skendleby Hall, Spilsby, Lincolnshire, would resolve the difficulty of the compound householder by letting the tenant pay his rate to the non-provided school and get a receipt which the landlord could present to the tax collector. In the case of the large business enterprise, such as a railway company, its allocation could be set up according to the wishes of shareholders in proportion to their stock on a three-year basis. Archbishop Bourne preferred the allocation of rates among all the schools of a district on a per capita basis as a more equitable way of reflecting the wishes of breadwinners whose manner of lodgings did not result in direct payment of rates.[28]

Some Catholics questioned the effectiveness of earmarking rates and how their schools would fare under it. The Tablet saw several obstacles in applying to England the schemes used in Canada. Many classes of people—renters of houses and flats and lodgers—paid no rate. Until the system of compounding for rates was abolished or radically altered, the proposal to let individuals assign their educational rate was unwise. A single Nonconformist grocer who had invested his savings in a street of workmen's cottages could manipulate at his pleasure the indirect rates paid by fifty or a hundred poverty-stricken Catholic families. The

---

* Both John Redmond and his younger brother William, also a member of parliament, joined in requesting the Board of Education to prepare a memorandum on the school rating systems in Quebec and Ontario. Commons, March 9, 1908, pp. 1118-19.

Church of England would possess the natural advantage of a State connection. For the prestige of public relations, persons unattached to any church might assign their educational rate to the Established Church. Msgr. Brown was worried over the allocation of the educational rate of commercial properties. He estimated that in London where the ratable value was £41,000,000, those of the City of London (£5,000,000) and the City of Westminster (£5,500,000), both largely business areas,[29] would redound to the gain of Anglican schools. For the rest, he saw a loss of revenue to Catholic Education Council schools in the twin factors of scattered parishioners living in rating areas where they had no schools and Roman Catholic children attending schools of the hierarchy in rating areas outside their own residential districts.[30]

Many Anglicans were prepared to recognize the need for special treatment of Catholics. While Rev. Wilfrid John Richmond, headmaster from 1901 to 1903 at St. Edmund's School, Hindhead, Surrey, and subsequently Chaplain, Lincoln's Inn, would concede them only facilities in single school areas, he thought that no principles would be violated in cities where a variety of schools were within easy reach of children. The nation must suffer some inconvenience in making exceptions for minorities. Canon Henson felt that it was absurd to jeopardize a settlement simply to feed the national ego that a unified school system must prevail. Catholics were so sharply marked off in point of religion from the general multitude of English folk that the isolation which they claimed could be readily granted on grounds of common sense. He would let them have their own schools wherever their numbers were sufficient and have these managed directly from Whitehall. Lathbury declared that they were for the most part a well-defined group and as a rule their children could be collected easily in the schools attached to their churches and directed by their clergy. The danger that a multiplicity of small schools would present itself could be dismissed, for the bulk of Catholics were concentrated in large towns where separate schools for them would be practical. And teachers from Catholic orders whose salaried needs were low would cut to a small amount the margin of subscriptions necessary.[31]

Some Anglicans were hostile to any special treatment for Catholics. One St. John Browne, London, asked what signal service they had rendered to the country that they alone among Christians should receive preferential consideration. The Liberal Party was accused of being prepared to make terms with this intransigent minority for political reasons. The Asquith Government needed the eighty votes of the Irish Nationalist Party and so hesitated to incur their enmity by any hostile move against English Catholic schools. To submit to the Roman Catholic demand, warned Athelstan Riley, was to abdicate the role of the Established Church as Christ's Church in England. It would mean that henceforth the Roman body would be the only one bringing up its children for entrance into church membership. In the meanwhile, especially where general religious instruction was given, Anglican children would labor under an admixture taught by untested teachers, perhaps even Agnostics. The *Guardian* hoped that Anglicans would reveal the same steadfastness in behalf of their own schools as Papists were doing. The implication that Protestants could be lumped together spiritually was to be resented. All denominations should be placed on an equal footing.[32]

Nonconformists were no less divided on the issue of special treatment for Catholics. Some signified willingness to accept this solution. Rev. A. J. French, onetime Wesleyan Methodist clergyman, Leeds, Yorkshire, felt the Romanist answer to "what must I do to be saved" was so at variance with that of Anglican and Nonconformist as to warrant Catholics being left out of account in any concordat. There was the further favorable circumstance that most of the parochial schools could be filled with a homogeneous student body. So they might well be allowed to continue teaching their own children in their own way. The great majority were Irish and had habits and customs distinct from those of the English community. The differences between the two peoples and their religious loyalties were broadly marked on the pages of history. The *Baptist Times* noted that "English history is the real difficulty and we can understand that a Roman Catholic would not care to have his children taught the history of the time of Bloody Queen Mary from the Protestant standpoint." George White offered a novel suggestion for meeting their needs in a strictly national system. He would dispense with the simple Bible teaching, appoint Catholic teachers, and then before or after school hours allow dogmatic teaching by priests.[33]

Some Nonconformists opposed vigorously any partiality to Catholics. To recognize their claim was to admit the entire sectarian position. High Churchmen could make out no less a case for public funds. To be logical, what Nonconformists refused to Anglicans they should not accord to Catholics. Dr. Clifford was incensed at the fact that Ultramontanism along with the High Church Party had been responsible for the defeat of the Liberal Government's bills. It was time that Rome fell into line with the aspirations of modern civil communities to get rid of all compulsion in the matter of religious beliefs.[34]

Rev. Hollowell expressed annoyance at the contention that council schools stood in the same relation to Free Churchmen as their voluntary schools did to Roman Catholics, each offering its own brand of Christianity. A council school was only acceptable to a Nonconformist because it omitted his distinct doctrines, while a parochial school was conducted for sectarian purposes and was closed to teachers who would not take a religious test. Catholics were no different from Anglicans in wanting to carry on the propaganda of their church in State-paid institutions. It was an abuse of the sacred name of religious equality to require the public to become the agent and paymaster of tyranny over conscience. Rev. Hollowell admonished the nation that "we shall cut a pretty figure if we praise the courage of the French democracy while we kneel to Rome in our own country."[35]

Nonconformist opponents of special treatment singled out America as a country where Catholic demands for separate schools had not been admitted. There they had to foot the entire bill themselves. That was the necessary price of revolt against democracy and of anti-civic conduct. A. Lees (perhaps Rev. Andrew Lees of London) asserted that "the question of ever giving a cent of State aid to a denominational or sectarian school had been settled forever in the States and this issue the Catholics never raise." † For that matter, Rev. Hollowell observed that while perhaps one million Catholic children in America attended parochial schools, more went to the common schools without apparent spiritual injury.‡ Many Catholic teachers had seen their way clear to accept employment in State schools. Rev. Hollowell referred to a letter from Pope Leo XIII which Msgr. Francis Satolli, in 1893 the first Apostolic delegate to the United States, read to American bishops at a Catholic assembly gathered in New York City in 1892.[36] The statement stipulated that when no parochial school was available, attendance at a State school was acceptable.* As the *Christian World* saw it, the authority of the Pope over English Catholics was fully as absolute and he could require an accommodation to the circumstances of a Protestant nation.[37]

---

† This statement would not hold true today in the United States, where parochial schools are receiving financial aid indirectly. See A. W. Johnson (1934), 332 pp.; Butts (1950), 230 pp.; Thayer (1951), 257 pp.

‡ An article written (for the *Annual Report of the Commissioner of Education* (U.S.), 1903, I, pp. 1089-90) by Rev. Morgan M. Sheedy, St. John's Rectory, Altoona, Pennsylvania, offers some concrete figures. According to the Catholic Directory for 1900 there were 10,774,989 Roman Catholics in the United States of whom 963,683 went to parochial schools—almost one-half of the Catholic children of elementary school age in the country.

* The *Christian World* (March 22, 1906) recalled the Concordat of 1801 between Pius VII and Napoleon as an example of a compromise with so-called religious principles. For the sake of an alliance with Napoleon and the revenues which it produced, the Pope retreated on the issue of strict orthodoxy in France.

CHAPTER TEN

THE JEWISH POSITION

LITERATURE on the religious controversy in the English schools bracketed Jewish children along with those of Roman Catholics as minority groups meriting special consideration. However, Jewish commentators were not encountered very frequently in the discussion of the various concordats. Perhaps it was a hesitancy to adopt a strident tone in a Christian land acknowledging the principle of religious liberty. Perhaps it was the realization that the nation accepted the need for adjustments in their case and only the details remained to be ironed out. At any rate, the facts summarized here have had to be gathered mostly from general documentary sources.

The Israelite population in England and Wales between 1902 and 1914 was not large, numbering about 120,000 out of a total population of some 32,000,000. Presuming a ratio of 20% to be of school age, it can be estimated that about 25,000 Jewish children attended elementary schools. The Jews possessed twelve voluntary schools distributed as follows: London—8, Manchester—1, Liverpool—1, Birmingham—1, Hull—1.[1] In 1906 the total number of accommodations was 11,358 and the average attendance 10,120; in 1911 the figures read 9,863 and 9,159 respectively.[2] In these schools the teaching staff comprised men and women of Jewish persuasion. The religious instruction was given in the tenets of the Hebrew faith and in the Hebrew language. The school calendar made due provision for the observance of their sacred days and holidays. The Chief Rabbi in each city supervised the religious instruction in their voluntary schools.[3]

The number of Jewish children in attendance at council schools may be estimated at some 15,000 or more. Perhaps London can serve as the best illustration of their treatment in the nonsectarian schools. Since they were concentrated mainly in the East End, some concessions were possible. Teachers of Jewish faith were selected to staff the schools in the district. The Chief Rabbi was allowed to draw up a syllabus of religious instruction which was confined to the Old Testament. On Jewish holidays the schools were permitted to close. It might be noted in passing that apparently these steps were taken despite regulations to the contrary. During the London School Board controversy of 1893-94 over the proposed use of the Doctrine of Trinity in board schools, the fact was brought out that the arbitrary selection of Jewish teachers for the East End schools ignored the operating principle of no tests for teachers. Again, the fact was disclosed that the special syllabus had been introduced without the sanction of the London School Board. However, no action followed and the community continued to acquiesce in the de facto privileges.[4]

In addition, in the council schools, the Jewish community itself, through the Chief Rabbi, organized classes in which the more distinctive doctrines of the Hebrew faith were taught in the Hebrew tongue to its children. The cost of the program was raised by contributions and the expenses included the salaries of the teachers, the rent of the schoolrooms, and the cost of books and equipment. It was given outside school hours. Annual reports of the London Jewish Religious Education Board, the central administrative organization, show that in 1902 there were 8,620 scholars on the roll and 7,198 in average attendance while in 1914 it was down to 7,007 and 6,206 respectively. That the Jewish community was not entirely happy with the conditions might be deduced from a memorandum submitted by the London Jewish Religious Education Board on the occasion of the Birrell Bill. The complaint was registered that they had to pay rent for the use of council school buildings after school hours. The position was that no charge should be made, seeing that all other expenses were borne by the Jews. Nothing, however, came of their protests.[5]

Subsequently, in 1908, during the deliberations on the McKenna and Runciman Bills, some comments by Jewish leaders are available confirming the balance of advantages. On the occasion of a dinner in April 1908, held to raise funds for the London Jewish Religious Education Board, the second Baron Rothschild, member of the well-known banking family, presided and spoke. He acknowledged graciously that the Jews in England had every reason to be grateful for the treatment accorded them in educational matters. The cost of Jewish voluntary schools was almost completely defrayed by the State. The cost of those council schools which were allowed to function essentially Jewish in character were entirely defrayed by the State. This might be compared to the lot of Jews in Poland and Russia where only 5% were able to get an education and then amidst trying circumstances.[6]

At the same time it was made plain that the Jewish people believed religion should be in the forefront of education. Lord Rothschild regarded both voluntary and council schools as invaluable agencies in fostering the Hebrew faith of Jewish children and in unfolding the kind of moral life society expected them to live when they grew up. The Very Rev. Hermann Adler, Chief Rabbi of London, applied these values to the compromise proposals offered by the government in 1908. He doubted whether Jewish voluntary schools could survive under the new contracting-out terms. He questioned likewise whether facilities twice weekly in transferred or council schools would be sufficient to acquaint Jewish children with their spiritual heritage. Nor would the right of teachers to volunteer credal instruction be of any assistance to Israelites. The thinly scattered incidence of Jewish children in most schools would militate against teachers of that faith being engaged by many education committees. At best the Jewish community would have to rely upon a peripatetic teacher. Nevertheless, Chief Rabbi Adler expressed the hope that the Jews would make whatever contribution possible to help settle the religious controversy and so "avoid the onrush of a flood of secularism."[7]

CHAPTER ELEVEN

THE SECULARIST POSITION

SECULARISTS followed closely the various concordats offered the nation. They condemned any scheme for a national system which included facilities in school hours with the right of teachers to volunteer. The spectacle would be something to behold, observed John M. Robertson, if the Atheist, Theist, Positivist, Unitarian, Swedenborgian, Christadelphian, and Christian Scientist as well as members of the larger sects demanded that instruction in their own "isms" should be available to their children. Pan-denominationalism would spell pandemonium. Religion would emerge as a divider and classrooms would be the scene of sectarian recrimination. Religious tests would be riveted upon teachers. Ralph Morley, then a schoolmaster and in 1929 Labour M.P., declared that a Freethinker or a Unitarian would find it impossible to get a school. Any hope for the recruitment of a gifted staff of teachers would be shattered. The permanent effect would be to endow all the churches as joint controllers of education. At least the current situation held out some glimmer of hope that the fierce rivalry between Anglicans and Nonconformists might open the door to the secular solution. But a scheme featuring facilities could well entrench religion behind a solid front of Christian bodies and spell doom for a progressive educational program.[1]

Lord Stanley of Alderley described the absurd pageant unfolded by facilities thus:

> The idea of the municipally paid secularist lecturer teaching in one classroom that the Bible is faulty and mischievous in its science, history, ethics, and spiritual ideals; in another classroom the ordinary Protestant teaching the traditional view of the Bible as the sole authoritative basis of conduct and hope; in a third the High Church Anglicans dwelling on the authority of the Church and the need of the Sacraments as a means of grace; in a fourth the Roman Catholic claiming to be the only authorized teacher on behalf of the one true Church outside of which there is

deadly peril, if not certainty of spiritual death—such a curious medley, to say nothing of the Jew, firm in his splendid isolation, is hardly to be contemplated as a practical scheme for use in the elementary schools.[2]

Secularists would consider facilities only if the scheme called for religious bodies to teach their own doctrines at their own expense outside the school hours.* If parents were so anxious for their children to receive definite denominational instruction, then they should show the interest to have them attend. The regular staff should be put on the same footing as civil servants, and the sects ought to find teachers from the outside. During the debate on the McKenna Bill in the spring of 1908, MacDonald presented a full dress survey of the opportunity at hand in the *Fortnightly Review*:

> We stand today at a point where we seem to be hemmed in by walls of denominational strife on all sides but one. But we are afraid to move out in that direction. . . . The way bears an ugly name . . . and hitherto the people have not been willing to enter upon it. Mr. McKenna, however, has begun to explore. . . . [Why not widen his idea for transferred schools] that before or after school hours their children will be taught denominational, but, during school hours, secular subjects only. . . . It would place a heavy burden upon the church and the family. But surely that is not all disadvantage either? We are told that parents demand religious instruction. Would it not be a good thing to compel them to take some trouble to see that their children attended . . . by making the exercises special and not ordinary parts of the timetable? . . . The nation is sick of this interminable and unchristian squabble. If half a dozen men on both sides were compelled to hold their tongues or were forbidden to use the organization of the churches for political purposes, the vast majority of parents would allow a settlement to be made, for the people desire their children to be educated by teachers selected solely for their capacity to impart knowledge, and to train the best that is in a child's personality. Will not the Church, in all its sections and fragments, remember the political advice once given by its Head, and rendering unto Caesar the things that are Caesar's and to God the things that are God's, rest content?[3]

Any scheme of general religious instruction was regarded as spawning the same vices of discord and educational retrogression. Teachers could not look forward to a career geared to competency in the secular subjects. Snowden declared that it would be impossible to prevent reli-

---

* George E. O'Dell, Ethicist, wondered whether even such a concession was desirable. It would mean that the State was making it easy to give religious instruction. The children were collected together compulsorily already and classrooms would be available. *Ethics*, Feb. 17, 1906.

gious tests if the staff were expected to give the daily Bible lesson. The
school managers would be concerned to know if a teacher were willing
to do so. Teacher applicants who professed such affiliations as Unitarian, Positivist, or Jew would be ruled out automatically. William
A. Appleton, secretary of both the Amalgamated Lace Makers and the
General Federation of Trade Unions, predicted that the problem of
finding an acceptable syllabus would turn the nation into a "spiritual
cockpit." No man alive could shape a dogmatic teaching acceptable to
all the creeds. The very fact that a selection from the Bible would have
to be made to prevent incessant quarrels showed how unsuitable and
unfit the Holy Scripture was as a school manual. And even given an
agreed-upon syllabus and teachers of Christian conviction, religious
peace was by no means assured. Halley Stewart, president of the Secular Education League and Liberal M.P., thought no teacher could remain neutral and avoid giving the Bible his bias. Teachers were spiritual
beings too and it would be strange if they did not convey to their pupils
their own views of the Bible as an authoritative text.[4]

As a matter of fact, the scheme of general religious instruction favored Nonconformists, anchored as it would be, like Cowper-Templeism currently, to the Bible. The passive resister traded on the esteem
which the Bible possessed as the symbol of the Reformation spirit and
proceeded on the supposition that the teacher would be content to give
the Bible an orthodox Protestant interpretation. But the passive resister
should know that neither Anglican nor Roman Catholic would go along
with merely the teaching of Hebrew folklore and Hebrew history and
should face up to the fact that undenominationalism was as sectarian
to the sacerdotalist as the latter's catechism and formulary were to him.
Halley Stewart recalled the warning of the Congregational pulpit orator, Rev. Joseph Parker, in 1894, to his fellow Nonconformists that the
Bible would never bring peace:[5]

> There is no Bible upon which all Christian parties are agreed. One
> party says that surely the historical parts . . . might be read, to which
> another party replies that the historical parts . . . are especially to be
> avoided, because they are critically incorrect and in many instances
> glaringly contradictory. One party says "Read the Bible" because of its
> divine revelations to the human soul; to which another party replies
> "The one thing that is distrusted is the claim on behalf of the super-
> natural or the ultra-historical." Some say "Read the life of Jesus"; and
> others say that there is no trustworthy life of Jesus to be obtained; to
> some the Bible is historical; to others it is ideal. Which Bible, then, or
> which view of the Bible, is to be recognized in schools sustained by the
> compulsory contributions of all classes of the community.[6]

Nonconformists were blamed not only for the religious settlement already rooted in the schools, but also for the persistent circulation of concordat schemes. Halley Stewart asked how Nonconformists could reconcile their historic brief that religion was the business of privately-organized bodies with their insistence that the State endow general religious instruction. Alexander Maccallum Scott, barrister and private secretary to Winston Churchill during World War I, could not understand these advocates of Disestablishment who denied the right of the State to interfere with the religious convictions of men and women and yet held that up to fourteen years of age it was the State's duty to act as their religious instructor. Nonconformists complained bitterly and justly, commented S. H. Swinny, editor of the *Positivist Review*, that publicly-supported voluntary schools to which many of their children had to go taught the doctrines of the Anglicans. Yet they saw no objection to the teaching of Nonconformity at public expense in council schools. Nonconformists would defy the law rather than pay for religious teaching offensive to them. Yet they would levy rates on all to provide the religious teaching of which they approved but others resented. If it were wrong to tax Nonconformists, it was equally wrong to tax Positivists for the dissemination of doctrines which they disapproved. The latter were citizens with rights as strong as those of any other section of the population.[7]

Unitarians followed their own intellectual trail in arriving at the secularist position. If in the debates on the government bills from 1902 to 1914 they were arrayed most of the time with the Nonconformists against the Anglicans, they despaired of saving religious instruction in the schools. Unitarians would like to see Bible reading accompanied by simple historical explanations and the inculcation of elementary Christian ethics. But the facts showed that the teaching of Evangelical Christianity was pursued in a form obnoxious not only to Unitarians, Agnostics, and Jews but also to Anglicans and Roman Catholics. Past experiences indicated undenominationalism on many lips implied simply education in the theology of some definite segment of the Church of Christ. Nonconformists as well as Anglicans were against an ideal "Board School Religion" which taught the theism and ethics of Christ and left the denominations a clear field through the home and the church to add their own superstructures. Indeed, Unitarians admitted, there would be logical difficulties in justifying public endowment of pure Christian Theism if those members of the community who refused to affirm the existence of the Deity chose to raise conscientious objections. Jews and Agnostics dissented from according to Jesus first place as the exponent of Theism which Christian teachers would undoubtedly give

Him. Therefore, the only fair solution was the secular one and any religious instruction should be out of school hours and at the expense of denominations.[8]

The demand of Catholics for special treatment was opposed as untenable. Ryan termed the thesis that dogma must permeate all teaching as not true to life. How could the dogma of Trinity be made to enter the arithmetic lesson or the dogma of the Immaculate Conception the geography lesson? The very fact that there were some non-Catholic teachers in Roman Catholic schools showed "that the doctrine that Catholic dogma must cover all teaching is really only used for dialectical purposes." In everyday commercial life a Roman Catholic did not inquire into the religious faith of the directors of the bank in which he deposited his money or of a prospective purchaser of his goods on credit terms. Snell felt that if the Roman Catholic could make good his claim that his religion should be taught at the expense of the State, then every other citizen could legitimately demand the same thing. Jew, Positivist, Theist, Theosophist, Spiritualist, Ethicist—all merited rights equal to those of the Roman Catholic. Was the latter prepared to insist upon the State providing for the teaching of Atheism as well as for Catholicism? And even if he were, the bedlam would be the end of general community interest in educational matters. The Roman Catholic Church could and should provide for the religious instruction of its children outside the schools.[9]

Secularists took active steps to keep their own solution before the nation. On February 4, 1907, at a meeting presided over by George Granville Greenwood, the Secular Education League was formed to acquaint the public with the viewpoint "that the sole responsibility for religious education rests with parents and churches and there shall be no teaching of religion in state-supported elementary schools in school hours or at public expense." Halley Stewart was named president and Harry Snell served as secretary. A general council of 97 prominent persons was designated as an advisory body, including Thomas Burt, Arthur Henderson, J. Ramsay MacDonald, Philip Snowden, Peter Curran, John M. Robertson, George W. Foote, Graham Wallas, Havelock Ellis, Sir Arthur Conan Doyle, Frederic Harrison, J. A. Hobson, George Meredith, H. G. Wells, Israel Zangwill, Rt. Rev. Mitchinson, Rev. R. J. Campbell, Rev. Stewart D. Headlam, and Charles F. G. Masterman. One of the refusals was from Dr. Clifford who replied that he was for secular education plus the Bible.[10] Foote commented "that is like soda-water plus whiskey. The latter is not teetotalism and the former is not the secular solution." By September 1906, Snell claimed that the league had a membership over 1,000 including more than 300 clergy of every Protestant denomination.[11]

The subsequent record of its progress is somewhat sporadic. A journal was published irregularly, known as the *Secular Education Chronicle*. Leaflets presenting aspects of the secular brief were distributed from time to time. Demonstrations were held and leading members spoke. The league was particularly active during the General Election of January 1910, seeking out candidates for their stand on the religious issue in the schools. Stewart complained that the activities of the Secular Education League were boycotted in the columns of the dailies whose sympathies with church and chapel were sufficiently strong to violate the spirit of freedom of the press. A canvass of *The Times* discloses only a few references to their meetings and of the most meager kind and relegated to obscure corners.[12] More items, but principally of an announcement nature, are to be found in journals devoted to non-Christian views.[13]

Great hope for the spread of the secular solution was pinned on the Labour movement. In the commons, MacDonald struck the keynote when he declared that the Labour parliamentary members all owed what education they had to the board schools and that the children of the people whom they represented had no chance of education except that obtained in an elementary school. If the schools were imperfect, poor, and twisted by sectarian clashes, then these children had no other chance of being turned out upon the world as motivated citizens. The annual conferences of both the Labour Party and the Trades Union Congress passed resolutions in favor of a secular school system.† However, the debates at both gatherings grew increasingly acrimonious. A Roman Catholic bloc constituted the chief opposition. Its two protagonists were James Sexton, general secretary of the National Union of Dock Labourers, and James O'Grady, delegate for the National Amalgamated Furnishings Trade Association and Labour M.P. They challenged the right to inject the school issue into a movement devoted to industrial ends. Working men of all faiths contributed funds for the improvement of their material conditions of life. If the agitation for the secular solution were persisted in, it could split wide open the ranks of the proletariat. It might be added that the Labour Party in parlia-

---

† The Labour Party record of its resolutions in favor of the secular solution is as follows: 1906—817,000 for and 76,000 against; 1907—627,000 for and 122,000 against; 1909—739,000 for and 234,000 against; 1910—650,000 for and 120,000 against. The Trades Union Congress record of its resolutions in favor of the secular solution is as follows: 1907—1,239,000 for and 126,000 against; 1908—1,433,000 for and 131,000 against; 1910—827,000 for and 81,00 against; 1911—717,000 for and 120,000 against.

ment refrained from invoking party discipline on divisions connected with the various education bills.[14]

Subsequently, secularists were somewhat disappointed at developments in the Labour movement. Increasing friction generated between Catholics and secularists at the Labour Party conferences induced that body in 1911 to exclude the topic of secular education from future agenda.[15] Similarly, in 1912 the decision was taken at the Trades Union Congress, in the face of the disruptive tendencies of the sectarian question, to exclude it from the annual sessions.[16] The margin of victory was narrow, 952,000 votes for and 909,000 votes against the resolution. Snell disputed the theory that Labour should restrict itself to economic matters. The Catholic argument that trade unions were formed to better the terms of toil and not to dictate to a man how he should educate his children was deplored. Good education was a necessary prelude to more ideal factory conditions; adequate schooling meant that ignorance would be wiped out and so lead to demands for higher wages and social benefits. More, the working classes should be concerned to assure their children of an opportunity to develop their latent powers. Apart from the effect it might have in weakening the offensive for secular education, Henry Mayers Hyndman, founder of the Social Democratic Federation, felt that the reactionary step taken would reflect upon the ability of Labour to undertake its duties in a democratic Commonwealth.[17]

Picton made much of the fact that the school policy of greater Anglo-Saxondom had been determined solely by educational reasons and not by sectarian rivalry. He singled out as the main exceptions Transvaal (about to adopt a bill to secure two and one-half hours of instruction per week in "Bible history") and Quebec; in these two lands the population had not yet become as much interested in historical criticism as people in England. But Australasia, which had most fully inherited the religious proliferations of the mother country, had wisely adopted the other alternative and taught the creed of none. Facilities were restricted to religious instruction out of school hours by voluntary effort. It was made the trust of the Christian societies and left to their zeal. He quoted an extract from a British bluebook on the facilities system in Victoria:[18]

> The law directs that no State school teacher shall give any other than secular instruction in any State school building, but it assigns as one of the duties of the Board of Advice "to direct with the approval of the Minister what use shall be made of school buildings after the children are dismissed from schools or on days when no school is held therein,"

and under this provision religious instruction can be given on school days (though not by the teacher) *after* the ordinary school hours. . . .[19]

Vain efforts in Australasia currently to introduce general religious instruction in the schools was proof of how well sold their peoples were on the secular system. Picton noted that in Victoria an attempt was made by means of a Royal Commission in 1900 to propose a system like that of the London School Board and specimen lessons on the Bible were drawn up. But, in December 1900, the Legislative Council threw out a bill to hold a referendum on the question.[20] Mrs. Hypatia Bradlaugh Bonner followed the further action in 1904 when a referendum was held. On the two questions which had to do with possible types of religious material to be used in the schools, a small majority was in favor of a scheme of scriptural lessons and hymns. However, on the main question: "Are you in favor of the Education Act remaining secular as at present?" the answer was 84,000 Yes and 58,000 No.[21] A. D. McLaren, member of the National Secular Society, analyzed the referendum held in Queensland in May 1910 on the question: "Are you in favor of Bible teaching in the State schools?" Despite a victory for the affirmative, 68,107 to 50,849, McLaren regarded the latter number as more significant.[22] From his correspondence and his reading of Brisbane newspapers, the information suggested that the negative vote was collected without any pressure and nearly equaled an affirmative vote amassed through extremely aggressive efforts. All this confirmed to McLaren that the secular system had for thirty years given general satisfaction.[23]

The socialist weekly, *Justice*, opened its columns to a New Zealander, James Thorn, who described how his countrymen had resisted encroachments upon their secular education system. The religious leaders were hopeful when women were enfranchised that they would be able to command a majority but the people of New Zealand remained steadfast.[24] The very figures relating to school attendance testified to this fact.[25] For the year ending March 1906, there were 139,302 scholars in State schools and 17,131 in private and denominational schools, of whom 11,948 went to Roman Catholic schools.[26]

Both Picton and Gould came forward to praise the United States, where churches were given no role in the State schools. Writing in 1907, Picton explained that, while in many schools the custom was kept up of reading at the commencement of school a few verses from the Bible "without note or comment," it was largely a survival of Puritan traditions in America. Writing in April 1914, after a tour through the Middle West where he lectured on moral education, Gould encountered the same usages. While some of the states permitted the reading of a few Bible verses without comment at the opening of each day and scriptural passages were included in school literature, the elaborate syllabuses taught in England were absent. The result had been to free the energies of Americans to think in terms of education rather than to balance the claims of jealous and quarreling sects. Such frustrations as minimizing the number of schoolplaces needed in a district lest a sectarian monopoly be disturbed by its inability to raise subscriptions for an enlargement or repressing the enterprise of more efficient council schools lest they attract more scholars were unknown in America. American commercial and scientific progress were ample evidence that no ecclesiastical barrier stood between the people and their intellectual aspirations.[27]

Picton had explanations for those countries where either separate schools or general religious instruction seemed satisfactory. In Ireland, to have insisted upon "simple Bible teaching" would have added insult to Irish sensibilities. Concurrent endowment was inevitable there with the Catholic preponderance in population statistics. In Scotland the answer was that the universality of Presbyterianism in one form or another made a system of local option possible. In Germany, where two great denominations held sway, the plan to teach creeds was at least plausible.‡ But if that fact, for example, had not apparently hindered the development of education in Prussia, it was because religious belief did not express itself so much a matter of individual conviction as in England. While Germans were not less religious in sentiment, they had not generally that idea of the duty of personal accountability which animated the innumerable English sects. Their confirmations and first communions were very much a matter of social routine, like the "coming-out" of girls or the assumption of the modern substitute for the *toga virilis* of boys. Rate-supported catechetical and scriptural lessons were of no consequence and this indifference made sectarianism powerless for harm to the secular program of the schools.[28]

Secularists did not fail to drive home on every occasion the disastrous

---

‡ McLaren questioned whether the scheme in Germany really worked smoothly. He quoted the chapter on "Children and Education" in the 1909 edition of *Our German Cousins* published by the *Daily Mail* (this special supplement was distributed in October 1909 but neither the files of the British Newspaper Library Museum nor the offices of the *Daily Mail* contain a copy). Here the statement is made that "there is always a quarrel going on between the two great Churches. The Catholics demand the erection of dual confessional schools where they have not previously existed and Lutherans demand the abolition of the dual confessional school where it already exists." *Freethinker*, Oct. 17, 1909. See Fife (1918), p. 357.

effect that the religious wrangle was having upon the secular program of the schools. Edward R. Pease, longtime secretary of the Fabian Society, regarded as disgraceful how "the free expenditure of public funds is grudged first by one side and then the other, lest their opponents should gain some unfair advantage." The Secular Education League drew up a damning arraignment of the damage done the school system. It diverted the attention of local authorities from the civic side of education. It lost the services of the potentially ablest members of the teaching profession. It paralyzed the faculties of the teacher for the lay subjects, forced as he was to struggle with his conscience on religious matters. It made difficult focussing children's minds on their school work, caught as they were in the middle of a sectarian struggle for their tender souls. Hyndman, reviewing the progress of education by 1911, expressed the harsh judgment that "our politicians and journalists are still engaged in their pitiful religious squabbling as to how best to keep the children of the old country ignorant or at the best half-taught in the name of their holy Christian religion."[29]

Robertson accused the churches of deliberately demanding the "atmosphere" type of school to stifle civic education for the masses. In two articles he developed a stern indictment against the malevolent influence of Christianity upon learning.[30] During the later centuries of the Roman Empire the Christian Church allowed the pagan grammar schools to die out and the higher clergy displayed little disposition to enlighten the laity. The monastic and cathedral schools of the "dark ages" were only to train youth for the priesthood.* The promotion of universities in the later middle ages was channeled along ecclesiastical lines. In the seventeenth century the Church of England, once it was convinced that the ability to read was a prime cause of schism within the Anglican fold, ceased to extend popular schooling. Rather it allowed grammar schools to be taken away from the poorer classes and turned over to the children of the middle and upper strata. It was the rivalry of the British and Foreign School Society which brought forth the schools of the National Society in the nineteenth century. Even then the purpose remained sectarian and was directed toward fostering church membership. The schools would never be free to mature until Church influence was at an end—and the stakes were high, for Great

---

* Robertson cited as his source Neander, *General History of the Christian Religion and Church* (Bohn, 1852, new ed. rev.), VI, p. 112. Dr. August Neander's statement is: "The synods of the ninth century were very decided in resolving that the increase and prosperity of Christianity depended in great part on the right discharge of the predicatorial office, . . . hence they would naturally be led to insist on the necessity of establishing special schools for the education of religious teachers."

Britain's hope of prosperity in the competitive modern world depended upon a sound secular education.[31]

Robertson dwelt at length upon the progress of secular education in Western society. Where a State Church prevailed the results had been disastrous.[32] In Belgium the number of illiterates in 1890 was 27%. In Spain (68.1% in 1889) and Italy (61.9% in 1881) matters were still worse, although the advance of anticlerical opinion was accompanied in both by a lessening number of illiterates. In Russia, under the Greek Orthodox Church, education was at the lowest level in Christendom, with only 30% of army recruits being able to read and write. Despite the heritage of a glorious intellectual past, in Greece, under the same sacerdotal system 75% of the women (and 30% of army recruits) could neither read nor write. Robertson noted the admirable progress in lands not hamstrung by a State Church. In Switzerland, where Catholicism had 40% and Protestantism 58% of the population, the number of illiterates was 1%, although the Roman Catholic cantons were less strict on compulsory attendance than the Protestant cantons. In countries where the authoritarian forces were most effectively matched by forces of dissent and democracy as in Scotland, Holland, and Germany, the record was impressive.† In countries where the secular system was fully operative like the British colonies, the United States, and France,‡ the achievements were spectacular.[33]

However, secularists denied that their solution would mean the removal of all references to religion, thereby eliminating a wealth of beautiful literature from the school program. Philip Whitwell Wilson, secularist by reluctance and Nonconformist at heart, could not imagine a classroom with the Scriptures excluded. He likened a nation's culture to an arch with the Holy Writ as the keystone. Unless the student mastered it, he had little chance to appreciate "Shakespeare, Milton, Macaulay, Ruskin, Carlyle, or indeed any great English book, sacred or secular, poetry or prose, history or fiction." The Bible was a book of life, the inspiration of allegory, painting, and poetry, and a guide for the statesman and the man of commerce. Surely no one desired to plunge history into the predicament which existed in science when it was

---

† Scotland (1889) recorded 1.9% males and 2.8% females who signed only by a mark. Holland (1890) recorded 7.21% of conscripts who could neither read or write. The German Empire (1896) recorded 0.11% of recruits who could neither read nor write.

‡ Victoria (1891) registered 2.33% of its population as unable either to read or to write. France (1899) registered 4.8% of conscripts who could neither read nor write. The United States (1890) registered an average of 13.3% illiterates thus: native whites, 6.2%; foreign whites, 13.1%; colored 56.8%.

treated as a branch of theology. There could be no thought of permitting questions of creed to block the beneficent avenue of historical
inquiry.[34]

Secularists protested that they harbored no such reactionary
thoughts. Rev. Stewart D. Headlam shuddered at the thought of excis-
ing references to the Bible from the great works of English literature
which came in the ordinary way into the reading and recitation lessons.
Gould declared that the idea of erasing the name of God from schoolbooks or forbidding the employment of biblical allusions as almost
too absurd for discussion. No sane educationist would propose the
deletion of theological terms—God, Creation, Christ, Revelation, Sacraments, Blessed Virgin—from school instruction. Geography and history involved acquaintance with folklore, mythology, and the cere-
monial rites of nations in their habitats and in their evolution through
the ages. He pointed out the ridiculousness of a teacher being able "to
borrow a parable from Buddha, a verse from Zoroaster, a legend from
the Hindu drama, a tale from the Japanese Shinto, an ode from Confucius, but not a narrative from the Jewish Bible or the Christian
Evangel." No reasonable person would object to theistic expressions
remaining in the schoolbooks in much the same way as was the case at
present. Extracts from Milton, Cowper, Wordsworth, and Tennyson,
interspersed as they were with spiritual language, should still be freely
taught even though related to Christian thought.[35]

Gould had ready at hand examples of literature strewn with visions
of the supernatural that were highly desirable reading for children. He
related Sir Walter Scott's description of the Hermit of Engaddi upon
the occasion of his interview with King Richard in the crusading novel,
Talisman:[36]

> His dress of shaggy skins, his uncombed and untrimmed hair and
> beard, his lean, wild, and contorted features, and the almost insane fire
> which gleamed from under his bushy eyebrows, made him approach
> nearly to our idea of some seer of Scripture, who charged with high mis-
> sion to the sinful Kings of Judah or Israel, descended from the rocks and
> caverns in which he dwelt in abstracted solitude, to abash earthly
> tyrants in the midst of their pride, by discharging on them the blighting
> denunciations of Divine Majesty.

Here was to be found biblical lore and the teacher would be wanting in
common sense if he declined to explain the passage lest he trench on
the religious sensibilities of his pupils. Again, there was Dante's Divine
Comedy, the very title of which introduced the subject of theism.
Would any teacher be so idiotic as to carry a pupil through the regions

of Inferno, Purgatory, and Paradise without an explanatory word as
to their eschatological imagery? Again, suppose the teacher chose to
recite the funereal lines from Milton's *Lycidas*: "So Lycidas sunk low,
but mounted high / Through the dear might of Him who walked the
waves."[37] Surely no one could object to a few words of elucidation by
the teacher suggesting conceptions of death.[38]

Neither Protestant protagonist was inclined to let the advocates of
the secular solution establish their ready affirmation that the lay subjects would still be enriched by materials divinely-inspired. Anglicans
pondered the predicament of a teacher when he dealt with the subject
of history. *The Times* propounded a series of blunt questions. What
was a teacher to do with the ecclesiastical conflicts of the middle ages?
What was a teacher to do with the religious implications of the seventeenth century civil wars? Nor would the teacher's task be any simpler
when he dealt with literature, "with Milton, for instance, and Bunyan."
Samuel Butcher quoted Dr. Butler, President of Columbia University,
as stating that not only was the absence of religious instruction in
American common schools as such to be regretted but it had had a
saddening effect upon the teaching of *belles-lettres*. To the average student, "the First Book of *Paradise Lost* is an enigma. The epithets, the
allusions, even many of the proper names are unfamiliar. This is due
to the ignorance of the Bible."[39] As the *Churchman* saw it, religion must
enter under full sail when humanities were studied. It was impossible to devise any treatment which would not offend the consciences
of one or another class of ratepayers.[40]

Nonconformists offered their forecasts of the cultural riches that
would be lost under the pruning knife of secularism. Rev. Hollowell
observed that the teacher would find literature a barren subject if he
had to eliminate the religious ideas which suffused it. There were
many passages in Longfellow, Lowell, Whittier, Cowper, Tennyson,
and Shakespeare which were deeply and perhaps more Christian than
some parts of the Bible. The best writings of the world were replete with
theological asides. Biblical speech and content were woven into the
very texture of the best English works. The *Methodist Times* employed a vivid imagination to suggest where secularism might carry
England as it had the Australian state of Victoria: ". . . The days of the
week being named after the Scandinavian deities must not be mentioned in schools, . . . that names of months are a veritable Roman
theogony; also the computation of years from the birth of our Saviour
would offend the ears of Hebrew children and a description of school
terms in which the words Easter, Whitsuntide, and Christmas entered would be tabooed. . . . The history of the revised calendar of

the French Revolution is a standing monument to the folly of the secularist policy."[41]

The logicality of secularism would make history the most difficult of all lessons to give free from any bias. Rev. James Hope Moulton, tutor in the classics, Wesleyan College, Westbury-on-Trym, near Bristol, asserted that a glance at an Anglican or Roman Catholic account of Oliver Cromwell would be enough to verify how little "dry light" already existed where ecclesiasticism thrust itself forcibly upon the lay subjects. The result would be as bad if secularism applied the scissors. The *Examiner* affirmed that the Bible was the key to all history. Without it no child could understand the story of the Commonwealth. Yet if one understood the full import of secularism, there could hardly be a discussion of the attendant religious issues. Supposedly the Reformation would have to be eliminated because it required some explanation of Luther's spiritual views. Presumably an account of Puritanism would have to be eschewed because it involved discoursing on the essence of salvation. Harvey offered an especially keen observation on the secularist dilemma in the lay subjects:

> If the State attempts to shut all religious teaching out of the only school life which it will recognize, it must mutilate that life; in the end, it can only succeed in its endeavor to be impartial by fixing blinkers upon the eyes of its officials and its teachers. History and literature must remain half taught and half understood and their noblest passages must be forgotten or unstudied. Such an attempt must break down either by the influence of religious teaching coloring and permeating a curriculum nominally non-religious, or by the definite substitution for the religious intolerance of the past of a new anti-religious intolerance, no less dogmatic and no less illiberal.[42]

CHAPTER TWELVE

POSTSCRIPT

STRATEGY OF ATTRITION

W HAT FURTHER COURSE to pursue in the face of the failure to enact remedial legislation was debated earnestly in Nonconformist ranks. It was granted that the Liberal Government should be supported in its struggle to curb an arrogant House of Lords behind whose rampart denominationalists had resisted successfully the several measures proposed between 1906 and 1908 to establish popular control and no religious tests for teachers. But there was no certainty that a reduction in the power of the lords would assure a satisfactory measure. After all, the Liberal Government was susceptible to political considerations and would probably prefer a compromise for vote-getting purposes. Dr. Clifford favored a reinvigoration of the passive resistance movement and warned that its cessation would be a sign to the country that Nonconformist grievances were a thing of the past. To crowd the magisterial courts once again would keep alive the essential fact that the Education Act of 1902 was a Bishop's Act. The public should not be allowed to forget that a "non-elected oligarchy of peers and bishops . . . carry on the work of Charles I, ruling us with the same arbitrary . . . selfishness and greed that sent the Stuarts to the block." The spectacle of the distraint of goods and imprisonment would keep kindled the nation's imagination that Great Britain must emancipate itself from the insufferable grip of ecclesiasticism.[1]

However, many Nonconformists wondered if the story of statistics did not suggest the best strategy, namely, the efflux of time. By this they meant that if the line could be held against any further aid to voluntary schools, patience would bring a complete victory in the end. The reasoning was that despite the grant of rate aid by the Education Act of 1902 the cost of structural alterations and the construction of new schools had taxed the resources of church educational associations. The *Westminster Gazette* emphasized that over the span of years from 1901 to 1907 not only had council schools forged ahead but voluntary schools were actually on the decline. Whereas the former had increased their accommodations by 800,000 (from 2,881,155 to 3,651,537), the latter had lost 300,000 (from 3,729,261 to 3,410,530).[2] Nor did the succeeding years alter the trend of statistics. Rev. Horne contrasted the figures for 1910-11 with those of 1900-01. In terms of accommodations the voluntary schools dropped from 3,790,000 to 2,826,000 while the council schools increased from 2,880,000 to 3,980,000 schoolplaces.[3] Even more significant was the breakdown of voluntary school accommodations for 1910-11. If one considered that the Wesleyans with 69,000 and British and Foreign School Society schools with 109,000 places were practically run on undenominational lines, it meant that 4,160,000 places could be counted on the side of council schools as against 2,648,000 in denominational schools (Church of England, Roman Catholic, Jewish). The logic of events was steadily reducing the magnitude of the problem. The voluntary schools were not flourishing.[4]

Anglicans were not oblivious of the danger that the mere passage of time might dissolve the dual system. Some were genuinely alarmed at the failure of the Church of England to hold its own. Archbishop Davidson, speaking before the Representative Church Council on December 4, 1908, in behalf of his negotiations with Runciman, confessed himself quite concerned that 550 Church schools with accommodations for more than 160,000 children had been closed in the last three years in contrast to an increase of 1,050 council schools with accommodations for 478,000 children.[5] Bishop Edwards of St. Asaph found no comfort in the Report of 1910 published by the National Society. Comparing the years 1906 and 1909 the story was one of steady decline in average attendance (from 1,945,587 to 1,829,486).[6] The *Guardian* lamented the further diminution in accommodations of voluntary schools according to the Board of Education Report for 1911-12. It was sad reading to find that the number of places lost totaled 153,000 in 1910, 68,000 in 1911, and 28,000 in 1912. The *Guardian* would have been even sadder had it known that for 1911 the correct figure was 267,908 instead of 68,000.[7] Great energies would be needed to halt the downward trend both in the growing obsoleteness of many voluntary schools and the low rate of new construction.[8]

Still other Anglicans saw nothing to fret about in the aggregate figures of Church schools and accommodations. John Gilbert Talbot, Conservative M.P. for Oxford University and an active Churchman, contested the significance of the statistics for the period to 1909. Referring to the figures from 1901 to 1907, the vital facts were that more than one-half of the voluntary schools lost belonged to the Wesleyan and Undenominational (including British and Foreign School Society) bodies and that even at the current mortality rate of three a week it would be eight years before the total of voluntary schools was reduced to 10,000.* It was a matter of regret that 457 Anglican schools with accommodations for 132,536 should have been lost in those six years, but even this decline was rather the result of increasing the space requirement to ten square feet per child. Again, referring to the figures issued by Runciman (that in 1905-06 the Church of England had 11,377 schools, Wesleyans 345, and Undenominationals 689 and in 1907-08 the Church of England had 11,180 schools, Wesleyans 294, and Undenominationals 602), Talbot had his own interpretation of their meaning.[9] While the net loss was 337 (correctly, 335), Wesleyans and Undenominationals accounted for 138. Even more salutary for the Anglican case was the fact that its loss was 100 schools a year on a total of 11,377 whereas that of the other two together was 69 on a total of 1,046 schools. In short, the net loss of Church schools was less than one per cent per annum during a period of incessant anxiety over proposed destructive legislation. At that rate, it would take ten years before the total of Church schools was reduced to 10,000. Anglicans could take heart that they were not in imminent danger of being overwhelmed.[10]

Even more assuring were the statistics from 1909 to 1914. Referring to a study issued by the Board of Education for the decennium from 1902 to 1911, the School Guardian frankly deplored the further decline in Church schools from 11,711 to 10,952.[11] But the proportion of losses had been slowed down so that if in 1909 the figure was 11,102, it held at 10,952 in 1911, a tribute to noble efforts in a period when the onslaught of a Nonconformist-inspired Liberal Government was heavy. Particularly comforting to Rev. Taylor was the story contained in the Board of Education Report for 1911-12. Where the Guardian had chosen to emphasize the dismally large aggregate number of places lost, Rev. Taylor stressed the encouraging fact of an ultimate decrease in the number of places lost. While his set of figures too differed from those in the governmental bluebook, the interpretation of an ultimate slowing down in the number of places lost was correct: 1910, 178,000; 1911, 153,000; 1912, 28,000.[12] What had been happening was that the weaker schools had fallen by the wayside under the administrative at-

---

* A table of statistics prepared by the Board of Education for the period from 1902 to 1911 supports Talbot's calculations for the years from 1901 to 1907. In 1902 the Church of England had 11,711 schools, the Wesleyans 458, and the Undenominationals 644. The total shrinkage was 875 and that of the Wesleyans and Undenominationals together came to 438 or approximately one-half. Parl. Papers, 1911, LIX, Cd. 6002, p. 3.

tack of the Liberal regime. The stronger ones were being strengthened. The Church of England record was an honorable one, if far from satisfactory. This was hardly the time to talk of compromise or surrender.[13]

TRAINING COLLEGES

A more active campaign was favored among Nonconformists to enable their young people to obtain the necessary preparation for the teaching profession. The Board of Education was pressed to break the monopoly of the sectarians in denominational training colleges. McKenna responded on July 8, 1907, by announcing a new set of regulations designed to open up places in church-connected training colleges. First, no applications for admission into existing institutions could be rejected on the grounds of faith or for refusal to attend or to abstain from attending any place of worship or class in religious instruction in the college or elsewhere. The date set for effectiveness was August 1, 1908. Second, no new training college would be recognized in the future unless it complied with certain conditions: 1) no religious tests for the instructional staff, 2) no majority from a particular denomination on the governing board, 3) no compulsory class for the teaching of any catechism or formulary. In regard to the last-mentioned item, only the right of entry at the request of parents was to be permitted. Third, grants would not be available for sectarian hostels attached to the new training colleges. The date of effectiveness for the second and third regulations was set for August 1, 1907.[14]

Anglican reaction was instant and explosive. The new regulations would destroy the denominational character of their training colleges. The *Saturday Review* predicted that the admission of students of any and of no religion—Turk, Jew, infidel, heretic—would drive a wedge into their corporate life. The chapel service was the keystone and to permit the many exemptions that must follow would play havoc with the spiritual atmosphere. To have persons present treating with indifference or even active hostility an important facet of their daily life could endanger the morale of Anglican students. Indeed, one ill-conditioned person of perversive character could undermine the religious observances. The *Morning Post* asked if Jewish students would be indulged in their special foods and Sabbath services. Dr. Davidson predicted that denominational training colleges, weakened as their spiritual basis must become, would be equally powerless to provide an adequate preparation for teachers of Cowper-Templeism in council schools. Obviously the consequences could be fatal for the Christian outlook of the nation as a whole.[15]

What a breach of trust these regulations were! Subscriptions had been raised on the understanding that the State wanted the church associations to set up training colleges. Charles T. D. Acland used the figures of Sir Patrick Cumin, secretary to the Committee of Council on Education, submitted in 1886 to the Cross Commission, to illustrate the past sacrifices of Anglicans. The Church of England had contributed £271,185 compared to £92,613 by the State for building construction.[16] For the past twelve years, Dr. Davidson estimated that Anglicans had spent £210,000 more to enlarge and repair their colleges.[17] True it might be, agreed Rev. C. E. Brooke, St. John the Divine Vicarage, London, that the bulk of maintenance aid came from the State.[18] But the answer here was a matter of bookkeeping. It was not the training college which received the public money but the student who earned it by winning a King's Scholarship. The student could take the stipend to any college he chose. Only for sake of convenience was it paid in bulk to the training college after the completion of the student's education. Rev. Cleworth was fond of drawing an analogy with the admiralty which paid a private firm for building a ship but did not on that account claim to control all other work done in the yard where the ship was built.[19]

Anglicans failed to see where the current distribution of accommodations was unfair to Nonconformists. As Rev. Stevenson computed the figures, the number of places open to students with a preference for nonsectarianism was greatly in excess of those for Anglicans. Whereas the Church of England had 3,337 places, the Nonconformists could count 1,397 places in Wesleyan and Other Undenominational training colleges, 3,541 places in local day training colleges, and 801 places (including 484 in Church of England institutions) for day students in all the residential colleges.[20] In short, at the present moment, Nonconformists had over 5,700 places open to them. Furthermore, declared Dr. Davidson, the future had been even brighter with the expansion plans of the Church of England for more hostels and lodging houses open to Nonconformists.[21] Instead, noted Rev. Cleworth, the new regulations would dry up the religious sources eager to help construct new denominational training colleges and hostels. The government was making no attempt to increase accommodations, simply displacing students of the Anglican faith to make room for those with other credal affiliations.[22]

Anglicans were bitter at the apparent ruse of the Liberal Government to do by administrative regulation what they could not do by legislation.

The question of religious teaching in the schools had always been treated as of cardinal importance and so a matter for parliamentary action. The *Spectator* accused Nonconformists of having said to the government "that even if you cannot destroy Church predominance in the Voluntary Schools by Act of Parliament, you can make the Church exceedingly uncomfortable in the training colleges and produce indeed a state of things so intolerable that they will be glad to come to a compromise." Militantly the *Standard* called for resistance to the regulations, even to the extent of closing all the training colleges and leaving the government to find its own accommodations.† The National Society sought the advice of its lawyers and received the counsel that compliance with McKenna's regulations would be a violation of trust deeds. If McKenna persisted in his intention, then the denominational training colleges would have to accept the loss of exchequer grants and withdraw their approximately 4,000 places. In due course Dr. Davidson transmitted this information to McKenna, offering at the same time, on behalf of the governing bodies of the Anglican institutions, the alternative of an accelerated expansion of the hostel system.[23]

The Roman Catholic Church was no less angered by McKenna's training college regulations. The *Catholic Times* proclaimed that their colleges were to their teachers "what the seminaries are to our clergy." The pedagogue instructed "for Heaven and earth and so needs a special preparation in a special atmosphere for his sacred office." It was a matter of concern to envisage an Agnostic plying his anti-Christian crusade among Catholic students. At every turn the religious services would be mocked—the common prayer, Mass, reception of the Sacraments, the sermon. Cardinal Bourne reminded the nation of past financial sacrifices, stressing that from 1863 to 1905 the total maintenance fund was £409,000 and of this £93,000, or 22% came from subscriptions.[24] In the last five years the *Tablet* estimated that £150,000 had been spent upon the expansion of their training colleges at the encouragement of the State, a tremendous effort by a small and at that a very poor minor-

---

† A few Anglicans favored accepting the new regulations. They reasoned that the proportion of subscriptions to exchequer aid was steadily declining and at the moment it amounted to slightly less than 5% of the total. The important thing was to assure the Christian tone of training colleges and the pressure upon the government should be rather for making religious instruction available to students in all institutions. *Churchman*, Sept. 1907, pp. 516-17, Feb. 1908, pp. 66-67; The *Times*, Jan. 9, 1908, 6a (Percival), Feb. 5, 1908, 19b (Memorial of group of Churchmen to Prime Minister). For the year ending July 31, 1906, voluntary subscriptions were £22,806, exchequer grants £224,538, total receipts of fees and books £308,304. *Parl. Papers*, 1908, LXXXV, Cd. 3886, p. 374.

ity.[25] The Nonconformist grievance of no places for their children could be matched by the plight of Catholic youths whose training colleges (numbering 7 with accommodations for 631 students) were too few to admit all of them.[26] Certainly the nonsectarian character of the day colleges was hardly inviting for the hierarchy to place their stamp of approval upon them. Cardinal Bourne headed a deputation on July 25, 1907, to protest to Asquith and McKenna that the admission of students without reference to their religious beliefs would mean the destruction of the denominational foundation of Roman Catholic training colleges. Cardinal Bourne informed McKenna bluntly that his new regulations would not be obeyed.[27]

Surprisingly, Nonconformists were not impressed with the prospective benefits of McKenna's new regulations. There was no guarantee that religious tests would be eliminated for admission to denominational training colleges. Rev. Hollowell was positive that Anglicans would find some way to select their own youths for most of the places. There was nothing to suggest that Anglican management had been eliminated. The Established Church would still have the right to appoint a clergyman as principal and to exact a religious test from college staff members. As the Daily Chronicle saw it, all that Nonconformist students would escape was the necessity to attend the daily service in the college chapel. No provision was made for any other kind of religious worship within the residential campus. Indeed, given perchance a greater number of Nonconformist students at denominational training colleges under the new regulations and the potential of proselytism could increase, a conscience clause notwithstanding. In short, the regulations erred not in severity but in excessive indulgence toward sectarian interests.[28]

The Anglican contention that their heavy financial sacrifices merited special consideration was challenged. The Westminster Gazette referred to statistics prepared in 1906 by the Board of Education that between 1839 and 1862 Anglican contributions amounted to £165,668 and exchequer grants to £368,301, a ratio of more than two to one in favor of the State. Again, between 1863 and 1905, Anglican contributions amounted to £508,000 and exchequer grants to £3,418,000, a ratio of six to one.[29] Rev. W. Harper Fox, Congregational minister, Bury, Lancashire, confined himself to a comparison of maintenance recepits for the year 1900-01, listing Anglican contributions as £15,882 and exchequer grants as £149,548, a ratio of ten to one.[30] The Daily Chronicle offered a comparison for 1905, listing Anglican contributions as £27,135 and exchequer grants as £369,329, a ratio of fourteen to one.[31] For such progressively smaller outlays, denominationalists had no right to post figuratively over the entrances to their colleges the sign that "no Nonconformists need apply." Dr. Clifford matched Rev. Cleworth in drawing an analogy, picturing the cool reception a Rationalist would receive if he offered to put in every town a library, provided the shelves were restricted to books issued by the Rationalist press.[32]

Nonconformists placed greater hope for the future in the provisions outlined for new training colleges. In these the ban against religious tests for admission could be enforced effectively. Rev. Hollowell welcomed the stipulation that the majority of the governing body must not be of one particular denomination. Admittedly, it would be better to have the entire membership and not just a majority severed from denominational ties. It was a distinct gain to have the new training colleges required to assemble their instructional staffs without regard for religious affiliations. However, Nonconformists manifested stubborn opposition to the Anglican proposal for each set of training colleges to accept hostels. The suspicion was voiced that if hostels were permitted in the new training colleges, Anglicans would aim to exploit theirs as an instrument of sectarian incubation. Nonconformists had no intention to ask for protection of their youths as communicants but rather as citizen students. The *Nation* informed Anglicans that nothing less than national training institutions, State-supported and State-controlled and free from every shadow of ecclesiasticism, would be accepted.[33]

A *modus vivendi* was arrived at in June 1908, between the Church of England training colleges and the Board of Education. The former agreed to make available 50% of the vacancies in the coming September term to those not of the Anglican faith. These students would be housed in the college itself, or in annexes, hostels, and lodgings approved by the Board of Education. This compromise was to be for the coming year only to allow for a period of review. The Catholic Church refused to enter into any agreement to admit non-Catholic students and apparently did not suffer any penalties.[34]

Reaction in Anglican circles varied. On the one hand, the *School Guardian* felt that the avoidance of litigation over trust deeds and the possible loss of grants were worth the admission of some non-Anglican students. Furthermore, assuming an average of equality in intellect and character between Nonconformist and Anglican applicants, the chances were that the proportion of Nonconformists admitted would be far less than 50% of the total matriculations. So in effect the temporary arrangement would not bear too marked a departure from that now operating in denominational training colleges. On the other hand, Rev. Taylor regarded the compromise as an abandonment of trust deeds. While it was only "for a year" and "without prejudice," it would have to run for two years since that was the length of the full course for students. In the meanwhile, where there were no hostels, non-Church students would be mingling with Church students. The consequence could only be a secularized atmosphere.[35]

Nonconformists tended to look on the brighter side of the *modus vivendi*, withal their previously severe strictures against the McKenna regulations. The *Westminster Gazette* believed that the withdrawal by the Church of England of the plea that trust deeds forbade compliance would strengthen its leadership with the nation. In turn it could foreshadow an acknowledgment by the Established Church that changing conditions had made obsolete the theory of education as an ecclesiastical function. If this came to pass, then peace in the broader field of State education was yet possible. The *Daily News* allowed its imagination to dwell upon the significant possibility that the dignity of the teaching profession itself would be enhanced. While one could duly record the great contribution of the churches to education during centuries when the nation at large cared nothing about it, the fact remained that the patronage of the privileged orders affixed a stigma of inferior social status upon the teacher. As Charlotte Yonge's novels would testify, the teacher became identified with the upper strata of servants.[‡] This tradition still persisted and lent its peculiar sting to the profession. How noticeably different was the bearing and mental sturdiness of students in the training colleges attached to the universities. The more strenuous intellectual life provided prospective teachers with an exhilarating anticipation of their role in society. For the future, therefore, if the final goal must be an end to the denominational training colleges, it should be not merely to eliminate sectarianism but also a humiliating social view which could not be tolerated in a modern democracy.[36]

The sequel to the *modus vivendi* brought strange developments. Anglicans did not cease in their efforts to salvage the religious atmosphere of denominational training colleges. While the National Society noted that in the first two years the number of Nonconformists admitted annually was only 170 out of 1,600 or slightly more than ten per cent, the time would come when the maximum was reached and then a grave situation must occur. Hoare contended, moreover, that the steady expansion of day training colleges had lessened the need for

---

‡ An example may be found in Charlotte M. Yonge, *The Carbonels* (New York: 1895), p. 93. Mrs. Carbonel, seeking a teacher for her children, inquires about a widow at her old home site who had once been a servant in the family. Mrs. Carbonel recalled her to be a good religious person who could read and calculate well enough for any possibly advanced scholars and, to boot, was an accomplished needlewoman.

opening places in denominational institutions.* As a matter of fact, by 1914, a new danger confronted Anglicans. The National Society expressed itself as worried by the growing number of places unfilled in its training colleges. The *School Guardian* had its analysis of the problem. Local authorities, blessed with unlimited funds, had expanded their facilities unnecessarily. Again, the general impression circulating that the teaching profession was overcrowded discouraged recruits. Naturally the competition for applicants between day and denominational training colleges was intensified. Dr. Davidson accused the former of questionable tactics. Not only did they offer attractive scholarships but they also resorted to the sly argument that the cost falling upon the rates would be diminished proportionately with the receipt of capitation grants for each student. Since the day training colleges in the main still paid no attention to religious instruction, Dr. Davidson protested that a monopoly of teacher training in their hands would let in secularism by a side wind.[37]

Statistics of training colleges today show that a marked change has occurred in the number of students handled by the various institutions. According to tables prepared by the Ministry of Education for 1956-57 the disposition of training colleges and students is as follows: local authorities—64 (12,632); Church of England—25, (5,210); Roman Catholic—13 (1,958); Wesleyan—2 (475); Undenominational—9 (1,292). Thus the passage of time has seen the day training colleges forge ahead. Further, grouping together those of the local authorities, Wesleyans, and Undenominationals as nonsectarian, the number of places open on a non-credal basis is double that controlled by the denominationalists (Anglican and Roman Catholic).[38]

ACT OF 1944

What has the present-day generation in England and Wales done with the explosive inheritance of the religious issue? The facts suggest that the idea of a concordat based on general religious instruction plus supplementary facilities has gained considerable ground. This most recent development is the result of the Act of 1944.[39] The stimulus for

---

* A comparison of training college accommodations for 1902 and 1913 (*Parl. Papers*, 1902, XXIV, Cd. 1275, p. 45; 1914-16, L, Cd. 7674, pp. 216-17) is as follows:

	1902		1913	
	Colleges	Places	Colleges	Places
Denom.	45	4,454	48	5,846
Day	17	1,426	19	3,738

this measure came from the need to bring up-to-date many of the dilapidated school buildings. The sacrifices of the British nation against the Hitler onslaught should have tangible meaning. The returning war heroes should be assured, among other things, that their children would have a better chance to fulfill their destiny as dignified human beings. The voluntary schools were offered two choices in connection with the prospective heavy expense of reconstruction involved for them. If they chose to become controlled schools and accept the designation of two-thirds of their managers by the local authority, then the State would bear the entire cost. If they chose to become aided schools and permit only one-third non-foundation managers as heretofore, then the State would bear one-half the cost.

The central issue now as before was the Christian basis of the various types of State schools. Where church educational associations chose to bear one-half the cost and so place their schools in the category of those aided, their retention of two-thirds of the managers would enable them to continue to name the teachers and to dictate the content of the religious instruction. But in the controlled as well as the council schools a new settlement would prevail. Religious instruction was to be compulsory and in accordance with an agreed syllabus to be drawn up by a conference including Nonconformist and Anglican representatives, branch agents of the teachers' association, and the local authority. The Cowper-Temple clause excluding catechisms or religious formularies distinctive of particular denominations would govern the content of the agreed syllabus and the Victorian timetable conscience clause would be available for objectors. While the majority of the staff were to be selected without religious tests, it was specified that one-fifth (excluding the head teacher) were to be picked for fitness to give the religious instruction and were to be known as reserved teachers. In order to use this corps of specialists to the fullest extent, the religious lesson could be set for any period during the school day. In addition, in the controlled school, two days of credal instruction could be substituted for the children of those parents who so desired.

Some interpretation is possible as to the implementation of the Act of 1944 for the years in which it has operated. The Catholic Church, which manifested the greatest opposition to the measure, chose to have its schools become aided and accepted under protest the financial burden to meet fifty per cent of the cost of reconstruction. The Church of England followed a middle course, allowing about one-half of its schools to become controlled. In terms of statistics, as of January 1958, and bearing in mind that computations today are of departments rather than schools and that there has been a separation of elementary and secondary grades, they are as follows for the Church of England: out of 7,836 schools 4,323 have become controlled, 3,294 aided, and 219 are in an indeterminate status.[40] In the matter of the general religious instruction for controlled and council schools, both Anglicans and Non-conformists would appear to have cooperated closely in drawing up agreed syllabuses.[41] Moreover, local authorities have been very generous to publish them in bound printed form. The number in use is very large and some, notably those of Durham and Cambridgeshire, have been adopted by other counties.

Undoubtedly, the prospect of attrition and anxiety over the future of the British Isles as a Protestant nation provided the impetus for the *eirenicon* between Anglicans and Nonconformists assuring religious instruction in all State schools. In this respect it might be interesting to note as of January 1958 the comparative figures of schools and average attendance with those of 1911, lumping together controlled and aided as voluntary schools.[42] In 1911 the figures read as follows: Church of England, 10,952 (1,750,094); Roman Catholic, 1,073 (293,391); Wesleyan, 223 (56,181); Jewish, 12 (9,159); Undenominational, 490 (82,389). In January 1958 the figures read as follows: Church of England, 7,836 (859,426); Roman Catholic, 1,697 (418,797); Others (Wesleyan, Jewish, Undenominational),† 215 (27,663). Save for the Catholic Church, the voluntary schools were steadily declining. In contrast, the council schools in 1911 and 1958 numbered 8,006 (2,164,591) and 13,977 (3,202,529) respectively. Patently the most telltale figure was the average attendance record and where in 1902 the Church of England taught more than one-half of the nation's pupils, in 1958 it was less than one-fifth. The specter that the efflux of time might dissolve the religious issue had been no chimera and probably influenced a more receptive mood for a compromise between the Church of England and the Free Churches.

---

† For more comparable detailed figures the Ministry of Education Report for January 1956 lists Wesleyan, 100 (13,332); Jewish, 8 (2,092); Undenominational, 114 (14,162). *Education in 1956: Being the Report of the Ministry of Education and the Statistics of Public Education For England and Wales* (Cd. 223), p. 92.

CHAPTER THIRTEEN

CONCLUSION

H OW FAR in this instance one can go beyond unfolding the true record of the past is a moot question. Despite the well-known proclivity of Englishmen for compromise solutions, nothing seemingly could budge many participants from their adamant positions. To assume the role of a tribunal of final review and say who was right and who was wrong would seem to ask the impossible, even of a Solomon. Obviously the gravamen of any judgment must center about the conception of the role of the school in society. Few will cavil with the thesis that education should seek to mold a youth versed in the tools of knowledge and possessed of high ethical ideals. The critical issue is the contention of the churches of the need for an intimate relationship between Christian bodies and the schools. The assurance that the nation would remain spiritual in outlook and be guided by sound moral principles should be treasured achievements of the schools. The position of secularists was that the heterogeneous incidence of religion in the British Isles posed a problem for freedom of conscience if the schools were used to foster church membership. However the religious syllabus might be framed, there would be children and teachers with contrary spiritual convictions. Moreover, a morality emphasizing a positive social conscience was not the same as the church idea of a personal conduct code. In the end the inevitable conflict of interests must have an adverse effect upon the secular program.

But for this study to single out the thesis of any one plaintiff as possessing the best case is to risk the validity of the research as an objective account of the past. Apart from the truth of the statement that all facts are relative, where the area of man's thinking is the highly sensitized one of religion, the plaintiffs could well charge that personal views influenced the judgment. The real and ultimate solution must rest with a nation to register its collective thinking and not for a self-assertive fountain of justice in the form of an individual to press forward his views. However, so great was the division of opinion among Englishmen that an actual stalemate developed, dented only by partisan advantages reaped in the fluctuating fortunes of political warfare. Yet it would appear worthwhile to parade the human and institutional elements whose welfare were the objects of the debate. Perhaps their introduction on the stage before the spotlight may serve to point up the facts in the case.

The most immediate figure to discuss is the parent. Occasionally in the literature the statement is encountered that the average parent was satisfied with whatever religious instruction his child was receiving. The religious squabble was put down as one "made in Germany," unrealistic and concocted. Extremists on all sides were accused of maliciously stirring up a hornet's nest. Probably some parents could honestly say that the dual system with its twin functions of religious and civic education met the needs of their children. Probably some parents were indifferent and did not want to be embroiled in a troublesome controversy. But the documentary material belies any attempt to establish as a sweeping generalization the impression of an artificial quarrel. The letters and articles dispatched to editors recounting tribulations are too numerous to be dismissed with lightness. Many parents were concerned that their children's schooldays were neither happy nor rewarding ones. Presumably the exchanges of confidence in the intimacy of the hearth suggested incongruous situations in the classroom due to the particular nature of a school's religious life, for from parents of all faiths and no faiths came hot words of indignation, attesting to the undeniable presence of a real problem.

Whether the child experienced the deep concern of its parents is a matter of conjecture. One naturally looks in vain for documentary material in youthful handwriting to convey in written words what went on in the inner recesses of the mind. The articulation of a child is to be sought in his queries, his chatter, and his outward demeanor. And even at that, it would appear to depend on a child's psychological make-up and his upbringing as to how much his stability was affected. Where impressionableness and environment had been conducive to a consciousness of piety, confusion toward the spiritual world often must have reigned. At best, perhaps an aggrieved parent might derive some balm in the hope that his child possessed the fortitude to extract the most good from a difficult situation. At worst, if the final product was a bruised soul, then the aggrieved parent must live with the knowledge that his child had trying days ahead to adjust himself to a world of harsh balance. At any rate, for many parents the writhing fact that the school often was turned into an instrument for transmitting religious intoleration did not endear education to him.

The teacher was still another central figure in the religious controversy. As Anglicans and Catholics would picture him, he treasured his calling as a sacred office to train children to become active communicants. As Nonconformists would see him, he welcomed the opportunity to diffuse a Christian spirit among his charges. As Rationalists would analyze him, he was distraught to find himself the catspaw of feuding sectaries and his professional duties in civic education subordinated. Each school of thought could count disciples rallying to its point of view. But the literature of the period is also replete with epistles from the teaching profession which suggest that the best of all worlds was not always present. Even for voluntary school teachers, if many radiated inward happiness in the performance of a pastoral function, they resented the penalty of inferior material rewards. For those teachers in council schools whose religious convictions were at odds with the syllabus they had to use, the hour devoted to reverence was a source of constant frustration. At best, those who regarded teaching as their life work could hope that the inner rewards would serve to reconcile them to the inroads made upon their conceptions of infinity. At worst, those whose tender souls opened to the floodgates of bitterness under the strain of spiritual embarrassment probably lost much of their zeal for the educational career.

Nor were the churches free from being rent asunder by the divisions within their ranks as to what policy to follow. The Established Church found itself no less embroiled with school matters than with doctrinal practices. True it is that Anglican resistance to the several measures of the Liberal Government presented a fairly united front. True it is, too, that Anglicans were one in their insistence upon positive Christian instruction as the only worth-while type of religious lesson. But there was no concealing the deeper cleavages when the question of a concordat cropped up. The High Church party, numbering in its ranks the Cecil family, Bishop Talbot of Rochester, and Athelstan Riley, was adamant upon the retention of the dual system modified perhaps by universal facilities. Only thus would there be any assurance that church membership would be in the forefront of educational aims. The Low Church party, to which Bishop Percival of Hereford and Canon Henson subscribed, was ready to accept a national system based upon the theme of a fundamental Christianity. Such a firm foundation, joining all children of Protestant faith in corporate worship would make easy the addition of the superstructure. The Moderate Church party, in whose camp understandably were to be encountered both archbishops, Dr. Frederick Temple and Dr. Randall Davidson, sought to chart a middle course. The Established Church should be not only the shepherd of its own flock but also the symbol of the Reformation to all Protestants. That responsibility could best be discharged by supporting a national system embracing effective general Christian instruction plus a real opportunity for credal lessons to fructify as a standard bearer of the best in religious instruction.

Nonconformists were no more united in their views of the proper solution of the school controversy. They were one in resisting the Balfour Act of 1902. They supported undenominational religious instruction as the finest foundation for later adding the superstructure. They were arrayed together for the establishment of a national system, predicated on the twin principles of popular control and no tests for teachers. But on the other side of the ledger there was the persistence of the Wesleyans in retaining their own schools. Again, Nonconformists differed measurably in their reactions to the various concordat proposals. One pivotal point was the question of facilities. Some, like Dr. Clifford, were not averse if facilities were given out of school hours and using only outside personnel. Some, like Rev. Hollowell, would not approve any kind of facilities, fearful that an overtone of sectarianism would prevail in the schools. Another pivotal point was the nature of the simple Bible reading. Where most Free Churchmen conceived of these lessons as definitely impregnated with the supernatural character of Christianity, Dr. Clifford would stress rather a non-theological use of the Scriptures. Some voices were raised for the application of the traditional principle of separation of Church and State to the field of education. Their fewness is to be explained perhaps by the twin factors of Romanism and Agnosticism whose growing strength made perilous the secular solution. The greater number of Free Churchmen were determined that the fruits of the Protestant Reformation must be preserved, even at the sacrifice of a nobler vision of spiritual vibrancy.

Catholics were not entirely free from friction among themselves. When the hierarchy chose to speak with finality, unity of thought and action were achieved. But there was latitude for a limited time to examine the various aspects at each stage of the school controversy. Perhaps it is the hierarchical conception of democracy employed to bring forth clearly the issues involved prior to the pronouncement of the line to be followed. Certainly Catholics were one in their conviction that the role of education was to form the practicing communicant. Where they differed was in the degree of adjustment necessary to arrive at the desired goal under particular circumstances. Because they were living in a predominantly Protestant country some Roman Catholics, Abbot Ford, for example, would explore all possible concordats. Again, there were differences of opinion over political strategy. Where the *Tablet* inclined to the Tory Party, the *Catholic Herald* preferred the Liberal Party. The relative weight which the Irish Nationalist Party should give to Home Rule and the survival of English Catholic schools reflected this cleavage. However, especially after the Liberal Government had suffered the defeat of the Runciman Bill, the hierarchy came forward to state boldly the official position as that of separate schools with generous financial support. Whatever risks Protestants might be ready to take in compromising the virility of Christianity in England and Wales, the Roman Catholic Church would insist upon the school as a spiritual shelter on the road to salvation.

Non-Christians—Agnostics, Positivists, Rationalists, Freethinkers, and Ethicists, among others—were alert to the future of their own fortunes. To be sure, they joined hands with any Christians who favored the secular solution. But this union was naturally a combination of strange bedfellows. On the one hand, secularists who claimed Jesus as the hope of redemption had no intention that their stand on the school issue should tell against Britain as a Christian nation. If their advocacy of the secular solution was partly conditioned by the conviction that the sectarian strife was affecting adversely educational progress, they were also sure that the spiritual life of the country would benefit. School religion often seemed to contain a secularizing catalyst. On the other hand, non-Christians were not preoccupied with saving Christianity. It was a matter of propriety not to press such thinking too heavily while the conflict raged over school religion. The immediate object was to gather strength from all quarters to uproot conventional theology from the schools. Then, at least, and especially if moral instruction of a non-theological nature were taught in the schools, their children as pupils and teacher candidates would find a happier climate in the schools. Further, given relief from the Christian incense in the schools, it would be easier to win their own children over to their notions of infinity.

Some pertinent comments seem in order on the effect of sectarianism upon the progress of education in England and Wales. The foregoing facts should indicate that the secular program was not the beneficiary of the embattled adversaries. The enthusiasm of students, teachers, and parents for the civic purpose of education was subject to constant vitiation. The support of public opinion for the State schools had always been difficult to achieve because of the close tie between the substantial citizenry and the privately-supported schools. How much more loathe must have been the inclination of people to take an interest in the State schools when called upon to express an opinion on the religious issue. In short, the penalty was that, save for a few indomitable souls, the field of education would be abdicated to those spurred by credal interests. The progress made by the Board of Education to improve the schooling opportunities of children was painfully slow and tedious.

Moreover, the lay subjects themselves were swept into the vortex of the religious issue. While it is true that commentaries on this topic were not abundant, they were sufficient to indicate an awareness of the problem. The classical aspects of elementary education included both history and literature. In the case of history, whether it related to the British Isles or the Continent, the teacher faced difficulties in presenting the Protestant Reformation. One might like to believe that the teacher treated the material from the vantage point of the potential enrichment of Christianity on the theory that rival churches would outdo themselves in acts of ennobling piety to attract worshippers. Again, in the case of literature, especially that of England from the seventeenth century on, an appreciative acquaintance required an open treatment of many facets of Christian theology. But the acuteness of the controversy over the use of the school to foster church membership weakened any objective approach. More likely the teacher was a victim of the charged atmosphere and presented either a biased and harsh account or one so cautious as to strip the story of any human warmth. In short, under the existing pincer of aroused religious passions, the ability of the lay subjects to promote the cultural side of man's nature was beset with tensions.

Catapulting the status of the religious issue to the present time, the decision of today's generation in England and Wales obviously has been to continue the partnership between the churches and the State in the field of education. It will be recalled that the Act of 1944 recognized the presence of voluntary schools in the form of aided schools with two-thirds of the managers to be appointed by church educational associations as heretofore. Again, religious instruction was made compulsory in all elementary schools, and in the transferred (controlled) and council schools the right was granted to use a portion of the regular staff as a corps of specialists to give the Cowper-Temple lessons. From the Protestant point of view, the Christian tone in the schools was especially strengthened by the agreement between Anglicans and Nonconformists to participate in drawing up the religious syllabus in the various localities. It is important to hope that the decision represents a nation fully cognizant of the manifold ramifications for spiritual vitality, religious liberty, and educational progress. The tribulations from 1902 to 1914 should be a sharp reminder that the step ought not to have been taken lightly. If it is mere submission to the pressure of aggressive interests, then troubles galore are being stored up in the future for both religion and the schools. At any rate, if the principle of freedom of conscience is to be pursued in the form of a religion of the majority settlement with the rights of minorities duly respected, the new measure will certainly challenge the quest for human dignity in the universal sense.

NOTES

NOTES

CHAPTER ONE: INTRODUCTION

1. For general literature on English education see Adamson, *English Education, 1789-1902* (1930); Barnard, *A Short History of English Education From 1760 to 1944* (1952); Birchenough, *History of Elementary Education in England and Wales From 1800 to the Present Day* (1938, 3rd ed.); Curtis, *History of Education in Great Britain* (1950, 2nd ed.); Smith, *A History of English Elementary Education, 1760-1902* (1931).

2. For some interesting illustrations of the employment of the Bible in the lay subjects see Birchenough (1938), pp. 274-75.

3. For a glimpse into the story of the religious issue after 1870 see Adams, *History of the Elementary School Contest in England* (1882); Halévy, *Imperialism and the Rise of Labour* (1951, 2nd rev. ed.), p. 163 ff.

4. *Parl. Papers*, 1901, LVI, Cd. 568, p. 134.

5. *Ministry of Education*, 1902, Bill Papers, No. 22.

6. Halévy (1951, 2nd rev. ed.), pp. 196-98.

7. Halévy (1951, 2nd rev. ed.), pp. 199-200; Webb, *Our Partnership* (1948), pp. 253-55.

8. *The Times*, July 4, 1901, 12c.

9. Dugdale, *Arthur James Balfour* (1937), I, pp. 236-40; Fitzroy, *Memoirs* (1925, 3rd ed.), I, pp. 63-81.

10. Amery, *The Life of Joseph Chamberlain* (1951), IV, pp. 478-508.

11. Amery (1951), IV, pp. 491-92.

12. Dugdale, *Arthur James Balfour* (1937), pp. 241-43.

13. For an account of the opposition in the Liberal Party see Haldane, *An Autobiography* (1929, 2nd ed.), p. 148; Spender, *The Life of the Right Hon. Sir Henry Campbell-Bannerman* (1923), II, pp. 81-84.

14. For the clauses of the Balfour Bill as it went through the legislative stages see *Parl. Papers*, 1902, I, Bills 138, 303, 304, 309. For the definitive provisions see Public General Acts, 2nd year, Edward VII, 1902, Chapt. 42, pp. 126-47. For secondary literature see Adamson (1952), pp. 245-47; Curtis (1950), pp. 315-19; Smith (1931), pp. 347-49.

CHAPTER TWO: PASSAGE OF THE ACT OF 1902

1. *Church Times*, Jan. 3, 1902 (Maclagan); *Ministry of Education*, 1902, Bill Papers, No. 10a.

2. *Parl. Papers*, 1901, LVI, Cd. 568, p. 134.

3. *Parl. Papers*, 1902, LXXVIII, Cd. 1139, pp. 76, 79.

4. *Guardian*, May 28, 1902 (Miller); *School Guardian*, April 19, 1902; Moorhouse, *The Education Bill* (1902), pp. 7-8.

5. The breakdown (*National Society*, Annual Report, 1902, p. 14) is as follows for the period from 1870 to 1900:

	Buildings	Maintenance
Day Schools	£8,407,751	£20,060,319
Training Colleges	£ 166,400	£ 437,647

6. *Parl. Papers*, 1902, LXXVIII, Cd. 1139, pp. 60-64.

7. *Parl. Papers*, 1902, LXXVIII, Cd. 1139, p. 7.

8. *School Guardian*, April 26, 1902; *The Times*, Sept. 16, 1902, 8e-f (Rev. E. F. Taylor); Dymott, *The Case for the Voluntary School* (1902), p. 1; MacColl, *The Education Question and the Liberal Party* (1902), pp. 5, 78-79.

9. *Parl. Papers*, 1902, LXXVIII, Cd. 1139, p. 71.

10. *National Society*, Annual Report, 1902, p. 11.

11. *Manchester Guardian*, Aug. 7, 1902 (Cleworth); *School Guardian*, July 5, 1902; *Standard*, April 28, 1902; Humphreys, *The Plain Truth about the Education Bill* (1902), p. iii; Moorhouse, *The Education Bill* (1902), p. 5.

12. Amery (1951), IV, pp. 487-89.

13. *Church Times*, March 27, 1902; *Guardian*, March 26, April 2, 1902; *Pall Mall Gazette*, March 25, 1902; *School Guardian*, March 29, April 5, 1902; *Western Mail* (Cardiff), May 17, July 11, 1902.

14. For the several successful amendments see *Parl. Papers*, 1902, I, Bills 303, 309.

15. There is no command paper to verify this estimate with regard to teachers' dwellings and a check with the Ministry of Education produced no file papers on the subject.

16. For the year ending Aug. 31, 1901, educational endowments yielded an income of £123,761 to the Church of England, £611 to Wesleyans, £2,677 to Roman Catholics, and £26,917 to the British (and Foreign School Society) and other schools—a total of £153,966. *Parl. Papers*, 1902, LXXVII, Cd. 1139, pp. 70-73.

17. For the year ending Aug. 31, 1901, the breakdown of income resources indicated that school fees netted the Church of England £121,815, Wesleyans £29,981, Roman Catholics £7,163, and the British (and Foreign School Society) and other schools £31,161 —a total of £190,210. *Parl. Papers*, LXXVIII, Cd. 1139, pp. 70-72.

18. *Church Times*, March 27, Dec. 19, 1902; *Lords*, Dec. 10, 1902, p. 560 (Moorhouse); *Manchester Guardian*, Dec. 15, 1902 (Cleworth); *School Guardian*, July 5, 1902; *The Times*, Dec. 13, 1902, 12d (P. V. Smith).

19. *Parl. Papers*, 1902, I, Bill 138, pp. 3-4.

20. *Church Times*, March 27, 1902; *Guardian*, March 26, May 14, 1902; *School Guardian*, April 5, 1902; *Standard*, Nov. 5, 1902.

21. *Daily News*, Oct. 8, 1902 (Taylor); *Guardian*, April 16, May 14, 1902; *School Guardian*, June 21, 1902; *The Times*, April 19, 1902, 13d-e (Bishop Talbot of Rochester); MacColl, *The Education Question and the Liberal Party* (1902), pp. 48-49; Moorhouse, *The Education Bill* (1902), p. 4.

22. *Morning Post*, Oct. 20, 1902; *Lords*, Dec. 2, 1902, p. 408 (Percival); *Pilot*, May 3, 1902; *The Times*, July 30, 1902, 8b (Percival), Aug. 2, 1902, 6f (Wilson).

23. For a sampling of adverse Anglican opinion see *Church Times*, July 18, Oct. 17, 1902; *Commons*, July 30, 1902, p. 170 (A. Griffith-Boscawen); *Guardian*, July 2, 1902; *The Times*, July 31, 1902, 5e (J. J. Scott), Aug. 6, 1902, 4f (Lacey).

24. *Tablet*, Jan. 25, 1902, Supplement (Glancey), May 10, Dec. 27, 1902 (ed.).

25. *Catholic Herald*, May 9, 1902; *Catholic Times*, April 4, May 16, Dec. 19, 24, 1902; *Dublin Rev.*, July 1902, pp. 26-30 (Glancey); *Tablet*, Dec. 20-27, 1902.

26. For literature on the operation of the cumulative vote in school board contests see Adams (1882), *passim*.

27. *Catholic Times*, May 16, Oct. 3, 31, Dec. 24, 1902; *Tablet*, Oct. 4, 1902; *Ministry of Education*, 1902, Bill Papers, No. 320, Letter, Cardinal Vaughan to Lord Talbot, Nov. 4, 1902.

28. *Catholic Times*, Oct. 17, 1902; *Commons*, July 30, 1902, pp. 141-46 (Dillon); *Tablet*, Oct. 25, Nov. 1, 1902 (Ford), July 19, Sept. 6, Oct. 25, 1902 (ed.); *The Times*, Aug. 5, 1902, 8e (J. G. Snead Cox).

29. *Catholic Herald*, Oct. 3, 10, 24, 1902; *Catholic Times*, Oct. 10, Dec. 5, 1902; *Tablet*, Oct. 11, 1902, p. 579 (Vaughan), Dec. 6, 1902, pp. 888-89 (John Redmond).

30. Rev. Blomfield's figures can be arrived at thus: 1) in 1870 contributions per scholar were 7s. 0d. and school fees were 8s. 4d. out of a total income of £1 5s. 6d. per scholar and 2) in 1901 contributions were 6s. 8d. and school fees were 1s. 7d. out of a total income of £2 5s. 4d. *Parl. Papers*, 1902, LXXVIII, Cd. 1139, pp. 74, 76.

31. *Baptist Times*, Sept. 19, 1902 (Blomfield); *Christian World*, April 24, 1902; Clifford, *The Fight Against the Education Bill* (1902), pp. 19-20; Gibson, *An Appeal to British Justice on the Education Question* (1902), pp. 12-14.

32. For the official figures upon which Dr. Macnamara based his statistics see *Parl. Papers*, 1902, LXXVIII, Cd. 1139, pp. 16-19.

33. *Commons*, May 5, 1902, p. 654 (Bryce), Oct. 27, 1902, p. 870 (Lloyd George); *The Times*, Aug. 28, 1902, 4e (Macnamara); Gibson, *An Appeal to British Justice on the Education Question* (1902), p. 21; Macnamara, *The Education Bill* (1902), pp. 15-17.

34. *Parl. Papers*, 1900, LXV, Part 1, Cd. 109, pp. 74-84, 90. The year 1898 was the last one in which grants were broken down for the two school systems and thereafter the block grant system was employed.

35. National Education Association, *The Education Crisis; A Defence of Popular Management in Public Education* (1902), 96 pp.

36. *Parl. Papers*, 1883, XXV, Cd. 3706-1, p. 190.

37. *Parl. Papers*, 1902, LXXVIII, Cd. 1139, p. 5.

38. *New Liberal Rev.*, Sept. 1902, pp. 165-66; *Speaker*, Sept. 27, 1902 (Edmund Robertson); Gibson, *An Appeal to British Justice on the Education Question* (1902), pp. 20-21.

39. *Parl. Papers*, 1901, XIX, Cd. 757, p. 359.

40. For the space regulation see *Parl. Papers*, 1902, LXXVIII, Cd. 1332, 13 pp.

41. *Speaker*, May 24, 1902 (Woodhead).

42. For 1901 the school rate amounted to £3,340,975. *Parl. Papers*, 1902, LXXVIII, Cd. 1139, p. 79.

43. Hollowell in *Daily Chronicle*, April 28, 1902; in *Daily News*, Sept. 27, 1902; in *The Times*, April 28, 1902, 9f.

44. There is a reference in the debates that information on teachers' residences had been laid on the table but there is no command paper to verify these figures. Inquiries to the libraries of the commons and the lords and to the Ministry of Education produced no documentary memorandum. *Commons*, Nov. 19, 1902, p. 1345.

45. Martin, *The Education Bill, 1902* (1902), p. 7.

46. *Baptist Times*, Nov. 28, 1902 (White); *British Weekly*, Nov. 27, Dec. 18, 1902; *Daily News*, Nov. 21, 1902; *New Liberal Rev.*, Jan. 1903, p. 778 (Clifford); *Speaker*, Nov. 22, Dec. 20, 1902; *Westminster Gazette*, Nov. 19, 21, 1902.

47. *British Weekly*, April 3, Nov. 6, 27, 1902; *Daily Chronicle*, Nov. 4, 1902; *Daily News*, Nov. 5, 1902; *Manchester Guardian*, Nov. 6, 1902; *Monthly Messenger*, May, Dec. 1902; *Speaker*, Nov. 8, 1902; *Westminster Gazette*, April 4, 14, May 22, 1902.

48. *Baptist Times*, Sept. 19, 1902 (Blomfield); *British Weekly*, April 10, Aug. 14, 1902; *Daily News*, March 25, Nov. 13, 1902; *Manchester Guardian*, July 16, 1902 (Elliot); *Speaker*, Nov. 22, 1902; Armstrong, *The Government Assault on Education* (1902), pp. 61-64.

49. *Baptist Times*, May 2, 1902; *Commons*, May 6, 1902, pp. 851-52 (Griffith), p. 902 (Macnamara), Oct. 27, 1902, p. 874 (Macnamara). *Daily Chronicle*, Oct. 28, 1902; *Methodist Times*, Dec. 11, 1902.

50. *Agnostic Journal*, Nov. 8, 1902; *Literary Guide and Rationalist Rev.*, Aug. 1, 1902 (Picton).

51. For Morley's statement of himself as a Positivist see *Recollections* (1917), II, p. 297.

52. *Labour Leader*, June 7, 1902 (Hardie); *The Times*, Nov. 4, 1902, 9e (Alderley).

53. For Balfour's concession see *Commons*, Oct. 28-30, 1902.

54. *British Weekly*, July 24, 1902; *Commons*, May 8, 1902, 1102-03 (Lloyd George); *Daily Chronicle*, Nov. 10, 1902 (Rogers); *Daily News*, Oct. 29, 1902.

55. *British Weekly*, July 24, Sept. 11, 1902; *Commons*, March 24, 1902, p. 911 (Compton-Rickett), July 21, 1902, p. 861 (Bryce); *Examiner*, April 17, 24, 1902.

56. *British Weekly*, June 25, 1902 (Jowett); *Commons*, May 8, 1902, p. 1099 (Lloyd George); *Liberal Magazine*, April 1902, p. 158 (Birrell); *Monthly Messenger*, May 1902; Perks in *The Government Education Bill*, pamphlet No. 5, Oct. 15, 1902, p. 29 (Liberal Publication Dept.).

57. *Church Times*, Oct. 31, 1902 (Lacey); *Commons*, March 24, 1902, pp. 877-78 (Richard Jebb); *School Guardian*, May 17, 1902; MacColl, *The Education Question and the Liberal Party* (1902), pp. 27-28, 54-56.

58. *Church Times*, Sept. 26, 1902; *Lords*, Dec. 10, 1902, pp. 613-14 (Sheepshanks); *Pilot*, July 5, 1902 (ed.), April 26, 1902 (Curtoys); *The Times*, May 27, 1902, 4a-b (Davidson).

59. For Rev. Robert Dale's statement see A. W. W. Dale (his son), *The Life of R. W. Dale of Birmingham* (1899), p. 280.

60. For Rev. Dymott's statistics see *Parl. Papers*, 1871, XXII, Cd. 406, p. 1 and 1903, LI, Cd. 1476, p. 16.

61. *Daily News*, Sept. 23, 1902 (Dymott); *Empire Rev.*, Oct. 1902, pp. 221-23 (Bishop Talbot of Rochester); *Pilot*, May 24, 1902; *The Times*, April 12, 1902, 11d-e; Dymott, *The Case for the Voluntary School* (1906), p. 2.

62. *British Weekly*, April 10, 1902; *Commons*, May 8, 1902, p. 1148 (White); *Pilot*, May 17, 31, 1902 (Bartlet); *The Times*, April 9, 1902, 6f (Massie); Gibson, *An Appeal to British Justice on the Education Question* (1902), pp. 7-8.

63. *Commons*, July 7, 1902, p. 944 ff.

64. *Parl. Papers*, 1902, XXIV, Cd. 1275, p. 47.

65. The report of the Board of Education tabulated 45 residential training colleges accommodating 4,273 plus 181 day students and 17 day training colleges accommodating 700 students. Since the course of study was for two years, it works out roughly at 2,700 students taken in annually. *Parl. Papers*, 1902, XXIV, Cd. 1275, p. 45.

66. Presumably Bruce obtained his information from data in the files of the Ministry of Education.

67. *Parl. Papers*, 1902, LXXVIII, Cd. 1139, pp. 114, 118.

68. *Baptist Times*, Sept. 19, 1902 (Blomfield); *Commons*, July 2, 1902, pp. 575-78 (Macnamara); *Daily News*, July 4, 1902 (Macnamara); *Speaker*, May 31, 1902 (Bruce); Clifford, *The Fight Against the Education Bill* (1902), pp. 40-41.

69. *Lords*, Dec. 9, 1902, pp. 388-89 (Bishop Jacob of Newcastle), pp. 389-90 (Londonderry); *Pilot*, May 3, 1902; *School Guardian*, July 12, Dec. 13, 1902.

70. *Baptist Times*, May 16, 1902; *Daily Chronicle*, Oct. 4, Dec. 17, 1902; *Examiner* July 10, 1902; *Manchester Guardian*, Sept. 9, 1902.

71. *Examiner*, July 31, 1902; *Liberator*, Dec. 1902; *Presbyterian*, May 15, 1902 (Gibson); Clifford, *The Fight Against the Education Bill* (1902), p. 52 ff.

72. For the details of these by-elections in Bury, North Leeds, Sevenoaks, Devonport, East Toxteth, and Cleveland see *Annual Register, 1902*.

73. *Baptist Times*, April 25, 1902; *Daily News*, Sept. 25, 1902 (ed.), (Evans); *Manchester Guardian*, May 9, 1902; Clifford, *The Fight Against the Education Bill* (1902), p. 12.

74. For Dr. Temple's speech see *The Times*, June 9, 1896, 14b. Archbishop Temple died in December 1902.

75. *Baptist Times*, April 25, 1902; *British Weekly*, Aug. 14, 1902; *Daily News*, Sept. 25, 1902 (Evans); *Examiner*, Dec. 11, 1902; *Methodist Times*, Sept. 25, 1902; *Westminster Gazette*, May 31, 1902 (Hughes).

76. *Christian World*, Sept. 4, 1902; *Daily Chronicle*, Sept. 22, 1902; *Friend*, Sept. 5, 26, 1902 (John Stephenson Rowntree); *Manchester Guardian*, Sept. 19, 1902; *Methodist Recorder*, Sept. 18, 25, 1902.

77. *Church Times*, June 20, 1902; *Pall Mall Gazette*, Dec. 9, 1902; *Spectator*, Sept. 27, Dec. 27, 1902; *Standard*, Sept. 24, 1902; *The Times*, April 10, 1902, 9d, Dec. 16, 1902, 9d.

78. For Colonel Kenyon-Slaney's speech see *Commons*, Oct. 31, 1902, pp. 1311-16.

79. *Church Standard*, Jan. 1903; *Pall Mall Gazette*, Nov. 1, 1902; *Record*, Nov. 7, 1902; *Spectator*, Nov. 8, 1902; *Standard*, Nov. 1, 14, 1902; *The Times*, Nov. 1, 1902, 11e (ed.), Nov. 7, 1902, 8d (Henson).

80. *Church Times*, Nov. 7, 1902; *Guardian*, Nov. 12, 1902; *Pilot*, Nov. 1, 8, 1902; *The Times*, Nov. 12, 1902, 12e (Riley), Nov. 5, 1902, 11e-f (Bishop Gore of Worcester), Dec. 4, 1902, 12b-c (Lord Hugh Cecil).

81. *National Society*, Annual Report, 1872, pp. 39-40.

82. For the Attorney-General's ruling see *Commons*, Dec. 1, 1902, p. 848 (Sir Robert Finlay).

83. *Church Times*, Nov. 21, Dec. 12, 1902 (ed.), Dec. 5, 1902 (Riley); *Guardian*, Nov. 19, Dec. 3, 1902; *The Times*, Nov. 12, 1902, 12e (Knox).

84. *Church Times*, Dec. 19, 1902; *Guardian*, Dec. 17, 1902; *Pilot*, Dec. 6, 1902; *School Guardian*, Dec. 20, 1902.

85. *Baptist Times*, Nov. 14, 1902; *British Weekly*, Nov. 13, Dec. 4, 1902; *Examiner*, Nov. 13, 1902; *Liberator*, Jan. 1903; *Methodist Recorder*, Nov. 6, 1902; *Westminster Gazette*, Nov. 14, 24, 28, 1902.

CHAPTER THREE: ACT OF 1902 IN OPERATION (1903-06)

1. For this martial song see Evans, *James Hirst Hollowell* (1911), p. 85.

2. *British Weekly*, Dec. 18, 23, 1902, Jan. 1, 15, April 30, June 4, 1903; Evans, *James Hirst Hollowell* (1911), pp. 85, 92 ff; Townsend, in Edmund C. Rawlings, *Free Churchman's Guide to the Education Act, 1902* (1903), pp. 64-67.

3. *Tablet*, Jan. 28, 1905.

4. *Baptist Times*, Jan. 8, Aug. 5, 1904; *British Weekly*, July 16, 1903, Nov. 24, 1904; Jan. 19, Dec. 28, 1905; *Crusader*, Jan. 25, 1906 (Hollowell); *North American Rev.*, March 1905, pp. 430-34 (Clifford).

5. *Methodist Recorder*, Jan. 8-29, Feb. 5, 1903; *Methodist Times*, Jan. 1, 1903 (Perks), Jan. 8, 1903 (Lidgett); *The Times*, Jan. 9, 1903, 10e (Hollowell); Smart, *Ought Nonconformists to Uphold the Education Act?* (1903), pp. 7-10.

6. For an account of the proceedings of the Wesleyan Methodist Conference see *Methodist Recorder*, July 23, 30, Aug. 6, 1903.

7. *Baptist World Congress*, 1st, Proceedings, London, July 11-19, 1905, p. 48 (Clifford); *The Times*, Sept. 25, 1903, 9e (Lloyd George); Smart, *Ought Nonconformists to Uphold the Education Act?* (1903), pp. 12-14, 23.

8. *National Society*, Annual Report, 1904, p. 12.

9. *Daily News*, Nov. 29, 1905; Martin, *The Education Rate and Passive Resistance* (1903), p. 6; Smart, *Ought Nonconformists to Uphold the Education Act?* (1903), pp. 26-27; Welsh, *The Capture of the Schools* (1903), pp. 30-32.

10. *Manchester Guardian*, Sept. 22, 1904 (Hollowell); *Westminster Gazette*, Dec. 15, 1903, Jan. 25, 1904; Martin, *The Education Rate and Passive Resistance* (1903), pp. 4-5.

11. *Manchester Guardian*, Jan. 26, 1903 (Elliot).

12. In 1902 there were 62 training colleges and 5,880 places. *Parl. Papers*, 1906, LXXXIX, Cd. 2782, p. 115.

13. The breakdown for admission to British and Foreign School Society training colleges is as follows: Episcopalians (32.6%), Congregationalists (19%), Wesleyans and other Methodists (17.5%), Baptists (15.9%), Presbyterians (7.2%), Other Denominations (7.8%). *Educational Record*, June 1904, p. 565.

14. *Parl. Papers*, 1906, LXXXIX, Cd. 2782, pp. 418-20.

15. *Christain World*, Dec. 3, 1903, Feb. 9, 1905; *Contemporary Rev.*, March 1906, pp. 384-85 (Macnamara); *Daily News*, Feb. 12, 1906 (Macnamara); *The Times*, June 11, 1904, 4f and June 18, 1904, 17f (Evans).

16. The findings of the royal commission are contained in *Parl. Papers*, 1906, XXXIII, Cd. 3040 and XXXIV, Cd. 3072. Subsequently bills were introduced without success to deal with ecclesiastical disorders.

17. *Baptist Times*, Dec. 9, 1904 (Clifford); *British Weekly*, Oct. 1, 1903; *New Liberal Rev.*, Feb. 1903, pp. 21, 35 (Clifford); *The Times*, May 15, 1903, 7e-f (Lloyd George); Smith, *Conscience and the Education Rate* (1903), p. 8.

18. *Daily News*, Oct. 30, 1903; *New Liberal Rev.*, Feb. 1903, pp. 17-19, 23-25 (Clifford); *Review of Reviews*, Jan. 1903, Feb. 1903; Smith, *Conscience and the Education Rate* (1903), p. 8.

19. *Daily Chronicle*, Oct. 3, 1903, Nov. 23, 1904; *Westminster Rev.*, Jan. 1904, pp. 37-44 (Reed); Burns, *An Argument Addressed to Thoughtful Nonconformists Against "Passive Resistance."* (1904), pp. 4-13.

20. For an example of Dr. Davidson's active interest in their behalf see *The Times*, Dec. 15, 1903, 12a-b.

21. *Church Times*, June 12, 1903; *The Times*, Aug. 28, 1903, 5e-f and Sept. 15, 1903, 11f (Eglen), May 7, 1904, 16f and June 1, 1904, 6f (David C. Anderson); Sanday, *Justice in Education* (1904), pp. 21-22.

22. *Church Times*, Jan. 2, 1903 and Feb. 5, 1904 (Riley); *Pilot*, Jan. 10, 24, 1903; *School Guardian*, Feb. 14, 1903; Headlam, *The Education Act, 1902* (cir. 1903), p. 23.

23. By 1906 the number of recognized pupil teacher centers was 364 and the number of students 23,683. *Parl. Papers*, 1906, LXXXV, Cd. 3255, p. 93. For literature see Sandiford, *The Training of Teachers in England and Wales* (1910), pp. 59-61.

24. *Church Times*, Oct. 13, 1905 (ed.), Aug. 25, 1905 (Houghton); *Pilot*, Feb. 14, 1903; *School Guardian*, July 25, 1903.

25. The specific sum was £45,054,973. *National Society, Annual Report*, 1903, pp. 15-16.

26. The sum listed in respect of school board loans outstanding in September 1902 was £33,564,133. *Parl. Papers*, 1903, XX, Cd. 1763, p. 41.

27. *Parl. Papers*, 1903, LI, Cd. 1476, p. 73.

28. *Church Times*, Dec. 23, 1904 (Cleworth); *School Guardian*, Aug. 15, Dec. 19, 1903, Nov. 4, 1905; *The Times*, Dec. 15, 1903, 12a-b (Davidson), Sept. 19, 1904, 4f (Cleworth).

29. *Daily Telegraph*, June 5, 1903; *Pilot*, May 9, 1903; Betts, *Education and Passive Resistance* (1904), p. 13; Hammond, *Passive Resistance—Positive Wrong* (1903), pp. 5-6; Wordsworth, *Education Rates and Religious Instruction* (1905), pp. 5-11.

30. *Church Times*, June 12, 1903; *Morning Post*, Feb. 4, 1903; *The Times*, Jan. 13, 1904, 7d-e; Hammond, *Passive Resistance—Positive Wrong* (1903), pp. 7-8.

31. *Catholic Herald*, Dec. 5, 1902; *Tablet*, Dec. 19, 1903, Oct. 1, 1904, March 24, 1906.

32. For the years 1870 to 1901 Roman Catholics expended £2,021,945 on their schools. Presumably the difference to make up the total of £4,000,000 is to be found in expenditures before 1870. As of August 31, 1901 the accommodations in the 1,053 Roman Catholic schools stood at 400,730. *Parl. Papers*, 1902, LXXVIII, Cd. 1139, pp. 7, 79.

33. *Catholic Herald*, Sept. 9, 1904, May 26, 1905; *Catholic Education Council, Annual Report*, 1905, p. 30; *Daily News*, Feb. 12, 1906 (Russell); *Manchester Guardian*, March 26, 1906 (Rothwell).

34. *Parl. Papers*, 1903, LI, Cd. 1476, pp. 7, 18-21.

35. *Month*, Dec. 1903, pp. 572-77 (Strappini).

36. *Freethinker*, May 10, 1903 (Cohen); *Literary Guide and Rationalist Rev.*, Sept. 1, 1903 (Gould); *New Age*, Sept. 3, Oct. 8, 1903 (Ryan).

37. Lloyd George in *Commons*, April 26, 1904, pp. 1207-08; in *Free Church Year Book*, 1903, pp. 88-91; in *The Times*, Jan. 17, 1903, 12e-f. Cf. Edwards, *David Lloyd George* (1929), I, pp. 262-69; Halévy, *Imperialism and the Rise of Labour* (1951, 2nd rev. ed.), pp. 208-09, 376.

38. *Parl. Papers*, 1904, LXXV, Cd. 2041, 11 pp.

39. For the story of its passage by the Balfour Government see *Commons*, April 26, July 15, Aug. 5, 1904; *Lords*, Aug. 11, 12, 1904.

40. Lloyd George in *Independent Rev.*, Sept. 1904, p. 484; in *The Times*, May 3, 1905, 8a.

41. *Crusader*, Sept. 22, 1904 (Hollowell); *Daily Chronicle*, Aug. 6, 15, Sept. 17, 1904; *Daily News*, Aug. 12, Sept. 17, Oct. 8, 1904; *Examiner*, Oct. 13, 1904.

42. *Crusader*, Dec. 28, 1903 and Jan. 8, 1904 (Hollowell); *Daily News*, Dec. 18, 1903; *Speaker*, Feb. 14, 1903; Welsh, *The Capture of the Schools* (1903), pp. 10, 18; White, *The Case Against the Education Act* (1905), p. 9.

43. *Daily Telegraph*, April 27, 1904; *Morning Post*, Nov. 25, 1904; *Pilot*, Dec. 12, 1903 (Compton); *The Times*, April 27, 1904, 9c-d.

44. *Daily Telegraph*, May 16, 1905; *Morning Post*, Feb. 27, 1905; *Western Mail* (Cardiff), April 27, Aug. 11, 1904.

45. The Ministry of Education Reference Library contains a collection of most of these leaflets. *Church Schools' Emergency League Leaflets*, First to Sixth Series (Nos. 1-71), 1904—Jan. 1908 (published in Manchester).

46. *Church Times*, Oct. 30, 1903; *Guardian*, Aug. 17, 1904 (Cleworth); *Morning Post*, Oct. 28, 1905; *School Guardian*, May 28, 1904 (Cleworth).

47. *Catholic Education Council*, Annual Report, 1904: *Catholic School Committee*, Annual Report, 1903; *Tablet*, Jan. 3, 1903, April 1, Oct. 28, 1905 (ed.), Nov. 24, 1904 (Ford).

48. *Parl. Papers*, 1903, III, Bills 154, 216, 279, 312; *Statutes* (Great Britain), 3 Edward VII, 1903, c. 24, pp. 31-33; Webb, *The London Education Act, 1903* (1904), 19 pp.

49. *Commons*, April 28, 1903, pp. 752-53 (Channing); *Daily Chronicle*, April 9, 1903; *Liberator*, May 1903; *Presbyterian*, April 16, 1903.

50. *Daily News*, April 29, 1903; *Manchester Guardian*, April 8, 1903; *Speaker*, May 2, 1903.

51. *Church Times*, April 17, 1903; *Guardian*, April 15, 1903; *Lords*, July 28, 1903, pp. 485-86 (Percival); *Pilot*, April 4, 11, 18, 1903; *School Guardian*, April 11, 1903; *Standard*, July 23, 1903.

52. *Catholic School Committee*, Annual Report, 1903, pp. 4-5; *Commons*, May 18, 1903, p. 1038 (T. P. O'Connor); *Tablet*, April 11, May 30, 1903.

53. For Bishop Lang's questions see *The Times*, Jan. 18, 1904, 8a.

54. *The Times*, March 8, 1904, 12c.

55. Bishop Lang appended a list of candidates whose answers were acceptable. *The Times*, March 3, 1904, 8a.

56. *Church Times*, March 11, 1904; *Guardian*, March 2, 1904; *The Times*, Jan. 18, 1904, 9c-d, Feb. 24, 1904, 11f-12a (ed.), Dec. 16, 1903, 14b (Letter by Bishops Ingram of London and Talbot of Rochester), Jan. 18, 1904, 8a (Lang).

57. *Daily Chronicle*, Feb. 26, 1904; *Daily News*, Jan. 18, Feb. 26, March 3, 7, 1904; *Examiner*, Dec. 24, 1903, Feb. 25, March 10, 1904; *Speaker*, Dec. 19, 1903.

58. *Catholic Herald*, Jan. 8, Feb. 12, March 4, 11, 1904.

59. London County Council, *Report of the Education Committee*, April 7, 1904, "On the Survey and Inspection of Non-Provided Schools," 227 pp.

60. *Christian World*, April 20, 1905; *Daily Chronicle*, April 17, 1905; *Daily News* April 17, 1905; *Independent Rev.*, June 1905, pp. 163-69 (Bruce); *Speaker*, April 22, 1905.

61. *London County Council Report*, 1905, p. 10.

62. *Church Times*, April 28, 1905; *Guardian*, April 19, 1905; *Pall Mall Gazette*, April 17, 1905; *Standard*, April 18, 1905; *The Times*, April 17, 1905, 12a, April 18, 1905, 7e-f.

63. *Catholic Herald*, April 21, 1905; *Catholic Times*, April 28, 1905; *Tablet*, April 22, May 13, 1905.

64. London County Council, S. O. No. 3497, 39 pp.

CHAPTER FOUR: THE LIBERAL GOVERNMENT'S PROPOSALS

1. For literature on Free Church Council see E. K. H. Jordan, *Free Church Unity* (1956), 254 pp.

2. *Free Church Chronicle*, Jan., April 1906.

3. For secondary literature see Fitzroy, *Memoirs* (1925, 3rd ed.), I, p. 287; Haldane, *An Autobiography* (1929, 2nd ed.), p. 218; Halévy, *The Rule of Democracy, 1905-1914* (1952, 2nd rev. ed.), Book I, pp. 64-73; Spender (1923), II, pp. 274-77.

4. Parl. Papers, 1906, I, Bills 160, 317, 327, 365.

5. Parl. Papers, 1908, II, Bill 112.

6. Parl. Papers, 1908, II, Bill 376.

7. Parl. Papers, 1902, LXXVIII, Cd. 1336, pp. iii-iv.

8. The reports of the National Society do not carry any estimates of the total repair bill for the years 1902 to 1905. Rather oddly, the sum of £3,000,000 shows up in *Church Schools' Emergency League Leaflet*, XLII, April 1906, p. 88.

9. *Blackwood's Magazine*, May 1906, pp. 736-38; *The Times*, April 24, 1906, 11a-b (Ridgeway), April 19, 1906, 8d and Feb. 27, 1908, 12e (Cleworth); Knox, *Elementary Education* (1908), p. 5.

10. *Blackwood's Magazine*, May 1906, pp. 736-37; *Commons*, Dec. 12, 1906, pp. 415-16 (Butcher); *Guardian*, Dec. 2, 1908 (Williams); *The Times*, April 11, 1906, 9c-d (ed.), Nov. 24, 1908, 10b-c (Knox); *Ministry of Education*, 1908, No. 113, Letter, Dr. Davidson to McKenna, April 11, 1908.

11. Parl. Papers, 1906, XC, Cd. 3219, 3 pp.

12. *Church Times*, Feb. 28, 1908; *Commons*, May 7, 1906, p. 1023 (Wyndham); *Commonwealth*, Jan. 1909, pp 1-3; *Guardian*, May 16, 1906, May 27, Nov. 25, 1908; *School Guardian*, April 14, 1906; *Western Mail* (Cardiff), April 10, 1906.

13. *Guardian*, July 4, 1906; *Record*, May 4, 1906; *Standard*, June 21, 1906; *The Times*, July 3, 1906, 9e-f.

14. *Commons*, July 3, 1906, pp. 1710-18 (Lough).

15. *Church Times*, April 24, 1908; *Commons*, Feb. 24, 1908, p. 1418 (Lord Robert Cecil); *Pall Mall Gazette*, July 4, 1906; *School Guardian*, July 7, 1906; *The Times*, Nov. 23, 1906, 15a-c (Davidson).

16. *Catholic Herald*, Nov. 28, 1908; *Catholic Times*, April 20, 1906; *Month*, May 1906, p. 455 (Smith); *Tablet*, April 21, 1906; Gallwey, *Mr. Birrell's Education Bill* (1906), p. 6.

17. *Catholic Herald*, April 13, 1906; *Month*, Sept. 1906, 232-34 (Smith).

18. *Catholic Times*, June 22, 1906; *Month*, Sept. 1906, pp. 226-32 (Smith); *Tablet*, June 2, Oct. 6, 1906.

19. *Catholic Herald*, Nov. 28, 1908; *Catholic Times*, March 6, 1908; *Tablet*, Nov. 28, Dec. 5, 1908; *Westminster Gazette*, Nov. 24, 1908 (Brown).

20. *Manchester Guardian*, Sept. 25, 1906 (Hollowell); *Methodist Times*, May 17, 1906; *Speaker*, May 5, Dec. 22, 1906 (Bruce); *Westminster Gazette*, Oct. 4, 1906; Society for the Liberation of Religion From State-Patronage and Control Leaflet, *Where Is the Robbery?* (June 1906), 4 pp.

21. *Daily Chronicle*, March 23, 1908; *Commons*, Nov. 25, 1908, pp. 433-37 (Hutton); *Daily News*, April 28, 1906; *Manchester Guardian*, Nov. 26, Dec. 9, 1908 (Hollowell); *The Times*, Nov. 30, 1908, 9c (Hollowell).

22. *British Congregationalist*, Feb. 27, May 21, Dec. 3, 10, 1908 (Horne); *British Weekly*, April 26, 1906, March 12, 1908; *Daily Chronicle*, March 23, Dec. 3, 1908; *Manchester Guardian*, May 16, Sept. 10, 1906 (Hollowell); *Methodist Times*, May 17, 1906; *The Times*, April 21, 1906, 12b-c (Hollowell), Dec. 4, 1908, 11a (Clifford).

23. For the negative see *Manchester Guardian*, July 5, 1906; *Methodist Times*, April 19, 1906; *Westminster Gazette*, July 3, 1906; J. L. Paton (his son), *John Brown Paton* (1914), pp. 394-99.

24. For the Irish National School scheme see *Parl. Papers*, 1906, XXIX, Cd. 2773, pp. 116-17.

25. For the affirmative see *British Weekly*, May 10, 1906; *Commons*, July 2, 1906, p. 1449 (Perks); *Examiner*, July 5, 1906 (Horne); *Monthly Messenger*, May, 1906; *South Wales Daily News*, July 3, 1906.

26. *Examiner*, April 12, 1906; *Manchester Guardian*, Nov. 26, Dec. 9, 1908 (Hollowell); *Methodist Times*, May 17, Nov. 1, 1906; *Speaker*, May 5, June 23, 1906 (Bruce); *Westminster Gazette*, Nov. 23, 1908 (Clifford).

27. *Commons*, June 25, 1906, pp. 715-20 (MacDonald); *Ethical World*, March 15, 1908; *Freethinker*, April 19, Dec. 6, 1908 (Secular Education League Manifestoes); *Justice*, March 7, 1908 (Rothstein); *Literary Guide and Rationalist Rev.*, Dec. 1, 1908 (McCabe); *New Age*, May 10, 1906.

28. *Commons*, May 23, 1906, p. 1309 (MacDonald); *Literary Guide and Rationalist Rev.*, May 1, July 1, 1906 (Gould); *Positivist Rev.*, May 1, 1906 (Gould).

29. *Freethinker*, April 29, 1906 (Foote); *Literary Guide and Rationalist Rev.*, June 1, 1906 (McCabe).

30. For Gould's own account of his correspondence with the London School Board see *Literary Guide and Rationalist Rev.*, June 1, July 1, 1912; *Manchester Guardian*, Jan. 4, 1902; Gould, *The Life Story of a Humanist* (1923), pp. 66-71.

31. *Commons*, May 7, 1906, p. 1080, Feb. 24, 1908, pp. 1408-09, and Nov. 25, 1908, pp. 526-27 (MacDonald); *Fortnightly Rev.*, April 1908, p. 709 (MacDonald); *Freethinker*, May 6, 1906 (Foote); *Literary Guide and Rationalist Rev.*, Dec. 1, 1908 (McCabe); *Manchester Guardian*, April 24, 1906 (Harrold Johnson).

32. *Commons*, May 21, 1906, p. 961 (MacDonald), May 28, 1906, pp. 116, 156 (Maddison); Wilson, *Liberty and Religion* (1906), p. 32.

33. *Parl. Papers*, 1906, I, Bill 365.

34. Birrell, *Things Past Redress* (1937), pp. 191-92; Dugdale (1937), II, pp. 19-21; Fitzroy (1925, 3rd ed.), I, 309-11; Lee, *King Edward VII* (1927), II, pp. 460-63; Newton, *Lord Lansdowne* (1929), pp. 355-58; Earl of Oxford and Asquith, *Fifty Years of Parliament* (1926), II, p. 44; Petrie, *The Life and Letters of the Rt. Hon. Sir Austen Chamberlain* (1939-40), I, pp. 192-98; Spender (1923), II, pp. 303-11.

35. *Parl. Papers*, 1908, LXXXII, Cd. 4421, 19 pp.; *The Times*, Nov. 28, 1908, 9c (news item), Nov. 11, 1908, 6d and Nov. 30, 1908, 9b (Lidgett), Dec. 4, 1908, 10c-f (ed.); Lord Parmoor, *A Retrospect* (1936), pp. 99-100.

36. *Baptist Times*, Jan. 10, March 14, 1913, Feb. 13, 1914; *British Weekly*, April 10, 1913; *Christian World*, Aug. 28, 1913; *Free Church Chronicle*, June 1913; *Free Church Year Book*, 1914, pp. 113-14; *Methodist Times*, Feb. 12, May 14, 1914.

37. Ministry of Education, 1913-14, Box 104, I (L), (N), (P), (Q), (R).

CHAPTER FIVE: FOSTERING CHURCH MEMBERSHIP

1. *Church Times*, Jan. 5, 1906; *Commons*, May 6, 1902, pp. 845-46 (Lord Hugh Cecil); *Saturday Rev.*, Oct. 6, 1906; *The Times*, May 23, 1908, 11f (Riley); Sedgwick, *Pedagogus* (1909), pp. 6-8.

2. A bluebook was published in 1906, during the height of the struggle over the Birrell Bill, containing many of the diocesan syllabuses. *Parl. Papers*, 1906, XC, Cd. 3074, 99 pp.

3. *Commonwealth*, Jan. 1909, pp. 16-17; *Contemporary Rev.*, Feb. 1911, p. 186 (Lathbury); *The Times*, May 27, 1902, 4a-b and Aug. 26, 1903, 6a-b (Davidson); Henson, in Stephens (1905), pp. 237-40; Knox, *Pastors and Teachers* (1902), p. 76; Wace, *Religious Education and National Schools* (1906), p. 9.

4. *Commons*, May 28, 1906, p. 186 (Lord Robert Cecil); *The Times*, Jan. 22, 1907, 3b-c (Davies), May 12, 1906, 8b-c (Bishop Ingram of London); Strong, *Undenominationalism* (1906), pp. 7-10.

5. *Church Times*, Jan. 31, 1908; *School Guardian*, June 21, 1902; *The Times*, April 14, 1902, 7c-d, April 28, 1902, 9d-e, and May 21, 1902, 10e-f (MacColl); MacColl, *The Education Question and the Liberal Party* (1902), p. 26.

6. *Commonwealth*, Nov. 1904, pp. 341-42 (Rogers); *The Times*, Feb. 24, 1906, 10a-b (Strong), Sept. 3, 1903, 8e (Legge); Gore, *Objections to the Education Bill* (1906), pp. 6-9; Sanday, *Justice in Education* (1904), p. 7.

7. *Commonwealth*, March 1908, pp. 65-67 (Rev. H. S. Holland); *Pilot*, Aug. 2, 1906 (Stevenson); *The Times*, Oct. 1, 1902, 4d-e (Mackarness), Aug. 5, 1903, 8f and Nov. 5, 1903, 9e (Davidson).

8. *Lords*, May 7, 1904, p. 708 (Bishop Edwards of St. Asaph); *Westminster Gazette*, Feb. 8, 1906 (Lathbury); Cleworth, *The Education Crisis of 1906* (1906), p. 17; Wakeford, *The Education Crisis of 1906* (1906), pp. 25-26.

9. *The Times*, Jan. 7, 1907, 8c (Lord Hugh Cecil).

10. *Monthly Rev.*, Feb. 1905, pp. 140-41 (Ottley); *Pilot*, May 24, 1902 (Rev. Edward Lyttelton); *The Times*, April 14, 1902, 9c (Riley), Aug. 30, 1902, 4e-f (Beeching), Jan. 2, 1906, 9b (Rev. William Gascoyne-Cecil).

11. See A. W. W. Dale (his son) (1899), pp. 555-57.

12. *Commons*, Nov. 26, 1902, pp. 527-28 (Platt-Higgins); *Monthly Rev.*, Feb. 1905, pp. 141-43 (Ottley); *Pilot*, Aug. 2, 1902 (Stevenson), June 14, 1902 (MacColl); *The Times*, May 21, 1902, 10e-f (MacColl).

13. Booth, *Life and Labour of the People in London, Third Series; Religious Influences, Summary* (1903), VII, pp. 394-432.

14. *Commons*, Feb. 24, 1908, p. 1422 (Lord Robert Cecil); *Monthly Rev.*, Feb. 1905, pp. 141-43 (Ottley); *The Times*, Nov. 18, 1903, 6f (Rev. William Gascoyne-Cecil); Lang, *The Principles of Religious Education* (1906), p. 30.

15. *Commonwealth*, June 1902, pp. 162-65 (Masterman); *Westminster Gazette*, April 28, 1902 (Masterman).

16. A visit to the archives of the London County Council and the National Society yielded no documentary evidence of these calculations. Perhaps Dr. Davidson had a special check made.

17. For literature on the Bible and archaeological findings see Sayce, *The "Higher Criticism" and the Verdict of the Monuments* (1894), 575 pp.

18. *Lords*, July 28, 1903, pp. 463-64 (Davidson); *Pilot*, May 14, 1904 (ed.), June 14, 1902 (MacColl); *Record*, March 18, 1904; *The Times*, Aug. 26, 1903, 6a-b (Davidson), May 27, 1902, 4a-b (Temple).

19. *Commons*, May 6, 1902, p. 844 (Lord Hugh Cecil); *Manchester Guardian*, May 26 and Oct. 2, 1902 (Wilson); *Standard*, Dec. 12, 1902; *The Times*, Oct. 6, 1902, 8c (Tilby); Nunn, *The New Education Bill* (1908), p. 4.

20. *House of Lords, Sessional Papers*, 1888, XIX, No. 311, 408 pp. The findings may also be studied in the Cross Commission Inquiry of 1888—*Parl. Papers*, 1888, XXXVI, Cd. 5485—IV, 408 pp.

21. *The Times*, Jan. 12, 1906, 4f (Chambers); Beeching, *Religio Laici* (1902), pp. 253-54.

22. *House of Lords*, Sessional Papers, 1895, X, No. 2, 645 pp.

23. Visits and inquiries to the National Society, British Museum, Lambeth Palace, House of Lords Library, and many other places failed to yield a copy of the analysis published by the National Society in 1895.

24. *Commons*, May 10, 1906, p. 1539 (Lord Robert Cecil); *Lords*, July 4, 1904, p. 414 (Davidson); *The Times*, Oct. 1, 1902, 4d-f (Mackarness), May 27, 1902, 4a-b (Temple).

25. *Commons*, April 23, 1907, pp. 1582-84 (Lord Robert Cecil), Aug. 23, 1907, pp. 1448-49 (Sherwell); *Lords*, Aug. 3, 1906, pp. 1519-20 (Percival).

26. A. H. D. Acland, *Problems of Education* (1905), p. 4.

27. *House of Lords*, Sessional Papers, 1906, XIII, No. 115, Part I, p. iv.

28. *House of Lords*, Sessional Papers, 1906, XIII, No. 155, Part I, 137 pp.

29. *Lords*, July 26, 1906, pp. 1373-78, 1380-85 (Davidson); National Society, *Analysis of the Return to an Order of the House of Lords, dated May 4, 1906* (1906), 39 pp.; *The Times*, July 27, 1906, 9c-d.

30. Mudie-Smith, *The Religious Life of London* (1904), p. 68.

31. *Lords*, Dec. 4, 1902, pp. 2152-53 (Midleton); *The Times*, Sept. 3, 1902, 8e (Horsfall); Carnegie, *The Church and the Schools* (1905), pp. 41-42; Henson, *The Education Act and After* (1903), pp. 47-52.

32. *The Times*, Sept. 3, 1902, 8e (Horsfall); Carnegie, *The Church and the Schools* (1905), pp. 42-43; Henson, *The Education Act and After* (1903), pp. 52-53; Wilson, *The Day-School and Religious Education* (1907), pp. 5-9.

33. For literature see Johnson, *The Legal Status of Church-State Relationships in the United States* (1934), 332 pp.; Butts, *The American Tradition in Religion and Education* (1950), 230 pp.; Thayer, *The Attack Upon the Secular School* (1951), 257 pp.

34. Perhaps the reference is to Rev. Josiah Strong's widely circulated book, *Our Country: Its Possible Future and Its Present Crisis* (New York: 1891, rev. ed.), pp. 85-110.

35. *Commons*, May 8, 1906, p. 1237 (Butcher); *Manchester Guardian*, Nov. 16, 1908 (Horsfall); Jephson, *Report on Elementary Education in the United States* (1904), pp. 77-78.

36. Rev. Papillon cited the *Education Review* (New York) issue of December 1899 as containing the speech of Dr. Butler in an article entitled "The Unsolved Problem of Religion in Education." While there is an article by Dr. Butler in this issue, it is called "Religious Instruction and Its Relation to Education," pp. 425-36, and it does not contain the quoted statement. Instead, the article discusses Sunday schools in terms of potential positive good if well organized (pp. 433-36). This article is a reprint of a speech delivered in New York City, October 14, 1899, under the auspices of the Sunday School Commission of the Diocese of New York.

37. For literature on Victoria see *Parl. Papers*, 1900, XXII, Part I, Cd. 417, pp. 308-309; Browne, *Education in Australia* (1927), p. 84; Sweetman, Long, and Smyth, *A History of State Education in Victoria* (1922), pp. 145-46.

38. Rev. Beeching got his figures from a speech of Bishop Moorhouse of Manchester, delivered to the Church Congress in 1892 at Folkestone. For Bishop Moorhouse's speech see *Guardian*, Oct. 12, 1892, p. 1535. For the figures cited see *Victorian Year-Books*, 1883-84, p. 543 and 1890-91, II, p. 391.

39. *Church Quarterly Rev.*, Oct. 1902, p. 181; *Fortnightly Rev.*, May 1908, pp. 909-10 (Rees); *Guardian*, Feb. 3, 1904 (Papillon); Beeching, *Religio Laici* (1902), p. 247.

40. *Dublin Rev.*, July 1906, pp. 157-59; *Month*, April 1906, pp. 345-46, June 1906, p. 579, and Sept. 1906, pp. 234-36 (Smith); *The Times*, Feb. 6, 1906, 12a (Father Bernard Vaughan).

41. *Commons*, May 9, 1906, pp. 1381-82 (O'Brien); *Dublin Rev.*, July 1902, p. 11 (Glancey), July 1906 (ed.); *Lords*, Aug. 2, 1906, p. 1243 (Lord Killanin).

42. *Commons*, May 7, 1902, pp. 1004-05 (Dillon); *The Times*, July 19, 1902, 6f (Cardinal Vaughan); Burton, *Catholic Education and the Duties of Parents* (1906), pp. 4-5; Lilly, *Education, True and False* (1905), p. 13.

43. *Commons*, Nov. 25, 1902, p. 408 and Dec. 2, 1902, pp. 1028-29 (Bryce), May 5, 1902, p. 721 (Perks); *Nineteenth Century and After*, May 1902, p. 854 (Bryce); *South Wales Daily News*, Oct. 22, 1902, May 12, 1906.

44. For literature on the Scottish system see Balfour, *The Educational Systems of Great Britain and Ireland* (1903, 2nd ed.), p. 128; Curtis (1918), II, p. 358; Stewart (1927), p. 120.

45. Bryce in *Commons*, Nov. 25, 1902, p. 408 and Dec. 2, 1902, pp. 1028-29; in *Nineteenth Century and After*, May 1902, p. 854.

46. For literature on the German system see Fife, *The German Empire Between the Two Wars* (1918), pp. 336-38; Helmreich, *Religious Education in German Schools* (1959), p. 60 ff; Hughes, *The Making of Citizens* (1902), p. 67; Ross, *The Schools of England and Germany* (1894), pp. 124-25.

47. *Commons*, May 9, 1906, p. 1322 (Bryce); *The Times*, Dec. 7, 1906, 8b (Horton), May 16, 1906, 13a (Bryce); Horton, in Stephens (1905), p. 269; J. L. Paton (his son), *John Brown Paton* (1914), pp. 400-01.

48. For Dr. Clifford's figures see *Daily News*, Jan. 15, 1902, p. 3. The compiler of these statistics was Howard Evans and his annual computations are to be found in this newspaper from 1897 on.

49. *Commons*, May 8, 1902, p. 1107 (Lloyd George); *South Wales Daily News*, May 4, 1906; *The Times*, April 9, 1902, 6e-f (Hughes); Clifford, *Clericalism in British Politics* (1902), p. 37; Horton, in Stephens (1905), pp. 277-81.

50. *Commons*, May 9, 1906, p. 1322 (Bryce); *Nineteenth Century and After*, Aug. 1906, p. 342 (Rogers); *The Times*, Nov. 1, 1904, 7c (Glover); Horton, in Stephens (1905), p. 274; Paton, *Shall There Be Bible Instruction in the National Schools?* (1905), 4 pp.

51. For board school syllabuses see *Parl. Papers*, 1888, XXXVI, Cd. 5485-IV, pp. 337-93.

52. *Daily Chronicle*, May 21, 1906; *Fortnightly Rev.*, May 1, 1902, pp. 836-37 (Macnamara); *New Liberal Rev.*, March 1902, pp. 193-94 (Macnamara); Birrell (1937), pp. 185-88.

53. Dr. Clifford in *Baptist Times*, Aug. 30, 1907; in *British Weekly*, June 14, 1906; in *Daily News*, Nov. 5, 1903; in *Manchester Guardian*, Nov. 22, 1911; in *Morning Post*, April 18, 1906; in *The Times*, Jan. 12, 1906, 4c, Jan. 5, 1907, 8b.

54. For the official statistics see *Annual Report of the Commissioner of Education* (U.S.), 1903, II, pp. 2444-48.

55. *Parl. Papers*, 1902, XXVIII, Cd. 837, p. 5.

56. *Commons*, Dec. 2, 1902, pp. 1028-29 (Bryce), May 10, 1906, pp. 1565-66 (Massie); *Crusader*, Nov. 16, 1905 (Clifford); *Friend*, April 20, 1906 (John S. Rowntree); *Speaker*, Oct. 11, 1902 (Woodhead).

57. *Daily News*, July 18, 1907 (Mundella); *The Times*, Oct. 6, 1902, 8c and Jan. 16, 1906, 15a (Evans).

58. For an interpretive article on the state of religion in Wales at the time see C. R. Williams "The Welsh Religious Revival, 1904-5," *British Journal of Sociology*, Sept. 1952, pp. 242-59.

59. *Daily News*, Nov. 23, 1906 (Macnamara); *The Times*, Dec. 18, 1906, 11b and Dec. 22, 1906, 12f (Macnamara); Wilson, *Liberty and Religion* (1906), p. 66.

60. *Daily News*, July 18, 1907 (Mundella); *Manchester Guardian*, Nov. 22, 1911 (Clifford); *Morning Post*, April 18, 1906 (Clifford); *Speaker*, May 19, 1906; *The Times*, Jan. 3, 1914, 3d (Clifford).

61. *Christian World*, Nov. 16, 1911; *Examiner*, May 31, 1906; *Monthly Messenger*, May 1906; *The Times*, Sept. 20, 1907, 4b (Clifford).

62. *Manchester Guardian*, Nov. 19, 1906 (Rev. James Hope Moulton); *The Times*, Sept. 24, 1906, 4f (Hollowell), Jan. 10, 1907, 4d (Clifford); *Westminster Gazette*, April 19, 1906 (ed.), Jan. 10, 1907 (Theobald).

63. For a description of the London School Board religious controversy see *Examiner*, Dec. 24, 1903 (Hugh B. Philpott); Philpott, *London at School* (1904), pp. 105-09; Riley, *Religious Teaching in Board Schools* (London: 1893), 12 pp.

64. For Archbishop Benson's speech see *Guardian*, July 18, 1894.

65. *Commons*, May 9, 1906, p. 1321 (Bryce); *Lords*, Dec. 4, 1902, p. 1217 (Earl Spencer).

66. *Clarion*, June 1, 1906 (Quelch); *Commons*, May 7, 1906, pp. 1084-85 and Feb. 24, 1908, p. 1409 (MacDonald); *Fortnightly Rev.*, April 1908, pp. 710-11 (MacDonald); *Freethinker*, June 1, 1902 (Cohen).

67. *Commons*, May 23, 1906, pp. 1313-14 (MacDonald); *Fortnightly Rev.*, April 1908, p. 710 (MacDonald); *Literary Guide and Rationalist Rev.*, June 1, 1902 (Gorham); Headlam, *Secular Schools* (1906), pp. 12, 21; Snell, *Secular Education* (cir. 1908), p. 8.

68. *Commons*, May 7, 1906, p. 1085 (MacDonald); *Fortnightly Rev.*, April 1908, p. 711 (MacDonald); *Freethinker*, Aug. 18, 1907 (Cohen); *Justice*, Nov. 1, 1903 (Hunter).

69. *Commons*, May 9, 1906, p. 1327 (Dillon).

70. *Manchester Guardian*, Jan. 13, 1903 (Coller); *Westminster Gazette*, April 12, 1902 (Picton).

71. *Statistical Register of Victoria*, 1901, Part IX, Social Conditions, p. 6.

72. *Literary Guide and Rationalist Rev.*, Sept. 1, 1902 (Picton); *Ethics*, Nov. 21, 1903 (Johnson).

73. *Manchester Guardian*, Jan. 13, 1903 (Coller); *The Times*, May 19, 1906, 10e (Hardie); *Truth*, May 8, 1902, May 16, 1906.

74. *Justice*, Dec. 12, 1902, Sept. 30, 1905; *Literary Guide and Rationalist Rev.*, Nov. 1, 1902 (Gould); *Positivist Rev.*, Dec. 1902 (Frederic Harrison); *Social Democrat*, July 15, 1904.

75. *Daily News*, May 10, 1902 (Hopps), March 16, 1904 (Johnson); *Freethinker*, May 25, 1902 (National Secular Society), Dec. 7, 1902 (Cohen); *Reformer*, July 15, 1903, p. 415 (Robertson); *Truth*, Dec. 11, 1902, Sept. 10, 1903; MacDonald, *Socialism and Society* (1905), pp. 151-52.

76. *Ethical World*, April 15, 1912 (Callaway); *Freethinker*, May 13, 20, 1906 (Foote); *Literary Guide and Rationalist Rev.*, Aug. 1, 1910 (Callaway); *Manchester Guardian*, June 8, 1906 and June 29, 1908 (Picton).

77. *Daily News*, May 10, 1902 (Hopps); *Freethinker*, Oct. 27, 1903 (Russell), May 14, 1905 (Foote); *Labour Leader*, Dec. 5, 1903 ("M."); *Literary Guide and Rationalist Rev.*, Nov. 1, 1903 (Greenwood); *New Age*, Sept. 8, 1910; Picton, *The Bible in School* (1907), pp. 60-61.

78. Holmes, *What Is and What Might Be* (1911), p. 101.

79. MacDonald in *Commons*, May 7, 1906, pp. 1081, 1083-84 and May 23, 1906, pp. 1308-09; in *Fortnightly Rev.*, April 1908, p. 712.

80. The statistics on the Welsh districts were obtained from the Return of 1906 to the lords' request for information on the extent of religious teaching in council schools. Whereas MacDonald gives the number of county councils having no religious instruction in Cardigan and Carmarthen as 66 out of 70 and 62 out of 100 respectively, the bluebook contains the figures 60 out of 75 and 69 out of 104 respectively. *House of Lords*, Sessional Papers, 1906, XIII, No. 115, Part I, pp. 83-85.

81. *Fortnightly Rev.*, April 1908, pp. 712-13, 715 (MacDonald); *Leicester Pioneer*, Feb. 17, 1906 (MacDonald); *Literary Guide and Rationalist Rev.*, June 1, 1906 (McCabe); Holmes, *What Is and What Might Be* (1911), p. 94n.

82. MacDonald, *Socialism and Government* (1909), I, pp. 39-40.

83. MacDonald in *Commons*, May 7, 1906, p. 1081; in *Fortnightly Rev.*, April 1908, p. 709.

84. For this letter see *Democracy* (later the *Ethical World*), Feb. 23, 1901. MacDonald refers also to this letter in *Fortnightly Rev.*, April 1908, p. 709.

85. Picton in *Ethics*, June 6, 1903; in *Literary Guide* and *Rationalist Rev.*, Aug. 1, Sept. 1, 1902, March 1, July 1, 1908; in *Nation*, Jan. 25, 1908; in *Westminster Gazette*, Aug. 8, 1903; in *The Bible in School* (1907), pp. 37-41.

86. Reginald John Campbell, *The New Theology* (1907), 268 pp.

87. T. K. Cheyne, *Bible Problems and the New Material for Their Solution* (New York: 1904), pp. 58-60; see also *Encyclopaedia Biblica* (1899-1903), preface.

88. *Manchester Guardian*, Jan. 30, 1908 (Picton); *The Times*, July 7, 1906, 6e and Sept. 4, 1906, 9e (Greenwood); Picton, *The Bible in School* (1907), pp. vii-viii, x-xi, 12-14, 33, 38, 74n; Snell, *Secular Education* (cir. 1908), p. 7.

89. For the specific remark by Nevinson see *Westminster Gazette*, Oct. 15, 1906. His other articles are in the issues of Oct. 16, 17, 18, 19, 21, 1906.

90. Picton in *Literary Guide and Rationalist Rev.*, Jan. 1, 1907, March 1, July 1, 1908; in *Manchester Guardian*, Jan. 30, 1908; in *Nation*, Jan. 25 and Feb. 8, 1908; in *The Bible in School* (1907), pp. viii-ix, 24, 28-29, 32-33, 40, 42.

91. MacDonald in *Commons*, Nov. 25, 1908, p. 531; in *Fortnightly Rev.*, April, 1908, pp. 711-13; in *Margaret Ethel MacDonald* (1912), p. 62.

92. Picton in *Literary Guide and Rationalist Rev.*, Jan. 1, 1907; in *The Bible in School* (1907), pp. 17-18, 75.

93. MacDonald in *Commons*, May 23, 1906, pp. 1313-14; in *Fortnightly Rev.*, April 1908, pp. 710, 713.

CHAPTER SIX: INCULCATING MORALITY

1. *School Guardian*, Sept. 20, 1902 (Dymott); Egerton, *A Plea for Church Schools* (1906), pp. 12-14; Henson, *Religion in the Schools* (1906), pp. 39-40; MacColl, *The Education Question and the Liberal Party* (1902), pp. 87-89.

2. *The Times*, July 28, 1902, 12e (MacColl); Dymott, *The Case for the Voluntary School* (1902), p. 3; Lang, *The Principles of Religious Education* (1906), p. 5; MacColl, *The Education Question and the Liberal Party* (1902), pp. 82-83.

3. *Commons*, April 9, 1906, p. 1043 (Anson); *The Times*, Dec. 22, 1903, 5a-b (Rev. Wm. Gascoyne-Cecil); Carnegie, *The Church and the Schools* (1905), pp. 37-38; Cleworth, *The Education Crisis of 1906* (1906), p. 9.

4. Stephen (1883), III, p. 366.

5. *Commons*, May 8, 1906, p. 1224 (Evelyn Cecil); *School Guardian*, Sept. 20, 1902 (Dymott); *Standard*, Jan. 2, 1905 (Bishop Edwards of St. Asaph); Smith, *Dr. Clifford on Education* (1903), p. 9.

6. *Commons*, May 5, 1902, pp. 749-50 (Lyttelton).

7. *Parl. Papers*, 1895, CVIII, Cd. 7725, Part I, p. 72.

8. *Parl. Papers*, 1906, CXXXV, Cd. 2871, Note 1, pp. 32-33.

9. The official annual figure per 100,000 for graver offenses for the period 1857-59 is 93.81. *Ibid.*, pp. 34-35.

10. The official annual figures per 100,000 for less grave offenses for the periods 1857-59 and 1900-04 are 175.44 and 138.30 respectively. *Ibid.*, pp. 34-35.

11. The official annual figures per 100,000 for non-indictable offenses for the periods 1857-59 and 1900-04 are 1760.54 and 2228.79 respectively. *Ibid.*, pp. 34-35.

12. *Church Quarterly Rev.*, Jan. 1908, pp. 323-24 (Rees); *Independent Rev.*, July 1906, p. 19 (Wilson); Wilson, *Education and Crime* (1905), pp. 7, 11-12.

13. An inquiry at the Home Office on August 20, 1957 confirmed his figures.

14. Jones, *The Moral and Religious Condition of Wales* (1906), pp. 34-35.

15. *Parl. Papers*, 1902, CXVII, Cd. 953, p. 30.

16. *Daily News*, Sept. 11, 23, 1902 (Dymott); *Independent Rev.*, July 1906, p. 20 (Wilson); *School Guardian*, Feb. 22, March 22, 1902; Wilson, *Education and Crime* (1905), pp. 13-14.

17. For some references to their lamentations see Charles W. Eliot "Lawlessness," *Putnam's Magazine*, April 1909, p. 91; Hall, *Adolescence, Its Psychology* (1904), I, p. xviii; Harper, *The Trend in Higher Education* (1905), p. 70.

18. *McClure's Magazine*, Dec. 1904, p. 168. Its editor cited as the source of his statistics the compilations maintained by the *Chicago Tribune* for twenty-three years.

19. For Wilson's statistics see Bliss, *The New Encyclopaedia of Social Reform* (1908), pp. 334-36. The eleventh United States census report gives the slightly different figures of 290 prisoners in 1850 and 1,315 in 1890. *U.S. Census, 11th, 1890*, III, Part II, p. 6.

20. *Church Quarterly Rev.*, Jan. 1908, pp. 320-22 (Rees); *Independent Rev.*, July 1906, p. 21 (Wilson); *Manchester Guardian*, April 15, 1909 (Horsfall); *The Times*, Sept. 27, 1902, 12f (Horsfall); Horsfall, *The Amendment of the Education Act of 1902* (1905), pp. 5-9.

21. These several figures can be confirmed in *Victorian Year-Book*, 1890-91, II, pp. 190-91.

22. *Church Quarterly Rev.*, Oct. 1902, p. 181; *Independent Rev.*, July 1906, p. 19 (Wilson); Beeching, *Religio Laici* (1902), pp. 244-46.

23. For literature on New Zealand see Campbell, *Educating New Zealand* (1941), pp. 45-49; *Parl. Papers*, 1900, XXII, Part I, Cd. 417, pp. 635-36 (New Zealand); Paton (1914), Handbook No. 8.

24. Official figures approximate those cited by de Winton. See *New Zealand Official Year-Book*, 1904, pp. 108, 154.

25. *The Times*, Feb. 4, 1905, 15b (de Winton).

26. For literature on New South Wales see *Parl. Papers*, 1900, XXII, Part I, Cd. 417, pp. 223-24; Browne (1927), pp. 5-6, 29; Paton (1914), Handbook No. 2; *Official Year-Book of New South Wales*, 1904-05, pp. 545-46.

27. For his statistics Rev. Rees listed these sources: T. A. Coghlan, *A Statistical Account of Australia*, 1903-04, pp. 545-49, 553-54; *Statistical Register of the State of*

Victoria, 1905, p. 10; *Official Year Book of New South Wales*, 1904-05, pp. 577-83; *New South Wales Statistical Register for 1905*, p. 1098.

28. For original statement of E. T. Drake see *Victorian Year-Book*, 1905, p. 398.

29. *Church Quarterly Rev.*, Jan. 1908, pp. 313-20 (Rees); *Fortnightly Rev.*, May 1908, pp. 906-08 (Rees).

30. *Parl. Papers*, 1906, CXXXV, Cd. 2871, pp. 11, 34-35.

31. The official figure is 16,553. *Statistical Register of Victoria*, 1904, Part VI, p. 13.

32. *New South Wales Statistical Register for 1905*, p. 1122.

33. *Church Quarterly Rev.*, Jan. 1908, pp. 315, 320 (Rees).

34. For literature on France see Bracq, *France Under the Republic* (1910), pp. 212-34; Farrington, *The Public Primary School System of France* (1906), pp. 82, 107-08; Hayes, *France: A Nation of Patriots* (1930), pp. 35-36; Reisner (1922), pp. 81-86, 101.

35. *Compte Général de L'Administration de la Justice Criminelle*, 1904, p. xiv.

36. *Annuaire Statistique de la France*, 1905, p. 28.

37. *Church Quarterly Rev.*, Jan. 1908, pp. 308-13 (Rees); *The Times*, March 16, 1906, 4a-b (Bishop Wilkinson for Europe, North and Central).

38. Edgar Loening, *Jahrbücher für Nationaloekonomie und Statistik*, LXXVII, July —Dec. 1901, pp. 2-3. An English translation of Loening's report is to be found in *Annual Report of the Commissioner of Education* (U.S.), 1904, I, pp. 703-04.

39. *Church Quarterly Rev.*, Jan. 1908, pp. 307-08, 325-26 (Rees); *Independent Rev.*, July 1906, pp. 18-19 (Wilson); *The Times*, March 16, 1906 4a-b (Wilkinson); Shadwell (1906), II, pp. 393-98; Wilson, *Education and Crime* (1905), p. 8.

40. *Catholic Herald*, Feb. 23, 1906; *Month*, Dec. 1906, pp. 612-16 (Smith); Lilly, *Education, True and False* (1905), pp. 13-15; *International Moral Education Congress*, 1908, pp. 41-42 (Maher).

41. Shadwell (1906), II, pp. 390-92.

42. For literature on *morale laique* see Bracq (1910), pp. 235-351; Farrington (1906), pp. 106-07; Reisner (1922), pp. 83-86.

43. *Catholic Herald*, Sept. 23, 1911; *Commons*, Nov. 4, 1902 p. 688 (Healy); Burton, *Catholic Education and the Duties of Parents* (1906), pp. 4-5; Myers, in Sadler, *Moral Instruction and Training in Schools* (1908), II, pp. 51-69; Bourne, *The Maintenance of Religion in the Schools* (1908), I, pp. 10-11.

44. *Parl. Papers*, 1906, LXXXV, Cd. 3043, vii, p. 3.

45. *Month*, Dec. 1906, pp. 602-16, June 1909, pp. 584-92 (Smith).

46. For the three addresses see Sadler (1908), I, pp. 88-93, 166-80 (Maher), pp. 372-74 (Brown), II, pp. 51-69 (Myers).

47. *Month*, Nov. 1908, pp. 450-52 (Smith).

48. *Commons*, May 8, 1906, p. 1187 (Lloyd George); *Daily News*, June 20, 1902; *Manchester Guardian*, Sept. 6, 1902; *The Times*, April 29, 1905, 13f (Lloyd George).

49. *Daily Chronicle*, May 7, 1906; *Manchester Guardian*, Sept. 6, 1902; *The Times*, Aug. 5, 1903, 8e-f (Paton), July 28, 1903, 5f (Horton); Beet, in Stephens (1905), pp. 349, 367-69.

50. *Commons*, May 23, 1906, p. 1336 (Runciman); *Contemporary Rev.*, June 1913, p. 778 (Compton-Rickett); *Free Church Chronicle*, April 1904; Beet, in Stephens, (1905), pp. 350-56.

51. Clifford in *Crusader*, Nov. 16, 1905, July 1906; in *Daily News*, May 31, 1904, Jan. 12, Feb. 12, 1906; in *New Age*, Jan. 5, 1905; in *The Times*, Jan. 12, 1906, 4c; in *The Fight Against the Education Bill* (1902), p. 37.

52. The writer is indebted to Mr. J. K. Elliot, Chief Education Officer for the Manchester Education Committee, for a letter, dated November 12, 1956, containing

extracts from the triennial reports of the Manchester School Board for 1891, 1897, 1900. Utilizing only the 1897 triennial report, the numbers of Protestant and Roman Catholic children in industrial schools were 343 and 394 respectively out of a school roll of 44,198 board school, 33,721 Church of England, 3,949 British, 3,044 Wesleyan, and 14,166 Roman Catholic Church. These are not far off the figures cited by Evans.

53. Commons, May 5, 1902, pp. 656-57 (Bryce); The Times, July 21, 1902, 10f (Evans).

54. Lord Avebury, The Use of Life (London: 1902), p. 42.

55. Education Department Bulletin, New York, No. 424, May 1908, p. 22 (Reid).

56. Baptist Times, Jan. 10, 1908; Westminster Gazette, Dec. 8, 1902 (Williams).

57. South Wales Daily News, June 1, 1906; Wilson, Liberty and Religion (1906), p. 66.

58. Manchester Guardian, Sept. 14, 1907 (Hollowell); Whitwell, Liberty and Religion (1906), pp. 75-76.

59. Joseph Henry Crooker, Religious Freedom in American Education (Boston: 1903), p. 35.

60. Manchester Guardian, April 26, 1909 ("National Education"); The Times, Oct. 21, 1907, 9a (Clifford).

61. British Congregationalist, Sept. 29, 1910; The Times, Dec. 7, 1906, 8b (Horton).

62. Daily Chronicle, Feb. 8, 1906 (Stead); Ethics, Feb. 17, 1906 (O'Dell); Review of Reviews, Feb. 1906, pp. 116-17 (Stead); The Times, May 29, 1905, 9f (Johnson).

63. Ethics, Feb. 17, 1906 (O'Dell); Fortnightly Rev., April 1908, p. 710 (MacDonald); Freethinker, April 27, 1902 (Cohen); Literary Guide and Rationalist Rev., Sept. 1, 1902 (Picton).

64. International Journal of Ethics, Oct. 1904, p. 40 (Thompson); Literary Guide and Rationalist Rev., Jan. 1, 1907 (Picton); McCabe, The Truth About Secular Education (1906), pp. 81-85; Picton, The Bible in School (1907), pp. 32, 70-71; Thompson, Essays in Revolt (1905), pp. 64-70.

65. Fortnightly Rev., April 1908, pp. 712-13 (MacDonald); International, May 1908, pp. 68-69 (Johnson); Literary Guide and Rationalist Rev., June 1, 1906 (Gould); Manchester Guardian, Feb. 9, 1905 (Picton).

66. Ethics, Jan. 14, 1905 (Merriman); Hibbert Journal, Jan. 1906, p. 402 (Furnell); Picton, The Bible in School (1907), pp. 46-47.

67. Justice, Sept. 21, 1912 (Ralph Morley); Manchester Guardian, March 16, 1906 (Johnson); Snell, Secular Education (cir. 1908), p. 13; Spiller, Report on Moral Instruction (1909), pp. 14-15, 26.

68. Ethics, Nov. 15, 1902 (Spiller).

69. Fortnightly Rev., April 1908, pp. 710-11 (MacDonald).

70. Ethics, Feb. 6, 1904 (Snell); Justice, Feb. 19, 1914 (Morley); Literary Guide and Rationalist Rev., Nov. 1, 1903 (G. G. Greenwood, pseud. Forester); Progress, Jan. 1909, p. 26 (Spiller); Socialist Rev., Aug. 1909, pp. 436-38 (Ransom); Spiller, Report on Moral Instruction (1909), p. 15.

71. Commons, Nov. 25, 1908, p. 531 (MacDonald); Ethics, Dec. 6, 1902 (Sullivan), Feb. 6, 1904 (Snell); Fortnightly Rev., April 1908, p. 714 (MacDonald); Picton, The Bible in School (1907), pp. 43-44.

72. Parl. Papers, 1907, XCIV, Cd. 3691, p. 350.

73. Commons, May 10, 1906, p. 1554 (Snowden), Nov. 25, 1908, p. 531 (MacDonald); Fortnightly Rev., April 1908, p. 714 (MacDonald); Picton, The Bible in School (1907), p. 45n.

74. Hayward, *The Reform of Moral and Biblical Education* (1902), p. 48. In this book Dr. Hayward developed his own ideas, advocating that a judicious mixture of the better features of both Bible and non-theological lessons could best foster the moral sense of youth.

75. Richard Harcourt, *The Great Conspiracy Against Our American Public Schools* (San Francisco: 1890), p. 40.

76. McCabe in *Literary Guide and Rationalist Rev.*, June 1, 1906; in *The Truth About Secular Education* (1906), p. 67.

77. *Victorian Year-Book*, 1905, p. 398.

78. *Freethinker*, May 27, 1906 (Cohen).

79. *The Times*, May 14, 1906, 4e-f.

80. For his sources in compiling his statistics McCabe used the *Statesman's Year-Books*, 1892 and 1905.

81. McCabe in *Literary Guide and Rationalist Rev.*, June 1, 1906; in *The Truth About Secular Education* (1906), pp. 64-67.

82. A more extended statement on the Secular Education League is to be found in Chapter Eleven, pp. 202-03.

83. For all the statistics cited by the Secular Education League see *Victorian Year-Book*, 1909-10, pp. 525-27 and *Official Year Book of the Commonwealth of Australia*, 1908, pp. 760, 763-64.

84. *Secular Education Chronicle*, No. 8, Dec. 1911; Secular Education League, *Secular Education and Crime* (1912), 4 pp.

85. Webb's *Supplementary Edition of Mulhall's Dictionary of Statistics* (1911), p. 173.

86. *Revue Des Deux Mondes*, "Les Jeunes Criminels, L'Ecole et la Presse," 1897, p. 418 (Alfred Fouillée); *Statesman's Year-Books*, 1901, 1902, 1905.

87. *Freethinker*, Oct. 20, 1912 (Secular Education League); *Literary Guide and Rationalist Rev.*, June 1, 1906 (McCabe); McCabe, *The Truth About Secular Education* (1906), pp. 58-62; Secular Education League, *Secular Education and Crime*, (1912), 4 pp.

88. For the official graduated syllabus of moral instruction see *Ethics*, Nov. 22, 1902.

89. *Ethics*, Sept. 12, 1903 (A. J. Waldegrave); *International Journal of Ethics*, July 1904, p. 418 and Oct. 1904, pp. 28-38 (Thompson); Spiller, *Report on Moral Instruction* (1909), pp. 46-59, 65-72; Thompson, *Essays in Revolt* (1905), pp. 35-62.

90. *Fortnightly Rev.*, July 1908, pp. 70-71 (Grove); *Literary Guide and Rationalist Rev.*, Aug. 1, 1906, March 1, 1907, April 1, 1909 (Gould); Spiller, *Report on Moral Education* (1909), pp. 31-33.

91. *Commons*, May 7, 1906, p. 1083 (MacDonald); *Ethical World*, Sept. 5, 1910; *Freethinker*, April 13, 1902 (Watts); *Literary Guide and Rationalist Rev.*, Feb. 1, 1906 (Declaration of Agnostics and Freethinkers).

92. Edward Carpenter, ed., *Chants of Labour: A Song Book of the People, With Music* (No. 12), pp. 18-19.

93. *The Day of Days*, in *Collected Works of William Morris*, With Introduction by his daughter, May Morris (London: 1921), IX, p. 115.

94. *Commons*, March 16, 1909, pp. 996-1005 (Gooch), p. 1007 (Collins); *Ethical Rev.*, June 2, 23, 1906 (Coit); *Ethics*, March 3, 1906 (Coit); *The Times*, Oct. 14, 1907, 11e (Johnson).

95. *Ethical World*, Jan. 15, 1908; *Hibbert Journal*, Jan. 1906, pp. 403-04 (Furnell); *International Journal of Ethics*, July 1906, pp. 409-11 (Oliphant); *Justice*, April 14, 1906 (Maxted), May 15, 1909 (ed.).

96. For a copy of the original manifesto of the Moral Instruction League see *Ethics*, March 25, 1905.

97. *Positivist Rev.*, Aug. 1, 1905 (Gould); Gould, *The Life Story of a Humanist* (1923), p. 85; *London County Council, Education Committee Minutes*, Oct. 28, 1908, pp. 3277-78; *Parl. Papers*, 1907, LXII, Cd. 3594, pp. 3-4; *Moral Instruction League, Annual Report*, 1906, pp. 4-12.

98. *Commons*, March 16, 1909, pp. 996-1000 (Gooch); *Moral Instruction League, Annual Report*, 1906, pp. 4-12; Johnson, *Moral Instruction in the Elementary Schools in England and Wales* (1908), 46 pp.

99. *International*, May 1908, pp. 71-75 (Johnson); *The Times*, Sept. 26, 1908, 8d (Johnson); Johnson "Moral Instruction in France," in Sadler (1908), II, pp. 1-50; McCabe, *The Truth About Secular Education* (1906), pp. 70-79; Spiller, *Report On Moral Instruction* (1909), pp. 125-305.

100. *Agnostic Annual and Ethical Rev.* (1906), pp. 19-20 (Gould), (1907), pp. 47-50 (Bonner); *Ethical World*, June 15, 1907; *International Journal of Ethics*, July 1909, pp. 416-17 (Mackenzie); *Literary Guide and Rationalist Rev.*, Aug. 1, 1910 (Gould).

101. *Agnostic Journal and Eclectic Rev.*, Sept. 8, 1906 (Baylis); *Daily News*, April 17, 1909 (Chesterton); *Ethical World*, April 15, 1909 (Spiller).

CHAPTER SEVEN: UNIVERSAL FACILITIES

1. *Pilot*, Aug. 23, 1902, Jan. 10, Oct. 3, 1903, Jan. 2, 1904; *Saturday Rev.*, Jan. 25, March 29, 1902.

2. While official figures for 1901-02 did not yet establish the fact of more scholars in board schools, the margin was being narrowed; voluntary—1890 (2,260,559), 1900 (2,448,877), 1901 (2,492,536); board—1890 (1,457,358), 1900 (2,177,253), 1901 (2,239,375). *Parl. Papers*, 1902, LXXVIII, Cd. 1139, pp. 60-64 and 1903, LI, Cd. 1476, p. 7.

3. Official figures for London school accommodations are: board (567,071), voluntary (250,309). *Parl. Papers*, 1903, LI, Cd. 1476, p. 12.

4. *Manchester Guardian*, Aug. 5, 1902 (Rev. F. E. Powell); *Pilot*, Aug. 23, Sept. 13, 1902, Feb. 14, 1903, Jan. 2, 1904; *Saturday Rev.*, March 29, 1902, April 22, 1905.

5. *Pilot*, April 5, May 10, 17, July 26, Aug. 16, 1902, Jan. 2, 1904; *Saturday Rev.*, April 22, 1905; *Westminster Gazette*, Oct. 2, 1905 (Lathbury).

6. This quotation is a summary offered by Dr. Dale's son reflecting the spirit of his father's appreciation of the past role of the Christian churches. A. W. W. Dale (his son) (1899), p. 268.

7. *Nineteenth Century and After*, Jan. 1903, p. 7 (Lathbury); *Pilot*, May 17, June 7, Aug. 23, Sept. 13, Nov. 1, 1902, Jan. 2, 1904; *Saturday Rev.*, April 22, 1905.

8. For Chamberlain's amendment see *Commons*, May 22, 1906, p. 1243.

9. *Parl. Papers*, 1911, LIX, Cd. 6002, 3 pp.

10. *Church Times*, Dec. 23, 1909; *Saturday Rev.*, May 26, 1906, Jan. 11, 1908, June 7, 1913; *School Guardian*, March 11, 1911 (Seaborne); *The Times*, Feb. 13, 1907, 18a-c (Lathbury).

11. For a list of such Anglican schemes see Riley, Jackson, and Sadler, *The Religious Question in Public Education* (1911).

12. For Canon Henson's figures on the number of school teachers see *Parl. Papers*, 1904, LXXV, Cd. 2000, pp. 45-47.

13. *Guardian*, March 23, 1904; *Pilot*, Aug. 15, 1903, March 19, 1904; *Saturday Rev.*, Nov. 7, 1908; *Westminster Gazette*, Dec. 13, 1904 (Henson); Russell, ed., *Malcolm MacColl; Memoirs and Correspondence* (1914), p. 277, citing Letter, MacColl to Lord Salisbury, June 15, 1902.

14. For literature on the Drury-lane Day Industrial School see *London County Council Report with Regard to Industrial Schools, 1870 to 1904*, pp. 47-48; Spalding, *The Work of the London School Board* (1900), pp. 146-47.

15. *Church Times*, March 11, 1904; *Daily Mail*, May 8, 1906 (J. J. Cockshott); *Manchester Guardian*, Feb. 9, 1904 (Cleworth); *National Rev.*, May 1906, p. 362; *Saturday Rev.*, March 5, 1904.

16. For literature on the Prussian mixed schools see Helmreich (1959), p. 61; Hughes (1902), p. 67; Ross (1894), pp. 124-25.

17. *Parl. Papers*, 1902, XXVII, Cd. 836, p. 407.

18. *Church Times*, Jan. 22, 1904 (Cleworth); *Saturday Rev.*, March 5, 1904.

19. For literature on right of entry in Australasia see Browne (1927), pp. 38, 84, 180, 245-246, 315, 389; Paton (1902-14), Handbook Nos. 2, 4, 5, 6, 7; *Parl. Papers*, 1900, XXII, Part I, Cd. 417, pp. 223-24, 308-09, 419-20, 458, 470, 547-48, 635-36.

20. *Church Times*, Dec. 4, 1903 (Wells); *The Times*, April 6, 1906, 3f (Cyril Jackson).

21. For Lord Hugh Cecil's amendment see *Commons*, Nov. 25, 1904, p. 406.

22. *Church Quarterly Rev.*, Jan. 1902, pp. 466-67; *Commons*, Nov. 20, 1902, p. 401 (Lord Hugh Cecil); *School Guardian*, May 17, 1902, Oct. 10, 1903; *The Times*, Aug. 26, 1903, 6a-b (Davidson); Beeching, *Religio Laici* (1902), pp. 260-63.

23. *Church Quarterly Rev.*, Oct. 1907, pp. 15-17 (Rogers); *Church Times*, March 15, 1907 (Cleworth); *School Guardian*, July 4, 1908; *The Times*, Jan. 9, 1908 9c (Steer); Wordsworth, *The Education Question* (1906), p. 11.

24. For literature on the history of the Parents' League see *National Society, Annual Reports*, 1908, p. 25, 1909, p. 8; *Official Year Book of the Church of England*, 1908, p. 636, 1909, p. 639; *The Times*, July 14, 1908, 12e-f.

25. *Parents' League Leaflet*, 1909, XII and XV.

26. Thorpe, *The General Election and the Education Question* (1909), pp. 9-17.

27. Lawder-Eaton obtained his statistics from a statement to the commons by Joseph Albert Pease, President of the Board of Education. *Commons*, July 24, 1913, p. 2239 (Pease).

28. *Church Quarterly Rev.*, April 1912, pp. 24-25 (Bishop Whitcombe of Colchester); *Guardian*, Aug. 1, 1913; *Saturday Rev.*, Nov. 5, 1910, (Hoare); *School Guardian*, Feb. 4, 1911; *The Times, Educational Supplement*, Sept. 2, 1913, p. 141 (Lawder-Eaton).

29. *The Times*, July 4, 1901, 12c.

30. *National Society, Annual Report*, 1912, pp. 35-36; *The Times*, Nov. 21, 1913, 4d (Canterbury House of Laymen).

31. *Guardian*, April 23, 1902 (Ingram); *School Guardian*, March 4, 1911; *Spectator*, Aug. 16, 1902 (Rev. H. Lee-Warner); *The Times*, Feb. 2, 1912, 11d (Lang), Feb. 10, 1914, 4f (Davidson); Nunn, *The New Education Bill (Nov. 1908) Examined* (1908), pp. 3-5.

32. For literature on Quebec and Ontario see McCutcheon, *Public Education in Ontario* (1941), pp. 70-72; Weir, *The Separate School Question in Canada* (1934), pp. 131-41; 181-86; Ross, *The School System of Ontario (Canada)* (1896), pp. 148-51.

33. Guardian, May 2, 1906 (Rev. George H. Sharpe); The Times, Dec. 27, 1906, 10f and April 17, 1906, 5c (Redmayne), Jan. 1, 1907, 4b (Ridgeway), Dec. 27, 1906, 10e-f (Cleworth).

34. Church Quarterly Rev., April 1912, p. 10 (Bishop Whitcombe of Colchester); Guardian, May 2, 1906, Aug. 8, 1908 (Hope), Feb. 10, 1911 (Sadler); The Times, Jan. 9, 1907, 11b-c (Hope).

35. For an account of the adoption of the right of entry at Drury-lane see London School Board, Proceedings, XLIII, June 27, 1895—Nov. 28, 1895, pp. 83-84.

36. Church Times, Jan. 10, 1902 (Riley); Parents' League Leaflet, 1909, XII; The Times, May 23, 1902, 6a-b (Riley), Nov. 12, 1906, 10c (P. V. Smith); Westminster Gazette, Nov. 2, 1903 (Gascoyne-Cecil).

37. For literature on Scotland see Balfour (1903), p. 182; Curtis (1950), pp. 542-46; Sir Henry Craik, The State In Its Relation to Education (1896, new and rev. ed.), pp. 158-59, 163-64.

38. Parl. Papers, 1908, XXVII, Cd. 4291, pp. 17, 19-20.

39. Commons, June 20, 1906, pp. 205-06 (Butcher); Commonwealth, Jan. 1902, pp. 10-12 (Lord Hugh Cecil); Empire Rev., May 1906, p. 316 (Elliott); Parents' League Leaflet, 1909, XII; School Guardian, Jan. 25, 1908; Spectator, Nov. 21, 1908 (Baines).

40. Horsfall presented a detailed description of the Prussian system in a pamphlet entitled, Professor Rein's System of Religious Instruction for Schools (1905), 33 pp.

41. Church Quarterly Review, Jan. 1904, pp. 405-07; School Guardian, June 2, 1906, Jan. 25, 1908; Spectator, Jan. 6, 1906 (Horsfall); The Times, June 11, 1902, 11d-e; Horsfall, The Amendment of the Education Act of 1902 (1905), pp. 10-13.

42. For literature on Switzerland see Brooks, Government and Politics of Switzerland (1918), pp. 333-34; Adams and Cunningham, The Swiss Confederation (1889), pp. 189-209.

43. For literature on Holland see Parl. Papers, 1902, XXVI, Cd. 835, pp. 321-33.

44. For literature on Belgium see Annual Report, Commissioner of Education (U.S.), 1898-99, I, pp. 93-98; Goris, Belgium (1946), pp. 99-100; Parl. Papers, 1897, XXV, Cd. 8447, pp. 258-65; Rowntree, Land and Labour: Lessons from Belgium (1911), pp. 257-82.

45. Church Times, Dec. 11, 1908; Commons, May 28, 1906, p. 171 (F. S. Powell); Pall Mall Gazette, Oct. 5, 1906; School Guardian, Jan. 25, 1908; Westminster Gazette, Oct. 4, 10, 24, 1907, Feb. 27, 1908 (Clement F. Rogers).

46. Guardian, Sept. 7, 1904 (Whitworth); Nineteenth Century and After, April 1902, pp. 545-46 (Fletcher); Spectator, Dec. 30, 1905; The Times, Oct. 15, 1910, 9a and Jan. 28, 1908, 12c (Diggle).

47. Blackwood's Magazine, May 1908, p. 763, Dec. 1908, p. 872; Modern Churchman, Oct. 1912, p. 319 (C. T. D. Acland); Pilot, Sept. 17, 1902 (Lacey), Feb. 7, 1903 (S. M. B.); The Times, Jan. 28, 1908, 12c (Diggle), Educational Supplement, Sept. 2, 1913, p. 141 (Lawder-Eaton).

48. Modern Churchman, Oct. 1912, p. 317 (C. T. D. Acland); Pilot, Aug. 23, 1902 (Curtoys); Saturday Rev., March 15, 1902 (Macleane); Spectator, April 26, 1902 (Fletcher).

49. For literature on the Birmingham experiment see Adams (1882), p. 298; Gulley (1926), pp. 121-22.

50. Church Times, Nov. 30, 1906 (Bell); Nineteenth Century and After, May 1908, p. 699 (Knox).

51. For Dr. Moorhouse's statement see Guardian, Oct. 12, 1898, p. 1535.

52. *Nineteenth Century and After*, April 1902, p. 546 (Fletcher); *Pall Mall Gazette*, May 11, 1906; *The Times*, Nov. 19, 1903, 12d (Chandler); Henson, *Religion in the Schools* (1906), p. 55.

53. The official figure is 159,281. *New Zealand Official Year Book*, 1908, p. 190.

54. *East and the West*, July 1908, pp. 244-45 (Neligan); *Pilot*, June 21, 1902 (Flavell); *The Times*, Nov. 27, 1908, 11e (Neligan).

55. For the Transvaal story see *Transvaal, Report of the Religious Instruction in Schools Commission*, 1904-05, 271 pp.; Bot, *A Century of Education in the Transvaal, 1836-1936* (1936), p. 87; Malherbe, *Education in South Africa* (1925), p. 341.

56. *Guardian*, April 13, 1904 and Dec. 2, 1908 (Nash).

57. For literature supporting this adverse comment on the poor results of religious instruction in Germany in terms of spirituality see Barker (1915), pp. 462-63; *Contemporary Rev.*, Oct. 1906, p. 522 (Barker); Dawson (1894), I, pp. 316-32.

58. *Church Quarterly Rev.*, Jan. 1908, pp. 325-26 (Rees); *Church Times*, Jan. 3, 1902 (Lacey); *Commons*, Nov. 26, 1908, p. 786 (Kennaway); *Pilot*, Sept. 27, 1902 (Lacey).

59. *Church Times*, Oct. 31, 1902 (Lacey); *Nineteenth Century and After*, April 1902, p. 547 (R. C. Fletcher); *Pilot*, Aug. 16, 1902 (Talbot); *Western Mail* (Cardiff), March 30, 1903.

60. *Baptist Times*, Aug. 30, 1907 (Clifford); *British Weekly*, April 3, July 31, 1902; *Christian World*, Dec. 28, 1905 (Clifford); *Examiner*, July 23, 1903, March 31, 1904; *Manchester Guardian*, July 22, 1902.

61. *Christian World*, Dec. 28, 1905 (Clifford); *Daily News*, Nov. 12, 1908 (Clifford); *Examiner*, July 17, 1902; *The Times*, Nov. 12, 1908, 8b (Clifford).

62. *Contemporary Rev.*, Dec. 1902, pp. 811, 820-21 (Spender); *Methodist Times*, Nov. 21, 1907, Jan. 25, 1912, April 17, 1913.

63. *Baptist Times*, Aug. 30, 1907 (Clifford), Jan. 17, 1908 (ed.); *Daily News*, Nov. 12, 1908; *Methodist Times*, Sept. 12, 1907, Nov. 17, 19, 1908.

64. *Commons*, March 24, 1902, pp. 939-40 (Bryce), May 8, 1902, p. 1136 (Asquith), Nov. 25, 1902, pp. 439-40 (Lloyd George); *Daily Chronicle*, Oct. 3, 1907; Wilson, *Liberty and Religion* (1906), pp. 57-58.

65. *Liberator*, July 1906, Jan. 1908; Society for the Liberation of Religion From State-Patronage and Control Leaflet, *Little Billy and the Inalienable Right of Parents* (June 1906), 4 pp.

66. *Christian World*, Nov. 19, 1908, March 27, June 5, 1913; *Nation*, June 8, 1907 (Hollowell); *Westminster Gazette*, May 23, June 2, 1906.

67. *British Weekly*, Aug. 29, 1907 (Compton-Rickett); *Crusader*, Feb. 16, 1905 (Hollowell); *Daily Chronicle*, Oct. 24, 1904; *Liberator*, Oct. 1902, Aug. 1904; *Presbyterian*, Feb. 15, 1906.

68. *British Weekly*, Jan. 30, 1908; *Christian World*, Oct. 27, 1910; *Manchester Guardian*, Dec. 3, 1902; *Westminster Gazette*, Oct. 28, 1902; Welsh, *The Capture of the Schools* (1903), p. 24.

69. See *Transvaal, Report of the Religious Instruction in Schools Commission*, 1904-05, 271 pp. The Northern Counties Education League published this report in pamphlet form in October 1905 as evidence of the impracticality of facilities.

70. *Commons*, Nov. 25, 1902, pp. 413-14 (Bryce), Dec. 12, 1906, p. 461 (Birrell); *Manchester Guardian*, Dec. 29, 1904 (Clifford); *The Times*, Dec. 11, 1906, 12d and Feb. 3, 1912, 12a (Clifford).

71. Wilson, *Liberty and Religion* (1906), pp. 74-75.

72. Hollowell, *Reply to Mr. Balfour's Address to the Deputation of the National Free Church Council* (1902), p. 7.

73. For Dawson's own description of the Prussian educational system see *The German Empire, 1867-1914, and the Unity Movement* (1919), II, p. 325.

74. *The Times*, Aug. 5, 1902, 8e-f (Dawson).

CHAPTER EIGHT: GENERAL RELIGIOUS INSTRUCTION

1. *Contemporary Rev.*, Sept. 1910, pp. 281-83 (Shakespeare); *Fortnightly Rev.*, May 1902, p. 838 (Macnamara); *Free Church Chronicle*, April 1904; *Free Church Year Book*, 1904, pp. 88-89; *Methodist Times*, July 3, 1902.

2. *Fortnightly Rev.*, Nov. 1903, pp. 808-09 (Macnamara); *Friend*, Feb. 16, 1906; *Manchester Guardian*, Oct. 10, 1902; *Methodist Times*, July 30, Sept. 17, 1903; *The Times*, Sept. 18, 1902, 6d-e and Sept. 14, 1903, 8f (Macnamara).

3. *Christian World*, Dec. 28, 1911; *Crusader*, Feb. 5, 1904 (Hollowell); *Daily News*, Jan. 30, 1904 (Macnamara), Nov. 12, 1908 (Clifford); *Methodist Recorder*, Nov. 12, 1908; *Methodist Times*, April 16, 1908.

4. *Liberal Magazine*, Dec. 1903, p. 709 (Horton); *The Times*, Nov. 16, 1903, 10f (Clifford), Aug. 31, 1903, 8e-f (Horton); Hodgkin, *National Education* (1906), pp. 19-20.

5. *Contemporary Rev.*, Feb. 1908, p. 145 (George White); *Methodist Times*, Dec. 17, 1908 (Lidgett); *Westminster Gazette*, Aug. 9, 31, 1906 (Bayly).

6. For literature on Ontario see Bourinot, *How Canada is Governed* (1938, 3rd ed.), pp. 248-49; McCutcheon (1941), pp. 74-80; Ross (1896), pp. 148-53; Siegfried, *The Race Question in Canada* (1907), pp. 77-78.

7. These statistics were prepared in May 1896 by the Chicago Woman's Educational Union. Letters of inquiry were sent to State Superintendents of Public Instruction who in turn sent the questions along to city and county superintendents. *Annual Report of the Commissioner of Education* (U.S.), 1897-98, III, pp. 1539, 1560-61.

8. *British Weekly*, Jan. 1, 1903 (Hollowell); *Commons*, May 6, 1902, pp. 912-13 (Macnamara), July 2, 1902, p. 566 (Lloyd George); *Daily News*, Jan. 7, 1904 (Hollowell); *The Times*, Sept. 18, 1902, 6d-e (Macnamara).

9. For literature on the adoption of general religious instruction in Queensland see Browne (1927), pp. 245-46; Paton (1914), Handbook No. 5.

10. Harvey in *Educational Record*, June 1912; in *Nation*, July 9, 1910.

11. *Baptist Times*, Oct. 9, 1903 (Whitley).

12. *Parl. Papers*, 1911, LIX, Cd. 6002, 3 pp.

13. *Guardian*, Nov. 25, 1908; *Manchester Guardian*, June 20, 1906 (Screeton); *The Times*, Feb. 4, 1907, 7b-c (Percival), Jan. 23, 1906, 10e (Wakefield).

14. *Nineteenth Century and After*, April 1908, pp. 551-52 (Henson); *Record*, Feb. 9, 1906; *The Times*, Jan. 28, 1908, 12c (Diggle), Oct. 18, 1904, 10a (Henson), May 22, 1908, 9c (Ridgeway).

15. *Independent Rev.*, Feb. 1907, pp. 149 (Henson).

16. *Independent Rev.*, Feb. 1907, pp. 148, 155 (Henson); *The Times*, May 18, 1908, 6d (Ridgeway); Bruce, *Dr. Gore and Religious Education* (1906), p. 14; Henson, *Religion in the Schools* (1906), pp. vii-viii, 116.

17. John Milton, *Paradise Regained*, Book IV, Lines 361-63.

18. *Spectator*, April 28, 1906; *The Times*, May 26, 1906, 16a (Diggle), Feb. 4, 1907, 7b-c (Percival); Henson, *Religion in the Schools* (1906), p. 55.

19. *House of Lords, Sessional Papers*, 1906, XIII, No. 115, Part I, pp. 57, 62, 67, 72, 99, 101.

20. Morley (1923), II, pp. 307-08.

21. For the catechisms of the Church of England and the Free Church Council see Knox, *Pastors and Teachers* (1902), pp. 195-99, 289-97.

22. *Independent Rev.*, Feb. 1907, p. 149 (Henson); *The Times*, Jan. 6, 1905, 8a and Oct. 21, 1910, 12d (Edwards); Nov. 4, 1903, 10e and Nov. 5, 1903, 9e (Davidson); Henson, *The Education Act and After* (1903), pp. 69-70.

23. *Independent Rev.*, Feb. 1907, p. 158 (Henson); *The Times*, April 7, 1906, 10a (Carpenter), Jan. 17, 1907, 10c-d (Henson); Henson, *Religion in the Schools* (1906), pp. 14-15.

24. *Manchester Guardian*, April 27, 1907 (Cremer); *Spectator*, Feb. 17, 1906, Feb. 29, 1908; *The Times*, April 7, 1906, 10a (Carpenter), Feb. 13, 1906, 8b-c (Wilson), June 8, 1908, 7f (Rev. M. G. Glazebrook); Henson, in Stephens (1905), p. 246.

25. *Guardian*, April 20, 1904 (Rev. J. Frome Wilkinson); *Manchester Guardian*, April 27, 1907 (Cremer); *The Times*, March 3, 1906, 8c (Rev. W. Moore Ede), Oct. 24, 1908, 7a (Papillon), Oct. 27, 1910, 7a (Edwards).

26. *The Jamaica Day School Catechism* (London: 1907, 4th ed.), 28 pp.

27. For the article written by Bishop Smyth of Lebombo see *East and the West*, April 1906, pp. 121-34.

28. *Fortnightly Rev.*, June 1, 1906, pp. 1011-12 (Carpenter); *The Times*, April 7, 1906, 10a (Carpenter), Nov. 4, 1905, 4c (Henson).

29. Christopher, *An Example From India* (1906), 24 pp.

30. *The Times*, March 24, 1906, 5b (Emery).

31. Correspondence with the Department of Education of New South Wales reveals that Inspector Lobban's statement is not to be found in any of its official reports for the period of his service. But the suggestion is made, and seems a likely possibility, that— since Lobban and Bishop Frodsham were personally acquainted—it might be assumed that the quotation came from an exchange of letters between the two.

32. Bishop Frodsham in *Guardian*, July 25, 1913; in *Manchester Guardian*, Nov. 15, Dec. 15, 29, 1913; in *Morning Post*, March 9, 1914; in *The Times, Educational Supplement*, Aug. 5, 1913, p. 123.

33. For the debate in the London School Board see *School Board for London, Minutes of Proceedings*, XL, Dec. 1893—May 1894 and XLI, June—Nov. 1894.

34. See Riley, *Religious Teaching in Board Schools: Being an Account of the Great Religious Controversy on the London School Board in 1893, With an Appeal to All Christian People in the Metropolis* (London: 1893), 12 pp.

35. *Manchester Guardian*, Feb. 4, 1907 (Cleworth); *The Times*, May 19, 1906, 7d (Knox), Jan. 4, 1907, 6c-d (Wace), Oct. 27, 1902, 3d (Riley), Aug. 29, 1902, 8c (Taylor); *Westminster Gazette*, Oct. 31, 1905 (Lathbury).

36. *Church Times*, Nov. 13, 1903; *Morning Post*, Oct. 17, 1902 (Nicholson); *School Guardian*, Feb. 1, Sept. 13, 1902; *The Times*, Jan. 15, 1907, 11c-d (Lord Hugh Cecil), Feb. 16, 1906, 7c (Gore).

37. *Blackwood's Magazine*, May 1908, p. 763; *Manchester Guardian*, Nov. 13, 1908 (Knox); *Nineteenth Century and After*, May 1908, pp. 698-99 (Knox); *School Guardian*, Feb. 28, 1903.

38. *British Weekly*, Oct. 23, 1902 (ed.), Jan. 1, 1903 (Hollowell); *Christian World*, March 16, 1905, Jan. 18, 1906; *Commons*, July 14, 1902, p. 193 (Jones); *Daily News*, May 31, 1904 (Clifford); *Free Church Year Book*, 1904, p. 102 (Hollowell).

39. *Baptist Times*, Nov. 25, 1904 (Wishart); *British Weekly*, Oct. 23, 1902; *Crusader*, Jan. 22, 1904 (Hollowell); *Daily News*, May 7, 1902; *Manchester Guardian*, April 24, 1902 (Elliot).

40. *Commons*, Nov. 3, 1902, p. 1451 (Yoxall); *Examiner*, Jan. 1, 1903; *Westminster Gazette*, Dec. 10, 1906 (ed.), Nov. 19, 1908 (Mundella); Brock (1902), p. 7.

41. *Church Times*, Jan. 25, 1907; *Commonwealth*, Feb. 1906, pp. 41-42 (Holland); *Conservative and Unionist*, March 1908, p. 38 (F. E. Smith); *The Times*, Oct. 8, 1902, 8b (Lord Hugh Cecil), May 17, 1902, 5d-e (C. T. D. Acland).

42. *Churchman*, Sept. 1903, p. 670; *Pilot*, May 14, 1904; *The Times*, Aug. 18, 1903, 9f (Davidson).

43. *Church Times*, Jan. 18, 1907 (Burnie); *Manchester Guardian*, Jan. 6, 1908 (Cleworth); *Nineteenth Century and After*, Jan. 1903, p. 12 (Lathbury).

CHAPTER NINE: THE ROMAN CATHOLIC POSITION

1. *Month*, April 1906, p. 347 (Smith); *The Times*, Nov. 5, 1903, 9e (Hedley); Bourne, *The Catholic Attitude on the Education Question* (1906), p. 22; Rickaby, *The Rights of Minorities* (1905), pp. 3-4.

2. *Month*, April 1906, pp. 346, 351-52 (Smith); *Tablet*, March 3, 1906, pp. 350-53 (Bourne); *The Times*, Feb. 6, 1906, 12a (Father Bernard Vaughan); Bourne, *The Maintenance of Religion in the Schools* (1908), pp. 7-8; Lescher, *The School Question* (1906), pp. 5-7.

3. For the New South Wales figures furnished by Rev. Glancey see *Parl. Papers*, 1900, XXII, Part I, Cd. 417, p. 223n.

4. *Catholic Times*, Oct. 6, 1905; *Dublin Rev.*, July 1902, p. 22 (Glancey), July 1906, p. 164 (ed.); *The Times*, July 19, 1902 6f (Cardinal Vaughan); Bourne, *The Education Act of 1902* (1904), pp. 13-14.

5. *Parl. Papers*, 1906, XXX, Cd. 2942, p. 8.

6. *Dublin Rev.*, July 1902, pp. 6-7 (Glancey), Jan. 1907, pp. 134-38 (Brown); *Month*, Sept. 1906, p. 241 (Smith); *Tablet*, Oct. 25, 1902, Dec. 17, 1904.

7. For literature on the Victorian strife to 1900 see Sweetman, Long, and Smyth, *A History of State Education in Victoria* (1922), pp. 147-49; Victoria, *Report of the Royal Commission on Religious Instruction in State Schools*, 1900, 445 pp.; *Parl. Papers*, 1900, XXII, Part I, Cd. 417, pp. 393-408.

8. *Dublin Rev.*, July 1902, pp. 4-6 (Glancey).

9. For literature on Ontario and Quebec see Bourinot (1918), pp. 245-53; McCutcheon (1941), pp. 74-80; Ross (1896), p. 134 ff; Siegfried (1907), pp. 66-73, 75-77; Weir (1934), p. 128 ff, p. 174 ff.

10. For literature on Manitoba see Ewart, *The Manitoba School Question* (1894), 413 pp; Siegfried (1907), pp. 80-84; Weir (1934), pp. 35-37.

11. *Dublin Rev.*, July 1902, pp. 6-7 (Glancey).

12. For literature on Prussia see Dawson (1918), II, p. 326; Fife (1918), pp. 355-56; Helmreich (1959), p. 60 ff; Hughes (1902), p. 67; *Parl. Papers*, 1886, Cd. 4752, pp. 12-14 (Matthew Arnold).

13. *The Times*, July 19, 1902, 6f (Cardinal Vaughan).

14. Goodier, *Side-Lights From the Continent on the Education Question* (1906), pp. 6-11.

15. *Parl. Papers*, 1911, LIX, Cd. 6002, 3 pp.

16. *Catholic Herald,* Feb. 15, 1908; *Catholic Times,* May 30, 1913; *Tablet,* Sept. 6, 1902, Sept. 24, 1904, Dec. 23, 1911; Windle, *The Catholic Aspect of the Education Question* (1904), p. 12.

17. In 1904 there were 4,235 Roman Catholic parishes with schools in which 1,031,378 children were in attendance. *Annual Report of the Commissioner of Education* (U.S.), 1904, II, p. 2305.

18. *Catholic Times,* Nov. 15, 1907; *Dublin Rev.,* July 1902, pp. 7-8 (Glancey); *Manchester Guardian,* April 30, 1907 (Patrick Lynch); McNabb, *The Secular Solution to the Education Difficulty* (1909), p. 4.

19. As of 1901, the figures for France read 3,864,189 in public primary schools and 1,662,611 in private primary schools, Hayes (1930), p. 37. For literature see also Bracq (1910), pp. 212-34; Farrington (1906), p. 82; Hughes (1902), pp. 106-07.

20. For a brief reference to the Italian experience see Croce, *A History of Italy* (1929), pp. 68, 177.

21. Goodier, *Side-Lights From the Continent on the Education Question* (1906), pp. 12-45.

22. *Catholic Times,* Jan. 29, 1904, Aug. 9, 1907; *Commons,* May 7, 1906, p. 1072 (Belloc); *Tablet,* March 3, 1906, p. 351 (Bourne); Belloc, *Catholics and the Education Bill* (1906), p. 8; Bourne, *The Education Act of 1902* (1904), pp. 12-14; Burton, *Catholic Education and the Duties of Parents* (1906), pp. 6-12.

23. *Catholic Herald,* March 21, 1908, March 19, 1910, April 8, Sept. 9, 1911, March 2, 1912, Jan. 18, 1913.

24. *Commons,* May 1908, pp. 1703-04 (John Redmond); *Manchester Guardian,* Jan. 17, 1908 (Richardson); *Tablet,* Jan. 4, 25, 1908 (ed.), June 13, 1908 (Doughan).

25. For literature on earmarking in Ontario and Quebec see McCutcheon (1941), pp. 70-74; Ross (1896), pp. 148-50; Siegfried (1907), pp. 66-73, 75; Weir (1934), pp. 118-49.

26. For 1905 the Report of the Ontario Minister of Education lists 428 Roman Catholic schools, an increase of 9 over 1904. *Parl. Papers,* 1908, LXXXIII, Cd. 4143, p. 7.

27. *Commons,* May 10, 1906, p. 1507 (John Redmond); *Month,* Aug. 1906, pp. 164-69 (Smith).

28. *Guardian,* May 16, 1906 (Gainsford); *Tablet,* March 14, 1908, pp. 430-32 (Bourne).

29. The figures cited by Msgr. Brown would be correct for 1904. *Statistical Abstract for London,* 1908, X, Issued Under Standing Order of the London County Council, pp. 11-12.

30. *Tablet,* March 14, 21, 1908 (ed.), Feb. 10, 1906 and April 11, 1908 (Brown).

31. *Commonwealth,* May 1904, pp. 147-48 (Richmond); *Independent Rev.,* Feb. 1907, p. 159 (Henson); *Manchester Guardian,* July 16, 1902 (Horsfall); *Westminster Gazette,* Oct. 2, 1905 (Lathbury).

32. *Guardian,* Jan. 3, 1906; *Manchester Guardian,* April 7, 1903 (Cleworth); *Pilot,* Aug. 22, 1903 (St. John Browne); *The Times,* Jan. 29, 1906, 8c and Feb. 3, 1906, 11c (Riley).

33. *Baptist Times,* April 8, 1904; *Contemporary Rev.,* Feb. 1908, pp. 145-46 (White); *Methodist Recorder,* May 1, 1902 (French); *Methodist Times,* Feb. 2, 1905; White, *The Case Against the Education Act* (1905), p. 15.

34. *Crusader,* Sept. 1906 (Clifford); *Examiner,* March 8, 1906; *Free Church Year Book,* 1909, p. 21 (Clifford); *Westminster Gazette,* Sept. 26, 1905.

35. *Manchester Guardian,* March 20, 1907 (Hollowell); *The Times,* Aug. 31, 1908, 4d (Hollowell); *Westminster Gazette,* Oct. 4, 1905 (Hollowell).

36. For the text of Msgr. Satolli's address see *The New York Times*, Dec. 8, 1892, p. 9, col. 4.

37. *Christian World*, March 22, 1906; *Crusader*, Feb. 11, 1904 (Hollowell); *Daily News*, April 12, 1902 (A. Lees); *Manchester Guardian*, April 4, 1903, April 19, 26, Sept. 14, 1907 (Hollowell); Wilson, *Liberty and Religion* (1906), p. 58.

CHAPTER TEN: THE JEWISH POSITION

1. *Ministry of Education*, 1906, Bill Papers, B 12.

2. *Parl. Papers*, 1911, LIX, Cd. 6002, 3 pp.

3. For available secondary literature on the Jewish position see Philpott, *London at School* (1904), p. 113; Riley, Sadler, and Jackson (1911), pp. 275-85; Webb, *London Education* (1904), pp. 200-02.

4. *Extract From the Report of the School Management Committee of the 6th October 1893*, Introducing Motion 14 to Send a Letter to the Education Department With Reference to Religious Instruction to Jews and Roman Catholics, 14 pp.; *School Board for London, November 1894*, Return With Regard to Religious Instruction in the Schools of the School Board for London (Ordered by the House of Lords Through the Education Department), 26 pp.

5. Jewish Religious Education Board (London), Annual Reports, 1902-14; *Jewish Year Books*, 1902-14; *Ministry of Education*, 1906, Bill Papers, B 12.

6. *The Times*, April 8, 1908, 12d (news item).

7. *The Times*, April 8, 1908, 12d (news item), Nov. 27, 1908, 11d (Adler).

CHAPTER ELEVEN: THE SECULARIST POSITION

1. *Agnostic Annual and Ethical Rev.*, 1906, pp. 17-18 (Gould); *Justice*, Sept. 21, 1912 (Morley), Jan. 14, 1905 (ed.); *Literary Guide and Rationalist Rev.*, April 1, 1908, (Robertson).

2. *Nineteenth Century and After*, March 1906, p. 376 (Alderley).

3. *Commons*, Feb. 24, 1908, pp. 1407-08 (MacDonald); *Fortnightly Rev.*, April 1908, pp. 715-16 (MacDonald); *Literary Guide and Rationalist Rev.*, April 1, 1908 (Robertson); *New Age*, April 14, 1904; *Reformer*, July 15, 1903, p. 416 (Robertson).

4. *Daily News*, Feb. 12, 1906 (Snowden); *Literary Guide and Rationalist Rev.*, Feb. 1, 1906 (Gould); *Nineteenth Century and After*, April 1911, pp. 751-53 (Stewart); *Trades Union Congress*, Sept. 4-9, 1905, p. 142 (Appleton).

5. *The Times*, Oct. 11, 1894, 14d-e (Parker).

6. *Agnostic Annual and Ethical Rev.*, 1906, p. 15 (Gould); *Daily Chronicle*, Feb. 8, 1906 (Stead); *Freethinker*, Sept. 1, 1907 (Foote); *Justice*, Sept. 21, 1912 (Morley); *Nineteenth Century and After*, April 1911, pp. 751-52 (Stewart).

7. *Clarion*, June 19, 1914 (Snell); *Freethinker*, June 9, 1912 (Stewart); *Positivist Rev.*, Feb. 1, 1909 and July 1, 1912 (Swinny); Scott, *National Education* (1906), p. 15; Snell, *Secular Education* (cir. 1908), pp. 5-7.

8. *Christian Life and Unitarian Herald*, May 6, 1905, Jan. 12, 1907; *Inquirer*, Nov. 14, 21, 1903, March 19, 1904, Feb. 10, 1906.

9. *Clarion*, June 19, 1914 (Snell); *Literary Guide and Rationalist Rev.*, April 1, 1906 (Ryan); *Socialist Rev.*, April 1911, p. 132 (Snell); Scott, *National Education* (1906), p. 16.

10. For an indirect reference to Dr. Clifford's answer see *Crusader*, Feb. 1907 (Hollowell).

11. *Clarion*, Sept. 4, 1908 (Snell); *Freethinker*, Dec. 13, 1908 (Foote); *Positivist Rev.*, May 1, 1907, pp. 118-19 (Swinny); Snell, *Men, Movements, and Myself* (1938), p. 176.

12. *The Times*, Feb. 5, 1907, 3f, March 25, 1907, 7a, Sept. 20, 1907, 7f, Oct. 14, 1907, 10d, Nov. 8, 1907, 8d, March 5, 1908, 9f, Dec. 2, 1908, 8c.

13. *Freethinker*, Jan. 2, 1910 (Secular Education League); *Nineteenth Century and After*, April 1911, p. 743 (Stewart); Snell, *Men, Movements, and Myself* (1938), p. 176 ff.

14. *Labour Party* Annual Conferences, 1906-10; *Commons*, April 9, 1906, pp. 1056-57 (MacDonald); *Trades Union Congress*, Annual Conferences, 1907-08, 1910-11.

15. *Labour Party*, Annual Conferences, Feb. 1-3, 1911, p. 90.

16. *Trades Union Congress*, Annual Conference, Sept. 3-7, 1912, pp. 177-84.

17. *Nineteenth Century and After*, April 1911, pp. 745-46 (Stewart); *Socialist Rev.*, April 1911, pp. 129-33 (Snell); Hyndman, *Further Reminiscences* (1912), p. 529.

18. For Picton's reference see *Parl. Papers*, 1900, XXII, Part I, Cd. 417, pp. 308-09.

19. Picton in *Pilot*, Aug. 16, 1902; in *The Bible in School* (1907), pp. 56, 56n, 59-60.

20. For Picton's reference see *Parl. Papers*, 1900, XXII, Part I, Cd. 417, pp. 393-408; Sweetman, Long, and Smyth (1922), p. 149.

21. For a ready account of the 1904 referendum in Victoria see *London Tribune*, March 5, 1906 (W. H. Fitchett).

22. For literature on the Queensland referendum see Browne (1927), pp. 245-46; Paton (1902-14), Handbook No. 5; Wyeth (1955), pp. 168-70. In parliament Col. John E. B. Seely, Under-Secretary for the Colonies, in answer to a query, stated that the Queensland figures as given in newspapers were 69,321 (Yes) and 51,955 (No). *Commons*, July 4, 1910, pp. 1303-04.

23. *Freethinker*, May 9, 1909 and Aug. 14, 1910 (McLaren); *Literary Guide and Rationalist Rev.*, May 1, 1907 (Bonner); *Pilot*, Aug. 16, 1902 (Picton).

24. For available literature on New Zealand see Campbell (1941), pp. 49-52.

25. *Statistics of the Colony of New Zealand*, 1906, II, pp. 517, 529.

26. *Justice*, Oct. 9, 1909 (Thorn).

27. *Justice*, April 23, 1914 (Gould); *Literary Guide and Rationalist Rev.*, May 1, 1914 (Gould); Picton, *The Bible in School* (1907), pp. 56-57.

28. Picton, *The Bible in School* (1907), p. 59n, pp. 59-60.

29. *Freethinker*, Dec. 1, 1912 (Secular Education League); *International*, Dec. 1909, p. 19 (Pease); Hyndman, *The Record of an Adventurous Life* (1911), pp. 99-100.

30. McCabe offered a similar indictment against Christianity. McCabe, *The Truth About Secular Education* (1906), pp. 7-12, 15-32, 39, 45-48.

31. *Reformer*, June 15, 1903, pp. 332-37, July 15, 1903, pp. 400-13 (Robertson). These two articles were revised and expanded in 1943 by A. Gowans Whyte and are catalogued thus: J. M. Robertson and A. Gowans Whyte, *The Church and Education* (London: 1943), 32 pp.

32. Robertson's figures may be checked in *Statesman's Year-Books*.

33. *Reformer*, June 15, 1903, pp. 328-31 (Robertson).

34. Wilson, *Liberty and Religion* (1906), pp. 86, 91-93, 97.

35. *Ethical World*, June 15, 1907; *Literary Guide and Rationalist Rev.*, Sept. 1, 1907, Aug. 1 and Oct. 1, 1910 (Gould); Stewart D. Headlam, *Secular Schools* (1906), p. 26.

36. Sir Walter Scott, *Talisman* (1894), p. 272. Buckner Library edition.

37. Milton, *Lycidas*, lines 172-73.

38. *Literary Guide and Rationalist Rev.*, Sept. 1, 1907, Aug. 1 and Oct. 1, 1910 (Gould).

39. *Educational Review* (New York), Dec. 1899, p. 436 (Butler).

40. *Churchman*, Sept. 1903, p. 669; *Commons*, May 8, 1906, p. 1237 (Butcher); *The Times*, Sept. 5, 1903, 7c-d.

41. *Crusader*, May 25, 1905 (Hollowell); *Methodist Times*, March 1, 1906; *Speaker*, Aug. 16, 1902 (Hollowell); *The Times*, Aug. 5, 1903, 8e-f (Paton).

42. *Examiner*, Nov. 16, 1905, Jan. 11, 1906; *Manchester Guardian*, March 19, 1906 (Moulton); *Nation*, June 11, 1910 (Harvey); *The Times*, Aug. 5, 1903, 8e-f (Paton).

CHAPTER TWELVE: POSTSCRIPT

1. *Manchester Guardian*, Nov. 15, 1911 (Clifford); *The Times*, April 1, 1909, 12f and Jan. 2, 1912, 4b (Clifford); Clifford, *Ten Years of Protest Against the Intrusion of Churches Into State Schools: Passive Resistance*, June 1912-June 1913 (1913), 15 pp.

2. *Parl. Papers*, 1902, XXIV, Cd. 1275, p. 5; 1908, LXXXV, Cd. 4288, p. 15.

3. The official tabulation is as follows: voluntary schools, 1900-01 (3,729,261) and July 31, 1911 (2,826,594); council schools, 1900-01 (2,881,155) and July 31, 1911 (3,980,946). *Parl. Papers*, 1912-13, LXIV, Cd. 6338, pp. 15, 17.

4. *British Congregationalist*, May 29, 1913 (Horne); *Westminster Gazette*, Feb. 24, 1908.

5. For the slightly different official figures see *Parl. Papers*, 1911, LIX, Cd. 6002, p. 3.

6. *Parl. Papers*, 1911, LIX, Cd. 6002, p. 3.

7. The corrected breakdown is as follows: (1909) 3,246,411, (1910) 3,093,307, (1911) 2,825,399, (1912) 2,797,636. *Parl. Papers*, 1913, XLIX, Cd. 6934, p. 17.

8. *Guardian*, Aug. 8, 1913; *The Times*, Dec. 4, 1908, 10c-f (Davidson), April 27, 1910, 7a (Edwards).

9. *Commons*, April 6, 1909, p. 1134 (Runciman).

10. Talbot in *Manchester Guardian*, Dec. 15, 1908; in *Standard*, April 9, 1909; in *The Times*, Dec. 14, 1908, 6d.

11. *Parl. Papers*, 1911, LIX, Cd. 6002, 3 pp.

12. See Note 7 above for corrected figures.

13. *Morning Post*, Feb. 23, 1914 (Taylor); *School Guardian*, Dec. 16, 1911.

14. *Parl. Papers*, 1907, LXIV, Cd. 3597, pp. v-vi. The full text of the McKenna regulations can also be found in *The Times* (London), July 11, 1907, 8d.

15. *Morning Post*, July 31, 1907; *Lords*, July 25, 1907 (Davidson); *Saturday Rev.*, July 13, 27, 1907; *School Guardian*, July 13, 20, 1907; *The Times*, July 19, 1907, 4d (Stevenson).

16. *Parl. Papers*, 1886, XXV, Cd. 4863, pp. 54-55 (questions 1199-1200).

17. These figures are not contained in the annual reports of the National Society and were apparently supplied by its staff to the Archbishop of Canterbury.

18. For the period from 1863 to 1905 revenue sources for maintenance of Church of England training colleges are as follows: subscriptions (£508,022), endowments (£48,934), student fees (£587,988), exchequer grants (£3,418,564). *Parl. Papers*, 1906, XC, No. 233, 15 pp.

19. *Spectator*, July 20, 1907 (Cleworth); *The Times*, July 22, 1907, 18a-e (Davidson), Dec. 28, 1907, 9b-c (C. T. D. Acland); *Westminster Gazette*, Jan. 3, 1908 (Brooke).

20. *Parl. Papers*, 1908, LXXXV, Cd. 3886, p. 114.

21. By 1907 the Church of England had seven hostels handling 189 students and the day training colleges eighteen hostels handling 627 students. *Parl. Papers*, 1908, LXXXV, Cd. 4288, pp. 140-41, 386-87. For literature see Sandiford (1910), pp. 67-69.

22. *School Guardian*, July 20, 1907 (Cleworth); *The Times*, July 19, 1907, 4d (Stevenson), July 22, 1907, 18a-f (Davidson).

23. *Guardian*, Dec. 18, 1907; *Saturday Rev.*, Dec. 21, 1907; *Spectator*, July 27, 1907; *Standard*, Dec. 19, 1907; *The Times*, Dec. 18, 1907, 14a-c (Davidson).

24. *Parl. Papers*, 1906, XC, No. 233, p. 12.

25. The annual reports of the Catholic Education Council do not carry repair cost statistics.

26. *Parl. Papers*, 1908, LXXXV, Cd. 4288, pp. 140-41.

27. *Catholic Times*, May 24, July 19, 26, Aug. 2, 1907; *Month*, Aug. 1907, pp. 169-99 (Smith); *Tablet*, Aug. 3, Dec. 21, 1907; *The Times*, July 26, 1907, 4a-c (Deputation headed by Cardinal Bourne); Oldmeadow, *Francis Cardinal Bourne* (1940), I, pp. 343-46.

28. *British Congregationalist*, Aug. 1, 1907 (Hollowell), *Daily Chronicle*, Dec. 23, 1907; *Daily News*, Jan. 13, 1908; *The Times*, July 29, 1907, 13e (Hollowell); *Tribune*, Dec. 19, 30, 1907.

29. *Parl. Papers*, 1906, XC, No. 233, pp. 5, 11.

30. *Parl. Papers*, 1902, LXXVIII, Cd. 1139, pp. 108-09, 114.

31. *Parl. Papers*, 1906, LXXXV, Cd. 3255, p. 478.

32. *Baptist Times*, Sept. 6, 1907 (Clifford); *Daily Chronicle*, July 20, 1907; *Manchester Guardian*, July 29, 1907 (Fox); *The Times*, Sept. 4, 1907, 6d (Clifford); *Westminster Gazette*, July 12, 16, 1907.

33. *British Congregationalist*, Aug. 1, 1907 (Hollowell); *Daily Chronicle*, July 10, 1907; *Nation*, Sept. 7, 1907; *Westminster Gazette*, July 26, 1907.

34. *Parl. Papers*, 1908, LXXXIII, Cd. 4169, pp. xii-xiii, 7; *The Times*, June 29, 1908, 10c (official correspondence of the negotiations); Oldmeadow, *Francis Cardinal Bourne* (1940), I, p. 348.

35. For approval—*School Guardian*, July 4, 1908; *The Times*, June 29, 1908, 10e. For disapproval—*Church Times*, July 10, 1908 (Taylor); *School Guardian*, July 18, 1908 (Taylor).

36. *British Congregationalist*, July 9, 1908 (Fred Horne); *Christian World*, July 2, 1908; *Daily Chronicle*, June 29, 1908; *Daily News*, June 29, 1908; *Westminster Gazette*, June 29, 1908.

37. *Saturday Rev.*, May 8, 1909 (Hoare); *School Guardian*, Feb. 1, 8, 1913; *The Times*, June 3, 1913, 12c and June 18, 1914, 6b (Davidson).

38. *Ministry of Education, Statistical Return* No. 39 for 1956-57.

39. For ready access to the detailed provisions see Dent, *The Education Act, 1944* (1957, 6th ed.).

40. *Education in 1958: Being the Report of the Ministry of Education and the Statistics of Public Education for England and Wales* (Cd. 777), p. 142.

41. For an account see *Religious Education in Schools: The Report of an Inquiry Made by the Research Committee of the Institute of Christian Education Into the Working of the 1944 Education Act* (London: 1954).

42. *Parl. Papers*, 1911, LIX, Cd. 6002, 3 pp.; *Education in 1958: Being the Report of the Ministry of Education and the Statistics of Public Education For England and Wales* (Cd. 777), p. 142.

BIBLIOGRAPHY

BIBLIOGRAPHY

I. PUBLIC DOCUMENTS

A. Ministry of Education Files, 1902-14

B. Parliamentary Debates

House of Commons, 1902-14.
House of Lords, 1902-14.

C. Parliamentary Papers

1871, XXII, Cd. 406, "Report of the Committee of Council on Education; With Appendix, 1870-71."

1883, XXV, Cd. 3706-1, "Report of the Committee of Council on Education; With Appendix, 1882-83."

1886, XXV, Cd. 4863, "First Report of the Royal Commission Appointed to Inquire Into the Working of the Elementary Education Acts, England and Wales."

1888, XXXVI, Cd. 5485-IV, "Appendix to the Final Report of the Royal Commission Appointed to Inquire Into the Working of the Elementary Education Acts, England and Wales."

1893, XXVI, Cd. 7089, "Report of the Committee of Council on Education; With Appendix, 1892-93."

1895, CVIII, Cd. 7725, "Judicial Statistics, England and Wales, 1893, Part I—Criminal Statistics."

1896, I, Bill 172, "A Bill to Make Further Provision For Education in England and Wales."

1897, XXV, Cd. 8447, "Special Reports on Educational Subjects, 1896-97."

1897, LXVIII, No. 327, "Scheme for the Management of the Foundation Known as the Berrew School, in the Parish of Berrew, in the County of Montgomery, Regulated by a Scheme of the Charity Commissioners of the 24th July 1863."

1900, XXII, Part I, Cd. 417, "Special Reports on Educational Subjects, V, Educational Systems of the Chief Colonies of the British Empire."

1900, LXV, Part I, Cd. 109, "Return Showing the Expenditure From the Grant for Public Education in England and Wales in the Year 1899, And Expenditure From 1839 to 1899; the number of Elementary Day Schools on the Annual Grant List on the 31st August 1899; the Accommodation, Number of Scholars and Average Attendance in Those Schools; and Detailed Statistics of Inspected Schools, 1898-99."

1901, XIX, Cd. 757, "Report of the Board of Education, 1900-01, vol. II, Appendix to Report (Reports and Statistics)."

1901, LVI, Cd. 568, "Statistics of Public Elementary Schools, Evening Continuation Schools, and Certified Efficient Schools, For the Year Ended 31st August 1900."

1902, I, Bill 138, "A Bill to Make Further Provision With Respect to Education in England and Wales."

1902, I, Bill 303, "Education (England and Wales) Bill As Amended in Committee."

1902, I, Bill 304, "Education (England and Wales) Bill As Amended in Committee and on Consideration."

1902, I, Bill 309, "Lords Amendments to the Education (England and Wales) Bill."

1902, XXIV, Cd. 1275, "Report of the Board of Education For the Year, 1901-02."

1902, XXVI, Cd. 835, "Special Reports on Educational Subjects, VIII, Education in Scandinavia, Switzerland, Holland, Etc."

1902, XXVII, Cd. 836, "Special Reports on Educational Subjects, IX, Education in Germany."

1902, XXVIII, Cd. 837, "Special Reports on Educational Subjects, X, Education in the United States of America."

1902, XXIX, Cd. 1156, "Special Reports on Educational Subjects, IX, Education in the United States of America, Part 2."

1902, LXXVIII, Cd. 1139, "Statistics of Elementary Day Schools, Evening Continuation Schools and Training Colleges, 1900-01."

1902, LXXVIII, Cd. 1332, "Rules To Be Observed in Planning and Fitting Up Public Elementary Schools."

1902, LXXVIII, Cd. 1336, "Statement Under Administrative Counties and County Boroughs, of Public Elementary Schools Which Have Received Building Grants, Showing in Each Case the Amount of Such Building Grants and the Amount Subscribed by the Promoters At the Time (So Far As Records Exist), Also in the Case of Schools Which Have Been Transferred to the School Board or Closed the Year of Transfer or Closure, With Explanatory Memorandum and Appendix."

1902, CXVII, Cd. 953, "Judicial Statistics, England and Wales, 1900, Part I—Criminal Statistics."

1903, III, Bill 154, "A Bill to Extend and Adapt the Education Act, 1902, to London."

1903, III, Bill 216, "A Bill to Extend and Adapt the Education Act, 1902, to London, As Amended in Committee."

1903, III, Bill 279, "A Bill to Extend and Adapt the Education Act, 1902, to London, As Amended in Committee and on Consideration."

1903, III, Bill 312, "Lords Amendments to the London Education Bill."

1903, XX, Cd. 1763, "Report of the Board of Education for the Year, 1902-03."

1903, LI, Cd. 1476, "Statistics of Public Elementary Schools and Training Colleges, 1901-02."

1903, LI, Cd. 1509, "Provisional Code of Regulations for Public Elementary Schools and Training Colleges, With Schedules."

1904, LXXV, Cd. 2000, "Statistics of Public Elementary Schools, Pupil Teacher Centres, and Training Colleges, 1902-03."

1904, LXXV, Cd. 2041, "Report of a Public Inquiry Held Under Sections 16 and 23 of the Education Act, 1902, and Section 73 of the Elementary Education Act, 1870, by A. T. Lawrence, K.C., at Carmarthen, 24th and 25th March 1904."

1906, I, Bill 160, "Bill to Make Further Provision With Respect to Education in England and Wales."

1906, I, Bill 317, "Education (England and Wales) Bill As Amended in Committee."

1906, I, Bill 327, "Education (England and Wales) Bill As Amended in Committee and On Report."

1906, I, Bill 365, "Lords Amendments to the Education (England and Wales) Bill."

1906, XXIX, Cd. 2773, "Appendix to the 71st Report of the Commissioners of National Education in Ireland for the Year 1904, Section 11."

1906, XXX, Cd. 2942, "Report of the Committee of Council on Education in Scotland, 1905-06."

1906, XXXIII, Cd. 3040, "Report of the Royal Commission on Ecclesiastical Discipline."

1906, XXXIV, Cd. 3072, "Record of Commissioners' Attendances, Appendices, Index and Analysis of Evidence, IV, (Ecclesiastical Discipline)."

1906, LXXXV, Cd. 3255, "Statistics of Public Education in England and Wales, 1904-05-06."

1906, LXXXV, Cd. 3043, "Codes of Regulations For Public Elementary Schools with Schedules, 1906."

1906, LXXXIX, Cd. 2782, "Statistics of Public Education in England and Wales, 1903-04-05."

1906, XC, Cd. 3074, "Statement Showing Syllabuses of Religious Instruction Issued by Diocesan and Other Associations For the Use of Church of England Schools."

1906, XC, Cd. 3208, "Books and Papers on Religious Instruction in Schools."

1906, XC, No. 233, "Return Showing for Each of the Training Colleges for Elementary Teachers, Both Day and Residential, the Total Amounts Received Since Their Foundation for Maintenance from Voluntary Subscriptions and Endowments; From Students' Fees; and From Exchequer Grants."

1906, XC, Cd. 3219, "Statement Showing: 1. Number of Voluntary Schools in England and Wales Respectively, on 1st January 1906, in Urban Areas With a Population of 5,000 and Over; 2. Number of Voluntary Schools in England and Wales Respectively, on 1st January 1906, in Urban Areas With a Population of Less than 5,000; 3. Number of Voluntary Schools in England and Wales Respectively, on 1st January 1906, in Rural Areas, and Their Average Attendance for the Statistical Year Ended July 31st, 1905, With the Approximate Percentages to the Total Number and Average Attendance of All Voluntary Schools in England and Wales for the Same Period."

1906, XCIX, No. 138, "Return Showing the Declared Creeds and Denominations of the Prisoners in Each of His Majesty's Prisons in England and Wales, and Scotland on the 28th day of March 1906."

1906, CXXXV, Cd. 2871, "Judicial Statistics, England and Wales, 1904, Part I—Criminal Statistics."

1907, I, Bill 73, "Education (Special Religious Instruction) Bill."

1907, LXII, Cd. 3680, "Regulations Under Which Grants For the Building of New Public Elementary Schools in England and Wales Will Be Made by the Board of Education After the Passing of the Appropriation Act, 1907, During the Year Ending March 31st, 1908."

1907, LXIV, Cd. 3416, "Statement Showing the Number of Teachers (Excluding Pupil Teachers and Supplementary Teachers) Employed During the Statistical Year Ended on July 31st, 1906, in Voluntary Schools, in England and Wales, Classified by Denominations and the Total Amounts Paid to Them by Local Education Authorities in Respect of Salaries."

1907, LXIV, Cd. 3597, "Regulations for the Training of Teachers and for the Examination of Students in Training Colleges."

1907, LXII, Cd. 3594, "Codes of Regulations for Public Elementary Schools in England (Exclusive of Wales and Monmouthshire), With Schedules."

1907, LXVII, Cd. 3391, "Judgments of the Divisional Court, Court of Appeal, and House of Lords in the Case of the King vs. the County Council of the West Riding of Yorkshire."

1907, XCIV, Cd. 3691, "Statistical Abstract for the United Kingdom in Each of the Last Fifteen Years from 1892 to 1906."

1907, XCVIII, Cd. 3315, "Judicial Statistics (England and Wales), Part I—Criminal Statistics."

1908, II, Bill 112, "A Bill to Regulate the Conditions on Which Public Money May Be Applied in Aid of Elementary Education in England and Wales, and for Other Purposes Incidental Thereto."

1908, II, Bill 376, "A Bill to Make Further Provision With Respect to Elementary Education in England and Wales."

1908, XXVII, Cd. 4291, "The Seventy-Fourth Report of the Commissioners of National Education in Ireland, School Year, 1907-08."

1908, LXXXII, Cd. 3973, "The London County Council Syllabus Contained in a Return to an Order of the House of Lords, Numbered 115-1, 1906."

1908, LXXXII, Cd. 4036, "Statement Showing the Cases in Which the Board of Education Have Received Applications from Local Education Authorities for Special Grants for the Building of New Elementary Schools, and the Stage Which Each Case Had Reached on 31st March 1908."

1908, LXXXII, Cd. 4406, "Statement as to the Expenditure by the Local Education Authorities on the Maintenance (As Distinct from Administration and Loan Charges) of Public Elementary Schools for the Year Ended 31st March 1907."

1908, LXXXII, Cd. 4409, "Education (England and Wales) Bill No. 2, Draft Regulation Under Clause 2."

1908, LXXXII, Cd. 4421, "Correspondence Relating to the Education Bill."

1908, LXXXIII, Cd. 4143, "Memorandum on Special Rating for School Purposes in Quebec and Ontario."

1908, LXXXIII, Cd. 4169, "Regulations for the Training of Teachers for Elementary Schools (In Force from 1st August 1908)."

1908, LXXXV, Cd. 3886, "Statistics of Public Elementary Education in England and Wales, 1905-06-07."

1908, LXXXV, Cd. 4288, "Statistics of Public Education in England and Wales, 1906-07-08, Part I, Educational Statistics."

1908, CXXIII, Cd. 3929, "Judicial Statistics, England and Wales, 1906, Part I, Criminal Statistics."

1909, LXVII, Cd. 4737, "Regulations for the Training of Teachers for Elementary Schools (In force from 1st August 1909)."

1909, LXVII, Cd. 4746, "Syllabus of Lessons on 'Temperance' for Scholars Attending Public Elementary Schools."

1909, LXVII, Cd. 4783, "Circular as to Regulations for Religious Instruction in Training Colleges."

1909, XVIII, Cd. 4542, "Report of Public Inquiry Into Oxford Street (Church of England) School, Swansea, 1908."

1910, LXXI, Cd. 5355, "Statistics of Public Education in England and Wales, Part I, Educational Statistics, 1908-09."

1911, II, Bill 294, "Bill to Make Further Provision With Respect to Elementary Education in England and Wales."

1911, LIX, Cd. 6002, "Table Showing the Number, Accommodation, and Average Attendance of Public Elementary Schools in England and Wales During the Period 1902 to 1911."

1912-13, I, Bill 2, "Education Acts (Single School Areas) Amendment Bill."

1912-13, II, Bill 119, "Bill to Make Further Provision With Regard to Elementary Education in England and Wales."

1912-13, VII, Cd. 105, "Report and Special Report From Standing Committee A on the Education Acts (Single School Areas) Amendment Bill, With the Proceedings of the Committee."

1912-13, XXI, Cd. 6463, "Report of the Departmental Committee Appointed to Inquire Into Certain Questions in Connection With the Playgrounds of Public Elementary Schools, With Abstracts of Evidence."

1912-13, LXIV, Cd. 6338, "Statistics of Public Education in England and Wales, Part I, Educational Statistics, 1910-11."

1913, II, Bill III, "Bill to Make Further Provision With Regard to Education in England and Wales."

1913, II, Bill 278, "Bill to Amend the Law With Respect to Grants in Aid of Building, Enlarging, Improving, or Fitting Up Elementary Schools."

1913, XLIX, Cd. 6934, "Statistics of Public Education in England and Wales, Part I, Education Statistics, 1911-12."

1914, LXIV, Cd. 7516, "Building Regulations for Public Elementary Schools, Being Principles to be Observed in Planning and Fitting Up New Buildings in England."

1914-16, L, Cd. 7674, "Statistics of Public Education in England and Wales, Part I— Educational Statistics, 1912-13."

1958, Cd. 777, "Being the Report of the Ministry of Education and the Statistics of Public Education for England and Wales."

D. House of Lords, Sessional Papers

1888, XIX, No. 311, "Return to an Order of the House of Lords, dated 15th May 1888, for School Board Schools (Religious Teaching)."

1895, X, No. 2, "Return of the Regulations With Regard to Religious Instruction of the School Boards for England and Wales."

1904, III, No. 72, "A Bill Intituled An Act to Enable Local Education Authorities and Others to Make Arrangements With Reference to the Transfer of Public Elementary Schools."

1906, XIII, No. 115, Part I, "Education (Religious Instruction in Council Schools)."

1906, XIII, No. 115-1, Part II, "Education (Religious Instruction in Council Schools)."

1908, VI, No. 32, "A Bill to Amend the Acts Relating to Elementary Education in England and Wales."

II. REPORTS AND PROCEEDINGS

Baptist World Congress, Record of Proceedings, First, London, July 11-19, 1905, Second, Philadelphia, June 19-25, 1911.

Catholic Education Council, Annual Reports, 1904-14.

Catholic School Committee, Annual Reports, 1902-03.

Educational Record, With the Proceedings of the British and Foreign School Society, 1902-14.

Free Church Year Book (includes Reports of Annual Conferences), 1902-14.

International Moral Education Congress, Proceedings, London, Sept. 25-29, 1908.

Jewish Religious Education Board, Annual Reports, 1902-14.

Labour Party, Annual Reports, 1906-14.

Labour Representation Committee, Annual Reports, 1901-05.

Moral Instruction [later *Education*] *League,* Annual Reports, 1906-07, 1910, 1914.

National Protestant Church Union (moderate Church of England), Annual Reports, 1902-06.

National Society, Annual Reports, 1902-14.

National Union of Teachers, Annual Reports, 1902-14.

Official Year Book of Church of England, 1902-14.

Secular Education League, Annual Reports, 1909-11.

Secular Education League, Minutes, 1907-13.

Trades Union Congress, Annual Reports, 1902-13.

III. NEWSPAPERS AND PERIODICALS

A. Religious

Agnostic Annual and Ethical Review, 1902-07. Succeeded by *Rationalist Press Association Annual.*

Agnostic Journal and Eclectic Review (weekly), 1902—June 8, 1907. Suspended publication.

Anglo-Catholic (monthly), 1902-03. Suspended publication.

Baptist Times and Freeman (weekly), 1902-14.

British Congregationalist and Examiner (weekly), Aug. 2, 1906-14. Preceded by *Examiner.*

British Weekly (Nonconformist), 1902-14.

Catholic Herald (weekly), 1902-14.

Catholic Times (weekly), 1902-14. Published first in Liverpool and from 1910 on in London.

Christian (Nonconformist weekly—evangelical), 1902-14.

Christian Life and Unitarian Herald (weekly), 1902-14.

Christian World (Nonconformist weekly—evangelical), 1902-14.

Churchman (Anglican monthly), 1902-14.

Church Quarterly Review (Anglican), 1902-14.

Church Standard (Anglican quarterly), 1902—Aug. 1906. Suspended publication.

Church Times (Anglican weekly), 1902-14.

Commonwealth (Anglican monthly), 1902-14.

Companion (Anglican quarterly), 1904-14.

Crusader (Passive Resistance Movement weekly and monthly), April 15, 1903 (No. 6)—June 1907. Suspended publication.

Dublin Review (Catholic monthly), 1902-14.

East and the West (Christian Missions monthly), 1903-14.

English Church Review (Anglican monthly), I, 1910-14.

Ethics (Ethical Union weekly), 1902—March 17, 1906; succeeded by *Ethical Review* (weekly), March 24, 1906—June 30, 1906; suspended; resumed Oct. 6, 1906—Oct. 27, 1906; succeeded by *Ethical World* (monthly), Jan. 15, 1907-14.

Examiner (Congregationalist weekly), 1902—July 1906. Succeeded by *British Congregationalist and Examiner.*

Free Church Chronicle (National Council of the Evangelical Free Churches monthly), 1902-14.

Free Churchman (monthly), 1902-14.

Freethinker (weekly), 1902-14.

Friend (Society of Friends weekly), 1902-14.

Guardian (Anglican weekly), 1902-14.

Inquirer (Unitarian weekly), 1902-14.

Liberator (Society for the Liberation of Religion from State-Patronage and Control monthly), 1902-14.

Literary Guide and Rationalist Review (monthly), 1902-14.

Methodist Recorder and General Christian Chronicle (weekly), 1902-14.

Methodist Times (weekly), 1902-14.

Modern Churchman (Anglican monthly), I, April 1911-14.

Month (Catholic), 1902-14.

Monthly Messenger (Presbyterian), 1902-14.

Moral Instruction [later *Education*] *League Quarterly*, April 1905—Oct. 1914.

Pilot (Anglican weekly), 1902—May 21, 1904. Suspended publication.

Positivist Review (monthly), 1902-14.

Presbyterian (weekly), 1902—May 31, 1906; suspended publication; resumed Jan. 1911-14.

Rationalist Press Association Annual, 1908-14. Preceded by *Agnostic Annual and Ethical Review.*

Record (Anglican weekly—evangelical), 1902-14.

Reformer (Rationalist monthly), 1902—June 15, 1904. Suspended publication.

School Guardian (Anglican weekly), 1902-14.

Secular Education Chronicle (issued irregularly), 1907-14.

Tablet (Catholic weekly), 1902-14.

Treasury (Anglican monthly), 1902-14.

B. Labour

Clarion (Socialist weekly), 1902-14.

Fabian News (Socialist monthly), 1902-14.

Independent Labour Party News (Socialist monthly), 1902—Dec. 1903. Suspended publication.

Justice (Socialist weekly), 1902-14.

Labour Leader (Socialist weekly), 1902-14.

Leicester Pioneer (Labour weekly—J. Ramsay MacDonald column), 1905-14.

New Age (Guild Socialist weekly), 1902-14.

Social Democrat (Socialist monthly), 1902—Dec. 1913. Suspended publication.

Socialist Annual (Social Democratic Federation), 1906-14.

Socialist Review (Socialist monthly and quarterly), 1908-14.

C. Education

Board Teacher and London School Board Review (monthly), 1902-04. Succeeded by London Teacher and London Schools Review.

Educational Times and Journal of the College of Preceptors (monthly), 1902-14.

Journal of Education (monthly), 1902-14.

London Education Gazette (London County Council weekly), I, May 1904—Oct. 16, 1905. Suspended publication.

London Teacher and London Schools Review (monthly and weekly), 1904-14. Preceded by Board Teacher and London Schools Board Review.

Practical Teacher (monthly), 1902-14.

School (monthly), Jan. 1904—March 1909.

School Board Chronicle (weekly), 1902-03. Succeeded by School Government Chronicle and Education Authorities Gazette.

School Government Chronicle and Education Authorities Gazette (weekly), 1903-14. Preceded by School Board Chronicle.

School Manager (weekly), 1902—Dec. 16, 1905. Suspended publication.

Schoolmaster (weekly), 1902-14.

D. General

Albany Review (monthly—Nonconformist viewpoint), 1907-08. Suspended publication and preceded by Independent Review.

Blackwood's Magazine (monthly—Anglican viewpoint), 1902-14.

British Review (monthly—Anglican viewpoint), 1913-14.

Conservative (monthly—Anglican viewpoint), 1905-07. Succeeded by Conservative and Unionist.

Conservative and Unionist (monthly—Anglican viewpoint), 1908-May 1912. Preceded by Conservative and succeeded by Our Flag.

Contemporary Review (monthly), 1902-14.

Daily Chronicle (London—Nonconformist viewpoint), 1902-14.

Daily Mail (London—Anglican viewpoint), 1902-14.

Daily News (London—Nonconformist viewpoint), 1902-14.

Daily Telegraph (London—Anglican viewpoint), 1902-14.

Economist (weekly), 1902-14.

Edinburgh Review (monthly—Anglican viewpoint), 1902-14.

Empire Review (monthly), 1902-14.

English Review (monthly), 1908-14.

Fortnightly Review (monthly), 1902-14.

Gentleman's Magazine (monthly—Anglican viewpoint), 1902-Sept. 1907. Suspended publication.

Hibbert's Journal (quarterly), 1902-14.

Independent Review (monthly—Nonconformist viewpoint), Oct. 1903-March 1907. Succeeded by Albany Review.

International (monthly), Dec. 1907—Dec. 1909. Suspended publication.

International Journal of Ethics (quarterly), 1902-14.

Liberal Magazine (Liberal Party reprints), 1902-14.

Manchester Guardian (Nonconformist viewpoint), 1902-14.
Monthly Review (Anglican viewpoint), 1902-07. Suspended publication.
Morning Post (London daily—Anglican viewpoint), 1902-14.
Nation (London weekly—Nonconformist viewpoint), 1907-14. Succeeded *Speaker.*
National Review (monthly—Anglican viewpoint), 1902-14.
New Liberal Review (monthly—Nonconformist viewpoint), 1902-14. Suspended publication.
New Statesman (weekly), April 12, 1913-14.
Nineteenth Century and After (monthly), 1902-14.
Our Flag (monthly—Anglican viewpoint), June 1912-14. Preceded by *Conservative and Unionist.*
Pall Mall Gazette (London daily—Anglican viewpoint), 1902-14.
Progress (quarterly), Jan. 1906-14.
Quarterly Review (Anglican viewpoint), 1902-14.
Review of Reviews (London weekly—Nonconformist viewpoint), 1902-14.
Saturday Review (London weekly—Anglican viewpoint), 1902-14.
South Wales Daily News (Cardiff—Nonconformist viewpoint), 1902-08.
Speaker (weekly—Nonconformist viewpoint), 1902-Feb. 23, 1907. Succeeded by *Nation.*
Spectator (weekly—Anglican viewpoint), 1902-14.
Standard (London daily—Anglican viewpoint), 1902-14.
The Times (London daily—Anglican viewpoint), 1902-14.
Tribune (London daily—semi-official Liberal Government), published for two years, Jan. 15, 1906—May 3, 1908.
Truth (weekly—Nonconformist viewpoint), 1902-14.
Twentieth Century Quarterly, 1906. Suspended publication.
Western Mail (Cardiff daily—Anglican viewpoint), 1902-11.
Westminster Gazette (London daily—Nonconformist viewpoint), 1902-14.
Westminster Review (monthly), 1902-14.
World's Work (monthly), Dec. 1902—Nov. 1904; changed name to *World's Work and Play*, Jan. 1905—Dec. 1905; resumed title of *World's Work*, 1906-14.

IV. BOOKS AND PAMPHLETS

Acland, A. H. D. *Problems of Education* (London: 1905), 16 pp.
Allen, Bernard M. *Sir Robert Morant: A Great Public Servant* (London: 1934), 318 pp.
Amery, Julian. *The Life of Joseph Chamberlain* (London: 1951), IV.
Armstrong Richard A. *The Government Assault on Education* (Liverpool: 1902), 14 pp.
Balfour, A. J. *The Education Bill, 1902: Speeches and Letter, With Text of the Bill* (London: 1902), 36 pp.
Balfour A. J. *Letter From the Rt. Hon. A. J. Balfour, M.P., On the Criticisms of an Opponent of the Education Bill, 1902* (London: 1902), 15 pp.
Bayly, Elisabeth Pond. *Truth, Unity, and Concord: Thoughts on the Question of Religious Education in Our Day Schools* (London: 1905), 160 pp.
Bedingfield, C. H. *Education and the Rates* (Bristol: 1906), 16 pp.

Beeching, H. C. *Religio Laici: A Series of Studies Addressed to Laymen* (London: 1902), 270 pp.

Bell, G. K. A. *Randall Davidson, Archbishop of Canterbury* (Oxford: 1952, 3rd ed.), 1442 pp.

Belloc, Hilaire. *Catholics and the Education Bill: Some Suggested Amendments* (London: 1906), 16 pp.

Bettany F. G. *Stewart Headlam: A Biography* (London: 1926), 250 pp.

Betts, J. A. *Education and Passive Resistance: What Is the Fight About?* (London: 1904), 20 pp.

Bevan, Rev. J. O. *The Education Question in the Immediate Future: How to Deal With It* (Canterbury: 1909), 20 pp.

Birrell, Augustine. *Things Past Redress* (London: 1937), 317 pp.

Bourne, Francis Cardinal (Archbishop of Westminster). *The Catholic Attitude on the Education Question* (London: 1906), 24 pp.

—————. *The Education Act of 1902: The Difficulty and Its Solution* (London: 1904), 16 pp.

—————. *The Maintenance of Religion in the Schools* (London: 1908), 16 pp.

—————. *Pastoral Letter of the Archbishop and Bishops of the Province of Westminster on the Education Crisis* (London: 1906), 7 pp.

Bray, Reginald A. *The Town Child* (London: 1907), 333 pp.

Brock, Rev. William. *The Religious Difficulty in the Schools and the Education Bill* (Hampstead: 1902), 16 pp.

Brooke, Charles W. A. *A New Solution of the Elementary Education Controversy, Together With a Table of Educational Changes in England Since A.D. 1547* (London: 1908), 19 pp.

Bruce, Rosslyn. *Dr. Gore and Religious Education: A Protest* (Nottingham: 1906), 17 pp.

Buckle, Rev. D. P., ed. *Undenominationalism in Elementary National Education or Mr. Gladstone and School Boards* (Manchester: 1902), 36 pp.

Burns, Dawson. *An Argument Addressed to Thoughtful Nonconformists Against "Passive Resistance"* (London: 1904), 14 pp.

Burton, Rt. Rev. George Ambrose (Bishop of Clifton). *Catholic Education and the Duties of Parents* (London: 1906), 12 pp.

Byrt, G. W. *John Clifford: A Fighting Free Churchman* (London: 1947), 192 pp.

Carnegie, Rev. W. Hartley. *The Church and the Schools: A Churchman's Review of the Education Controversy* (London: 1905), 84 pp.

Chamberlain, Sir Austen. *Politics From Inside: An Epistolary Chronicle, 1906-1914* (New Haven: 1937), 647 pp.

Christopher, Rev. Canon A. M. W. *An Example From India: A Contribution to the Solution of the Education Question* (London: 1906), 24 pp.

The Church and the Teacher: An Urgent Plea For the Organization of Church People Trained in the Art of Teaching Children, With a Few Words on the Danger of Facilities (London: 1904), 2 pp.

Church Committee. *The Church and Education Since 1870* (London: 1903), 20 pp.

Church Schools' Emergency League Leaflets, First to Sixth Series, Nos. 1-71, 1904-08 (Manchester).

Claridge, W. *What Has the Church Done for Education?* (Manchester: 1907), 16 pp.

Cleworth, Rev. Thomas E. *The Education Crisis of 1906* (London: 1906), 17 pp.

Clifford, Dr. John. *Clericalism in British Politics: Letters On the Education Bill of 1902* (London: 1902, rev. ed.), 40 pp.

──────. *The Education Bill* (London: 1902), 8 pp.

──────. *The Fight Against the Education Bill: What Is At Stake* (London: 1902), 62 pp.

──────. *Ten Years of Protest Against the Intrusion of Churches Into State Schools: Passive Resistance, June 1912—June 1913* (London: 1913), 15 pp.

Cockshott, J. J. *Objections to the Education Bill Examined* (Southport: 1902), 12 pp.

Cole, Margaret, ed. *The Webbs and Their Work* (London: 1948), 544 pp.

Collett, John. *The Education Riddle Answered: How to Solve the Problem* (Cardiff: 1910), 35 pp.

Creighton, Louise, ed. *Life and Letters of Mandell Creighton, Sometime Bishop of London* (London: 1905, 5th imp.), 2 vols.

──────. *Life and Letters of Thomas Hodgkin* (London: 1917), 445 pp.

──────. *Thoughts on Education: Speeches and Sermons by Mandell Creighton* (London: 1902), 215 pp.

Cunningham, Rev. W. *The Meaning of Religious Education* (London: 1907), 8 pp.

Darlow, T. H. *William Robertson Nicoll: Life and Letters* (New York: 1925), 475 pp.

Davies, Rupert E., ed. *John Scott Lidgett: A Symposium* (London: 1957), 212 pp.

Dugdale, Blanche E. C. [his niece]. *Arthur James Balfour: The First Earl of Balfour* (New York: 1937), 2 vols.

Dymott, Rev. S. E. *The Case for the Voluntary School* (London: 1902), 4 pp.

The Education Crisis: Letters on the Subject (London: 1907), 27 pp.

Edwards, John Hugh. *David Lloyd George: The Man and the Statesman* (New York: 1929), 2 vols.

Egerton, Hakluyt (pseud. Arthur Boutwood). *The Maintenance of Denominational Teaching: A Note Upon Section 7 (1) of the Education Act of 1902* (London: 1905), 109 pp.

──────. *A Plea For Church Schools* (London: 1906), 46 pp.

Evans, Howard. *The Established Church and the Education of the People: A Brief History of the Education Struggle, With a Concise Statement of the Church Grievance* (London: 1903), 32 pp.

Evans, William. *James Hirst Hollowell* (Manchester: 1911), 166 pp.

Fairbairn, A. M. *Education: National or Denominational* (London: 1902), 33 pp.

Ferry, Rev. J. B. *A Straight Talk With the British People About the Schools; And About "Our Unhappy Divisions," and Their Remedy—Back to the Church* (London: 1907), 122 pp.

Fitzroy, Sir Almeric. *Memoirs* (New York: 1925, 3rd ed.), 2 vols.

Gallwey, Father. *Mr. Birrell's Education Bill: Selections From the Objections Urged Against It, A Memorandum* (London: 1906, 2nd ed.), 34 pp.

Gardiner, A. G. *The Life of Sir William Harcourt* (New York: 1923), 2 vols.

Gibson, Dr. J. Monro. *An Appeal to British Justice on the Education Question* (London: 1902), 36 pp.

Glancey, Rev. M. F. *The Education Bill* (London: 1902), 32 pp.

Goodier, Rev. Alban. *Side-Lights From the Continent On the Education Question: Three Lectures Given in the Church of the Immaculate Conception, Farm Street, April 1906* (London: 1906), 49 pp.

Gore, Rt. Rev. Charles (Bishop of Worcester). *Objections to the Education Bill 1906 In Principle and In Detail* (London: 1906), 27 pp.

Gould, Frederick James. *The Life Story of a Humanist* (London: 1923), 172 pp.

Graham, John W. *Education and Religion: An Address* (London: 1902), 47 pp.

Grier, Lynda. *Achievement in Education: The Work of Michael Ernest Sadler, 1885-1935* (London: 1952), 267 pp.

Haldane, Richard Burdon. *An Autobiography* (London: 1929, 2nd ed.), 355 pp.

Hamilton, Mary Agnes. *Arthur Henderson: A Biography* (London: 1938), 461 pp.

Hammond, Rev. Joseph. *Passive Resistance—Positive Wrong* (London: 1903), 8 pp.

Hayward, Frank Herbert. *The Reform of Moral and Biblical Education, On the Lines of Herbartianism, Critical Thought, and the Ethical Needs of the Present Day* (London: 1902), 248 pp.

Headlam, Rev. A. C. *The Education Act, 1902: A Church Policy* (London: cir. 1903), 29 pp.

Headlam, Rev. Stewart D. *The Place of the Schools in Secular Education: An Open Letter to the Teachers Under the London School Board* (London: 1903), 37 pp.

—————. *Secular Schools: A Lecture Given to the Guilds of St. Matthew* (London: 1906), 27 pp.

Henson, Herbert Hensley, *The Education Act And After* (London: 1903), 96 pp.

—————. *A Memoir of the Right Honourable Sir William Anson, 1843-1914* (Oxford: 1920), 242 pp.

—————. *Religion in the Schools: Addresses On Fundamental Christianity* (London: 1906), 137 pp.

Hoare, Samuel John Gurney. *The Schools and Social Reform: The Report of the Unionist Social and Reform Committee on Education* (London: 1914), 30 pp.

Hodgkin, Thomas. *National Education: A Retrospect and a Prospect* (London: 1906), 31 pp.

Holland, Bernard. *The Life of Spencer Compton, Eighth Duke of Devonshire* (London: 1911), 2 vols.

Hollowell, Rev. J. Hirst, *Recent Challenges to Our Faith: The Right to National Education, An Address* (Manchester: 1908), 16 pp.

—————. *Reply to Mr. Balfour's Address to the Deputation of the National Free Church Council* (London: 1902), 8 pp.

Holmes, Edmond. *What Is and What Might Be: A Study of Education in General and Elementary Education in Particular* (London: 1911), 308 pp.

Horne, C. Silvester. *A Popular History of the Free Churches* (London: 1903), 449 pp.

Horsfall, T. C. *The Amendment of the Education Act of 1902: By Passive Resistance or By a More Excellent Way? An Appeal to Nonconformists* (London: 1905), 16 pp.

Hughes, Rev. A. J. I. *The Reason of Our Resistance: A Contribution to the Education Question On the Appearance of Mr. Birrell's Bill* (London: 1906), 10 pp.

Hughes, Dorothea [his daughter]. *The Life of Hugh Price Hughes* (New York: 1904), 679 pp.

Humphrey-Davy, F. H. M. N. *How to Solve the Education Question* (London: 1906), 16 pp.

Humphreys, Rev. *The Plain Truth About the Education Bill* (Cambridge: 1902), xii pp.

Hyndman, Henry Mayer. *Further Reminiscences* (London: 1912), 545 pp.

—————. *The Record of an Adventurous Life* (New York: 1911), 407 pp.

Jephson, Arthur W. *Report on Elementary Education in the United States of America* (London: 1904), 79 pp.

Johnson, Harrold, *Moral Instruction in Elementary Schools in England and Wales: A Return Compiled From Official Documents* (London: 1908), 46 pp.

Jones, Rev. David. *The Moral and Religious Condition of Wales During the Last Thirty Years on the Testimonies of Welsh Nonconformists* (Bangor: 1906), 62 pp.

Jones, Thomas. *Lloyd George* (Cambridge, Mass.: 1951), 330 pp.

Kekewich, Sir George W. *The Education Department And After* (London: 1920), 358 pp.

Knox, Edmund Arbuthnott (Bishop of Manchester). *The Education Crisis of 1906: Two Sermons* (London: 1906), 23 pp.

——————. *Elementary Education (England and Wales) Bill, 1908* (Manchester: 1908), 12 pp.

—————— (Bishop of Coventry). *Pastors and Teachers: Six Lectures on Pastoral Theology* (London: 1902), 300 pp.

—————— (Bishop of Manchester). *Reminiscences of an Octogenarian, 1847-1934* (London: 1935, 2nd imp.), 336 pp.

Lang, Cosmo Gordon (Bishop of Stepney). *The Principles of Religious Education: Three Sermons Preached in St. Paul's Cathedral* (London: 1906), 32 pp.

Lee, Sir Sidney. *King Edward VII: A Biography* (New York: 1927), 2 vols.

Lescher, Father Wilfrid. *The School Question* (Hinckley: 1906), 16 pp.

Leslie, Shane, ed. *Letters of Herbert Cardinal Vaughan to Lady Herbert of Lee, 1867 to 1903* (London: 1942), 453 pp.

Lewis, Rev. J. P. *National Settlement of Religious Education* (London: 1906), 4 pp.

Liberal Publication Department, Pamphlets and Leaflets (London), 1902-14.

Lidgett, J. Scott. *Reminiscences* (London: 1928), 95 pp.

Lilly, A. L. *Sir Joshua Fitch: An Account of His Life and Work* (London: 1906), 255 pp.

Lilly, William Samuel. *Education, True and False* (London: 1905), 16 pp.

Lloyd-George, Rt. Hon. David. *The Government and Its Work: A Speech Delivered at Liverpool, May 24th, 1906* (London: 1906), 16 pp.

Lucas, Frederick. *Undenominationalism Or Cowper-Temple Religious Teaching* (London: 1906), 12 pp.

McCabe, Joseph. *A Hundred Years of Education Controversy* (London: 1907), 16 pp.

——————. *The Truth About Secular Education: Its History and Results* (London: 1906), 96 pp.

MacColl, Rev. Malcolm. *The Education Question and the Liberal Party* (London: 1902), 110 pp.

MacDonald, J. Ramsay. *Margaret Ethel MacDonald* (London: 1912), 270 pp.

——————. *Socialism and Government* (London: 1909), 2 vols.

——————. *Socialism and Society* (London: 1905, 2nd ed.), 186 pp.

——————. *The Socialist Movement* (New York: 1911), 248 pp.

McNabb, Rev. Vincent. *The Secular Solution of the Educational Difficulty* (London: 1909), 24 pp.

Macnamara, Dr. Thomas J. *The Education Bill and Its Probable Effects on the Schools, the Scholars, and the School-Teachers* (London: 1902), 34 pp.

——————. *The Education Bill of 1906: Explained and Defended* (London: 1906), 16 pp.

——————. *Elementary Education in 1902: Facts and Figures for the Education Bill Discussions* (London: 1902), 75 pp.

Marchant, Sir James. *Dr. John Clifford, C.H.: Life, Letters, and Reminiscences* (London: 1924), 312 pp.

Mark, H. Thiselton. *The New Movement in Education: With Special References to Elementary Education* (London: 1904), 107 pp.

——————. *The Teacher and the Child: Elements of Moral and Religious Teaching in the Day School, the Home, and the Sunday School* (London: 1902), 165 pp.

Marson, Rev. Charles L. *Huppim and Muppim* (Oxford: 1903, reprint), 16 pp.

Martin, Rev. David Basil. *The Education Bill, 1902* (Hereford: 1902), 9 pp.

──────. *The Education Rate and Passive Resistance* (Hereford: 1903), 8 pp.

Masterman, Lucy. *C. F. G. Masterman: A Biography* (London: 1939), 400 pp.

Maude, William C. *The Religious Rights of the Catholic Poor: A Handbook For Catholic Guardians* (London: 1910, 2nd ed.), 96 pp.

Meharry, Rev. John B. *The Education Bill* (London: 1903), 4 pp.

Memorandum On the Education Bill (1902): Its Provisions Considered; Objections Answered: Summary and Merits of the Bill (Dewsbury: 1902, 2nd ed.), 8 pp.

Methuen, Rev. P. E. O'B. *The Education Question, or Why Not Be Just* (Bath: 1909), 8 pp.

Moberly, Robert Campbell. *Undenominationalism As A Principle of Primary Education* (London: 1902), 24 pp.

Moorhouse, James (Bishop of Manchester). *The Education Bill: An Address to the Manchester Diocesan Conference* (London: 1902), 8 pp.

Morley, John Viscount. *Recollections* (London: 1917), 2 vols.

Mosely Education Commission to the United States of America, October-December 1903, Reports (London: 1904), 400 pp.

Mothersole, Hartley B. N. *The A.B.C. of the Education Question: Facts and Figures for the Man in the Street* (London: 1902), 8 pp.

Mundella, A. J. *The Education Question in London* (London: 1909), 16 pp.

Mylne, L. G. *Facts About the Education Act of 1902: A Sermon Preached in St. Mary's Church, Marlborough, Oct. 15, 1903* (London: 1903), 12 pp.

National Education Association. *The Education Crisis: A Defence of Popular Management in Public Education* (London: 1902), 96 pp.

──────. *The Education of the People and the Bill of 1902* (London: 1902), 42 pp.

National Society. *Analysis of the Return to an Order of the House of Lords, Dated May 4, 1906, Relating to Religious Instruction in Council Schools* (London: 1906), 39 pp.

──────. *Annotated Edition of the Education Bill, 1906: Text of the Bill as Introduced into the House of Commons, with Explanatory Notes* (London: 1906, rev. and enl. ed.), 44 pp.

──────. *Handbook [No. 3] Education Bill (1906): The Last Stage, Vindication of the House of Lords* (London: 1906), 53 pp.

──────. *Handbook to the Education Bill (1906) in the House of Lords: Memorandum On the Progress of the Bill Through the House of Commons With Full Text of the Bill As Amended Together With an Appendix Containing the Text of the Bill As Introduced Into the House of Commons, With Explanatory Notes* (London: 1906), 44 pp.

Neale, Harold S. *The Education Question: A Defence of the Government Bill* (1902), 8 pp.

Newton, Lord. *Lord Lansdowne: A Biography* (London: 1929), 536 pp.

Nunn, Rev. Joseph. *The Education Bill (1902) Examined Or the Proposed Extinction of the Voluntary School System by a Unionist Government* (London: 1902), 12 pp.

──────. *The New Education Bill (November 1908) Examined* (Manchester: 1908), 15 pp.

──────. *"Towards Educational Peace": An Examination of the Plan of the Educational Settlement Committee* (Manchester: 1911), 32 pp.

──────. *The West Riding Judgment* (London: 1906), 14 pp.

Oldmeadow, Ernest. *Francis Cardinal Bourne* (London: 1940), 2 vols.

Onlooker. *The Single-School Authority and the Education Crisis* (London: 1906), 25 pp.

Owen, Frank. *Tempestuous Journey: Lloyd George, His Life and Times* (New York: 1955), 784 pp.

Oxford and Asquith, Earl of. *Fifty Years of Parliament* (London: 1926), 2 vols.

——————. *Memories and Reflections, 1852-1927* (London: 1928), 2 vols.

Parents League Leaflets, 1909, Nos. XII, 7 pp. and XV, 6 pp.

Parmoor, Lord. *A Retrospect: Looking Back Over a Life of More than Eighty Years* (London: 1936), 350 pp.

Paton, John Brown. *Shall There Be Bible Instruction In the National Schools?* (London: 1905), 4 pp.

Paton, John Lewis (his son]. *John Brown Paton: A Biography* (London: 1914), 538 pp.

Pearson, Samuel. *The Duty of Disobedience: A Defence of Passive Resistance* (London: 1903, 2nd ed.), 47 pp.

Petrie, Sir Charles. *The Life and Letters of the Right Hon. Sir Austen Chamberlain* (London: 1939-40), 2 vols.

Philpott, Hugh B. *London At School: The Story of the School Board, 1870-1904* (London: 1904), 314 pp.

Picton, James Allanson. *The Bible in School: A Question of Ethics* (London: 1907, new ed., rev. and enl.), 79 pp.

Porter, S. Lowry. *The Education Bill of 1906: An Analysis and a Brief Survey of the Education Question From 1870* (London: 1907), 38 pp.

Powell, Helena L. *Religious Teaching in the Schools: A Paper Read Before the Cambridge District Association of Church School Managers and Teachers* (Cambridge: 1905), 8 pp.

Prestidge, G. L. *The Life of Charles Gore: A Great Englishman* (London: 1935), 547 pp.

Rawlings, Edmund C. *The Free Churchman's Guide to the Education Act of 1902: With a Sketch of the History of Popular Education in England and Wales by Rev. Wm. J. Townsend* (London: 1903), 273 pp.

Religious Education of Our Children With Regard to the Present Crisis: How Is It To Be Met? (London: 1902), 16 pp.

Rice, Wilfrid V. *Passive Resisters at Bay: Letters* (Blackburn: 1905), 12 pp.

Rickaby, Joseph. *The Rights of Minorities* (London: 1905), 16 pp.

Riley, Athelstan; Sadler, Michael E.; and Jackson, Cyril. *The Religous Question in Public Education: A Critical Examination of Schemes Representing Various Points of View* (London: 1911), 350 pp.

Robertson, J. M., and Whyte, A. Gowans. *The Church and Education* (London: 1943), 32 pp.

Rogers, James Guinness. *An Autobiography* (London: 1903), 300 pp.

Rowntree, B. Seebohm. *Poverty: A Study of Town Life* (London: 1902, 2nd ed.), 452 pp.

Russell, George W. E., ed. *Malcolm MacColl: Memoirs and Correspondence* (New York: 1914), 407 pp.

Sacks, Benjamin. *J. Ramsay MacDonald In Thought and Action: An Architect For a Better World* (Albuquerque, N. M.: 1952), 591 pp.

Sadler, M. E. *Moral Instruction and Training in Schools: Report of an International Inquiry* (London: 1908), 2 vols.

——————. *Teachers and the Religious Lesson* (London: 1909), 24 pp.

Sanday, William. *Justice in Education: A Word For Peace* (London: 1904), 32 pp.

Scott, Alexander Maccallum. *National Education: The Secular Solution the Only Way* (London: 1906), 16 pp.

Secular Education League. *Secular Education and Crime*, Tract No. 18 (London: 1912), 4 pp.

Sedgwick, Thomas Arnold. *Pedagogus: Sermons on the Education Question* (London: 1909), 106 pp.

Selbie, W. B. *The Life of Andrew Martin Fairbairn* (London: 1914), 456 pp.

Shadwell, Arthur. *Industrial Efficiency: A Comparative Study of Industrial Life in England, Germany, and America* (London: 1906), 2 vols.

Smart, Rev. Henry T. *Ought Nonconformists to Uphold the Education Act: The Principles at Stake* (London: 1903), 29 pp.

Smith, Frank. *Conscience and the Education Rate* (Hants: 1903), 8 pp.

Smith, Rev. Isaac Gregory. *Dr. Clifford On Education* (London: 1903), 11 pp.

Smith, Rev. Sydney, *The Education Bill: How Will It Work* (London: 1906), 22 pp. Reprint from *Month*, June 1906.

————. *Mr. Birrell's Education Bill* (London: 1906), 22 pp. Reprint from *Month*, May 1906.

Smythe, Robert J. *Religious Instruction in Schools* (London: 1907), 31 pp.

Snead-Cox, John George. *The Life of Cardinal Vaughan* (London: 1910), 2 vols.

Snell, Lord. *Men, Movements, and Myself* (London: 1938), 284 pp.

————. *Secular Education: The Only Way* (London: cir. 1908), 14 pp.

Sneyd-Kynnersley, E. M. *H.M.I.: Some Passages in the Life of One of H. M. Inspectors of Schools* (London: 1938), 358 pp.

Snowden, Philip Viscount. *An Autobiography* (London: 1934), 2 vols.

Society for the Liberation of Religion from State-Patronage and Control Leaflets. *Where Is the Robbery? Trust Church-Schools and Mr. Birrell's Bill* (London: 1906), 4 pp.

————. *Does the Education Bill Treat Church Schools Fairly?* (London: 1906), 4 pp.

————. *Little Billy and the Inalienable Rights of Parents* (London: 1906), 4 pp.

Somerton, Alexander. *Is Passive Resistance Right for the Citizen?* (London: 1904), 47 pp.

Soulsby, L. H. M. *The Religious Side of Secular Teaching* (London: 1907), 24 pp.

Spender, J. A. *The Life of the Rt. Hon. Sir Henry Campbell-Bannerman.* (London: 1923), 2 vols.

Spiller, Gustav. *Report On Moral Education (General and Denominational) And On Moral Training in the Schools of Austria, Belgium, the British Empire, etc.* (London: 1909), 358 pp.

————. *The Ethical Movement in Great Britain: A Documentary History* (London: 1934), 195 pp.

Stephens, Thomas, ed. *The Child and Religion* (London: 1905), 371 pp.

Stevens, Rev. H. W. P. *The Practical Working of the Education Act* (London: 1904), 11 pp.

Strong, Thomas Banks. *Undenominationalism* (London: 1906, 3rd ed., reprint), 21 pp.

Temple, W. *The Church and the Education Bill: Being a Speech Delivered to the Oxford Union Society, Thursday, April 26, 1906* (Oxford: 1906), 12 pp.

Temple, William (Bishop of Manchester). *Life of Bishop Percival* (London: 1921), 389 pp.

Terbutt, J. H. *The Education Imbroglio: An Easy Way Out of It* (London: 1906), 93 pp.

Thompson, Herbert Metford. *Essays in Revolt: Being a Discussion of What Should Be Taught At School* (London: 1905), 194 pp.

Thompson, J. *Forty-Four Years of the Education Question, 1870-1914: The Story of the People's Schools Simplified and Explained* (London: 1914), 228 pp.

Thorpe, John H. *The General Election and the Education Question: Points and Principles For Speakers and Electors* (Manchester: 1909), 39 pp.

Todd, Rev. J. C. *Undenominational Religion: What Does It Really Mean* (London: 1906), 14 pp.

Towards Educational Peace: A Plea of Re-Settlement in English Elementary Education Issued By the Executive Committee of the Educational Settlement Committee (London: 1910), 59 pp.

Vaughan, Herbert Cardinal (Archbishop of Westminster). *On the Religious Training of Children: Their Preparation For First Communion* (London: 1903), 40 pp.

Wace, Rev. Henry (Dean of Canterbury). *Religious Education and National Schools: Two Sermons* (London: 1906), 28 pp.

Wakeford, Rev. John. *The Education Crisis of 1906* (London: 1906), 11 pp.

Watson, E. W. *Life of Bishop John Wordsworth* (London: 1915), 409 pp.

Webb, Beatrice. *Our Partnership* (London: 1948), 544 pp.

Webb, Sidney (Lord Passfield). *The Education Act, 1902: How to Make the Best of It* (London: 1903), 20 pp.

──────────. *London Education* (London: 1904), 219 pp.

──────────. *The London Education Act, 1903: How to Make the Best of It* (London: 1904), 19 pp.

Welsh, Rev. Robert E. *The Capture of the Schools, Education: Secular or National* (London: 1903), 47 pp.

Wetters, Adolph C. *Religious Instruction and Training in the Day School* (Stockport: 1911), 23 pp.

White, George. *The Case Against the Education Act* (London: 1905), 16 pp. in William Stead, ed., *Coming Men on Coming Questions* (1905).

Wilson, Rev. James Maurice. *An Autobiography, 1836-1931* (London: 1932), 307 pp.

──────────. *The Day School and Religious Education: A Sermon Preached in Worcester Cathedral On Sunday, January 6, 1907* (London: 1907), 16 pp.

──────────. *Education and Crime: A Sermon Preached in the Parish Church of Rochdale in January 1905, On Denominational Schools and Subsequently Enlarged* (London: 1905), 16 pp.

Wilson, Philip Whitwell. *Liberty and Religion: A Reply to Certain Bishops* (London: 1906), 224 pp.

Wilson, Thomas. *A Lay Eirenicon: A Paper Read Before a Clerical and Lay Society At the House of Mr. R. L. Howard, at St. Albans, 8th February 1909* (London: 1909), 20 pp.

Windle, Bertram C. A. *The Catholic Aspect of the Education Question* (London: 1904), 16 pp.

Wolf, Lucien. *Life of the First Marquess of Ripon* (London: 1921), 2 vols.

Wordsworth, John (Bishop of Salisbury). *The Education Question* (London: 1906), 75 pp.

──────────. *Education Rates and Religious Instruction* (London: 1905), 16 pp.

V. REFERENCE MATERIALS

Adams, Francis. *History of the Elementary School Contest in England* (London: 1882), 349 pp.

Adams, Sir Francis Ottiwell, and Cunningham, C. D. *The Swiss Confederation* (London: 1889), 289 pp.

Adamson, John William. *English Education, 1789-1902* (Cambridge: 1930), 519 pp.

Balfour, Graham. *The Educational Systems of Great Britain and Ireland* (Oxford: 1903, 2nd ed.), 307 pp.

Barker, J. Ellis. *Modern Germany: Her Political and Economic Problems, Her Foreign and Domestic Policy, Her Ambitions, and the Causes of Her Successes and of Her Failures* (London: 1915, 5th and enl. ed.), 852 pp.

Barnard, H. C. *A Short History of English Education From 1760 to 1944* (London: (London: 1952, reprint), 400 pp.

Barnett, Mary G. *Young Delinquents: A Study of Reformatory and Industrial Schools* (London: 1913), 222 pp.

Binns, Henry Bryan. *A Century of Education: Being the Centenary History of the British and Foreign School Society, 1808-1908* (London: 1908), 330 pp.

Birchenough, Charles. *History of Elementary Education in England and Wales From 1800 to the Present Day* (London: 1938, 3rd ed.), 572 pp.

Booth, Charles. *Life and Labour of the People in London, Third Series: Religious Influences* (London: 1902), 7 vols.

Bot, A. K. *A Century of Education in the Transvaal, 1836-1936* (Pretoria: 1936), 173 pp.

Bourinot, John G. *How Canada Is Governed* (Toronto: 1918, 11th ed.), 371 pp.

Bracq, Charlemagne. *France Under the Republic* (New York: 1910), 376 pp.

Broderick, Sister Mary John. *Catholic Schools in England* (Washington, D.C.: 1936), 187 pp.

Brooks, Robert C. *Government and Politics of Switzerland* (Yonkers-on-Hudson: 1918), 430 pp.

Brown, Peter Hume. *A Short History of Scotland* (Edinburgh: 1951, rev. ed.), 350 pp.

Browne, George S., ed. *Education in Australia: A Comparative Study of the Educational Systems of the Six Australian States* (London: 1927), 461 pp.

Bryce, James. *The American Commonwealth* (New York: 1895, 3rd ed.), 2 vols.

Butts, R. Freeman. *The American Tradition in Religion and Education* (Boston: 1950), 230 pp.

Cammaerts, Emile. *A History of Belgium from the Roman Invasion to the Present Day* (New York: 1921), 357 pp.

Campbell, A. E. *Educating New Zealand* (Wellington: 1941), 189 pp.

Campbell, Rev. Reginald John. *The New Theology* (New York: 1907), 258 pp.

Craik, Sir Henry. *The State in Its Relation to Education* (London: 1896, new and rev. ed.), 188 pp.

Croce, Benedetto. *A History of Italy, 1871-1915* (Oxford: 1929), 333 pp.

Curtis, S. J. *Education in Britain Since 1900* (London: 1952), 317 pp.

——————. *History of Education in Great Britain* (London: 1950, 2nd ed.), 637 pp.

Dale, Alfred W. W. [his son]. *The Life of R. W. Dale of Birmingham* (London: 1899, 4th ed.), 771 pp.

Dawson, William Harbutt. *The German Empire, 1871-1914, and the Unity Movement* (London: 1919), 2 vols.

——————. *Germany and the Germans* (London: 1894), 2 vols.

De Montmorency, J. E. G. *National Education and National Life* (London: 1906), 287 pp.

——————. *State Intervention in English Education: A Short History from the Earliest Times Down to 1833* (Cambridge: 1902), 366 pp.

Dent, Harold C. *The Education Act, 1944: Provisions, Regulations, Circulars, Later Acts* (London: 1957, 6th ed.), 139 pp.

Dobbs, A. E. *Education and Social Movements, 1700-1850* (London: 1919), 257 pp.

Eaglesham, Eric. "Planning the Education Bill of 1902," in *British Journal of Educational Studies*, Nov. 1960, pp. 3-24.

Endean, Russell. *The Public Education of Austria, Primary, Secondary, Technical, Commercial, Et Cetera* (London: 1888), 57 pp.

Evennett, H. O. *The Catholic Schools of England and Wales* (Cambridge: 1944), 141 pp.

Ewart, John S. *The Manitoba School Question* (Toronto: 1894), 413 pp.

Farrington, Frederic E. *The Public Primary School System of France* (New York: 1906), 303 pp.

Fife, Robert Herndon. *The German Empire Between Two Wars: A Study of the Political and Social Development of the Nation Between 1871 and 1914* (New York: 1918), 400 pp.

Goris, Jan Albert, ed. *Belgium* (Los Angeles: 1945), 478 pp.

Gregory, Robert. *Elementary Education: Some Account of Its Rise and Progress in England, With Appendix* (London: 1905), 215 pp.

Gulley, Elsie. *Joseph Chamberlain and English Social Politics* (New York: 1926), 341 pp.

Gwynn, Stephen. *Ireland* (London: 1924), 252 pp.

Halévy, Elie. *Imperialism and the Rise of Labour* (London: 1951, 2nd rev. ed.), 442 pp.

——————. *The Rule of Democracy, 1905-1914* (London: 1952, 2nd rev. ed.), Books I and II.

Hall, G. Stanley. *Adolescence: Its Psychology* (New York: 1904), 2 vols.

Hamer, Frederick E. *The Education Controversy: A Critical and Historical Review, 1870-1909* (London: 1909), 44 pp.

Harper, William Rainey. *The Trend in Higher Education* (Chicago: 1905), 390 pp.

Hayes, Carlton, J. H. *France: A Nation of Patriots* (New York: 1930), 487 pp.

Helmreich, Ernst C. *Religious Education in German Schools: An Historical Approach* (Cambridge, Mass.: 1959), 365 pp.

Hughes, Robert E. *The Making of Citizens: A Study in Comparative Education* (London: 1902), 405 pp.

Johnson, Alvin W. *The Legal Status of Church-State Relationships in the United States, With Special Reference to the Public Schools* (Minneapolis: 1934), 332 pp.

Johnson, Alvin W., and Yost, Frank H. *Separation of Church and State in the United States* (Minneapolis: 1948, 2nd printing), 279 pp.

Jordan, E. K. H. *Free Church Unity: History of the Free Church Council Movement, 1896-1941* (London: 1956), 254 pp.

Lathbury, D. C. *Correspondence on Church and Religion of William Ewart Gladstone* (London: 1910), 2 vols.

Levasseur, Emile. *L'Instruction Primaire Aux Etats-Unis* (Paris: 1894), 108 pp.

Lowell, A. Lawrence. *The Government of England* (New York: 1918, new ed.), 2 vols.

Lowndes, G. A. N. *The Silent Social Revolution: An Account of the Expansion of Public Education in England and Wales, 1895-1935* (London: 1937), 274 pp.

McCutcheon, J. M. *Public Education in Ontario* (Toronto: 1941), 283 pp.

Malherbe, Ernest G. *Education in South Africa, 1625-1922* (Johannesburg: 1925), 521 pp.

Morley, John Viscount. *The Life of William Ewart Gladstone* (London: 1903), 3 vols.

Morrison, William Douglas. *Juvenile Offenders* (New York: 1900), 317 pp.

Mudie-Smith, Richard, ed. *The Religious Life of London* (London: 1904), 518 pp.

Neander, Augustus. *General History of the Christian Religion and Church* (London: 1851-58), 9 vols. Bohn edition.

Norwood, Cyril. *The English Tradition of Education* (London: 1929), 335 pp.

Paton, Walter B., compiler. *Colonial Handbooks* (London: 1902-14).

Reisner, Edward H. *Nationalism and Education Since 1789: A Social and Political History of Modern Education* (New York: 1922), 575 pp.

Religious Education in Schools: The Report of an Inquiry Made by the Research Committee of the Institute of Christian Education Into the Working of the 1944 Education Act (London: 1954), 157 pp.

Rogers, Alan. "Churches and Children—A Study in the Controversy Over the 1902 Education Act," in *British Journal of Educational Studies*, Nov. 1959, pp. 29-51.

Ross, George William. *The School System of Ontario (Canada): Its History and Distinctive Features* (New York: 1896), 203 pp.

——————. *The Schools of England and Germany* (Toronto: 1894), 243 pp.

Rowntree, Benjamin Seebohm. *Land and Labour: Lessons From Belgium* (London: 1910), 633 pp.

Sandiford, Peter. *The Training of Teachers in England and Wales* (New York: 1910), 168 pp.

Sayce, A. H. *The "Higher Criticism" And the Verdict of the Monuments* (London: 1894, 3rd ed. rev.), 575 pp.

Selby-Bigge, Sir Lewis Amherst. *The Board of Education* (London: 1934, 2nd ed.), 329 pp.

Siegfried, André. *The Race Question in Canada* (London: 1907), 343 pp.

Smith, Frank. *A History of English Elementary Education, 1760-1902* (London: 1931), 360 pp.

Spalding, Thomas Alfred. *The Work of the London School Board* (London: 1900), 276 pp.

Stephen, Sir James. *A History of the Criminal Law of England* (London: 1883), 3 vols.

Stewart, George. *The Story of Scottish Education* (London: 1927), 164 pp.

Strachey, Sir John. *India: Its Administration and Progress* (London: 1911), 557 pp.

Sweetman, Edward; Long, Charles R.; and Smith, John. *A History of State Education in Victoria* (Melbourne: 1922), 312 pp.

Thayer, Vivian T. *The Attack Upon the Secular School* (Boston: 1951), 257 pp.

Tropp, Asher. *The School Teacher: The Growth of the Teaching Profession in England and Wales From 1800 to the Present Day* (London: 1957), 286 pp.

Weir, George M. *The Separate School Question in Canada* (Toronto: 1934), 298 pp.

Whitehouse, John Howard. *A National System of Education* (Cambridge: 1913), 92 pp.

Wyeth, E. R. *Education in Queensland: A History of Education in Queensland and in the Moreton Bay District of New South Wales* (Melbourne: 1955), 214 pp.

INDEX

Acland, Arthur H. D., 60n, 90, 99.
Acland, Charles T. D., 90, 181-82, 216.
Act of 1944, 221-23, 229-30.
Alderley, Lord Stanley of (Fourth Baron), 29, 29n, 69n, 198-99.
Adler, Chief Rabbi Hermann, 197.
Anson, Sir William Robert, 11, 63n, 67.
Appleton, William A., 200.
Asquith, Herbert Henry, 13, 62, 75, 76, 218.
Australasia, v, 104, 127, 140, 187, 204. See also individual states.
Avebury, Baron (First), 125-26.

Baines, Talbot, 155.
Balfour, Arthur James, 11, 12, 16, 30, 32n, 39n, 54, 75, 150.
Balfour Bill of 1902, 13-15.
Barker, J. Ellis, 95.
Barnett, Rev. Samuel Augustus, 116.
Bartlet, Rev. Vernon, 33.
Baylis, Walter J., 141.
Bayly, Elizabeth Boyd, 171.
Beeching, Rev. Henry Charles, 85, 88, 93, 104, 105, 118.
Beet, Rev. Joseph Agar, 124.
Belgium, v, vi, 156-57, 187, 188, 208.
Bell, Rev. Andrew, 5.
Bell, J. Allen, 159.
Belloc, Hilaire, 189.
Benson, Edward White (Archbishop of Canterbury), 101.
Birmingham Experiment, 158-59, 162, 167, 178.
Birrell, Augustine, 31, 62, 75, 97, 151, 151n, 167.
Birrell Bill of 1906, 63, 64.
Blatchford, Robert, 34.
Blomfield, Rev. William E., 23.
Bonner, Mrs. Hypatia Bradlaugh, 141, 205.
Booth, Charles, 86, 116.
Bourne, Francis Cardinal (Archbishop of Westminster), 183-84, 189, 191, 217, 218.
Bradlaugh, Charles, 102, 106, 141.
Braithwaite, William C., 171n.
British and Foreign School Society, 5, 6, 46, 207, 213, 214.
Brooke, Rev. C. E., 216.
Brown, Msgr. W. F., 70, 123, 185, 192.
Browne, St. John, 192.
Brownrigg, Rev. J. S., 49n, 155.
Bruce, George Lewis, 34, 60, 70, 72.
Bruce, Rev. Rosslyn, 174.
Bryce, James, 13, 84n, 95, 96, 97, 99, 102, 125, 167.
Burnie, R. W., 182.
Burns, Rev. Dawson, 47.
Burrows, Henry W., 61n.
Burt, Thomas, 202.
Burton, George A. (Bishop of Clifton), 122, 189.
Butcher, Samuel Henry, 66, 91, 155, 210.
Butler, Dr. Nicholas Murray, 92, 210.

Callaway, Charles, 107.
Campbell, Rev. Reginald John, 111, 202.
Campbell-Bannerman, Sir Henry, 13, 62, 63.
Canada, v, 140, 153, 171, 185-86, 187, 191, 191n, 204.
Carnegie, Rev. W. Hartley, 91, 115.
Carpenter, W. B. (Bishop of Ripon), 175, 176, 177.
Catholic Education Council, 56, 184-85.
Catholic School Committee, 6, 8, 56, 58.
Catholic Union of Great Britain, 94.
Cecil, Lord Hugh, 10, 10n, 11, 20n, 28, 36, 81, 85, 149, 182, 226.
Cecil, Lord Robert, 10n, 11, 36, 68, 82, 86, 89, 226.
Chamberlain, Joseph, 11, 12, 18, 147, 154n.
Chambers, George Frederick, 88.

Chandler, F. J., 159.
Channing, Francis A., 57.
Chesterton, Gilbert K., 141.
Cheyne, Dr. Thomas K., 111.
Christopher, Rev. Alfred M. W., 177.
Church Committee, 88.
Church Schools' Emergency League, 55, 56.
Cleworth, Rev. Thomas E., 50, 56, 65, 84, 115, 149, 152, 182, 216, 219.
Clifford, Dr. John, 23, 27, 36, 38n, 42, 43, 46, 47, 71, 72, 82, 83, 96, 98, 100, 101, 107n, 125, 127, 140, 162, 164, 167, 171, 178, 180, 193, 202, 212, 219, 227.
Cockerton, T. B., 10.
Coghlan, Thomas A., 134.
Cohen, Chapman, 53, 105n, 106, 134.
Coit, Dr. Stanton, 128, 138-39.
Coller, Rev. W. E., 104, 105.
Collins, Sir William J., 138.
Comte, Auguste, 102.
Compton, Rev. Berdmore, 55.
Compton-Rickett, Joseph, 30, 166.
Conscience Clause, 6, 7-8, 15, 30-31, 32-33, 32n, 51, 63, 63n, 64, 65, 67, 71-72, 73-74, 165, 181.
Contracting-out, 64, 65, 67, 69-70, 71, 73, 75-76, 163-64, 164n, 190, 197.
Corporation Act of 1661, 130n.
Cowper-Temple, William Francis, 7, 100.
Cremer, Rev. F. Daustini, 176.
Crewe, Marquess of (First), 62, 75.
Criminal Statistics, 116-21, 125-26, 132-36.
Cross Commission, 216.
Crooker, Dr. Joseph Henry, 127.
Cumin, Sir Patrick, 216.
Curran, Peter, 202.
Curtoys, Rev. W. Frank, 32, 158.

Dale, Rev. R. W., 33, 86, 147, 159, 159n.
Davidson, Randall Thomas (Archbishop of Canterbury), 32, 48, 50, 67, 75, 76, 81, 83, 87, 89, 90, 102, 102n, 150, 170n, 175, 182, 213, 215, 216, 221, 227.
Davis, Rev. John Llewelyn, 82.
Davies, T. Llewelyn, 154n.
Dawson, William Harbutt, 95n, 168.
Devonshire, Duke of (Ninth), 24n.
De Winton, Wilfred Seymour, 118.
Diggle, John William (Bishop of Carlisle), 173, 174.

Dillon, John, 22, 22n, 94, 104, 121n, 184n.
Doughan, James, 190.
Doyle, Sir Arthur Conan, 202.
Drake, E. T., 119.
Drury-lane Day Industrial School, 154.
Dymott, Rev. Sidney E., 17, 33, 114, 115.

Earmarking Rates, 153-54, 154n, 164n, 191-92.
Education (Local Authority Default) Act, 53, 54, 55.
Edward VII, 75.
Edwards, Alfred George (Bishop of St. Asaph), 169n, 175, 177, 213.
Eglen, John P., 48.
Eliot, Dr. Charles William, 118.
Elliot, Rev. W. Hume, 28, 45, 181.
Elliott, Sir Charles, 155.
Ellis, Havelock, 202.
Emery, Rev. William, 177.
English Church Union, 36.
Evans, Howard, 36, 37, 44, 45, 99, 125.

Finlay, Sir Robert, 40.
Fitch, Sir Joshua, 99.
Fitchett, W. H., 160n, 172.
Fitzroy, Sir Almeric, 11, 62.
Flavell, Rev. T., 160.
Fletcher, Ven. Robert C., 161.
Foote, George W., 73, 74, 107, 107n, 202.
Ford, Rev. Hugh E., 22, 56, 183n, 228.
Forester, George. See Greenwood, George Granville.
Forster, William E., 7.
Forster Bill of 1870, 7.
Fouillée, Alfred Jules, 136.
Fox, Rev. W. Harper, 218.
France, v, vi, 3, 69n, 120, 122, 126-27, 135-36, 140, 187, 188, 190, 208, 208n.
Free Church Council, 62, 76, 83, 162, 169-70.
French, Rev. A. J., 193.
Frodsham, George Horsfall (Bishop of North Queensland), 177-78.
Furnell, Miss A. S., 129.

Gainsford, W. D., 191.
Gallwey, Rev. Peter, 68.
Gascoyne-Cecil, James Edward Hubert. See Salisbury, Fourth Marquess of.

Gascoyne-Cecil, Rev. William, 154.
Germany, including Prussia, v, vi, 3, 9, 46, 69n, 95-96, 95n, 126, 148-49, 155-56, 156n, 160-61, 168, 186, 189, 206, 206n, 208, 208n.
Gibson, Rev. J. Monro, 23, 25.
Gladstone, William Ewart, 7, 84, 84n, 106n, 107, 107-08n, 175, 179.
Glancey, Rev. M. F., 94, 184, 185-86, 187-88.
Glover, Dr. Richard, 97.
Gooch, George P., 138, 140.
Goodall, Rev. A., 66n.
Goodier, Rev. Alban, 186, 188-89.
Gore, Charles (Bishop, Birmingham), 179.
Gorham, Charles T., 103.
Gorst Bill of 1896, 37n, 51, 149n.
Gould, Frederick James, 33n, 52, 73, 74, 129, 137, 139, 139n, 141, 205-06, 209-10.
Greece, 208.
Greenwood, Granville George (pseud. George Forester), 108, 111, 131, 202.
Griffith, Ellis Jones, 28.
Grove, Lady Agnes, 137.

Haldane, Richard Burdon, 13.
Halévy, Elie, 10n, 62n.
Halifax, Viscount (Second), 36, 41.
Hall, Dr. Granville Stanley, 118, 118n.
Hammond, Rev. Joseph, 51.
Harcourt, Rev. Richard, 133.
Hardie, J. Keir, 30.
Harper, Dr. William Rainey, 118.
Harrison, Frederic, 105, 202.
Harvey, Thomas Edmund, 172, 211.
Hayward, Dr. Frank Herbert, 133.
Headlam, Rev. Arthur C., 152n.
Headlam, Rev. Stewart D., 103, 202, 209.
Healy, Timothy M., 122.
Hedley, John Cuthbert (Bishop of Newport), 183.
Helmreich, Ernst Christian, 161.
Henderson, Arthur, 202.
Henson, Rev. Herbert Hensley, 91, 114, 148, 160, 173, 174, 175, 176, 177, 192, 226.
Hoare, Samuel J. G., 152, 220-21.
Hobson, John Atkinson, 202.
Hodgkin, Thomas, 171.

Holland, v, 156, 188, 208, 208n.
Holland, Rev. Henry Scott, 182.
Hollowell, Rev. James Hirst, 26, 42, 43, 70, 71, 101n, 126, 166, 168, 170, 171-72, 180, 193-94, 210, 218, 219, 227.
Holmes, Edmond, 108, 109.
Hope, Sir Theodore C., 153.
Hopps, Rev. John Page, 106.
Horne, Rev. Silvester C., 71, 213.
Horsfall, Thomas C., 91, 92, 117-18, 156.
Horton, Dr. Robert F., 96, 127, 170-71, 170n, 181.
Houghton, Thomas, 49.
House of Lords Return, Religious Instruction in Schools (1888), 88.
House of Lords Return, Religious Instruction in Schools (1895), 89, 99.
House of Lords Return, Religious Instruction in Schools (1906), 90, 99, 175.
Huddersfield ("Godless"), 89, 99-100.
Hughes, Rev. Hugh Price, 37, 82.
Hughes, Robert E., 187n.
Hunter, Ernest E., 103.
Hutton, Alfred, 71.
Hyndman, Henry Mayers, 204, 207.

India, 83, 177.
Ingram, A. F. W. (Bishop of London), 152.
International Moral Education League, 123.
Ireland, 72, 155, 155n, 167, 187, 188n, 206.
Irish Nationalist Party, 22, 23, 63, 68n, 190, 192.
Italy, 3, 69n, 188, 208.

Jackson, Cyril, 149.
Jamaica Catechism, 177.
Japan, 140.
Jephson, Rev. Arthur, 92.
Jewish Religious Education Board (London), 196.
Johnson, Harrold, 104, 127, 140, 140n.
Jones, Rev. David, 117, 126.
Jones, David Brynmor, 180.
Jones, Rev. H. Gresford, 174n.
Jowett, Rev. J. H., 31.

Keating, Rev. Joseph, 93.
Kekewich, Sir George, 54n.
Kennaway, Sir John, 160.
Kenyon-Slaney, Col. William, 38.

Kenyon-Slaney Amendment, 15, 38-41, 48, 49, 58, 146, 182.
Knox, Edward A. (Bishop of Manchester), 65, 158, 178, 180.

Labour Party Annual Conf., 203-04, 203n.
Lacey, Rev. Thomas Alexander, 31, 161.
Lancaster, Joseph, 5, 25.
Lang, Cosmo Gordon (Bishop of Stepney), 58, 59.
Lansdowne, Marquess of (Fifth), 75.
Lathbury, Daniel C., 84, 147, 159n, 178-79, 182, 192.
Law, Rev. Thomas T., 62.
Lawder-Eaton, G., 152, 158.
Lee, Sir Sidney, 75.
Lees, A., 194.
Legge, Rev. Hugh, 83.
Leo XIII, 194.
Lidgett, Rev. J. Scott, 43, 75, 171.
Lilly, William Samuel, 94, 121.
Lloyd George, David, 13, 24, 30, 44, 53, 55, 164, 171.
Lobban (Senior Inspector for New South Wales), 178.
Local Option, 180-82, 184-85.
Loening, Dr. Edgar, 121.
London County Council School Buildings Report of 1905, 60, 61.
London Education Act of 1903, 56, 57.
London School Board Controversy of 1894, 101, 178-79, 179n, 196.
Londonderry, Marquess of (Sixth), 11.
Lough, Thomas, 68, 74.
Lyttelton, Alfred, 116.
Lyttelton, Rev. Edward, 116.

MacColl, Rev. Malcolm, 32, 82, 86, 87, 114, 115, 148.
MacDonald, J. Ramsay, vii, viii, 28n, 73, 74, 102, 103-04, 108-09, 110, 112, 113, 129, 130-31, 132, 138, 199, 202, 203.
MacDonald, Margaret Ethel, 112.
Mackarness, Ven. Charles C., 84.
Mackenzie, John S., 137n.
Maclagan, William Dalrymple (Archbishop of York), 16.
Macleane, Rev. Douglas, 158.
Macnamara, Dr. Thomas James, 24, 29, 45, 97, 99, 170, 171, 181.

Maddison, Frederick, 74.
Maher, Rev. Michael, 121, 123.
Markham, Rev. A. A., 44.
Marson, Rev. Charles, 82n.
Martin, Rev. David Basil, 27, 44.
Massie, Rev. John, 34.
Masterman, Charles Frederick G., 87, 202.
Maxted, Rev. E. G., 139.
McArthur, Charles, 40n.
McCabe, Joseph, 73, 109, 133, 135, 136, 139.
McKenna, Reginald, 62, 199, 215, 217, 218.
McKenna Bill of 1908, 63, 64.
McLaren, A. D., 205, 206n.
McNabb, Rev. Vincent, 188.
Meredith, George, 202.
Merriman, W. A., 129.
Midleton, Viscount (Eighth), 91.
Miller, Rev., 17.
Mitchinson, John (Assistant Bishop of Peterborough), 202.
Morant, Robert, 11, 16.
Moorhouse, James (Bishop of Manchester), 17, 19, 20, 21, 65, 118, 159.
Moral Instruction (Education) League, 139, 140n.
Morley, John, 30.
Morley, Ralph, 198.
Morrison, Rev. William D., 118, 118n.
Mosely, Alfred, 92n.
Mosely Commission, 92.
Moulton, Rev. James Hope, 211.
Mudie-Smith, Richard, 91.
Mundella, Anthony John, 24n, 100.
Myers, Rev. Edward, 122, 123.

Nash, Rev. J. O., 160.
National Education Association, 24.
National Education Union, 7.
National Passive Resistance League, 42.
National Protestant Church Union, 39.
National Secular Society, 53, 73, 106.
National Society, 5, 6, 8, 25, 31, 40, 44, 56, 65, 66n, 89, 90, 150, 153, 165, 207, 213, 217, 220, 221.
National Union of Teachers, 24, 24n, 157n.
Neander, Dr. Johann August William, 207n.
Neligan, Moore R. (Bishop of Auckland), 160.

Newcastle Commission, 6.
Nevinson, Henry W., 112.
New South Wales, Australia, 119-20, 134, 135, 149, 172, 177-78, 184, 185, 187n.
New Zealand, v, 104n, 118-19, 127, 135, 160, 187n, 205.
Nicholson, Rev. W. Trevor, 179.
Nicoll, Dr. W. Robertson, 43.
Non-Theological Moral Instruction, 120, 122-23, 136-40.
Norfolk, Duke of (Fifteenth), 22n.
Northern Counties Educ. League, 26, 26n.
Nunn, Rev. Joseph, 152-53.

O'Dell, George E., 128, 199n.
O'Grady, James, 203.
Oliphant, James, 139.
Ottley, Rev. Edward B., 85.

Parents' League, 150, 154, 165.
Papillon, Rev. Thomas L., 92.
Parker, Dr. Joseph, 111, 200.
Paton, Rev. John Brown, 96, 97.
Pease, Edward R., 207.
Pease, Joseph Albert, 76, 77, 189n.
Pennington, Canon, 31.
Penryhn, Lord (Llandegai), 24.
Percival, John (Bishop of Hereford), 20, 58, 89, 99, 226.
Perks, John Robert, 31, 43, 44.
Picton, James Allanson, 25n, 29, 85n, 104, 107, 110-11, 112, 128, 129, 137n, 204, 205, 206.
Pius VII, 194.
Platt-Higgins, Frederick, 86.
Poland, 196.
Powell, Helena, 146n.
Prussia. See Germany.

Queensland, Australia, 104n, 135, 149, 172, 185, 205.
Quelch, Harry, 102.

Redmayne, J. S., 153.
Redmond, John, 23, 191, 191n.
Redmond, William, 191n.
Reed, F. W. H., 47.
Rees, Rev. W. G. E., 116, 118, 119-21.
Reid, Whitelaw, 126.
Representative Church Council, 75-76, 213.

Richards, Henry Charles, 32n.
Richardson, Rev. George, 190.
Richmond, Rev. Wilfrid John, 192.
Rickaby, Rev. Joseph, 183.
Ridgeway, Charles John (Bishop of Chichester), 65, 153, 173.
Riley, Athelstan, 36, 39, 48, 86, 154-55, 178-79, 179n, 193, 226.
Ripon, Marquess of (First), 68n.
Roberts, Rev. J. Edward, 98n.
Robertson, John Mackinnon, 106, 198, 202, 207-08, 207n.
Robson, Edward R., 54n.
Rogers, Rev. Clement F., 83, 150, 156.
Rogers, Rev. James Guinness, 30, 97, 98n.
Rothschild, Baron (Second), 196, 197.
Rothstein, Theodore, 73, 73n.
Rothwell, Rev. Charles, 51.
Rowland, Wilfred J., 24n.
Rowntree, John Stephenson, 38.
Rowntree, Joseph, 37, 38.
Rowntree, Walter Smith, 37.
Royal Lancastrian Society, 5, 25.
Runciman, Walter, 62, 64.
Runciman Bill of 1908, 63, 64, 65, 75, 76.
Russell, Charles, 51.
Russell, George W. E., 107.
Russia, 9, 126, 196, 208.
Ryan, Frederick, 52, 202.

Sadler, Michael Ernest, 123.
Salisbury, Marquess of (Third), 10, 11.
Salisbury, Marquess of (Fourth), 11, 150.
Sanday, Rev. William, 48.
Satolli, Msgr. Francis, 194.
Scotland, 95, 155, 167-68, 171, 181, 182, 185, 189, 206, 208, 208n.
Scott, Alexander Maccallum, 201.
Screeton, Rev., 173.
Seaborne, J. H., 147.
Secular Educ. League, 135, 202-03, 207.
Sexton, James, 203.
Shadwell, Dr. Arthur, 120, 122.
Shakespeare, Rev. John H., 169.
Sheedy, Rev. Morgan M., 194n.
Sheepshanks, John (Bishop of Norwich), 32.
Sherwell, Arthur, 89.
Smart, Rev. Henry R., 43, 44.
Smith, Arnold, 136-37n.

Smith, Frank, 46, 47.
Smith, Frederick E., 182.
Smith, Rev. Isaac Gregory, 115n.
Smith, Rev. Philip Vernon, 154.
Smith, Rev. Sydney F., 68, 69, 93, 122-23,
    183, 184-85, 191.
Smyth, William Edmund (Bishop of Le-
    bombo), 177.
Snell, Harry, 103, 111, 202, 204.
Snowden, Philip, 74, 132-33, 133n,
    199-200, 202.
South Africa (Transvaal), 160, 167, 204.
South Australia, 104n, 135.
Spain, 208.
Spencer, Earl (Fifth), 101.
Spender, John Alfred, 163.
Spiller, Gustav, 130, 131, 141.
Stead, William Thomas, 127.
Steer, Rev. W. H. Hornby, 150.
Stephen, Sir James, 114, 116.
Stevenson, Rev. Morley, 84, 216.
Stewart, Halley, 200, 201, 202, 203.
Strappini, Rev. W. D., 52.
Strong, Rev. Josiah, 92.
Strong, Dean Thomas Bank, 83.
Sullivan, Dr. Washington, 132.
Sunday schools, 91, 91n, 92-93, 96-97, 99,
    100, 103, 104-05.
Swinny, S. H., 201.
Switzerland, 69n, 156, 188, 208.

Talbot, Lord Edmund, 22, 22n.
Talbot, Edward Stuart (Bishop of Roches-
    ter), 59, 226.
Talbot, John Gilbert, 213-14.
Taylor, Rev. Edward F., 20, 30n, 179, 214,
    214n, 219-20.
Temple, Frederick (Archbishop of Canter-
    bury), 32, 37, 87, 89, 227.
Test Act of 1673, 130n.
Theobald, Robert Masters, 101.
Thompson, Herbert M., 136.
Thorn, James, 205.
Thorpe, Rev. John H., 151.
Tilby, T. Martin, 88.
Townsend, Rev. William J., 42.
Trades Union Congress, 203-04, 203n.
Training Colleges, 6, 8, 9, 15, 34-35, 45-46,
    49, 49n, 87-88, 140, 215-21.
Transvaal, South Africa, 160, 167, 204.

United States of America, v, 9, 46, 69n,
    91-92, 92n, 95, 95n, 98n, 99-100, 99n,
    104, 105, 117-18, 122, 127, 133, 140,
    148n, 171-72, 187, 188, 189, 194, 194n,
    205-06, 208, 208n, 210.

Vaughan, Father Bernard, 184.
Vaughan, Herbert Cardinal (Archbishop of
    Westminster), 22, 23, 94, 184, 186.
Victoria, Australia, 93, 104-05, 104n, 118,
    119-20, 134, 135, 149, 159-60, 172, 185,
    187n, 204-05, 208n, 210.

Wakefield, Rev. Henry Russell, 173.
Wakeford, Rev. John, 84.
Wallas, Graham, 202.
Watts, Charles, 138.
Webb, Sidney (Lord Passfield), 10, 11,
    57n.
Wells, H. G., 202.
Wells, W. A. J., 149.
Welsh, Rev. Robert E., 44, 54, 166.
Wesleyan Day Schools, 6, 43, 44, 213, 214,
    223, 223n.
Western Australia, 135, 149, 172.
Whitbread Bill of 1807, 25, 25n, 165.
White, George, 27, 54, 171, 193.
Whitley, Rev. William T., 172.
Wilkinson, Rev. J. Frome, 176.
Wilkinson, Thomas Edward (Bishop of
    North and Central Europe), 120.
Williams, Lewis, 125-26.
Williams, Mrs. Watkins, 66.
Wilson, Ven. James Maurice, 20, 88, 116,
    117, 118, 120.
Wilson, Philip Whitwell, 74, 100, 126,
    164, 167, 208-09.
Wishart, James, 181.
Woodhead, Edgar T., 26, 99.
Wordsworth, John (Bishop of Salisbury),
    50.
Wyndham, George, 66.
Wynn, Rev. Walter, 100n.

Yonge, Charlotte, 136, 220, 220n.
Yoxall, James Henry, 181.

Zangwill, Israel, 202.

℄